RULE OF LAW FOR NATURE

"Human laws must be reformulated to keep human activities in harmony with the unchanging and universal laws of nature." This 1987 statement by the World Commission on Environment and Development has never been more relevant and urgent than it is today. Despite the many legal responses to various environmental problems, more greenhouse gases than ever before are being released into the atmosphere, biological diversity is rapidly declining and fish stocks in the oceans are dwindling.

This book challenges the doctrinal construction of environmental law and presents an innovative legal approach to ecological sustainability: a rule of law for nature that guides and transcends ordinary written laws and extends fundamental principles of respect, integrity and legal security to the non-human world.

CHRISTINA VOIGT is a Professor at the Department of Public and International Law, University of Oslo, Norway, where she works in particular on legal issues of climate change, sustainability and the interface between environmental and trade law.

RULE OF LAW FOR NATURE

New Dimensions and Ideas in Environmental Law

Edited by

CHRISTINA VOIGT

CAMBRIDGE
UNIVERSITY PRESS

University Printing House, Cambridge CB2 8BS, United Kingdom

Published in the United States of America by Cambridge University Press, New York

Cambridge University Press is part of the University of Cambridge.

It furthers the University's mission by disseminating knowledge in the pursuit of education, learning and research at the highest international levels of excellence.

www.cambridge.org
Information on this title: www.cambridge.org/9781107043268

© Cambridge University Press 2013

This publication is in copyright. Subject to statutory exception and to the provisions of relevant collective licensing agreements, no reproduction of any part may take place without the written permission of Cambridge University Press.

First published 2013

Printed and bound in the United Kingdom by CPI Group Ltd, Croydon CR0 4YY

A catalogue record for this publication is available from the British Library

Library of Congress Cataloguing in Publication data
Rule of law for nature : new dimensions and ideas in environmental law /
edited by Christina Voigt.
    p. cm.
Includes bibliographical references and index.
ISBN 978-1-107-04326-8 (hardback)
1. Environmental law, International.   2. Environmental protection.   3. Rule of law.
    I. Voigt, Christina, 1971– editor of compilation.
K3585.R85 2013
344.04'6–dc23
                                    2013022963

ISBN 978-1-107-04326-8 Hardback

Cambridge University Press has no responsibility for the persistence or accuracy of URLs for external or third-party internet websites referred to in this publication, and does not guarantee that any content on such websites is, or will remain, accurate or appropriate.

To my sons Oscar and Victor and their generation

CONTENTS

List of contributors x
Preface xiii

PART I **Environmental law at the crossroads: achievements, shortcomings and challenges** 1

1 Twelve fundamental challenges in environmental law: an introduction to the concept of rule of law for nature 3
   HANS CHRISTIAN BUGGE

2 Rule of law for nature in a kaleidoscopic world 27
   EDITH BROWN WEISS

3 Evolved norms: a canon for the Anthropocene 46
   NICHOLAS A. ROBINSON

PART II **A rule of law for nature: theories and reflections** 73

4 Grounding the rule of law 75
   KLAUS BOSSELMANN

5 The rule of Nature's law 94
   CORMAC CULLINAN

PART III **Designing a rule of law for nature: new dimensions and ideas** 109

6 Ecological proportionality: an emerging principle of law for nature? 111
   GERD WINTER

7 Sustainable development and the rule of law for nature: a constitutional reading 130
   LOUIS J. KOTZÉ

8 The principle of sustainable development: integration and ecological integrity   146
CHRISTINA VOIGT

9 The need to recognize a coherent legal system as an important element of the ecosystem approach   158
FROUKJE MARIA PLATJOUW

10 An emerging legal principle to restore large-scale ecoscapes   175
ANASTASIA TELESETSKY

11 Traditional norms and environmental law: the sub-Saharan African case study   191
CHIZOBA CHINWEZE, CHUKWUEMEKA JIDEANI AND GWEN Z. ABIOLA-OLOKE

PART IV **Nature's rights**   207

12 Rules of law for use and nonuse of nature   209
JAN LAITOS

13 Realizing nature's rule of law through rights of waterways   222
LINDA SHEEHAN

PART V **Procedural dimensions of a rule of law for nature**   241

14 Towards a new instrument for promoting sustainability beyond the EIA and the SEA: the holistic impact assessment   243
MASSIMILIANO MONTINI

15 Enforcing environmental responsibilities: an environmental perspective on the rule of law and administrative enforcement   259
ANNIKA K. NILSSON

16 Mechanisms for reviewing compliance with international environmental law open to private parties   275
CRISTINA VERONES

PART VI **Rule of law for nature and the role of companies and markets** 293

17 The green economy will not build the rule of law for nature 295
   REBECCA M. BRATSPIES

18 Taking nature seriously: can the UN Guiding Principles tame corporate profiteering? 312
   SURYA DEVA

PART VII **A rule of law for the oceans** 329

19 Conservation of marine biodiversity and the International Maritime Organization 331
   TORE HENRIKSEN

20 Implementing the rule of law for nature in the global marine commons: developing environmental assessment frameworks 347
   ROBIN WARNER

21 Using the public trust doctrine to achieve ocean stewardship 365
   MARY TURNIPSEED, MICHAEL C. BLUMM, DUNCAN E. J. CURRIE, KRISTINA M. GJERDE, PETER H. SAND, MARY C. WOOD, JULIE A. HAMBROOK BERKMAN, RYKE LONGEST, GAIL OSHERENKO, STEPHEN E. ROADY, RAPHAEL D. SAGARIN AND LARRY B. CROWDER

Index 380

CONTRIBUTORS

GWEN Z. ABIOLA-OLOKE, MD/CEO United Bank for Africa, Republic of Benin

JULIE A. HAMBROOK BERKMAN, Doctor, Managing Director, Foundation for the Good Governance of International Spaces, UK

MICHAEL C. BLUMM, Jeffrey Bain Faculty Scholar and Professor of Law, Lewis and Clark Law School, USA

KLAUS BOSSELMANN, Professor of Law, University of Auckland, Faculty of Law; Founding Director of the New Zealand Centre for Environmental Law at the University of Auckland, New Zealand

REBECCA M. BRATSPIES, Professor, CUNY School of Law; Director of the Center for Urban Environmental Reform, USA

EDITH BROWN WEISS, Francis Cabell Brown Professor of International Law, Georgetown Law, Washington DC, USA

HANS CHRISTIAN BUGGE, Professor emeritus in Environmental Law, University of Oslo, Department of Public and International Law, Norway

CHIZOBA CHINWEZE, Chemtek Associates, Nigeria

LARRY B. CROWDER, Science Director, Center for Ocean Solutions, Stanford University, USA

CORMAC CULLINAN, environmental lawyer, Cape Town, South Africa; research associate, Department of Public Law, University of Cape Town; Director of Cullinan & Associates Inc; Chief Executive Officer of EnAct International

DUNCAN E. J. CURRIE, Director, Globelaw, New Zealand

SURYA DEVA, Associate Professor, School of Law, City University of Hong Kong, Hong Kong SAR, China

LIST OF CONTRIBUTORS

KRISTINA M. GJERDE, Senior High Seas Policy Advisor, International Union for the Conservation of Nature (IUCN), Gland, Switzerland

TORE HENRIKSEN, Professor, Faculty of Law, University of Tromsø, Norway

CHUKWUEMEKA JIDEANI, Director General, Ethics and Corporate Compliance Institute of Nigeria, Abuja

LOUIS J. KOTZÉ, Professor of Law, North West University, South Africa

JAN LAITOS, Professor of Law and John A. Carver, Jr Chair in Natural Resources Law, University of Denver Sturm College of Law, USA

RYKE LONGEST, Clinical Professor of Law, Director, Duke Environmental Law and Policy Clinic, Duke University School of Law, Nicholas School of the Environment

MASSIMILIANO MONTINI, Professor of European Union Law, Department of Business and Law, University of Siena, Italy; Director and Founder of the University's Environmental Legal Team

ANNIKA K. NILSSON, Doctor of Laws, post doctoral research scholar, Faculty of Law, Stockholm University, Sweden

GAIL OSHERENKO, Project Scientist, Marine Science Institute, University of California, Santa Barbara, USA

FROUKJE MARIA PLATJOUW, Ph.D. student, University of Oslo, Department of Public and Internaitonal Law, Norway

STEPHEN E. ROADY, Attorney, Earthjustice, USA

NICHOLAS A. ROBINSON, University Professor for the Environment, Pace University and Gilbert & Sarah Kerlin Distinguished Professor of Environmental Law, Pace University School of Law; Professor Adjunct, Yale University School of Forestry & Environmental Studies; Chairman (1996–2004), Commission on Environmental Law, International Union for the Conservation of Nature and Natural Resources (IUCN), USA

RAPHAEL D. SAGARIN, Associate Research Scientist, Institute of the Environment, University of Arizona, USA

PETER H. SAND, Lecturer in Law, University of Munich, Germany

LINDA SHEEHAN, Executive Director, Earth Law Center, California, USA

ANASTASIA TELESETSKY, Associate Professor of Law, College of Law, University of Idaho, USA

MARY TURNIPSEED, Arctic Fellow, National Center for Ecological Analysis and Synthesis, University of California, Santa Barbara, USA

CRISTINA VERONES, Ph.D. candidate at the Graduate Institute of International and Development Studies in Geneva, Switzerland

CHRISTINA VOIGT, Professor of Law, University of Oslo, Department of Public and International Law, Norway

ROBIN WARNER, Associate Professor at the Australian National Centre for Ocean Resources and Security, University of Wollongong, Australia

GERD WINTER, Professor of Public Law, Forschungsstelle für Europäisches Umweltrecht (FEU), Fachbereich Rechtswissenschaft, Universität Bremen, Germany

MARY C. WOOD, Philip H. Knight Professor of Law, Faculty Director, Environmental and Natural Resources Law Program, University of Oregon School of Law

PREFACE

"Human laws must be reformulated to keep human activities in harmony with the unchanging and universal laws of nature." This is what "Our Common Future", the report of the World Commission on Environment and Development, demanded more than a quarter of a century ago.

Since then, a wide range of environmental laws and regulations has been adopted at different scales and levels. International environmental law has emerged and rapidly expanded in scope and quantity. Regional environmental law, in particular EU environmental law, is now defining and prescribing environmental quality and standards for member states. At the national level, most countries have one or several environmental laws in place.

These developments over the last forty years are remarkable and could easily be mistaken for success. But so far, environmental laws have only led to modest environmental gains. Main trends of environmental destruction continue almost unchanged. It appears that decades with widespread environmental legislation have not made much of a difference in putting the world on an environmentally sustainable track. The overall shift towards environmentally sustainable development remains a distant goal, as if environmental law never existed.

The World Commission's call has thus never been more relevant and urgent than today. Now, in 2013, more greenhouse gases than ever are put into the atmosphere, biological diversity is rapidly declining and fish stocks in the oceans are dwindling.[1] The outcome document of the 2012 Rio+20 UN Conference on Sustainable Development had heads of state and government "recognize the severity of the global loss of biodiversity and the degradation of ecosystems and emphasize that these undermine global development, affecting food security and nutrition, the provision of and access to water and the health of the rural poor and of people

---

[1] UNEP, *Global Environment Outlook 5*, 2012, at 461.

worldwide, including present and future generations."[2] At the same time, these heads of state and government recognized

> that planet Earth and its ecosystems are our home and that "Mother Earth" is a common expression in a number of countries and regions, and we note that some countries recognize the rights of nature in the context of the promotion of sustainable development. We are convinced that in order to achieve a just balance among the economic, social and environmental needs of present and future generations, it is necessary to promote harmony with nature.[3]

Environmental laws are without doubt essential for the protection of natural resources and ecosystems and reflect our best hope for the future of our planet.[4] Some see that environmental laws have flourished and expanded, but much needs to be done if the legal system is truly to promote "harmony with nature".

Present environmental laws and their implementation are not adequate to ensure the maintenance or – where damage has happened – restoration of the integrity of natural systems. This situation begs many questions: Why is the ever-growing norm density in environmental law not mirrored by accelerating good news of high environmental quality and sustainability? Why is it very difficult to achieve effective results with environmental law and what can be done to change this situation?

The contributors to this book have varying views on these questions and on how they should be met. Some criticize existing environmental laws as "legalizing pollution". Others are worried that, through environmental laws, the environment becomes a property to be used rather than preserved, and thus question the larger paradigm of which environmental law is only a part. While some point to important positive signs on which further development could built, others are concerned that environmental law is facing systemic, complex challenges and that it is not clear that we will be able to address effectively the problems facing our planet.

To remedy this situation, this book argues that a "rule of law for nature" is needed: a legal framework that extends to the environment the procedural and substantive legal principles enshrined in the "rule of law".

---

[2] Outcome of the Conference Rio+20, *The Future we Want*, A/CONF.216/L.1, 19 June 2012, para. 197.
[3] Ibid., para. 31.
[4] *Rio+20 Declaration on Justice, Governance and Law for Environmental Sustainability*, available at: www.unep.org/rio20/Portals/24180/Rio20_Declaration_on_Justice_Gov_n_Law_4_Env_Sustainability.pdf (last accessed 30 May 2013).

Historically, the concept of rule of law is deeply linked to the principle of justice, involving an ideal of accountability and fairness in the protection and vindication of rights and the prevention and punishment of wrongs. The rule of law refers to a principle of governance in which the state – the sovereign – is accountable to laws that are publicly promulgated, equally enforced and independently adjudicated, and that are consistent with international human rights norms and standards. The concept requires measures to ensure adherence to the principles of supremacy of law, equality before the law, accountability to the law, fairness in the application of the law, separation of powers, participation in decision-making, legal certainty, avoidance of arbitrariness and procedural and legal transparency.[5]

A "rule of law for nature" transposes these concepts from the original state–citizen dimension to a system of governance in which *all* persons, institutions and entities, public and private, including the state itself, are accountable to laws that aim at protecting the health, integrity and security of the environment. Hans Christian Bugge writes in his chapter: "It means that nature and natural values are protected by law from encroachments, deterioration and destruction in fundamentally the same way as citizens are protected by law ... Rule of law for nature means predictability, security and the absence of arbitrariness and bias in decisions that affect nature and the full accounting of environmental values in decision-making – be it by private interests or public authorities."[6]

In this book, a rule of law for nature is approached from different perspectives. They range from the proposition that unwritten higher law – the universal laws of nature – must guide and transcend ordinary written laws, to the view that fundamental principles of respect, integrity and legal security need to be extended to the non-human world, to the more moderate view that government has to exercise its power also in relation to the environment in accordance with well-established and clearly written rules, regulations and legal principles. It also marks the shift from a purely human-centred concept of law towards a concept of law that is recognizant of ecological realities.

---

[5] Report of the Secretary-General on the Rule of Law and Transitional Justice in Conflict and Post-Conflict Societies, 23 August 2010, S/2004/616. See also Declaration of the High-level Meeting of the General Assembly on the Rule of Law at the National and International Levels, Resolution adopted by the General Assembly, A/RES/6//1, 30 November 2012.
[6] See Chapter 1 by Hans Christian Bugge.

In doing so, this book challenges the doctrinal construction of environmental law and presents innovative legal approaches to ecological sustainability. As Edith Brown Weiss aptly puts it in her chapter: "We are at a critical juncture in … environmental law, in which we will need to forge new paths to address global environmental problems and to advance the rule of law for nature."[7] Forging of new paths is the aim of this book. Of course, not all answers can be given and all problems solved. Rather, it is hoped that the book stimulates further thinking and research in these important fields and that, as a consequence, a rule of law for nature takes shape.

Part I of this book sets out a diagnosis of the fundamental, complex and systemic shortcomings that environmental law faces. This Part also looks ahead to the major legal challenges that loom in the onset of the Anthropocene – the epoch in which humans have become the central force affecting our planet.[8]

Part II continues with a doctrinal reflection on a "rule of law for nature". What is meant by it? How can it possibly remedy the challenges mentioned above? What would a rule of law for nature require?

Third, and most importantly, the book looks for ways to reform environmental law-making, interpretation, implementation and enforcement. It presents innovative and constructive legal approaches to ecological sustainability. The book reflects on the legal status of nature and environmental functions. It shows how ecological goods and services can be better taken into account in decision-making and the implications of the rule of law in this respect.

In Part III, the book portrays a wide spectrum of innovative legal ideas and approaches to solving environmental challenges. It comprises global, transnational, regional as well as domestic perspectives, all informed and connected by the attempt to strengthen the legal protection of nature. The environment does not correspond to administrative or sovereign boundaries. In the same way, new environmental legal concepts can and should travel across boundaries and be implemented at all levels, whether international, regional or in national legal systems.

Part IV deals with the notion of rights for nature. Nature's rights resemble the ultimate legal recognition of intrinsic value and moral standing of the environment.

Part V then discusses various procedural aspects of a rule of law for nature, such as the merging of environmental and social impact

---

[7] See Chapter 2 by Edith Brown Weiss.
[8] See Chapter 3 by Nicholas A. Robinson.

assessments to provide a more comprehensive, holistic impact assessment, administrative enforcement of environmental laws and the possibility for legal review of compliance by states with their international legal obligations.

In Part VI, the role of companies and markets is analysed from the perspective of environmental improvements. Again, we find the argument here that nature should be bestowed with autonomous rights that operate as trump cards over other social goals.

Finally, in Part VII the book turns to the oceans and the fact that a large part of the Earth's marine environment is outside national jurisdiction. It asks how environmental protection of marine life can be strengthened and suggests, for example, the innovative application of the traditional public trust doctrine.

The authors represent different legal fields, though most of them are prominent scholars and practitioners in environmental law. Importantly, however, they bring together a wide spectrum of views from different parts of the world. As such, the book is a fruitful exercise in exchanging views and ideas on strengthening environmental protection through the rule of law. Moreover, the list of contributors is balanced in terms of age and gender.

It is hoped that the book will provide environmental law scholars, students, researchers, lawyers, judges and civil servants with compelling new perspectives upon the pressing issue of improving the quality of environmental protection. However, while focusing on *environmental* law, the book also provides important insights as to the law's potential for scholars working in other fields of law and to (environmental) social scientists who are not lawyers. As such, the book is a contribution to the environmental discourse, and aims at stimulating debate and further research on how to further the quality of our natural environment across disciplinary boundaries.

Christina Voigt

PART I

Environmental law at the crossroads: achievements, shortcomings and challenges

1

Twelve fundamental challenges in environmental law

An introduction to the concept of rule of law for nature

HANS CHRISTIAN BUGGE

1. Introduction

This introductory chapter reflects on the legal status of nature and the fundamental challenges in protecting nature through law. It presents and discusses the concept of rule of law and how this can be developed into stronger legal protection not only for human beings as citizens, but also for the protection of nature and natural values.

In 2012 forty years had passed since the first global United Nations Conference on the Human Environment in Stockholm. It was also twenty-five years since the report 'Our Common Future' – known as the Brundtland Report – was launched with its urgent call for 'sustainable development', and twenty years since the milestone United Nations Conference on Environment and Development in Rio de Janeiro.

Over this period an impressive body of environmental law has been adopted in all developed and most developing countries as well as at the international level. There are some important success stories, but there are also numerous examples of ambitions and objectives of environmental policy that have not been fulfilled.

In June 2012 world leaders and more than 15,000 representatives of the civil society gathered again in Rio de Janeiro for the 'Rio+20' conference to discuss the progress made and the future course: how to meet the double challenges of global environmental degradation and development needs. What came out of this conference were mainly affirmations of earlier commitments, with few new initiatives.[1] It did not lay a foundation for

---

[1] *The Future We Want*, A/CONF/216.L.1 of 22 June 2012, adopted at the UN General Assembly on 27 July 2012 as A/RES/66/288.

more effective international and national measures to protect the global environment, although this is urgently needed.

An important factual basis for the conference was the most recent UNEP (United Nations Environment Programme) Global Environmental Outlook (GEO5). This report opens with the following statement:

> The currently observed changes to the Earth System are unprecedented in human history. Efforts to slow the rate or extent of change – including enhanced resource efficiency and mitigation measures – have resulted in moderate successes but have not succeeded in reversing adverse environmental changes. Neither the scope of these nor their speed has abated in the past five years.[2]

The report shows that in spite of all the political objectives adopted, the economic and legal instruments established and changes in attitudes and efforts made, most important trends continue to go in the wrong direction. For example, the report states that 'the rate of forest loss, particularly in the tropics, remains alarmingly high'. With regard to freshwater sources, despite progress in some areas, 'there are concerns that the limit of sustainability of water resources, both surface and ground water, has already been reached or surpassed in many regions'. Furthermore, despite many global agreements on the issue 'there are continuing signs of degradation' of the marine environment due to pollution. And with regard to biodiversity 'substantial and on-going losses of species contribute to ecosystem deterioration. Up to two thirds of species in some taxa are threatened with extinction'. This happens in spite of the fact that protected areas now cover nearly 13 per cent of the total land area and 'policies, regulations and actions have been adopted to minimize the pressures on biodiversity'.[3]

GEO5 points to the need

> to consider policies and programmes that focus on the underlying drivers that contribute to increased pressure on environmental conditions, rather than concentrating only on reducing environmental pressures or symptoms. Drivers include, inter alia, the negative aspects of population growth, consumption and production, urbanization and globalization.[4]

Undoubtedly, these are all root causes of the worldwide environmental degradation, and they can only be met by fundamental political reforms.

---

[2] The Fifth Global Environment Outlook (GEO5) Summary for Policy Makers, United Nations Environment Programme (2012), 6.
[3] Ibid., 6–11.   [4] Ibid., 14.

The environmental crisis is deeply rooted in the dominant values of economic growth and material consumption of our civilization. We have to admit that to a large extent the environmental problems of our time are the negative side effects, and as such to a large extent an expected consequence, of our economic and social goals and ambitions. They are thus not only consciously 'accepted', but also – implicitly – wanted.

At this fundamental level, what is needed is to give environmental protection higher priority as a political goal, and limit economic growth and consumption in the traditional (material) sense. Some of the chapters in this book challenge the very paradigm of economic growth as we know it and the exploitation and destruction of nature that it by necessity entails.

The issue also has an ethical dimension. How we treat nature is fundamentally an ethical question. In modern civilization there is no such thing as a strong 'nature ethics' that directs and limits human action and works as a defence against destruction or degradation of nature. For decades there have been philosophical discussions on the moral status of nature, and on the moral obligations of humans towards nature.[5] There is a growing movement in the field of animal welfare and even animal rights that is beginning to influence methods and practice in animal husbandry in some Western counties in particular. But in reality there are still few ethical barriers in our societies against widespread destruction and degradation of nature, at least as long as the purpose of the degradation is economic development and human well-being in the short term. This obviously has important consequences for legal thinking and the role of law in this area.

In addition to these fundamental causes, an important challenge from the perspective of environmental law is the discrepancy between the political rhetoric and formally adopted environmental objectives and legislation on the one hand and what happens in reality on the other hand. GEO5 states generally that 'environmental deterioration demonstrates internationally agreed goals have only partly been achieved'.[6] The negative trends go contrary to the political ambitions and objectives of

---

[5] For general sources see, for example, Andrew Brennan and Yeuk-Sze Lo, 'Environmental Ethics', in: Edward N. Zalta (ed.), *The Stanford Encyclopedia of Philosophy (Fall 2011 Edition)*, available at: http://plato.stanford.edu/archives/fall2011/entries/ethics-environmental (last accessed 11 March 2013); Joy A. Palmer (ed.), *Fifty Key Thinkers on the Environment* (London: Routledge, 2001); and Christopher Belshaw, *Environmental Philosophy. Reason, Nature and Human Concern* (Chesham: Acumen, 2001).
[6] The Fifth Global Environment Outlook (GEO5) Summary for Policy Makers, United Nations Environment Programme (2012), 7.

environmental protection and sustainable development, as they have been laid down by both states and international organizations for several decades. The goal of long-term environmental sustainability is fully recognized; why don't we manage to achieve it?

While certainly agreeing with the need for fundamental changes in ethics, political priorities, economic systems and lifestyle, we should be deeply concerned with how law actually works, its limitations and weaknesses, and how it can be improved and strengthened. It has become evident that environmental law – generally speaking – does not work as effectively as the public and the politicians want it to work – and probably presume that it actually works. My assertion is that this is due to a number of fundamental problems and challenges inherent in law and the legal system itself when natural values are at stake. These have to be identified and analysed in order for us to understand and eventually overcome them – as far as possible. This introductory chapter aims to identify some of these problems and reflect on how ideas of a 'rule of law for nature' may serve. Other chapters in the book will elaborate further on specific perspectives and aspects of this broad theme.

2. The concepts of 'rule of law' and 'nature'

The concept 'rule of law' encapsulates the highest values and functions of law and the legal system in society: 'rule of law is the role of law'. As such, rule of law can also be regarded as a primary social value. In its broadest sense rule of law refers to the principle of governance where law is the supreme factor in the relationship between the authorities and the citizen as well as between citizens with conflicting interests. It means that all persons, institutions and entities, public and private, including the state itself, are governed by established laws and accountable to legal institutions.

Rule of law has both a procedural and substantial content. In the procedural sense the laws must be established by an open and democratic process, publicly promulgated and equally and objectively implemented and enforced. They must be controlled and adjudicated by an independent judiciary. Rule of law means security in the form of predictability. Citizens should be able to see and understand from the legal texts their rights and obligations in different situations. Substantially, rule of law now implies that the law complies with internationally recognized human rights norms and standards regarding fundamental rights and freedoms, personal security, protection of personal integrity and due process before the courts, with corresponding obligations for both the state and local authorities. Justice and fairness are implicit values in rule of law.

One person's freedom may harm other people's freedom, integrity and rights. Therefore, rule of law does not mean citizens'´full freedom, nor does it mean absolute security and physical integrity. What rule of law requires is that any limitation and restraint in personal freedom, and any encroachment upon the individual's security and integrity must be found necessary and proportionate in order to protect other citizens' rights and interests or important public objectives and values. Furthermore, they must be laid down in formal laws and based on a due process, including the right to have one's rights and legitimate interests defended before an independent judiciary.

Rule of law is an anthropocentric ideal. It concerns human beings in their capacity as members of the society and subjects to the state's formal authority. Its aim – and hopefully its result – is the fulfilment of freedom, security and integrity of humans. Defined in this way, rule of law is not concerned with or relevant for nature as a subject of legal rules.

The concept of a *'rule of law for nature'* has two main aspects. The first is the importance of rule of law in general as a prerequisite also for proper management of nature and natural resources. Together with weak social groups, nature – the environment – is particularly vulnerable to lack of law, and to poorly developed legal and political systems. To put it simply: nature needs good laws and strong and unbiased implementation and enforcement of the laws.

But even more, the law must provide stronger protection for natural values. The second and more radical meaning of rule of law for nature – which will be the main perspective and topic of this book – is that important elements of rule of law are extended beyond human beings as citizens to nature and natural values. Instead of being anthropocentric, rule of law for nature even means a better legal protection of nature from human activities that may threaten or damage nature. Substantially it aims at the integrity and security of nature. It means that nature and natural values are protected by law from encroachments, deterioration and destruction in fundamentally the same way as citizens are protected by law. Of course, this does not mean that it shall be protected at any price and regardless of any other conflicting goal or interest. But these goals or interests must be strong enough to justify the environmental damage, and there must be procedural rules that ensure that the trade-off is made with due regard to nature's value and all other relevant facts. Rule of law for nature means predictability, security and the absence of arbitrariness and bias in decisions that affect nature and the full accounting of environmental values in decision-making – be it by private interests or public authorities.

Rule of law for nature also requires an expanded concept of justice and fairness, which includes the non-human world. Laws are not fair – and acts implementing them do not comply with the rule of law – if they 'legalize' environmentally destructive behaviour without sufficiently important reason and a corresponding procedure. Ultimately, it means that nature and natural values have legal protection at a similar level as that of human beings as citizens.

Rule of law for nature may, therefore, in a short-term perspective, be in conflict with elements of rule of law for humans – as limitations to the fundamental rights and freedoms of people. However, the universally recognized objective of sustainable development implies that protection of essential parts of the environment is necessary to ensure peace and security, social and economic stability progress, human rights and widespread well-being in the long term.

The values of nature may be 'intrinsic', which means values independent of human interests, or 'instrumental' – contributing to people's material and spiritual welfare.[7] There is a fundamental legal difference between – on the one hand – nature as a value in itself and – on the other hand – nature as a means for the satisfaction of human needs and interests. However, they both need stronger legal protection.

When intrinsic values of nature are threatened, there is per definition no human interest in protecting them. Can they nevertheless be protected? This fundamentally challenges our legal system, which is developed to regulate human actions to meet social needs and solve conflicts between human interests. Here the idea of a rule of law for nature is truly radical and seems to require major legal innovations.

If, on the other hand, nature as instrumental value is threatened, people appreciating this value will presumably take action to prevent it, or at least consider taking action. Whether they will actually do it depends on the strength of their interest, possible costs of an action and conflicting interests, and other factors. Whether they will succeed in protecting their interest depends ultimately on the legal rules that regulate the actual conflict, and how they are applied. In reality, we here meet many of the same

---

[7] Instrumental value of nature has for some time been divided into 'user value', 'option value', and 'existence value'. For an early discussion of these concepts see David Pearce and Kerry Turner, *Economics of Natural Resources and the Environment* (Baltimore: Johns Hopkins University Press, 1990). They see 'existence value' as equal to intrinsic value.

fundamental problems in environmental law as we face in the protection of intrinsic values of nature, although to a varying degree. And most of the ideas of a 'rule of law for nature' are relevant for nature as both intrinsic and instrumental value.

3. Twelve fundamental problems in environmental law

When we want to analyse environmental law in order to better understand how it works – or why it does not always work as expected – we must be conscious of some deep-rooted problems in dealing with nature and the environment through legal means. In fact, we are here faced with a legal challenge that is fundamentally different from other issues in law. Some of these problems are grounded in the characteristics of environmental problems and in the special types of interests and conflicts we are faced with in this area of law. They may be described and categorized in several different ways. Here, I want in particular to highlight twelve fundamental problems. Several of them may be perceived as obvious and self-evident, but individually and indeed *in sum* they are essential to understanding and explaining the problems that face environmental law and policy.

3.1 Nature is self-regulating and complex; we cannot influence the laws of nature

It is special to environmental law that the *object* of its rules and regulations is something that cannot itself be regulated. We can destroy nature. We can protect and improve the conditions for natural processes and natural objects. But we cannot influence nature's own laws, how nature reacts to external influence such as pollution and other encroachments. We cannot stop the greenhouse effect itself or prevent toxic chemicals from being spread by wind and ocean currents all over the planet once they have been emitted into the air or water. We cannot order a pack of wolves to keep within a certain geographic area or by a simple decision ensure a certain environmental quality.

We can of course only regulate the environmental quality indirectly, by regulating human activities that may influence that quality. This is evident and indeed trite, but nevertheless fundamental and of utmost importance for the effectiveness of environmental law. It requires good knowledge of and respect for the laws of nature. Ideally, an adequate regulation of human activities must be based on clear objectives with regard to the environmental quality or values to be protected or attained, and sufficient knowledge about what regulation of human activity is needed in order to reach that objective. The complexity of nature's law and of the relations and mutual influences and dependences between the innumerable elements in the ecosystems make this task very difficult. Effects are not necessarily linear; unknown thresholds may appear, as when the pH level in a lake passes a level in which fish can no longer live. And since environmental degradation often is the combined and synergetic effect of many human activities (see below), it is difficult to keep the damaging influence on nature within the 'critical load'.

3.2 Many environmental problems are invisible

Not all but many environmental problems of modern society are neither seen nor felt by human beings. We cannot 'see' radioactivity, the levels of dioxins in breast milk or CO_2 in the atmosphere. They are not perceived until their effects become evident: health problems and increased mortality among certain social groups, reduction of plant or animal species in an area, and increase in global temperature. This 'simple' fact makes many effects of environmental disturbance very difficult to discover.

In order to prevent and combat this type of problem, 'invisible' facts must be made 'visible'. They must be identified and presented in such a way that they can be understood by decision-makers. This requires resources for research and competent and independent researchers. And the decision-making system must be able and willing to respect and act solely on the basis of scientific knowledge.

What does rule of law for nature mean and imply to meet this problem? Here we get into such issues as producer responsibility: producers' obligation to assess and know about the properties, characteristics and effects of their production as well as their products, and the obligation to make this knowledge known to the relevant decision-makers and to the public. This must be secured by law. Effective enforcement of this also depends on the capacity of public authorities to be aware of and identify the 'invisible' and enforce the necessary legislation in order to avoid unwanted effects.

3.3 Many environmental problems are marked by uncertainties

Partly due to the complexities of natural processes there is often a lack of certain knowledge about causes and effects of changes in the environment, creating scientific debate and controversies. Environmental policy and law must address uncertainties and 'moving targets' in its conception, adoption and implementation.

Uncertainty about facts is not unique for environmental policy and law. In many policy areas, not least in the social sector, both the causes of the problem and how to solve them effectively may be uncertain or unknown. A key issue in a conflict and a court case is often simply uncertainty or disagreements about facts. The job of judges is to make difficult decisions under uncertainty.

However, environmental policy and law is probably marked by uncertainty to a greater extent than most other social sectors. And the consequences of making the wrong decision may be more serious. The problems of the ozone hole and climate change are the two most important examples. Here it becomes particularly important to 'err on the right side' – to give nature 'the benefit of the doubt'. That is why the precautionary principle has been conceived first and foremost as a principle of environmental law and policy, at national as well as international level. However, this principle is clearly controversial, not least in the perspective of economic efficiency, and it is certainly not being implemented consistently, neither by international bodies nor within states.[8]

This is not the place to discuss the precautionary principle in any depth. It is, however, obvious that rule of law for nature implies a strict interpretation and implementation of the precautionary principle. It requires that law is 'organic' and flexible so as to meet changing circumstances and new insight. This may challenge the traditional rule of law value of legal security and predictability.

3.4 Nature cannot itself act legally; nature, the environment, does not itself have a voice in decision-making

This is another obvious fact of great importance. In any political process and court case that concerns natural values and natural objects, nature must be represented by a physical or legal person. Not only are material rules necessary to have nature protected. In addition, there must be systems that ensure a proper implementation and enforcement of the rules. Some must have both the right and the duty to see to it that proper weight is given to environmental values in decision-making and to take remedial action on behalf of nature.

---

[8] See for example Nicolas de Sadeleer (ed.), *Implementing the Precautionary Principle. Approaches from the Nordic Countries, EU and USA* (London: Earthscan, 2007).

From a philosophical perspective, this may be seen primarily as an issue of 'rights' for natural objects. An independent 'right' for natural objects, regardless of their usefulness to humans and society, may seem a logical consequence of recognizing nature's intrinsic value. The issue of 'rights' for nature and natural objects is undoubtedly a key point in a discussion about rule of law for nature. Rule of law for nature in essence means that law provides nature with a legal status that can withstand attacks on legal grounds and be defended in political and legal procedures. Or, as a legal minimum, that nature's intrinsic value has legal relevance and must be taken into consideration in the development of policy and the implementation of laws.

However, regardless of whether the law provides nature and natural objects with formal 'rights' or simply accepts that nature's intrinsic value is legally relevant, the crucial point is the possibility to – ultimately – defend natural values before the courts even if there are no human interests attached. This requires the fulfilment of three conditions. First, the intrinsic value of nature must be accepted as an interest that has legal standing in the sense that it can be defended in courts. Second, there must be persons or organizations with resources, competence and independence willing to represent nature. And, third, the judiciary system must accept legal standing for both the natural object and the representative. This was the main idea of and reasoning by Christopher D. Stone in his famous article 'Should Trees have Standing? Toward Legal Rights for Natural Objects'.[9] This issue is more relevant than ever. Various concepts of rights for nature, and how natural values can be defended in courts, will be discussed in later chapters in this book.

3.5 Many environmental goods and services are public goods in the economic sense

Many environmental goods and services are not the property of physical or legal persons, but can be enjoyed by everybody; they are 'public goods'. The air we breathe, the water cycle, biodiversity, a beautiful landscape and the services and values we get from these goods do not 'belong' to anybody, but they are of course fundamental for the functioning of nature and thus essential for any economic activity, for human welfare

---

[9] Christopher D. Stone, 'Should Trees have Standing? Toward Legal Rights for Natural Objects', 45 *Southern California Law Review* (1972) 450.

and – ultimately – for human survival. Nevertheless, as public goods their legal protection is weak at the outset.

The public goods character of many natural values and environmental services raises fundamental problems in both environmental economics and environmental law. They are defined as 'goods that one individual can consume without reducing their availability to another individual and from which no one is excluded'.[10] Public goods cannot be traded in the markets; they do not have a market price as it is impossible to keep non-paying people away. Harm to a public good will not damage property and entail liability that leads to costs for the harmful activity. Unless such external effects are fully internalized through adequate legal measures, this creates a 'market failure' in the economic sense. Since they are not subject to property rights and do not have a price in the market, they also have at the outset a weaker legal status than various types of property rights and easily identified economic interests. Without public law protection, they may easily be harmed, reduced or destroyed.

The destruction of a public environmental good may be a serious cost to society. Many people, today and in the future, may lose an environmental service or natural good that they value. Even if it is possible to ultimately go to court to defend such interests, for example in countries that accept legal actions based on *actio popularis* in certain environmental cases, this may nevertheless be unlikely. One factor here is the so-called 'rational apathy' syndrome, generally defined as a person's indifference to act on a case based on a reasoned and rational assessment of the possibility to influence the outcome.[11] Environmental cases offer an important example of this: each individual member of the public who loses an environmental good may find that the costs of trying to prevent this loss are too high in light of both the likelihood of winning and what he or she may gain by winning. In addition, the transaction costs of organizing a common action may appear too high. Nevertheless, the public's – and society's – loss in sum may exceed the gains or profit that may be the result of the environmental destruction. 'Rational apathy' is thus a threat to economic efficiency.

Another problem with public goods is the free-rider problem: a rational person will not contribute to the provision of a public good because he does not need to contribute in order to benefit. This also leads to market failure in another sense: the risk of overexploitation of environmental

[10] www.investopedia.com/terms/p/public-good.asp#axzz2IhArtH8m.
[11] www.businessdictionary.com/definition/rational-apathy.html.

goods and resources, usually referred to as 'the tragedy of the commons'.[12] This is not the place to discuss this issue in all its complexities. But the fact that a large part of the Earth's marine environment is a 'common' in the sense that it is outside national jurisdiction is of course an enormous problem for the sustainable management of the oceans and protection of marine life.[13]

We witness these types of market failures – and the corresponding weakness of legal protection – in many types of environmental issues and cases, at the local as well as the global level. These fundamental problems may not be overcome without a radical new approach to the legal treatment of public goods. One alternative may be to introduce a form of property rights into the public goods sphere. One example of this are such instruments as cap-and-trade in emissions. In the climate regime a price is put on 'carbon' – emissions of CO_2 – to abate climate change, the climate being the ultimate example of a public good. In this way, a market is created artificially to overcome the public good market failure.

A different approach would be to separate the legal treatment of natural public goods from the economic nature and treatment of public goods altogether: provide nature with legal status even if it is not made subject to property rights and the market. This is a key element in a broad 'rule of law for nature' concept. Here in reality we get into much of the same issues and problems as discussed under 3.4 above. Such stronger legal protection will also serve to correct the market failure in the economic sense.

3.6 Environmental values – and environmental harms – are difficult to price correctly in decision-making

Closely linked to the 'public good' character of most natural and environmental values is the problem of pricing such values. This is particularly important in decision-making where environmental values are at stake, and the decision is to be taken on the basis of cost–benefit analysis.

Many natural values are often described as 'non-economic' or 'immaterial'. This easily leads to misunderstandings. Most environmental goods and services have an economic value both for individuals and for society.

---

[12] However, as not least the laureate of the Sveriges Riksbank Prize in Economic Sciences in Memory of Alfred Nobel, Elinor Ostrom, has shown, commons may be managed in a sustainable way by local communities and organizations. Her research challenged the conventional economic wisdom about the need for government regulation of public resources.

[13] See the chapters by Tore Henriksen and Robin Warner in this book.

This is evident when pollution causes health problems or kills fish in a river, and when high noise levels reduce the market value of houses along a major road. But it is also often implicit, for example when people spend time and money on hiking in a pristine forest or mountain area. These are examples of instrumental value of environmental goods. It is even more difficult – not to say impossible – to put a meaningful price on nature's intrinsic value.

This remains a problem in spite of the many efforts in environmental economics to quantify environmental values in economic terms in a meaningful way in order to have efficient and 'optimal' management of the environment. The traditional methods, such as analyses of 'willingness to pay', 'willingness to accept' and 'hedonic pricing', have several weaknesses. One is that the result varies with the economic situation of the person involved. To simplify: it is more expensive to harm rich people than poor people. The more fundamental critique is that natural values, by such methods, are measured only by people living today and what they can afford, and are reduced merely to a kind of consumer good competing with other consumer goods and services. Future effects are minimized in the calculation due to discounting – a fundamental challenge in itself. Intrinsic natural values are – per definition – excluded altogether.

Considerable work has been done and is being done in research in environmental economics to find good ways of 'pricing' natural values, but problems seem to remain. New thinking seems to be required. At the same time, it has to be recognized by decision-makers (and economists) that the social and long-term costs of nature degradation and destruction cannot be fully measured and expressed in defined money terms. For this reason, until really new methods in valuing nature and environmental services are developed, a rule of law for nature seems to me to require limitations on the influence of economic methods and thinking in environmental governance.

3.7 *The problem of 'the small decisions paradox'*

Many environmental problems are the unwanted and inefficient cumulative effect of numerous actions and decisions that – individually – are both rational and economically efficient. This may seem a paradox. How can the sum of many individually efficient decisions give an inefficient result?

This phenomenon is a well-known problem in economic theory. In 1966 the American economist Alfred E. Kahn wrote the essay 'The

Tyranny of Small Decisions'.[14] The essay describes a situation where a number of decisions, individually small in size and time perspective, cumulatively result in an outcome that is not optimal in the economic sense, nor desired by the actors. A series of small, individually rational decisions can negatively change the context of subsequent choices, even to the point where desired alternatives are irreversibly destroyed. Kahn described the problem as a common issue in market economics that can lead to market failure. He gave as an example the loss of passenger train service to Ithaca, New York. Even though the majority of the inhabitants of Ithaca would have preferred to retain a passenger train service, they 'decided' to terminate the service through the combined effects of a series of small, independent decisions to travel by car, aeroplane and bus.

The concept has since been extended to areas other than economic ones, such as environmental degradation, political elections and health outcomes. Several authors have elaborated more particularly on the problem in relation to environmental law and governance.[15] Examples of so-called 'small decision effects' in the environmental field range from loss of landscape values, biodiversity and prime farmland to acid precipitation. Today, the climate problem can be seen as the 'ultimate example' of the tyranny of small decisions.

How can this be overcome through the development and implementation of environmental law? Several elements may together work in the right direction. The main point is that we must avoid environmental governance based mainly on a case-by-case application of the law. A case should not be decided in isolation, and solely on an individual cost–benefit analysis.

Generally speaking, this requires such instruments as comprehensive and effective spatial planning as a basis for individual permits and other decisions. The plans must include 'environmental caps' or clear environmental quality objectives as a legal framework within which the sum of the individual decisions must be kept. Environmental quality norms must be both adopted and respected. In theory, general cap-and-trade systems are particularly useful for environmental problems caused by innumerable small decisions.

---

[14] Alfred E. Kahn, 'The Tyranny of Small Decisions: Market Failures, Imperfections, and the Limits of Economics', 19 *Kyklos* (1966) 23–47.

[15] Generally recognized as one of the first is William E. Odum, 'Environmental Degradation and the Tyranny of Small Decisions', 32:9 *BioScience* (1982) 728–9.

If each case has to be treated individually, the decision-maker must consider it in relation to the established framework and ensure that the limits are not exceeded. From a legal point of view this may be a difficult task in practice, given the need for consistency and equality in the implementation of environmental law. It presupposes that the environmental quality norm has clear legal effect. It also requires that environmental impact assessments ideally take into account all factors that may influence the total picture. This must also include assessment of possible future scenarios. In brief, a 'holistic' rather than 'reductionist' perspective is needed to avoid the undesirable, cumulative effects of small decisions.[16] This is an important element in the concept of rule of law for nature.

3.8 Many environmental problems cross economic and social sectors both in their causes and their effects

The problem of the 'small decisions paradox' is underpinned by the fact that many environmental problems have many different and complex causes. This is evident with regard to air, water and marine pollution, climate change and loss of biodiversity. They are not the result of a single activity, but of innumerable activities, in nearly all economic and social sectors, with different and even conflicting objectives. A consistent and sustainable management of environmental quality requires cross-sector coordination and coherence of policy and law.

In actual fact, however, each factor that contributes to the problem is most often treated individually pursuant to legislation that is sector-based and highly fragmented: there are separate acts for various types of industry, mining, agriculture, forestry, fishery and aquaculture, different types of energy production, road, air and sea transport, tourism, such public services as health and education, and so on. For each sector there are special political goals, which do not necessarily take environmental side-effects properly into account. The different pieces of law have different objectives and criteria for decisions. They treat environmental values differently. Even if environmental law principles apply generally, they will often be interpreted and implemented in various ways. Generally speaking, they also have different procedures for decision-making. But they all have effect on the same natural objects or ecosystems.

The environmental legislation in the strict sense – laws with the main objective of environmental protection – may apply across sectors and at

[16] Ibid.

least partly be suited to meet this challenge. However, the environmental legislation itself – apart from not being strong enough – is also often quite fragmented, with separate acts for different types of pollution, for chemical substances and products, waste treatment, and different instruments for nature protection. To my knowledge, only a few countries have an overarching framework of environmental law.

Mechanisms for coordination and coherence, and for holistic planning, may be in place. In particular, there is a long tradition for comprehensive spatial and land-use planning in most of the industrial countries at least. However, the relationship between such systems and the various sector policies and laws are often unclear and controversial. Again, adequate environmental quality objectives with binding legal force seem to be the required logic and main element of a rule of law for nature to meet this challenge.

This touches on the issue of sector responsibility for environmental protection, which I shall revert to under section 4 below.

3.9 The most serious environmental problems cross administrative borders

Environmental problems cross boundaries between local communities, between counties and regions, and not least between states. The main environmental harm of a certain activity may appear far away from its source, and under other jurisdictions. Hence, different and mutually independent constituents may, on the one hand, get the benefits from the activity that harms the environment and, on the other hand, be the victims and incur the costs of the environmental degradation.

When the negative effects are only local or national, the decision-making institution is forced by the different interests in question to balance the benefits and costs. But when the activity is regulated by the party that in the main gets only the benefit, the imbalance becomes evident. This is the fundamental issue with such global problems as climate change. As an example, the government of Norway does not see any reason to reduce its petroleum production even if it is an important source of GHG emissions. Would this policy have been different if the small island states threatened by rising sea levels were populated by Norwegians?

The 'simple' answer is decision-making procedures and institutions that can ensure that all aspects and effects of an activity are treated equally and comprehensively regardless of existing administrative and national borders. This is complex and controversial, however. It inevitably challenges the fundamental principle of state sovereignty and it will often go against the general objective and trend of decentralization of authority to the local level in many countries.

3.10 Many environmental effects are long term

Future generations will be the victims. But future generations do not have a defined legal status either. Generally speaking, the role of law is to regulate actual conflicts – between persons and interests of the present day. Law and legal institutions are not well developed and only marginally equipped to regulate intergenerational conflicts. Politicians are concerned with the present and the next election, and future generations have no vote.

Concern for the future and intergenerational equity is the core idea of sustainable development as a political objective and legal principle. The needs of our descendants must not be compromised by the steps we take to solve today's problems. Edith Brown Weiss wrote her seminal book on the problem in 1989,[17] and legal theory has continued to discuss it and search for solutions.[18] In practice, we see some positive trends. For example, sustainable development has been adopted as a principle and objective in many national laws around the world. It follows that future interests and long-term effects should be taken properly into account when decisions on nature and natural resources are made. But we generally lack a developed legal doctrine and instruments that can ensure that this requirement is actually fulfilled. The economic dilemma of discounting future effects have not been solved either.

Some type of legal status with corresponding representation for future generations must be a key element in a rule of law for nature.

---

[17] Edith Brown Weiss, *In Fairness to Future Generations: International Law, Common Patrimony, and Intergenerational Equity* (Tokyo: United Nations University, 1989).
[18] See, for example: M. Fitzmaurice, 'Intergenerational Equity Revisited', in: Isabelle Buffard, James Crawford et al. (eds.), *International Law Between Universalism and Fragmentation – Festschrift in Honour of Gerhard Hafner* (Leiden: Brill, 2008), 195–231; P. Lawrence, 'Justice for Future Generations: Environment Discourses, International Law and Climate Change', in: B. Jessup and K. Rubenstein (eds.), *Environmental Discourses in Public and International Law* (Cambridge University Press, 2012), 536; and E. B. Weiss, 'Implementing Intergenerational Equity', in: M. Fitzmaurice, D. M. Ong et al. (eds.), *Research Handbook on International Environmental Law* (Cheltenham: Edward Elgar Publishing, 2011), 703.

3.11 Corruption

Corruption is another fundamental problem that has to be addressed in the perspective of rule of law for nature. 'The environment is a silent victim of corruption';[19] we cannot understand the massive destruction of nature in many parts of the world without recognizing corruption as one important cause.

Corruption takes many forms, from direct bribes to extortion and patronage. There are 'grey zones' where decisions and actions are influenced by political support, personal relations, cronyism and mutual services. Corruption can be organized from the top to the bottom of a system and even be linked to organized crime. Corruption in its most primitive as well as in its more subtle and hidden forms is likely to be found – to a varying degree – in all countries.

Corruption is not specific to the management of nature. It is a general problem that hurts many aspects and values of society. Nevertheless, nature and natural values are particularly vulnerable to corruption; 'trees have no money'. 'Corruption and the environment' is now appearing as an important political and legal issue on the international scene.[20] Several of the fundamental problems mentioned above contribute to facilitate corruption in the environmental field.

Broadly speaking, there are two main areas of corruption in this field: On the one hand, activities in various sectors that harm the environment may be accepted and permitted due to various types of corruption. Main examples are the timber industry and other exploitation of renewable resources, the sectors of mining, oil and gas, and major infrastructure projects such as big dams and highways.

On the other hand, there may be corruption within the environmental sector and administration itself, linked to the implementation and enforcement of environmental legislation, concerning for example waste disposal and illegal poaching. There may be bribery or other forms of corruption in environmental permitting systems and in the inspection and

---

[19] *Corruption and The Environment. A Project For Transparency International*, Environmental Science and Policy Workshop Columbia University, School of International & Public Affairs, April 2006.

[20] Main sources: *Corruption and the Environment*, Report for USAID by Management Systems International, authored by Svetlana Winbourne, November 2002, available at: http://pdf.usaid.gov/pdf_docs/PNACT876.pdf (last accessed 11 March 2013); and *Corruption, Environment and the United Nations Convention against Corruption*, United Nations Office on Drugs and Crime, February 2012.

the enforcement of environmental legislation. Recently, there has also been a growing concern over the risk of corruption related to national and international measures to combat climate change.[21]

The fundamental causes of corruption are the same in the environmental sector as in other sectors: the legislation may itself be inadequate and the legal frames for decisions may be weak, unclear or non-existent. There may be weak democratic institutions and a general lack of accountability, transparency and general awareness in the public sector. The legislation in this sector often provides the authorities with wide discretionary power. This may in part be natural and necessary (see below), but it makes the system vulnerable to biased decisions and corruption.

Here the idea of rule of law for nature gets the broader meaning I briefly touched upon in the introduction. The respect for and strengthening of rule of law in the general sense is a key to combat corruption and cronyism. Strategies to address corruption in the environmental sector include general reforms to improve transparency, accountability and citizen participation in the public sector. It requires the strengthening of inspection and enforcement systems, investigation capacity and criminal law. And it demands that citizens turn against corruption in their society in general and increase their understanding of corruption's detrimental effect on the environment in particular.[22,23]

3.12 *Plurality of values and complexity in decision-making*

The objective and role of environmental law is often to regulate complex problems and situations where a plurality of different and conflicting values and interests are involved. The issue is seldom simply to solve a conflict between A and B, as between a buyer and a seller, a landowner and a tenant, or a tortfeasor and the injured party in classical private law. Neither is it only between a public authority and the taxpayer or the social security client in public administrative law. In many such areas of law it is possible to lay down rather precise mutual rights and obligations of the

---

[21] *Global Corruption Report: Climate Change*, Transparency International, May 2011.
[22] For a general and thorough presentation and discussion of corruption as a fundamental issue of governance, see Susan Rose-Ackerman, *The Challenge of Poor Governance and Corruption* (Copenhagen: Consensus Challenge Paper, 2004).
[23] The UN Convention against Corruption was adopted in Mexico in 2003 and has been ratified by 165 states (as at 31 December 2012). Effectively implemented, this Convention will clearly also have a positive effect for nature protection worldwide.

parties, individuals as citizens and the public authority, in the legislation itself.

In environmental cases the situation is usually very different. Although such bilateral relationships may be at the core of an environmental conflict as well (for example between a polluting factory and its close neighbours, or between the authority and the private actor applying for a building licence or a pollution permit), most often there are a number of third-party interests involved in addition. These are of various types and strengths: multiple and often conflicting public interests, and several private interests that also may be in conflict. The interests range from clear short-term economic profit on the one hand, to uncertain long-term effects on ideal, 'soft' and disputed natural values at the other end of the spectrum. And nature as such is always a third party in itself.

The various public interests may be at different levels of decision-making. It is not uncommon that interests at different levels collide. For example, in some cases national nature protection measures are met by loud opposition from the local community because they make traditional activities and new economic development difficult. In other cases, the local community wants to protect natural values and protest against an infrastructure project that is deemed necessary by the national authorities.

Can these complex patterns of values, interests and conflicts be adequately regulated through clear-cut, precise legal rules? To some extent, yes – and to some extent such rules are necessary in order to protect nature adequately. The production and use of the most toxic substances may be – and in many countries are – simply prohibited. Endangered species may be – and are – protected by strict laws in some countries. And legally binding environmental quality norms may be – and should be – applied to important problems.[24]

However, if we take a closer look, there are often some types of further conditions and exception clauses in these legal instruments. This illustrates the problem with absolute rules and the difficulty of making conflict-solving in the environmental field merely a legal exercise. To some extent, environmental regulation has to be marked by broadly formulated rules that provide flexibility. They will explicitly or implicitly prescribe a balancing of environmental concerns against sector objectives in both

---

[24] For example, we see important developments in this direction in the environmental legislation of the EU, such as the Water Framework Directive and the directives addressing air quality in urban areas.

policy development and in individual cases. By doing so, what seems to be law becomes politics.

And the fundamental problems I have described all make it difficult for values in nature and interests in nature protection to get the proper weight in the balancing exercise.

This leads to the issue of procedural rules. Good, precise procedural rules for environmental cases are even more important when the substantial rules are vague. They ensure transparency, public participation, environmental impact assessments (EIAs), and cost-benefit analyses. But the final outcome still depends on the formulation of the substantial rule and is left to the discretion of the responsible authority.

As a basis for decisions, different interests are being brought into the process by the various stakeholders. But stakeholders have widely differing means and resources to influence decisions. For example, a developer with a strong economic interest, and arguing on the basis of the creation of new jobs and increased tax income, might allocate significant time and human resources to influence a municipal body's decision to build a shopping centre. Environmental interests are often represented only by concerned individuals or a local group, which – if they get the information about the development plan at all – can often only use their spare time (and spare money) for making the authorities aware of environmental concerns. For the municipality or the state authority, an unbalanced picture easily arises where many (strong) economic arguments speak against (few) environmental arguments – making the final decision in favour of the development rather easy and environmental destruction legal. This is often the real situation on the ground.

Rules that ensure information dissemination to and real participation by the public also raise a dilemma in the perspective of rule of law for nature: who participates? Do these types of rules in reality tend to favour the resourceful segment of the concerned public, and strong economic versus weak environmental interests? This is at the core of the 'not in my back yard' (Nimby) syndrome, that environmentally hazardous activities tend to be located in poor neighbourhoods and cause 'environmental injustice'. It may also work clearly against nature protection interests in the stricter sense. Unwanted activities and installations may more easily end up in pristine natural areas so as to avoid neighbourhood nuisance and protests altogether.

Of course some will maintain that such decisions simply reflect political priorities and are legitimate results of our democratic system. But they are marked by the imbalance in the interests and material on which decisions are taken. And all the fundamental problems of environmental law that I have described contribute to these results. It is my conviction that a strengthening of nature's legal position and protection, as I have sketched, is a prerequisite for a proper balance, and through this also a proper functioning of our democratic system.

4. The dilemma of 'attacking the problem at the source'

In the Brundtland Report, 'merging environment and economics in decision making' is one of the seven 'strategic imperatives' recommended by the World Commission on Environment and Development (WCED) to achieve sustainable development. This reflects the fundamental message in the report: 'development' and 'environmental protection' should no longer be seen as separate and often conflicting objectives, but as 'two sides of the same coin'. The report recognizes the difficulty of treating ecology and economy in combination, but presents an important perspective when it states:

> Approaches to environmental policy can be broadly characterized in two ways. One, characterized as the 'standard agenda', reflects an approach to environmental policy, laws, and institutions that focuses on environmental effects. The second reflects an approach concentrating on the policies that are the sources of those effects. These two approaches represent distinctively different ways of looking both at the issues and at the institutions to manage them.[25]

The solution, the Commission says, is to move away from the first approach, and adopt the second approach: this means to integrate environmental protection objectives into the policies of important sectors that are the cause of environmental problems. In a key section of the report called 'Getting at the Sources',[26] the Commission develops its reasoning as follows:

> Sustainable development objectives should be incorporated in the terms of reference of those cabinet and legislative committees dealing with national economic policy and planning as well as those dealing with key sectoral and international policies. As an extension of this the major central economic and sectoral agencies of governments should now be made *directly responsible and fully accountable* for ensuring that their policies,

---

[25] World Commission on Environment and Development, *Our Common Future* (Oxford University Press, 1987), 310.
[26] Ibid., 20 and 310.

programmes, and budgets support development that is ecologically as well as economically sustainable.[27]

However, empirical studies tend to show that real environmental policy integration is difficult, in spite of strong, ambitious and well-formulated policy objectives to this effect. In reality, it often requires changes in the objective and priorities of the authorities in question. And too often, and in the short term, to take the environment properly into account is perceived as a 'problem'. It requires that sector authorities work with objectives and issues that they often know little about, with which they do not identify and that they even may perceive as contrary to what they regard as their – and their organization's – primary 'mission'.[28]

So, we are again faced with a dilemma: protection of nature seems to require that each economic sector is 'directly responsible and fully accountable' for protecting nature and ensuring ecological sustainability of its policy and measures. But how can this be achieved when environmental protection goes against the objective and value of the sector? And given the fundamental problems I have described, with numerous small decisions in different, fragmented sector institutions and authorities, all valuing and weighing environmental issues differently?

International and national environmental law is influenced by important legal principles. These may serve to overcome the problems of fragmentation and differences in the balancing, provided that they are understood and applied consistently by the various authorities. This is unfortunately not always the case, at least not in Norway. The principles of environmental law laid down in important international declarations and treaties, in national public documents on environmental policy and in legal texts are often interpreted and applied inconsistently.

The legal challenges of sector responsibility relate to both procedural and substantial rules: how to ensure through legal means and instruments that environmental objectives are both fully integrated in sector policies and on an equal footing with sector objectives instead of being seen and treated as contrary to their primary objective. How can legislation work in such a way that the objectives of environmental protection are naturally internalized in sector objectives and in the application of

---

[27] Ibid., 314, emphasis added.
[28] William M. Lafferty, 'From Environmental Protection to Sustainable Development: the Challenge of Decoupling through Sectoral Integration', in: William M. Lafferty (ed.), *Governance for Sustainable Development. The Challenge of Adapting Form to Function* (Cheltenham: Edward Elgar Publishing Ltd, 2004).

sector policies, and are not something that need to be avoided? How can an instrument such as environmental quality objectives serve as a basis and framework for all decisions affecting a certain part of nature? And how can law contribute to ensuring 'accountability' of the various sector authorities in this respect?

Indeed, we need to strengthen rule of law for nature. The following chapters of this book will discuss possible ways forward in this direction.

2

Rule of law for nature in a kaleidoscopic world

EDITH BROWN WEISS

> Now I truly believe that we in this generation must come to terms with nature, and I think we're challenged, as mankind has never been challenged before, to prove our maturity and our mastery, not of nature but of ourselves.
>
> (Rachel Carson, *Silent Spring*, 1962)

We stand at a critical juncture in conserving our human environment and protecting nature. Scientists warn that while we have been living in the stable Holocene Epoch, we may be entering a new geological epoch – the Anthropocene – in which humans have become the central force affecting the planet. We are challenged as never before to work together to sustain the integrity and robustness of the environment and at the same time to ensure that everyone can benefit from it. Law has an important role, for it reflects our values and shapes our behavior. It obligates us to engage in certain practices and to refrain from others.

The special challenge confronting the rule of law and the protection of nature is that we are living now in a kaleidoscopic world, in which not only states but also transnational networks, corporations, nongovernmental organizations, ad hoc coalitions, and increasingly individuals shape and implement the rule of law for nature. At the same time, our environmental problems have become more complex and systemic.

In order to understand our ability to use international environmental law to address the problems, it is useful to analyze its evolution over the last four decades. We shall find that the field has flourished and expanded, but at the same time that much more needs to be done. And the path ahead is far from clear.

The author thanks Lydia Slobodian, Esq. for research assistance.

1. The path to today

Our concern for the environment is ancient and embedded in various religious and cultural traditions.[1] But the emergence of international and national environmental law happened recently – less than five decades ago. In 1970, when environmental law began to flourish, states were concerned with environmental issues within their country and to a lesser extent with transboundary pollution and protection of specific fauna and flora.

In 1972 states gathered for the first international conference on the environment: the Stockholm Conference on the Human Environment. The insertion of "human" before environment in the title of the Stockholm Declaration on the Human Environment reflected an important recognition that the issues were not just about conserving nature for nature's sake, but also about humans in relation to the environment. The world was quite different in 1972. States were still the central and largely unchallenged actors, and there were many fewer states than exist today. The United Nations had only 132 member countries.[2] An international intergovernmental organization dedicated to the environment did not yet exist. The United Nations Environment Programme was established only after the 1972 Stockholm Conference on the Human Environment. In 1972 few multilateral environmental agreements existed, and these were concerned mainly with sustainable use of specific living resources and with transboundary pollution problems. We did not yet have agreements on globally common resources, such as the high-level ozone layer, or on the complex problem of climate change, or on natural resources within national borders of concern to the international community, such as biodiversity and deserts.

At the national level, most countries did not yet have environmental legislation. In the United States, the 1969 National Environmental Policy Act was the first major piece of national environmental legislation, which required environmental impact statements for major federal activities significantly affecting the environment.[3] The United States established its national environmental agency, the Environmental Protection Agency,

---

[1] For more detail, see E. Brown Weiss, "The Evolution of International Environmental Law," 54 *Japanese Yearbook of International Law* (2011) 1–28.

[2] As of January 2013, the United Nations had 193 member states. UN, "Growth in United Nations Membership, 1945–present," available at: www.un.org/en/members/growth.shtml (last visited March 7, 2013).

[3] National Environmental Policy Act of 1969, 42 U.S.C. § 4321 et seq. (1969).

only in 1970.[4] Businesses did not have councils or networks that were concerned with environmental issues, and there were still relatively few non-governmental organizations focused on environment, especially outside North America and Europe.

In 1972 a central issue was the perceived conflict between economic development and environmental protection. Developing countries feared that a focus on environmental protection would be at the expense of economic development. A pathbreaking meeting of governmental and non-governmental experts from developed and developing countries, which took place in Founex, Switzerland, developed a conceptual framework for reconciling economic development and environmental protection.[5] This was essential to the success of the Stockholm Conference and laid the foundation for states to confirm sustainable development as the guiding normative framework in Rio de Janeiro twenty years later.

Since the Stockholm Conference, states have concluded hundreds of new international legal instruments concerned with environment or with important provisions related to environment. Some are formal binding agreements, while many others are non-legally binding instruments, or what is sometimes referred to as "soft law." In 1999 there were already more than 1,100 such international legal instruments, and the numbers have climbed dramatically since then.[6] The agreements and other instruments have expanded from focusing on individual species (whales, fur seals, and migratory birds) to protecting ecosystems and marine areas, from focusing on transboundary air and water pollution to depletion of the high-level ozone layer, and from single-focused problems, such as pollution by heavy metals or persistent organic pollutants, to the enormously complex systemic issues related to climate change.

International legal principles related to the environment have also developed during the last four decades. Principle 21 of the 1972

---

[4] Reorganization Plan no. 3 of 1970, 5 U.S.C. App. 202 (1970); Special Message from the President to the Congress About Reorganization Plans to Establish the Environmental Protection Agency and the National Oceanic and Atmospheric Administration, 9 July 1970; United States Environmental Protection Agency, "EPA History," available at: www.epa.gov/history (last visited March 7, 2013).
[5] *Founex Report on Development and Environment* (1971). The report is reprinted in M. O. de Almeida *et al.*, *Environment and Development; the Founex Report on Development and Environment, with Commentaries* (New York: Carnegie Endowment for International Peace, 1972).
[6] E. Brown Weiss, D. B. Magraw and P. C. Szasz, *International Environmental Law, Basic Instruments and References* (Dobbs Ferry, NY: Transnational, 1992, 1999), Vol. I (1992), Vol. II (1999) (Volume I provides a list of 900 such international legal instruments).

Stockholm Declaration on the Human Environment and a number of principles in the 1992 Rio Declaration on Environment and Development have become part of international law or are in the process of becoming so. In 1996 the International Court of Justice recognized the essence of Principle 21 of the Stockholm Declaration on the Human Environment as part of the corpus of international law. According to the Court, "the general obligation of States to ensure that activities within their jurisdiction and control respect the environment of other States or of areas beyond national control is now part of the corpus of international law relating to the environment."[7] In the later *Pulp Mills Case*, the Court pronounced the requirement for an environmental impact assessment for activities having a significant adverse transboundary impact, especially on a shared resource, to be a general rule of international law.[8]

At the national level, every country now has at least one environmental statute or regulation, usually several. These cover air pollution, water pollution, waste disposal, hazardous chemicals, forests, water, biodiversity, wetlands, and desertification, among other topics. In 2012 the United Nations Environment Programme (UNEP) established a new program on the Rule of Law and the Environment, to increase respect for environmental laws at the national and subnational level and to address them effectively in judicial and auditing proceedings.[9] Within the last fifteen years, states have become less concerned with negotiating new binding international agreements and much more concerned with implementing and complying with them. The UNEP adopted Guidelines on Compliance with and Enforcement of Multilateral Environmental Agreements and has published a manual on the subject.[10] States have increasingly established Implementation and/or Compliance Committees within multilateral environmental agreements to address issues of noncompliance by

---

[7] *Legality of the Threat or Use of Nuclear Weapons*, Advisory Opinion, ICJ Reports 1996, 226; *Gabčíkovo-Nagymaros Project (Hungary/Slovakia)*, Judgment, ICJ Reports 1997, 7.

[8] *Pulp Mills on the River Uruguay (Argentina v. Uruguay)*, Order of July 13, 2006, ICJ Reports 2006, 43. The Court did not consider any procedural requirements for the environmental impact assessment, such as transparency or public participation in preparing the assessment.

[9] UNEP, "Advancement of Justice, Governance, and Law for Environmental Sustainability," available at: www.unep.org (last visited February 25, 2013).

[10] UNEP decision SS.VII/4. United Nations Environment Programme, *Manual on Compliance with and Enforcement of Multilateral Environmental Agreements* (UNEP, 2006).

member states.[11] Market mechanisms have also been incorporated into the design and implementation of certain multilateral environmental agreements, such as the Kyoto Protocol.[12]

The actors who participate in developing, implementing, and interpreting international environmental law have expanded far beyond states to include international organizations, multilateral development banks, nongovernmental organizations, private sector business councils, industry associations, civil society, and, most importantly, individuals. The Rio+20 meeting in June 2012, on the occasion of the fortieth anniversary of the 1972 Stockholm Conference, resulted in a long document entitled *The Future We Want*. This document affirmed a list of policies and measures to protect the human environment in the future. Governments did not, however, launch significant new initiatives.[13] The Rio+20 Conference had the effect of highlighting the ever-greater need for actors, in addition to states, to become major leaders in protecting our human environment.[14] It brought to the fore the importance of engaging civil society in this quest. This development is consistent with the kaleidoscopic world, described below.

One of the most significant developments in the last two decades is that international environmental law has been increasingly joined with other areas of international law. The latter include international trade, international investment, economic development, human rights, and national security. Protection of the environment is no longer viewed in isolation from other issues. This has important implications for the rule of law and nature, because it brings relevant bodies of law to bear on the issue and provides a voice for protecting nature in deliberations in other fora.

---

[11] See, e.g., The Montreal Protocol on Substances that Deplete the Ozone Layer, September 16, 1987, United Nations Treaty Series, Vol. 1522 (No. 26369) (states established an Implementation Committee to address noncompliance with the Protocol).

[12] See, e.g., Arts. 6, 12, and 17 Kyoto Protocol to the United Nations Framework Convention on Climate Change, December 10, 1997, United Nations Treaty Series, Vol. 2303 (No. 30822).

[13] *The Future We Want*, Report of the United Nations Conference on Sustainable Development, Rio de Janeiro, Brazil, June 20–22, 2012, UN Doc. A/CONF.216/16.

[14] As with past conferences, there were dozens of side events and initiatives, including presentation of proposed normative documents. See, e.g., "Peoples' Sustainable Manifesto: For Action Beyond Rio+20," June 2012, available at: http://sustainabilitytreaties.org/pst-manifesto (last visited March 7, 2013); "Peoples' Sustainability Treaties: Alternative Pathway for a Sustainable Transition," available at: http://sustainabilitytreaties.org/draft-treaties (last visited March 7, 2013).

Finally, and essentially, environmental protection and thereby protection of nature are now seen as including issues of justice, for poor communities may suffer most from environmental degradation and the failure to implement sustainable development. This is especially relevant, since more than 1 billion people live in extreme poverty, and 2.6 billion live on less than $2 per day.[15] That is less than the cost of an espresso or a cup of tea in many countries. While sustainable development is predominantly in the interest of poor people, their voices are the most likely to be overlooked in the process of development, or in responding to environmental challenges. The current emphasis in international environmental law on transparency, access to information, public participation, and access to remedies could help to give a voice to poor communities and to poor people, and to ensure that sustainable economic development responds to local needs and cultural traditions.

These are the encouraging developments of the last forty years. Quite remarkably, we have witnessed the emergence and rapid growth of a new field of international law. Governments at all levels, industries, non-governmental organizations, transnational groups, and civil society more generally have become engaged with the issues. We may view this as a glass half-full, as one filled with accomplishment and promise, but still with much to do. Or we may look to the onset of the Anthropocene Epoch and the increasingly grave environmental problems facing our planet and conclude that the glass is half-empty, and that it is not clear if we can fill the glass. In this view there is serious doubt about whether we have the capacity and requisite intent to protect nature in the future and to ensure sustainable development for all people. We are at a critical juncture in international environmental law, in which we will need to forge new paths to address global environmental problems and to advance the rule of law for nature.

2. Path to the future

The path to the future is enormously challenging. We may be leaving the Holocene Epoch, in which nature held sway, and entering the Anthropocene Epoch, in which humans are the major force shaping the planet in profound ways.

Since the end of the Pleistocene geological epoch, about 11,500 to 12,000 years ago, we have been living in the geological epoch known

---

[15] World Bank, *World Development Indicators 2008: Poverty Data Supplement* (Washington, DC: World Bank, 2008).

as the Holocene. In geological time, this is considered a warm period, between glacial periods. In 2000 Nobel Laureate Paul Crutzen and Eugene Stoermer[16] observed that human activities have now assumed a central role in shaping the planet and suggested that accordingly we have now entered a new geological epoch called the Anthropocene. "Considering [the] ... major and still growing impacts of human activities on Earth and atmosphere, and at all, including global, scales, it seems to us more than appropriate to emphasize the central role of mankind in geology and ecology by proposing to use the term 'Anthropocene' for the current geological epoch. The impacts of current human activities will continue over long periods."[17] Humans are now a force of nature shaping the planet on a geological scale and at a far faster rate than traditional geological speed.[18]

There are many examples of our dramatic effects. One engineering project alone, the Syncrude mine in the Athabasca tar sands in Alberta, Canada, will move 30 billion tons of earth, which is twice the amount of sediment that flows down all the rivers of the world in one year.[19] The sediment in river flows is also shrinking. Over the last forty to fifty years, 50,000 large dams have reduced sediment flow in rivers by 20 percent.[20] Deltas, where many people live, are eroding faster than they can be replenished. Ninety percent of the world's fauna and flora lies in ecosystems significantly affected by human activity. The extinction rate of species has been accelerating and is far higher than during other geological periods, as biologists have long been warning us.[21] The impacts from human activities will only increase, as our population is expected to reach 10 billion by 2100.[22]

One of the most disturbing developments is that scientists have begun to warn that both the carbon cycle and the nitrogen cycle are accelerating, the latter by 150 percent. Moreover, within the last decade hydrologists

---

[16] P. J. Crutzen and E F. Stoermer, "The 'Anthropocene'," 41 *Global Change Newsletter: International Geosphere-Biosphere Programme* (2000) 17–18.

[17] Ibid., 17.

[18] See, e.g., W. Steffen, P. J. Crutzen, and J. R. McNeill, "The Anthropocene: Are Humans Now Overwhelming the Great Forces of Nature?" 36 *Ambio* (2007) 614–21.

[19] "Welcome to the Anthropocene," *The Economist*, May 26, 2011, available at: www.economist.com/node/18744401 (last visited May 31, 2013).

[20] Ibid.

[21] N. Meyers, *The Sinking Ark* (New York: Pergamon Press, 1979); E. O. Wilson (ed.) *Biodiversity* (Washington, DC: National Academy of Sciences, 1988) (comprehensive review of the global loss of species diversity); E. O. Wilson, *The Diversity of Life* (Cambridge, MA: Harvard University Press, 1992).

[22] United Nations Department of Economic and Social Affairs, "World Population Prospects, the 2010 Revision," available at: http://esa.un.org/wpp (last visited March 7, 2013).

have uncovered evidence that the hydrological cycle is speeding up,[23] with potentially devastating impacts from more frequent and intense severe storms, floods, and droughts. We are interrupting the natural processes of our planet, refashioning them, and, most importantly, accelerating them.

The Anthropocene Epoch sharply strengthens the fundamental message that all of us share a global environment, that we are for the foreseeable future locked into the same atmosphere and biosphere, and that what we do in one place, either individually or cumulatively, can significantly affect the local and global resilience and integrity of our planet. The scale and rapidity of change make action urgent. We could invoke the analogy of a ship that has a big hole in it, which is expanding rapidly. Something needs to be done to ensure that the ship stays afloat. UNEP's fifth edition of its *Global Environmental Outlook* concludes that the Earth's systems are being pushed to the limit and warns that "several critical thresholds are approaching or have been exceeded, beyond which abrupt and non-linear changes to the life-support functions of the planet could occur. This has significant implications for human well-being now and in the future."[24] The emergence of the Anthropocene Epoch raises issues of intergenerational equity as never before, for what we do today will have enormous impact on the welfare of future generations. The global impact of our activities and the rapid pace of change make actions urgent but also complicated in new and as yet not well-understood ways.

2.1 The kaleidoscopic world

We are now living in what may be termed a kaleidoscopic world, in which information technology is transforming the ways in which individuals, ad hoc coalitions, nongovernmental organizations, transnational networks, business associations, and other groups participate in governance at global, national, and local levels. Governments and the increasing array of international intergovernmental organizations are critical players, but the system is much more chaotic, and less hierarchical than before.

---

[23] "A Man-Made World," *The Economist*, May 26, 2011, available at: www.economist.com/node/18741749 (last visited May 31, 2013); P. J. Durack, S. E. Wijffels and R. J. Matear, "Ocean Salinities Reveal Strong Global Water Cycle Intensification During 1950–2000," 336 *Science* (2012) 455–8 (predicting that the hydrologic cycle may intensify by as much as 2.4 per cent with a global temperature rise of 2 to 3 degrees centigrade).

[24] United Nations Environment Programme, *Global Environmental Outlook 5*, 194, available at: www.unep.org/geo/geo5.asp (last visited May 31, 2013).

Opposite movements exist in the international system: toward greater integration and toward greater fragmentation. According to the 2011–2012 *Yearbook of International Organizations*, there are now over 30,000 active intergovernmental and international nongovernmental organizations, and if special international organizations and inactive ones are included, over 66,000.[25] At the same time fragmentation has increased within countries and across countries. Since 1648 we have lived, at least in the West, in a world dominated by sovereign, theoretically equally, independent states. It has been a hierarchical system, in which states reach agreements among themselves and are responsible for those activities that take place within their borders or jurisdiction. In recent decades scholars have written about transnational actors, networks, and other groupings, which have also become significant international actors. These are not states but are still formal groupings.

We are now entering a new stage in which informal groups, ad hoc coalitions, and individuals are becoming important actors in influencing the development and implementation of international and domestic environmental law, and in carrying out (or not carrying out) obligations to conserve the environment. States remain central, but the context in which they operate is in flux. This world context may be called the kaleidoscopic world. It is a world in which change occurs rapidly, in which communication is rapid, and in which shifting informal groups, ad hoc coalitions, and increasingly individuals are significant actors. Most importantly, we are living in a period in which there are rapid and often unforeseen changes with widespread effects.

Information technology is transforming the participation of peoples globally in political, economic, and social life. The technology makes possible ever-shifting ad hoc coalitions and informal groups and myriad individual initiatives. Information technology and social networking allow people to collaborate across time and place through Facebook, YouTube, blogs, Twitter, and their analogs in various countries. As of November 2011, BlogScope tracked more than 57 million blogs, with 1 billion posts. Blogs are read daily by 346 million people, in 81 different languages, with 900,000 unique blog posts on average every 24 hours.[26] Twitter reported

---

[25] Union of International Associations, *Yearbook of International Organizations (2011–2012)* (Leiden: Brill, 2012).
[26] BlogScope, www.blogscope.net (last visited June 2012). The site has been discontinued and channeled into www.sysomos.com (last visited February 10, 2013). The WordPress website reports 61,133,411 World Press sites as of early 2013: en/wordpress.com/stats (last visited February 10, 2013).

288 million users in December 2012, with 69 governments using Twitter.[27] Mobile phones are now widely used to communicate across borders and to help organize coalitions, which can lead to direct action within and across countries. While many poor people do not have direct access yet to mobile phones, their rate of access is sharply increasing, especially in Africa, Asia, and Latin America. The explosive developments in information and communication technology mean that groups and especially individuals can increasingly participate in the development, interpretation, and implementation of international law generally, and of environmental law at all levels. This may be characterized as "bottom-up empowerment."

International examples of bottom-up empowerment include the successful campaign to ban land mines,[28] or the so-called color and velvet revolutions in Ukraine and other parts of Central and Eastern Europe, and the Arab Spring. Nongovernmental organizations such as Greenpeace have used social media campaigns to engage the public and put pressure on multinational corporations worldwide. In a 2011 campaign to pressure Volkswagen to stop lobbying against European emissions regulations, Greenpeace employed an interactive website in which users competed against each other to gain points and levels through sharing the campaign, uploading images and films, and engaging other users. The campaign gained over 500,000 participants and may have contributed to Volkswagen's commitment to substantially reduce its average fleet emissions by 2020.[29] Greenpeace has also launched interactive campaigns addressing Shell's drilling in the Arctic, Nestlé's use of palm oil that allegedly is produced unsustainably, and deforestation

---

[27] "Google+ passes Twitter to become No. 2 social network," *CBC News: Business*, January 28, 2013, available at: www.cbc.ca/news/business/story/2013/01/28/google-plus-twitter.html (last visited March 7, 2013); DigitalDaya, *Research Note: World Leaders on Twitter: Ranking Report, Dec. 2012*, available at: www.digitaldaya.com/admin/modulos/galeria/pdfs/69/156_biqz7730.pdf (last visited May 31, 2013).

[28] "The International Campaign to Ban Landmines," available at: www.icbl.org/index.php/icbl/Library/News-Articles/%28offset%29/45 (last visited March 7, 2013).

[29] Greenpeace, "VW Darkside," available at: http://archive.is/8eji (last visited May 31, 2013) and http://euvsco2.org/ (last visited June 10, 2013); "VW commits to slashing fleet emissions to 95g/km by 2020," *BusinessGreen*, March 6, 2013, available at: www.businessgreen.com/bg/news/2252574/vw-commits-to-slashing-fleet-emissions-to-95g-km-by-2020 (last visited March 7, 2013); S. Ayech, "Greenpeace takes on Europe's biggest carmaker ... and wins!" *Greenpeace*, March 6, 2013, available at: www.greenpeace.org/international/en/news/Blogs/makingwaves/greenpeace-takes-on-the-worlds-biggest-carmak/blog/44214/ (last visited March 7, 2013).

caused by coal mining in India.[30] At the national level, a small coalition in the western United States organized 300,000 phone calls to the United States Congress within a 72-hour period for a pending climate bill.[31]

The kaleidoscopic world is characterized by rapid change and bottom-up empowerment. It is dynamic and in many ways informal. Unlike a real kaleidoscope, no one entity controls the interactions of the many actors in the kaleidoscope. Here a word of caution is necessary, for at the same time that bottom-up empowerment is occurring, top-down control becomes vastly easier through information technology. Certain governments or other powerful actors, even illicit ones, may soon be able to monitor nearly all communications and through crowdsourcing all meetings, which would give them unprecedented power. This could threaten, or even triumph over, democracy and the rule of law, and make it much harder for all actors, especially non-state actors, to respond flexibly and effectively to environmental challenges.

With this caveat, the kaleidoscopic world may provide an important key to dealing effectively with the global crises of the Anthropocene Epoch. Bottom-up empowerment of non-state actors through easy access to information and communications technology can provide fast, flexible, powerful ways to target specific environmental problems directly. It minimizes blockages and administrative costs. However, the very aspects of the kaleidoscopic world that could allow it to respond rapidly and effectively may at the same time undermine its ability to address problems on a more integrated and larger scale efficiently. States and communities within states may be faced with multiple different standards and requirements, with multiple demands for accountability, and with little coordination or mutual recognition between them.

---

[30] G. Levy, "Shell 'Let's Go' Campaign a Brilliant, Elaborate Hoax," *UPI.com*, July 17, 2012, available at: www.upi.com/blog/2012/07/17/Shell-Lets-Go-campaign-a-brilliant-elaborate-hoax-UPDATED/5651342541859 (last visited May 31, 2013); M. Hickman, "Online Protest Drives Nestlé to Environmentally Friendly Palm Oil," *Independent*, May 19, 2010, available at: www.independent.co.uk/environment/green-living/online-protest-drives-nestl-to-environmentally-friendly-palm-oil-1976443.html (last visited March 7, 2013); N. Hingwala, "Social Media Campaign Review: Green Peace India Forest Hero," *Social Samosa*, December 28, 2012, available at: www.socialsamosa.com/2012/12/social-media-campaign-green-peace-forest-hero (last visited March 7, 2013).

[31] S. Parry, "72 Hour Campaign Generates 300,000 Calls," Environmental Defense Fund Blog, March 15, 2010, available at: blogs.edf.org/climate411/2010/03/15 (last visited March 31, 2013).

Bottom-up empowerment represents a shift of power from a discrete number of dominant states to non-state actors, including private sector organizations and nongovernmental organizations, but also thousands of shifting coalitions and millions of individuals. While non-state actors may mobilize many discrete actions quickly for immediate and emotionally salient issues, their actions may not necessarily lead to effective treatment of systemic problems or of larger scale regional or global problems. Moreover, it may be more difficult to coordinate them and to effect integrated, strategic, and prolonged responses to long-term systemic problems such as climate change and global water scarcity. Confronting these problems requires not only creating widespread political will but also maintaining it over time.

The kaleidoscopic world is in many ways democratic in the sense that there are many fewer barriers to participation. It also implicitly carries a certain degree of anarchy within it. In this context, shared values will be the glue that keeps everything together, and makes possible the necessary widespread and sustained cooperation. These values have to be consistent with the great diversity of cultural traditions, and respect both present and future generations.

In a kaleidoscopic world, many of the actions we need to take to sustain the integrity and robustness of our environment will be voluntary in nature. The effectiveness of these for managing complex environmental problems depends upon shared values and shared concerns about common problems.

We are motivated to take voluntary actions when we want to achieve some benefit that we cannot achieve alone, such as forecasting weather and climate or monitoring ocean health, or when we want to prevent a deteriorating situation from becoming worse. In the latter case, all would suffer, such as by the spread of virulent diseases. In the kaleidoscopic world, we need to share the common value in conserving the robustness and integrity of our environment and in ensuring that all have access to and can benefit from it.

2.2 Legal instruments for the future

For the last century, which was dominated by states, binding international agreements served as the preferred mode of operation. Such agreements remain essential. However, informal legal instruments and unilateral, voluntary commitments by states and by non-state actors have emerged as important legal instruments to address environmental problems. They are becoming ubiquitous. Non-legally binding instruments (often referred to as soft law) have played an important role since the onset of modern international environmental law in 1972. The Stockholm Declaration on the Human Environment, which set forth Principle 21, is a non-legally binding instrument, as is the influential Rio Declaration on Environment and Development.[32] The 1992 legal instrument on forests specifies in its title that it is not binding: Non-Legally Binding Authoritative Statement of Principles for a Global Consensus on the Management, Conservation, and Sustainable Development of All Types of Forests. The negotiated title was intended to ensure that the document could not be read as a binding international agreement.[33] The World Charter for Nature, adopted by the United Nations General Assembly, is similarly not binding.[34] One of the most significant non-legally binding instruments is the Nuuk Declaration on Environment and Development in the Arctic, which led to the formation by states of the Arctic Council and the negotiation under its auspices of a binding agreement on Marine Oil Pollution Preparedness and Response.[35]

So-called soft law is often used as a first step to address new problems (followed by "hard" law), as a strategy to be able to respond flexibly to new scientific understanding of the problems or other developments, as a way to avoid the need for ratification by parliaments of binding agreements, and, perhaps most importantly, as a way to respond quickly to urgent developments.[36] While non-legally binding instruments have always been integral to states' actions on environmental issues, they have also now become widespread in other areas of international law.[37] They are

---

[32] Report of the United Nations Conference on Environment and Development (UNCED Report), Rio de Janeiro, June 3–14, 1992, A/CONF.151/26 (Vol. I) Annex I.

[33] Non-Legally Binding Authoritative Statement of Principles for a Global Consensus on the Management, Conservation and Sustainable Development of all types of Forests (UNCED Report), A/CONF.151/26 (Vol. III) Annex III.

[34] World Charter for Nature, United Nations General Assembly Resolution 37/7, October 28, 1982, UN Doc. A/RES/37/7.

[35] Nuuk Declaration on Environment and Development in the Arctic, September 16, 1993, reprinted in "The Arctic Environment: Second Ministerial Conference," 3 *Yearbook International Environmental Law* (1993) 687; Declaration on the Establishment of the Arctic Council, September 19, 1996, reprinted in 35 *International Legal Materials* (1996) 1382; D. Rothwell, "International Law and the Protection of the Arctic Environment," 44 *International and Comparative Law Quarterly* (1995) 280–312.

[36] E. Brown Weiss (ed.) *International Compliance with Nonbinding Accords* (Washington, DC: American Society of International Law, 1997).

[37] See, e.g., D. Shelton (ed.), *Commitment and Compliance* (Oxford University Press, 2003); C. Brummer, *Soft Law and the Global Financial System: Rule Making in the 21st Century* (Cambridge University Press, 2012).

increasingly recognized as important and effective legal instruments in themselves.

This form of law has expanded to include such instruments as standards, codes of conduct, good practices, and similar instruments. Non-state actors have initiated their own standards and certification programs. For example, to address the serious problem of disposal and recycling of electronic wastes, the nongovernmental Basel Action Network developed a certification system for recycling, which led to a competing certification standard supported by industry.[38] Some documents by non-state actors set forth more general expected norms of behavior. As part of the Rio+20 process, the Center for Environment and Development in Sri Lanka developed the Peoples' Sustainability Manifesto, which sets forth guiding normative principles and commitments to achieve sustainable development.[39] In the bottom-up kaleidoscopic world, we can expect such practices to increase.

The major new development in legal commitments is the use by states and by non-state actors of voluntary, unilateral commitments to take certain actions or engage in certain behavior. When states could not reach agreement on the Copenhagen Accord during the climate negotiations in December 2009, they nonetheless voluntarily and unilaterally made commitments to take certain measures to mitigate carbon dioxide emissions in the form of official communications to the United Nations Framework Convention on Climate Change (UNFCCC) Secretariat. These commitments are publicly available on the UNFCCC website.[40]

Since the year 2000 there have been a number of initiatives that solicit and publish voluntary commitments by states and private entities. The United Nations has created and hosts some of these. States and private

---

[38] "Basel Action Network Oversees the E-Stewards Certification Progam," available at: http://e-stewards.org/certification-overview (last visited March 6, 2013); "The Responsible Recycling Practices for Use in Accredited Certification Programs for Electronics Recyclers (R2) Offers a Competing Recycling Standard," *R2 Solutions*, available at: www.r2solutions.org (last visited March 7, 2013).

[39] "Peoples' Sustainability Treaties," available at: http://sustainabilitytreaties.org (last visited March 7, 2013).

[40] Commitments by developed country parties (Annex I Parties) in the form of quantified economy-wide emissions targets for 2020 are available at http://unfccc.int/meetings/copenhagen_dec_2009/items/5264.php (last visited May 31, 2013). Commitments by developing country parties to take nationally appropriate mitigation actions are available at http://unfccc.int/meetings/cop_15/copenhagen_accord/items/5265.php (last visited May 31, 2013).

organizations have organized others. In addition, several registries aggregate and publish commitments from multiple initiatives.

There are notable examples focused on sustainable development. As part of the Rio+20 Conference, states, international organizations, and major nongovernmental organizations and private corporations were invited to make voluntary commitments to take actions supporting sustainable development. Over 700 commitments were collected during the conference. The commitments are listed in an online registry, the United Nations Sustainable Development Knowledge Platform, discussed below.[41] In another example, the UN Secretary-General established the Sustainable Energy for All initiative in connection with the 2012 Year of Sustainable Energy.[42] It is designed to elicit commitments by governments, businesses, and civil society to take actions that contribute to securing global access to sustainable energy. The United Nations Global Compact, set up in 2000, was used in the run-up to 2012 to solicit commitments by corporations to further the Rio+20 program.[43] The commitments must specify measurable targets.

In addition to these United Nations-based initiatives, there are others that solicit voluntary, unilateral commitments. These include the Clinton Global Initiative,[44] which invites commitments from governments and non-state actors across the world; the Corporate Eco Forum,[45] a membership organization of large companies that publishes commitments relevant to sustainability; and sundry national initiatives such as China Going Green.[46]

---

[41] *United Nations Sustainable Development Knowledge Platform*, available at: http://sustainabledevelopment.un.org/index.php?menu=1348 (last visited March 6, 2013).

[42] United Nations, *Sustainable Energy for All*, available at: www.sustainableenergyforall.org (last visited March 6, 2013).

[43] "Overview of the UN Global Compact," United Nations Global Compact, available at: www.unglobalcompact.org/AboutTheGC (last visited March 6, 2013); "Rio+20: Action Pledges by Business Kick Off Rio Drive for Sustainability Solutions," *United Nations Global Compact News*, June 18, 2012, available at: http://unglobalcompact.org/news/246-06-18-2012 (last visited May 31, 2013). Commitments under the global compact are published at http://business.un.org/en/browse/commitments (last visited March 6, 2013).

[44] Clinton Global Initiative, available at: www.clintonglobalinitiative.org (last visited March 6, 2013).

[45] Corporate Eco Forum, available at: www.corporateecoforum.com (last visited March 6, 2013). Recent corporate commitments are listed in Corporate Eco Forum and The Nature Conservancy, *The New Business Imperative: Valuing Natural Capital* (2012), available at: www.corporateecoforum.com/valuingnaturalcapital (last visited March 6, 2013).

[46] Commitments made under the China Going Green initiative are listed in the NRDC Cloud of Commitments, discussed below. See www.cloudofcommitments.org/commitments (last visited March 6, 2013).

One of the most important developments is the establishment of international registries that compile and publish lists of unilateral commitments by governments and non-state actors. In the lead-up to Rio+20, several states and civil society organizations pushed for the creation of a compendium of commitments in the form of an internet-based registry to bring together the non-legally binding commitments. The Conference document, *The Future We Want*, explicitly endorsed this proposal,[47] which led to the establishment of the United Nations Sustainable Development Knowledge Platform. The Platform provides a searchable registry of commitments made as part of the Rio+20 Conference as well as commitments made under the Sustainable Energy for All and the Global Compact initiatives. As of March 2013, the Platform listed 1,377 commitments, worth an estimated $636,979 million.[48] This includes 416 commitments by governments, 154 by the United Nations and international intergovernmental organizations, and the rest by non-state actors. The Platform continues to receive voluntary commitments, which are expected to "announce and achieve concrete time-bound deliverables that advance sustainable development."[49]

A nongovernmental organization, the US-based Natural Resources Defense Council, maintains another important registry: the Cloud of Commitments.[50] The Cloud aggregates state and non-state actor commitments made in association with and subsequent to Rio+20, including those made under the Rio+20 Platform, the Global Compact, the Sustainable Energy for All initiative, the Corporate EcoForum commitments, and other platforms relevant to sustainable development. The commitments by non-state actors are noteworthy, for they involve large multinational companies whose revenues eclipse the economies of some countries. For example, Microsoft has pledged to achieve net carbon neutrality by 2013. BMW has promised to reduce product carbon dioxide emissions by 50 percent by 2020, relative to 1990 levels. Disney has committed to fund 6,000 acres of reforestation, including projects aimed at enhancing carbon sequestration. Corporations operating in the agribusiness, apparel,

---

[47] *The Future We Want*, Resolution 1: Annex, para. 283.
[48] United Nations Sustainable Development Knowledge Platform, available at: http://sustainabledevelopment.un.org/index.php?menu=1348 (last visited March 6, 2013).
[49] United Nations Sustainable Development Knowledge Platform, "About Sustainable Development in Action," available at: http://sustainabledevelopment.un.org/aboutcommitments.html (last visited March 6, 2013).
[50] Natural Resources Defense Council, "Cloud of Commitments," available at: http://cloudofcommitments.org (last visited March 6, 2013).

automotive, communication, construction, energy, finance, insurance, technology, and tourism sectors have posted commitments to take specific measurable and time-bound actions to help mitigate climate change. While these are an important part of the legal picture, they are certainly not sufficient to address the problems of climate change.[51]

Within countries, some provinces and local governments are also taking important initiatives to address global or regional environmental problems such as climate change. Examples include California's binding cap-and-trade program in greenhouse gas emissions and its projected program with provinces in other countries, including Brazil, Mexico, and Indonesia, for Reduced Emissions from Deforestation and Degradation (REDD).[52] Indeed, within the United States the most important commitments to address climate change have been taking place at the regional, state, and local levels. In a bottom-up kaleidoscopic world, commitments at provincial and local levels are likely to increase in number and importance. Some will be binding in the form of regulations and others non-binding or voluntary in nature.

2.3 Concluding reflections

The emerging kaleidoscopic world has led to an increase in the number of relevant participants in developing and implementing a rule of law for

---

[51] Table of commitments on file with author. Commitments are posted on the following websites: Clinton Global Initiative, www.clintonglobalinitiative.org/commitments/commitments_search.asp (last visited June 10, 2013); Natural Resources Defense Council, Cloud of Commitments, http://cloudofcommitments.org (last visited December 20, 2012); United Nations Sustainable Development Knowledge Platform, http://sustainabledevelopment.un.org (last visited December 20, 2012); UN Business, http://business.un.org/en/browse/commitments (last visited December 20, 2012); Corporate EcoForum and The Nature Conservancy, *The New Business Imperative: Valuing Natural Capital* (2012), http://corporateecoforum.com/valuingnaturalcapital (last visited May 31, 2013); Sustainable Energy for All, www.sustainableenergyforall.org (last visited December 20, 2012).

[52] California Code of Regulation, Title 17, Subchapter 10, Climate Change, Article 5, Sections 95800–96023 (2012), available at: www.arb.ca.gov/regact/2010/capandtrade10/candtmodreg.pdf (last visited June 24, 2013). In 2010 the Governor of California signed a memorandum of understanding with the Governors of Chiapas, Mexico and Acre, Brazil, in which they agreed to work together to reduce emissions from deforestation and forest degradation, which led to the establishment of the REDD Offset Working Group (ROW), which is currently engaged in the process of drafting and finalizing recommendations for incorporation of international REDD-based offsets into the state carbon trading program. REDD Offset Working Group, "About ROW," available at: http://stateredd.org/about-row (last visited March 7, 2013).

nature and a rapid proliferation in the kinds of legal instruments and relevant commitments. While this world offers great promise for engaging the public and private sectors in addressing issues at all levels, it also presents serious challenges to our ability to address problems effectively. In the Anthropocene Epoch we need a systemic overview of the health of the Earth's systems and of the impact of human activities on them. We likely need both macro coordination and management and bottom-up initiatives, with binding and nonbinding legal instruments and voluntary unilateral commitments. Even with all of this, it is not clear that in the kaleidoscopic world we will be able to address the complex, systemic problems facing our planet effectively.

Climate change illustrates the complexity of the problems we face, as no other problem does. The causes of human-induced climate change encompass not only energy issues, but also land use and our economic activity. Climate change takes place within the context of complicated interactions between the land, ice-covered areas, atmosphere, and oceans. This means that we need to assess the effects of human interventions in a broad systems context and to evaluate proposed obligations and practices in this light. As the noted naturalist John Muir observed, "When we try to pick out anything by itself, we find it hitched to everything else in the universe."[53]

In the kaleidoscopic world it may be difficult to ensure that on balance actions taken are consistent with treating the Earth as a system, or with local ecologies as systems. It may be easier in the sense that non-state actors undertaking nonbinding actions can circumvent administrative impediments or special interests. At the same time, it may be difficult to assess whether the totality of such actions are consistent with a systemic view of the problem.

A critical challenge in the kaleidoscopic world is to have effective monitoring of the outcomes of many discrete actions taken by thousands, indeed potentially millions, of actors. Satellite technology is increasingly able to monitor natural resources, such as fresh water and forests, to a degree not possible even a decade ago. But our ability to monitor the large-scale and small-scale effects of our activities on the environment will be critical to assessing our impact and to guiding future actions.

Accountability for actions will also be important, but complicated. While states need to be accountable for their actions, non-state actors

---

[53] J. Muir, *John Muir: The Eight Wilderness Discovery Books* (London: Diadem Books, 1992), 19.

must also be accountable. It is not clear how to accomplish this, and without large transaction costs. While transparency is essential, accountability still requires an actor with the requisite resources to be able to monitor and respond to another's performance, and in a timely way.

These are but a few of the serious challenges arising from a kaleidoscopic world. As we analyze our capacity to address environmental change and to protect nature in the Anthropocene Epoch, two points remain central: to consider actions systemically and, most importantly, to foster common values among all participants. Unless states and the myriad of non-state actors and millions of individuals share a common value in conserving the integrity and robustness of our environment and in ensuring that people can access and benefit from it, the bottom-up approach will not be effective in reaching the common good. We owe it to ourselves and to future generations to foster such common values.

3

Evolved norms

A canon for the Anthropocene

NICHOLAS A. ROBINSON

1. Introduction

Humans find themselves – *we find ourselves* – confronting existential challenges. Earth's sea levels rise and the climate changes, displacing human settlements. While colonizing all corners of the Earth, human instincts for gathering, collecting, and storing resources enhanced their survival, but at incalculable costs to other species and nature's cornucopia. Through creativity, humans have elaborated extraordinary economic regimes, rooted in their "hunter-gatherer" instinctive capacities. The human brain's capacity to learn and create fashioned many great civilizations, and also cultivated instincts to conserve nature, protect the environment, and strive to sustain the oceans and atmosphere. Yet the success of "economic instincts" has eclipsed the promise of humans' "ecological instincts."

Global change threatens human well-being and survival. In response, humanity's "ecological instincts," favoring stewardship and cooperation, predictably will advance, mitigating the force of their "economic instincts." In the "Anthropocene Epoch,"[1] survival of *Homo sapiens* is enhanced through sharing and sustaining nature's bounty. The transcendence of "ecological instincts" will occur incrementally and haphazardly. Ways to encourage a more robust and systematic guide through the Anthropocene emerge from identifying new legal principles based upon instinctive norms, which have evolved within all humans.

This chapter examines three of several instinctively known legal principles. They will constitute the foundations for a new rule of law for nature. They can do this because they already exist within human nature.

---

[1] Will Steffen, Paul J. Crutzen and John R. McNeill, "The Anthropocene: Are Humans Now Overwhelming the Great Forces of Nature?" 36:8 *Ambio* (December 2007) 614–21.

Otherwise insightful legal scholarship[2] and political commentary[3] pay scant attention to evolutionary biology's insights about law. Both evolutionary biology and jurisprudence are elegant human disciplines of learning, but they are not yet integrated. The former explores empirically what humans *are* (what is human nature?), while the latter examines in theory and sociocultural study what humans *do* in law-making and governance (what laws, like other tools, do humans shape in their relations with nature?). The Anthropocene's existential challenges lend urgency to efforts at learning from sociobiology about law.[4] Humans often unconsciously enact their laws based upon instinctual perceptions as evolved norms.

2. Compasses for uncharted landscapes

Evolved norms will enable humans to chart pathways through the unknown landscapes of the Anthropocene, with its disruptions unprecedented in cultural memory. Already humans are defining new relationships between themselves and nature. Understanding evolved norms enables the proclamation of legal principles about the reciprocities between ecological systems and human society. Principles based on evolved norms can sustain and promote resilience in human adaptations to changing environments.

Earth's landscapes are rapidly changing. Economic and ecological interests are alike at stake.[5] The World Bank advises that:

> Without further commitments and action to reduce greenhouse gas emissions, the world is likely to warm by more than 3°C above the preindustrial

---

[2] See, e.g., Nicholas A. Ashford and Charles C. Caldart, *Environmental Law, Policy and Economics – Reclaiming the Environmental Agenda* (Cambridge, MA: MIT Press, 2008); Douglas Kysar, *Regulating from Nowhere: Environmental Law and the Search for Objectivity* (New Haven: Yale University Press, 2010); Louis J. Kotzé, *Global Environmental Governance: Law and Regulation for the 21st Century* (Cheltenham: Edward Elgar, 2012); Burns H. Weston and David Bollier, *Green Governance – Ecological Survival, Human Rights and the Law of the Commons* (Cambridge University Press, 2013).

[3] Al Gore, *The Future: Six Drivers of Global Change* (New York: Random House, 2013).

[4] Steven Pinker, *The Blank Slate: The Modern Denial of Human Nature* (London: Penguin Books, 2002). Legal scholarship often assumes that law is written on *tabula rasa*. Humans invent any number of possible logical theories without inquiring what lies behind the blank slate.

[5] UN Environment Programme, *Global Environmental Outlook 5* (June 2012), available at: www.unep.org/geo (last accessed May 31, 2013). See also the Intergovernmental Panel on Climate Change, *4th Assessment Report (2007)*, available at: www.ipcc.ch (last accessed May 31, 2013).

climate. Even with the current mitigation commitments and pledges fully implemented, there is roughly a 20 percent likelihood of exceeding 4°C by 2100. If they are not met, a warming of 4°C could occur as early as the 2060s. Such a warming level and associated sea-level ... by 2100 would not be the end point: a further warming to levels over 6°C, with several meters of sea-level rise, would likely occur over the following centuries.[6]

At a 6°C level increase, Earth's human civilizations, and the existence of perhaps 90 percent of its flora and fauna, are not sustainable.[7] Uncharted landscapes lie ahead.

Why do humans ignore such warnings? Logic alone will not change complacency. The exercise of human reason alone is not motivating humans to deploy the many technologies *available today* that can avert extreme climate change. Evolutionary sciences offer explanations. Informed by sociobiology, laws may guide social adaptations in reaction to ecological disruption and fears for survival.[8] Each human's instincts have similar capacities, the result of evolution over millennia in the brain's capability to learn, grow, and shape social relations. Sociobiology identifies traits of human nature, which jurisprudence should regard as "evolved norms." Based on evolved norms, humans cultivate common legal expectations to guide behavior, which they in turn confirmed as general principles of law. Once evolved norms are recognized as organizing principles for how human communities and countries make choices

---

[6] *Turn Down The Heat: Why a 4°C Warmer World Must be Avoided,* A Report for the World Bank by the Potsdam Institute for Climate Impact Research and Climate Analytics, "Executive Summary," xii (November 2012).

[7] Other economic analysts concur. In November 2012 PriceWaterhouseCoopers (PwC) advised that, unless extreme measures are taken to decarbonize energy systems and the atmosphere, a 6°C rise in the earth's temperature results. See "Too Late for Two Degrees," PwC Low Carbon Energy Index 2012, available at www.pwc.com (last accessed May 31, 2013). Annually, the PwC Index features one core statistic: the rate of change of global carbon intensity: "This year we estimated that the required improvement in global carbon intensity to meet a 2°C warming target has risen to 5.1% a year, from now to 2050. We have passed a critical threshold – not once since 1950 has the world achieved that rate of decarbonisation in a single year, but the task now confronting us is to achieve it for 39 consecutive years." The radical impact on species survival has been noted: James Lovelock, *The Revenge of Gaia – Earth's Climate Crisis and the Fate of Humanity* (New York: Basic Books, 2006); Mark Lynas, *6 Degrees: Our Future On A Hotter Planet* (London: Fourth Estate, 2007).

[8] Edward O. Wilson, *Sociobiology: The New Synthesis* (Cambridge, MA: Belknap Press of Harvard University Press, 1975); Jerome H. Barkow, Leda Cosmides and John Tooby, *The Adapted Mind – Evolutionary Psychology and the Generation of Culture* (Oxford University Press, 1992).

about governing, they can help induce widespread cooperation for bolstering ecological and social resilience.

Environmental law provides the strophe for humans defining their "balanced and harmonious" relationship with nature.[9] Despite geographic and cultural differences, all nations have enacted similar environmental legislation. This elaboration of a new field of law in the space of just one generation is itself remarkable; humans can act rapidly to protect Earth's biosphere, locally and globally. Nonetheless, environmental reforms still only marginally control "economic instincts." Initiatives at "sustainable development" remain too insubstantial to avert irreversible changes to the planet,[10] and the "Rio Principles" no longer rally nations to action.[11]

A deeper rule of law for nature is emerging. The new legal canon grows out of evolved norms, which humans can deploy culturally to yield new legal relationships between nature and humans. New legal principles can again motivate ecological instincts. Concepts of evolutionary biology inform this analysis.

3. Acknowledging biological foundations for law

Since emerging as a species, humans have shaped Earth's natural systems. So great has been human hegemony over other species that humans have ushered into existence the Anthropocene Epoch, a new geological period. Emerging conditions on Earth rapidly depart from those of the past 10,000 years, when humans fashioned their civilizations during the Holocene Epoch. Since 1870 human impacts on Earth accelerated,[12] prompting governments worldwide to enact laws for nature conservation, environmental protection, and "sustainable development."[13] In 1992

---

[9] These words recur often in expressions of environmental rights, as in Article 225 of the Constitution of Brazil, or that of the Philippines. See *Oposa v. Factoran*, GR 10 101083 (July 30, 1993).

[10] Nicholas A. Robinson, "Beyond Sustainability: Environmental Management for the Anthropocene Epoch," *Journal of Public Affairs* (2012, John Wiley & Son), published online in Wiley Online Library (www.wileyonlinelibrary.com) DOI: 10:1002/pa.1432.

[11] See the insightful "Rio+20 Round-up" in 42:4–5 *Environmental Policy and Law* (August 2012) 210–39.

[12] See Clive Ponting, *A New Green History of the World*, Revised edition (New York: Penguin Books, 2007); John R. McNeill, *Something New Under the Sun: An Environmental History of the 20th Century* (New York: W. W. Norton & Co., 2000); and also James Gustave Speth, *Red Sky at Morning: America and the Crisis of the Global Environment* (New Haven: Yale University Press, 2004).

[13] UN World Commission on Environment and Development, *Our Common Future* (Oxford University Press, 1987).

the UN "Earth Summit" declared that "Humanity stands at a defining moment in its history," and embraced policies for "sustainable development."[14] Multilateral environmental agreements have been integrating national environmental legal systems, for example in protecting Earth's stratospheric ozone layer.[15] Yet ecological degradation from economic "business as usual" has not materially changed.

Downward environmental trends persist and deepen. John P. Holdren summed up the challenges humanity faces as follows: "Our options in this domain are three. They are mitigation, adaptation and suffering. If we do less mitigation and adaptation, we're going to do a lot more suffering."[16] Adaptations are unavoidable.[17] Some small island states will cease to be. Major coastal cities will become relics of their past glory. Yet in the wake of environmental disasters, legal innovations will emerge from local and national decision-making. As humans confront new geophysical and biological conditions, they will share solutions. Global communications over the Internet will disseminate and magnify effective adaptations from place to place.

Human reactions to a changing Earth will emerge in comparable ways, reflecting traits of human nature that evolved through Darwinian natural selection and evolution. These instincts are "hard-wired" into *Homo sapiens*. As "evolved norms," they motivate human behavior. By magnifying positive instincts to cope with the emerging conditions of the Anthropocene, humans can select evolved norms that advantage their well-being, and even survival. Communities and countries can encourage instincts to cooperate, share, and collaborate with resilience, using legal principles to do so. Naturally meanwhile, other traits, many fueling "economic instincts," will undercut the effectiveness of laws based on these evolved norms.[18] Inertia and "business as usual" perpetuate the habits that

---

[14] See Paragraph 1.1 in *Agenda 21*, the principal report of the Earth Summit at Rio de Janeiro, Brazil, UN Doc. A/Conf. 151 (1992). The annotated version of *Agenda 21* and the *travaux préparatoires* for UNCED are found in N. A. Robinson, *Agenda 21 and the UNCED Proceedings*, 6 volumes (New York: Oceana Publications, 1993).

[15] See L. Kurukulasuriya and N. A. Robinson, *Training Manual on International Environmental Law* (Nairobi: UNEP, 2006).

[16] "Meeting the Climate-Change Challenge," http://ncseonline.org/sites/default/files/Chafee08final.pdf (2008), reprinted in R. C. Hildreth, D. R. Hodas, N. A. Robinson and J. G. Speth, *Climate Change Law – Mitigation and Adaptation* (St. Paul: West, 2009).

[17] James Lovelock projects the possibility of remnant human settlements in habitats compatible for human life in polar latitudes, in *The Revenge of Gaia*.

[18] Humans can suppress an instinct for sharing, or could even build on other evolved traits (e.g., tribalism or fear of "others") in negative ways (such as cooperating to arm and attack an adversary, or to steal and hoard) that in the short term perpetuate environmental

are degrading to Earth's natural systems. Nonetheless, humans change. Human beings have evolved norms to lessen warfare, reduce killing, and design laws to confirm and extend more peaceful behavior.[19] Laws guide behavior toward social objectives, and already advance biological conservation. How might evolved norms function to accentuate the positive and discourage the negative tendencies of human nature toward nature? Sociobiology suggests some answers.[20]

Three evolved norms – *cooperation, biophilia, resilience* – can guide communities and countries as legal principles. There are others, such as *foresight* and *sharing*. The law already explicitly recognizes the duty of cooperation and implicitly acts as if it recognized others, such as biophilia. Describing the interplay of cooperation, biophilia, and resilience illustrates how humans can magnify positively evolved norms as legal principles while adapting the Anthropocene's new world.

Consider the emergence of "environmental rights." Evolved norms prompt different human communities and countries to enact congruent laws: since 1972, individually and independently, all nations have enacted comparable environmental law and 147 of the 192 United Nations member states now recognize a fundamental "right to the environment" in their constitutions.[21] To enforce environmental rights, more than fifty

---

impoverishment. Charles Darwin in *The Descent of Man* (London: Murray, 1871), vol. 1, 159–60, observes: "A tribe including many members who, from possessing in high degree the spirit of patriotism, fidelity, obedience, courage and sympathy, were always ready to give aid to each other, and to sacrifice themselves for the common good, would be victorious over most other tribes; and this would be natural selection." See also "Hoarding Taboo" in Matt Ridley, *The Origins of Virtue – Human Instincts and the Evolution of Cooperation* (London: Penguin, 1996), 243–6.

[19] Steven Pinker, *The Better Angels of Our Nature* (New York: Viking, 2011).

[20] E. O. Wilson projects further studies between biology and social sciences in *On Human Nature* (Cambridge, MA: Harvard University Press, 1978), 195–6: "The mind will be more precisely explained as an epiphenomenon of the neuronal machinery of the brain. That machinery is in turn the product of genetic evolution by natural selection acting on human populations for hundreds of thousands of years in their ancient environments. By a judicious extension of the methods and ideas of neurobiology, ethnology, and sociobiology a proper foundation can be laid for the social sciences ... [and even partial success of these studies] will lead directly to ... [study of] the conscious choices that must be made among our innate metal propensities. The elements of human nature are the learning rules, emotional reinforcers, and hormonal feedback loops that guide the development of social behavior into certain channels as opposed to others. Human nature is not just the array of outcomes attained in existing societies. It is also the potential array that might be achieved through conscious design by future societies."

[21] David R. Boyd, *The Environmental Rights Revolution – A Global Study of Constitutions, Human Rights, and the Environment* (Vancouver: University of British Columbia Press, 2012).

nations unilaterally have established new environmental courts and tribunals.[22] International declarations proclaim environmental legal principles.[23] Such law-making reflects social evolution, which can be understood through the insights of sociobiology.[24] To date, legal scholarship has largely ignored the evolutionary aspects of why and how humans create law, preferring instead to fashion laws and theory as if writing on a "blank slate," which Steven Pinker characterizes as a modern denial of human nature.[25]

Studies in law and sociobiology should begin in their own right. An impetus to do so now will be to explore how humans can leverage more effective efforts to cope with climate change. Environmental lawyers already depend on the environmental sciences and thus should welcome sociobiological studies.[26] For example, ecology teaches much about resilience,[27] but how should law promote resilience? Edward O. Wilson urges integrated studies across "the line between the great branches of learning,"

---

[22] Symposium on "Environmental Courts and Tribunals: Improving Access to Justice and Protection of the Environment Around the World," 28:2 *Pace Environmental Law Review* (Winter 2012), available at http://digitalcommons.pace.edu/pelr/vol29/iss2 (last accessed June 3, 2013).

[23] Elements of these principles are found in the 1992 Rio de Janeiro Declaration on Environment and Development, adopted by the UN General Assembly, UN Doc. A/Conf.151/26 (vol. I), 31 ILM 874 (1992); many nations have enacted the 1992 Declaration's principles into their national legislation. Other well-known statements of principles, premised *sub silentio* on evolved norms, are the UN World Charter for Nature, UN Res. 37/7, The UN Declaration on the Rights of Indigenous Peoples, UN Res. 61/295; the "Earth Charter" – a civil society restatement – available at: www.earthcharterinaction.org (last accessed June 3, 2013); and the Andean nations' proposed *pachamama* declaration, The Universal Declaration of the Rights of Mother Earth, adopted in 2010 at the World People's Conference on Climate Change and the Rights of Mother Earth in Bolivia, which recognizes Mother Earth as a living being with rights to life, to exist and to continue her vital cycles and processes free from human disruptions. Civil society groups encourage new concepts of "earth law"; see www.gaiafoundation.org (last accessed June 3, 2013).

[24] Charles Darwin, *The Origin of Species By Means of Natural Selection, or the Preservation of Favored Races in the Struggle for Life* (London: John Murray, 1859).

[25] Pinker, *The Blank Slate*.

[26] In one of the few scholarly articles on evolution and environmental law, William H. Rodgers, Jr., examined how evolution could be reflected in norms for transparency and sufficiency in property law: "Bringing People Back: Toward A Comprehensive Theory of Taking In Natural Resources Law," 10 *Ecology Law Quarterly* (1982–3) 205.

[27] Lance Gunderson, "Resilience, Flexibility and Adaptive Management," *Conservation Biology* (June 30, 1999), available at: www.consecol.org/vol3/iss1/art7 (last accessed June 3, 2013), and Lance H. Gunderson, Craig R. Allen and C. S. Holling, *Foundations of Ecological Resilience* (Washington, DC: Island Press, 2010).

which he posits is "not a line at all, but instead a broad, mostly unexplored domain awaiting cooperative exploration from both sides."[28]

Since events of the Anthropocene already impact society,[29] there is urgency to undertake joint scholarship in this "domain."[30] But legal action should not await the outcomes of further scientific study. In order to benefit from – and test – the hypothesis that humans can adapt more effectively to disruptions in the Anthropocene Epoch by magnifying positively their evolved norms, communities and countries will need to use these norms *before* sociobiology can confirm the evolutionary basis for the legal principles discussed here. Events are overtaking humanity, and the only other option, "business as usual," is discredited by events daily.

Those who would reject this Darwinian inquiry *ab initio* are many.[31] Beyond "creationists",[32] some may confuse it with the "Social Darwinism" of Herbert Spencer.[33] Others will reject it in favor of the legal positivism.[34]

---

[28] E. O. Wilson, "Sociobiology at Century's End", foreword to the 25th anniversary edition of *Sociobiology: The New Synthesis* (Cambridge, MA: Belknap Press of Harvard University Press, 2000), vii. Wilson notes that "The perceived dividing line is essentially the same as that between the scientific and literary cultures defined by C. P. Snow in 1959. It still fragments the intellectual landscape." See C. P. Snow, *The Two Cultures and the Scientific Revolution* (Cambridge University Press, 1959). This fragmentation has virtually blinded law to any possible inquiry into the role evolutionary science can play in elucidating law as a field of human endeavor and a regime ordering cultures.

[29] See A. Janku, G. J. Schenk and F. Mauelshagen, *Historical Disasters in Context* (New York: Routledge, 2012), 2–3 reciting the extreme climate disasters of 2011. The pattern repeats in 2012, with additional extreme storms, such as tornados that literally wipe out towns such as Joplin, Missouri in 2011, or such as the vast repeated floods that in two years wiped out fifty years of sustained socio-economic development in Pakistan's Indus River Valley in 2010 and 2011, or repeated typhoons that struck the Philippines and South East Asia, inundating Indo-China with floods the size of Spain in 2011, or Mega-Storm Sandy that crippled much of New York City and the Atlantic sea coast in New Jersey and New York in 2012. Similar extreme weather recurred in 2013. See Sarah Lyall, "Heat, Flood or Icy Cold, Extreme Weather Rages Worldwide," *New York Times* (January 11, 2013), 4, col. 1.

[30] Sociobiology has yet to tackle this theme. As Edward Wilson notes, this is part of wider inquiry: "Sociobiology is a flourishing discipline in zoology, but its ultimately greatest importance will surely be the furtherance of consilience among the great branches of learning." Wilson, "Sociobiology at Century's End," vii.

[31] Robert C. Clark, "The Interdisciplinary Study of Legal Evolution," 90 *Yale Law Journal* (1981) 1238.

[32] For example, "creationism" actively opposes the teaching and study of evolution. See the National Council for Science and the Environment, www.ncseonline.org (last accessed June 3, 2013).

[33] J. D. Y. Peel, *Herbert Spencer: The Evolution of a Sociologist* (New York: Basic Books, 1971).

[34] O. W. Holmes, Jr., *The Common Law* (Boston, MA: Little, Brown, 1881), 31–2.

Donald Elliott notes that "theories of social evolution were so firmly associated with Spencer's racist and imperialist ideologies that any voluntary theory of social phenomena was perceived as reactionary."[35] Some in the humanities[36] may find this inquiry distasteful, affronting a "romantic belief in the autonomy of the human spirit"[37] or because it denies a postmodernist repudiation of "the idea of 'real' reality and hence 'objective truths,'"[38] or finally due to "traditional humanistic dualism," a belief that sciences and the humanities "occupy irreducibly distinct ontological territories."[39] Current jurisprudence will be suspicious, since it generally characterizes law as either positivist (might makes right) or a function of natural law, or as a "social contract," or grounded in religion.[40] Throughout, resistance to sociobiology is rooted in human instincts that prefer the safety of a known status quo, which is so manifestly "evident."

Yet, as Joseph Carroll observes, sociobiology enables the study of higher cognitive functions that motivate "artistic activity and spiritual fulfillment consists in the need to envision a humanly meaningful order within the total order of nature."[41] The human brain develops laws to establish an intelligible social order within the total discipline of nature, the "laws of nature." Scant legal scholarship probes evolutionary biology and law,[42]

---

[35] E. Donald Elliott, "The Evolutionary Tradition in Jurisprudence," 85 *Columbia Law Review* 38 (1985) 76.

[36] Joseph Carroll, "Wilson's Consilience and Literary Study," 23 *Philosophy and Literature* (1999) 393–413, reprinted in J. Carroll, *Literary Darwinism* (New York: Routledge, 2012).

[37] Carroll notes, "a desire to remain within the methodological boundaries of purely discursive philosophy – to cling to Kant and Rousseau rather than to negotiate the new and difficult terrain of neurophysiology and cognitive psychology." Ibid., 73.

[38] Ibid., 75. Postmodernists see science as only another way of looking at the world, and not a verifiable form of knowledge itself.

[39] Ibid., 76–7. The repudiation or deprecation of human universals necessarily constitutes the main bastion of defense against Wilson's proposals to integrate science and humanistic study.

[40] Ridley observes in *The Origins of Virtue*, 264: "For St. Augustine the source of social order lay in the teachings of Christ. For Hobbes it lay in the sovereign. For Rousseau it lay in solitude. For Lenin it lay in the party. They were all wrong. The roots of social order are in our heads, where we possess instinctive capacities for creating not a perfect harmonious and virtuous society, but a better one than we have at present. We must build our institutions in such a way that they draw out those instincts." Contrary to Ridley's concern, religion can promote wider cooperation. Ridley, "Ecology as Religion" in *Origins of Virtue*, 211.

[41] Ridley, "Ecology as Religion," 80.

[42] One scholar engaging evolutionary biology and law is Rodgers in "Bringing People Back."

and promising early inquires remain disregarded.[43] Lawyers are creatures of their own legal systems, taking them for granted. Their careers are invested in the logic of their given system, which takes skill and is time-consuming.[44] Most have little opportunity to cultivate an interest in sociobiology. Nonetheless, human laws are cultural creations, enabled because of biologically evolved capacities. Comparable ethical concerns for nature are found in all legal traditions.[45] Common principles of law exist within civil law, common law, socialist law, Islamic law, and customary law regimes. Evolved norms about nature are prompting identification of new legal principles in many nations. This trend can be acknowledged empirically, whether or not lawyers accept the sociobiological perspectives discussed here.

As manifestations of evolved "hard-wired" norms, the three legal principles of cooperation, biophilia, and resilience already function. In all countries, laws exist to protect nature. Their weakness does not negate their promise. When maladapted "economic instincts" eclipse "ecological instincts," humans suffer the consequences, being part of nature. Buildings constructed on dewatered wetlands or in a flood plain are destroyed when returning rains inundate the settlements. Erosion can morph into desertification. Ecosystem resilience has limits. Hazardous wastes bioaccumulate in humans, and cancers result. To avert such unexpected harm, most countries have – again unilaterally – enacted environmental impact assessment laws.[46]

---

[43] A. G. Keller, "Law in Evolution," 28 *Yale Law Journal* (1918–19) 769.

[44] The dominant international economic order applies and refines rational choice theory with little perceived critique of "business as usual." See the critique in Donald P. Green and Ian Shapiro, *Pathologies of Rational Choice Theory: A Critique of Applications in Political Science* (New Haven: Yale University Press, 1994).

[45] See the journal *Environmental Ethics*, and Holmes Rolston III, *Environmental Ethics: Duties to and Values in the Natural World* (Philadelphia: Temple University Press, 1988). E. O. Wilson notes that "The constructs of moral reasoning, in this evolutionary view, are the learning rules, the propensities to acquire or to resist certain emotions and kinds of knowledge. They have evolved genetically because they confer survival and reproduction on human beings." E. O. Wilson, "Biophilia and the Conservation Ethic", in: S. Kellert and E. O. Wilson, *The Biophilia Hypothesis* (Washington, DC: Island Press, 1993), 38.

[46] Many nations enacted environmental impact assessment (EIA) laws after 1969 unilaterally. This pattern reflects a sociobiological instinct to act on a trait of human nature captured in the maxim "look before you leap." Once EIA was created and implemented in the USA through the National Environmental Policy Act of 1969, 42 USC 4321, the technique came to be adopted worldwide. The mandatory use of EIA was confirmed in Principle 17 of the Rio de Janeiro Declaration on Environment and Development (1992).

As life on Earth changes, so will the laws of humans. The new landscapes of the Anthropocene Epoch are both of the Earth[47] and in the minds of *Homo sapiens*. How well communities or countries respond to their new habitats will be a function of how well they apply evolved norms as legal principles.

4. Exploring sociobiology in the quest for a rule of law for nature

As moral animals,[48] humans hold in their brains instincts for norms that evolved over hundreds of thousands of years. Humans have learned to fashion rich civilizations, replete with laws and legal institutions, largely unaware of how their inborn human nature enables their creativity. Enrico Coen notes that: "The initial values are built into the pattern of neural connections we are born with, and arise through development. Learning then allows these connections to be modified through experience, so that we increase our chances of obtaining the desirable and avoiding the undesirable."[49] Humans evolved their capacity to learn, reason, and shape cultures and civilizations. Humans develop law to order their societies to further their creative efforts.

Legal scholarship largely ignores insights from evolutionary biology about how humans shape laws. In a thoughtful article, Donald Elliott reviews legal attitudes toward evolutionary biology. He critiques narrow concerns about "survival," rather focusing upon evolved capacities to learn.[50] Elliott notes that only A. G. Keller understood that legal

---

[47] The scientific dimensions of the shift to a new epoch are for the International Commission on Stratigraphy to determine whether a new epoch of geological time has supplanted the Holocene. See Anthropocene Working Group of the Subcommission on Quaternary Stratigraphy of the International Commission on Statigraphy, www.quaternary.stratigraphy.org.uk (last accessed June 3, 2013). Eugene Stroemer, Paul J. Crutzen, John R. McNeill, and Will Steffen each proposed that the Earth has left the Holocene Epoch and entered a new epoch. Crutzen and his colleagues entitled their essay "Are Humans Now Overwhelming the Great Forces of Nature?" 36:8 *Ambio* (December 2007).

[48] While Darwin observed that humans are unique in having an advanced moral faculty, he noted that: "Any animal whatever, endowed with well-marked social instincts, the parental and filial affections being here included, would inevitably acquire a moral sense or conscience, as soon as its intellectual powers had become as well developed, or nearly as well developed, as in man." Darwin, *The Descent of Man*, 71–2.

[49] Enrico Coen, *Cells to Civilizations – The Principles of Change that Shape Life* (Princeton University Press, 2012), 241.

[50] Namely, Richard Epstein, "A Taste for Privacy?: Evolution and the Emergence of a Naturalistic Ethics," 9 *Journal of Legal Studies* (1980) 665. Elliott observes that "Epstein's argument that evolutionary forces only operate in areas close to the 'raw nerve' of survival and propagation overlooks the fact that evolution may build into a society's value

principles were "natural" and not natural law.[51] Keller's insights into human nature and law merit further study.[52] Keller conceived cultural "mores" as being evolved characteristics of humans.[53] Keller's cultural mores[54] anticipate "evolved norms." Human "folkways" exist, and are not "planful. Those who practice them can seldom give rational excuse for so doing ... there is a cooperation and constant suggestion which is highly productive when it operates in a crowd, because it draws out latent power."[55] In Keller's view, "It is by adjusting its mores that a human group adapts itself to environment; the slower method by way of structural change is superseded by the swifter action of a specialised organ of adjustment."[56]

Sociobiology elucidates how humans evolved their capacity to create. One generation's successful mores are refined by the next. The brain creates laws, languages, arts, and commerce, all together. As Darwin observed, "The habitual use of articulate language is peculiar to man ... no philologist now supposes that any language has been deliberately invented; it has been slowly and unconsciously developed by many steps."[57] Darwin further observes, "A language, like a species, when once extinct ... never reappears."[58] Steven Pinker observes that "having a language is part of

---

system adaptive criteria which are proxies for the results of past evolutionary selection ... in law evolution may operate in terms of intermediate norms, which embody the results of past adaptation, as well as through outright extinction of individuals or groups ... Once the fundamental norm to minimize internal struggle is built into the legal system by evolution, it is possible to derive subsidiary legal principles from it." Elliott, "The Evolutionary Tradition in Jurisprudence," 84.

[51] Elliott, "The Evolutionary Tradition in Jurisprudence," 92, citing A. G. Keller, "Law in Evolution," 769, 783.

[52] E. Donald Elliott notes that Keller's concepts of cultural mores can be read "as though it had been written half a century later by sociobiologist E. O. Wilson." See Elliott, "The Evolutionary Tradition in Jurisprudence," 73.

[53] Keller, "Law in Evolution," 779–80.

[54] The concepts of "memes," discussed by Charles L. Lumsden and E. O. Wilson in *Genes, Mind, and Culture: The Coevolutionary Process* (Singapore: World Scientific, 2005), envision roles similar to Keller's "cultural mores." Genes and culture co-evolve, and cultural-biological units can correspond to neuronal networks that function as memory nodes. "Memes" were defined in Richard Dawkins, *The Selfish Gene* (Oxford University Press, 1989). Wilson accepted the term and function of the meme as the fundamental unit of cultural inheritance in *Consilience: The Unity of Knowledge* (New York: Knopf, 1998). The transmission of legal principles exists across civilizations, but how this functions is not being explored by jurists.

[55] Wilson, *Consilience*, 775–6.   [56] Ibid., 775.

[57] Charles Darwin, *The Descent of Man and Selection in Relation to Sex*, 2nd edition (New York: Hurst & Co., 1874), 101–2.

[58] Ibid., 106.

what it means to be human." He states that "All claims about a language instinct and other mental modules are claims about the commonalities among all normal people."[59] Laws, songs, and poems alike use language to define relationships with nature.[60]

While evolved norms do not compel any country's particular social, cultural, political, or legal human constructs, all legal systems do reflect the operation of evolved norms when crafting rules, processes, and institutions. Evolved norms dispose humans to act instinctively in comparable ways, when similar opportunities to act are present.[61] This not a deterministic argument.[62] Each human brain's realm of creativity and "free" choice in shaping laws is enormous, while supported by the same evolved norms.[63] Humans have evolved between 4,000 and 6,000 different languages. They also have evolved many distinct and varied legal systems.

[59] Steven Pinker, *The Language Instinct – How the Mind Create Language* (New York: HarperCollins 1994), 410 and 446.
[60] For example, the Wilderness Act in the USA, 16 US Code §1131(1)(C), reads: "Wilderness, in contrast with those areas where man and his own works dominate the landscape, is hereby recognized as an area where the earth and its community of life are untrammeled by man, where man himself is a visitor who does not remain." Comparable wilderness statutes have been enacted independently in South Africa, Australia, and elsewhere.
[61] The logic of acknowledging a biological foundation for human laws is observed by Joseph Ledoux in *The Emotional Brain – The Mysterious Underpinnings of Emotional Life* (New York: Simon & Schuster 1996), quoting Terrence Sejnowski with favor at p. 40: "Nature is more ingenious than we are. And we stand to miss all that power and ingenuity unless we attend to neurobiological plausibility. The point is, *evolution has already done it*, so why not learn how that stupendous machine, our brain works" (emphasis in original).
[62] E. O. Wilson, in "Consilience among the Great Branches of Learning," 127. *Daedalus* (1998) 145 gives reasons why social sciences resist consilience studies: "Their conceptions of human behavior come either from folk psychology – intuitive notions that seem right but are factually wrong – or from notions of the mind as an optimizing device for rational choice. They ignore contrary signs from genetics, neurobiology, cognitive psychology, and the many quirky properties of human nature." The insights of cognitive psychology and neurobiology remain to be applied to understand how law is fashioned in light of evolved norms. See Iain McGilchrist, *The Master and His Emissary – The Divided Brain and the Making of the Western World* (New Haven: Yale University Press, 2009).
[63] Stephen Jay Gould made a different assessment of Darwin's natural selection theory than does Edward O. Wilson. See, e.g., Stephen Jay Gould, *Ever Since Darwin* (New York: Norton, 1977), 45. Gould feared that social sciences would use biological determinism to justify social or political precepts or policies. Ibid., 258. Gould argued for "the triumph of Darwinian pluralism. Natural selection will turn out to be far more important than some molecular evolutionists imagine, but it will not be omnipotent, as some sociobiologists seem to maintain." Ibid., 270. Wilson has the better evidence. The full scope of the evolutionary studies stimulated by Darwin, including Wilson's insightful conceptualization of sociobiology, is discussed in Ernst Mayr, *The Growth of Biological Thought – Diversity, Evolution and Inheritance* (Cambridge, MA: Belknap Press of Harvard University Press, 1982).

From within their human instincts, humans learn and shape their cultural behavior, confirming these choices in laws. Steven Pinker's study of how humans over time used instinctive tendencies to abate violence[64] may be applied to human violence toward nature. Anthropological studies often examine how customary environmental law functions among indigenous people and tribal communities.[65] Darwin made observations about indigenous peoples in his own scholarship, but did not extend his thinking to how people formally establish social laws.

Evolutionary biology can be applied to environmental law-making. Some environmental laws are essentially instrumental, enacted separately in sectors for controlling water pollution, hunting, or hazardous wastes. More holistic laws seek to reunite humans and nature. Aldo Leopold explained that human "instincts" prompt competition among species, but "ethics" prompt cooperation, "perhaps in order that there may be a place to compete for," and the ethic "enlarges the boundaries of the community to include soils, water, plants, and animals, or collectively: the land."[66] Darwin wrote that "it is a truly wonderful fact – the wonder of which we are apt to overlook from familiarity – that all animals and all plants throughout all time and space should be related to each other in group subordinate to group, in the manner which we everywhere behold."[67] Both Darwin and Leopold reflect the evolved norm of biophilia.

Environmental legal principles reflect a love of nature, and humans cooperate to further this shared norm. Confronting the Anthropocene's emerging biological and geophysical conditions, humans will enact congruent reforms across different countries, thereby abating degradation of shared natural systems. This has been accomplished with laws to curb emissions of gases that deplete the stratospheric ozone layer.[68] Human instincts have been aligned to produce positive, cooperative action.

---

[64] Pinker, *The Better Angels of Our Nature*.
[65] See, e.g., Philippe Descola, *In the Society of Nature – A Native Ecology in Amazonia* (Cambridge University Press, 1884). Samuel Bowles and Herbert Gintis draw on anthropological studies for their sociobiological analysis in their work *A Cooperative Species – Human Reciprocity and its Evolution* (Princeton University Press, 2011).
[66] A. Leopold, "The Upshot," in: *A Sand County Almanac* (Oxford University Press, 1949), 203–4.
[67] Darwin, *The Origin of Species*, 105–8.
[68] See the 1985 Vienna Convention for the Protection of the Ozone Layer and 1987 Montreal Protocol on Substances that deplete the Ozone Layer, available at: www.unep.org/ozone (last accessed June 3, 2013), which is the first multilateral environmental agreement to have universal participation by all nations.

Reliance on the shared legal principles facilitates laws promoting resilient socio-ecological sustainability.

Among evolved norms,[69] cooperation, biophilia, and resilience may be selected for initial recognition as general principles of law because they are of fundamental importance in motivating humans to cope effectively with the ambient environment of the Anthropocene, to magnify their instincts for survival. Each evolved norm cohabits in human nature. These evolved norms become principles of law when countries and communities acknowledge them as such, and deploy them consciously to guide further human conduct. Communities and countries are accustomed to proclaiming legal principles in order to organize their policies and programs.

5. The principle of cooperation

Humans instinctively cooperate with one another, in the family, community, and more widely. Human laws recognize the duty to cooperate in order to promote conscious measures to better their conditions. Human beings have long recognized reciprocity, an evolved norm for cooperation with each other. The recognition is ancient. Confucius, when asked "Is there one word which may serve as a rule of practice all one's life?" replied, "Is not reciprocity such a word?"[70] All religions invoke this norm as a "golden rule," to treat others as one would wish to be treated.

Cooperation is both an ethical norm and a duty of good neighborliness, acknowledged to be a customary norm in all legal systems (e.g. *droit de voisinage*).[71] The work worldwide of the International Federation of Red Cross and Red Crescent Societies is premised on cooperation. Among nations, treaties of friendship have expanded to embrace collective security in the Charter of the United Nations.[72] Cooperation is a basic rule of international law.

Humans can maximize the trait of "cooperation," to make more pervasive use of the principle of cooperation. Within local communities, humans cooperate not because they are ordered to do so, but because doing so is fulfilling and they wish to do so. Governments and individuals

---

[69] Cooperation, biophilia, resilience, foresight, sharing (or sufficiency), and justice (including equity and environmental rights) can be restated as general principles of law.
[70] *The Analects of Confucius*, Book 15, Chapter 23.
[71] Jacqueline P. Hand and James Charles Smith, *Neighboring Property Owners* (Colorado Springs: Shepard's/McGraw Hill, 1988; annual updates published by Thomson West).
[72] Articles 55 and 56 in Chapter IX of the United Nations Charter.

alike instinctively cooperate when providing mutual aid for disaster relief, for example amidst the intense storm impacts induced by "climate change." Mutual aid agreements enable cooperation for fighting fires and supplying sister governments in time of great need.[73] Mutual hospitals and insurance agencies and universities all work effectively because of cooperation.

The evolutionary foundations for cooperation are thoroughly described in sociobiological scholarship by Samuel Bowles and Herbert Gintis,[74] who find that the human capacity for cooperation is an evolved human characteristic, and by Enrico Coen,[75] Mark Pagel,[76] and Matt Ridley.[77] Since humans are "hard-wired" to cooperate, environmental law can draw on cooperative instincts to further its remedial provisions. Laws are more robust when relying explicitly on cooperation. In the future, environmental law will need to do more to frame procedures to promote cooperation and trust, and to expand human awareness of reciprocity to include other animals and ecosystems. Cooperation stems from compassion. Cultural ethics can broaden the scope of compassion, and laws can encourage a needed collective vision: "We are all in this together." Darwin cherished the "wonder" that all life is related.[78]

Cooperation can be cultivated. Strong reciprocity, a willingness to apply rules to punish those who do not cooperate, reduces the likelihood of free-riders. Institutions can co-evolve to build more robust cooperation.[79] Designing laws giving primacy to cooperation is not always easy. The UN Convention on Biological Diversity's decisions reflect strong cooperation based on shared concerns for nature and securing life on Earth,[80] while the UN Framework Convention on Climate Change illustrates weak cooperation, in which nations are more concerned with securing what they deem their fair share of economic growth, and the objective is "business

---

[73] Nicholas A. Robinson, "Forest Fires as a Common International Concern: Precedents for the Progressive Development of International Environmental Law," 18:2 *Pace Environmental Law Review* (2001) 459–504.
[74] Bowles and Gintis, *A Cooperative Species*.
[75] Coen, *Cells to Civilizations*, 2012 edn.
[76] Mark Pagel, *Wired for Culture: The Natural History of Human Co-operation* (London: Allen Lane, 2011).
[77] Ridley, *The Origins of Virtue*.
[78] Darwin, *The Origin of Species*, 106.
[79] Bowles and Gintis, *A Cooperative Species*, Chapters 7 and 9.
[80] See the "Strategic Plan for Biodiversity 2011–2020 and the Aichi Targets," Conference of the Parties of the Convention on Biological Diversity, available at: www.cbd.int/sp/targets (last accessed June 3, 2013).

as usual."[81] Moreover, within a country or community corruption, greed, and bias can work to frustrate cooperative instincts, and laws combat these antisocial acts. Cooperation may be extended too narrowly, to one's immediate clan or nation, and may not be applied when needed, as when a state denies access to refugees or environmentally displaced persons, or other migrants. Systems of common property rights can be designed to engender cooperation,[82] as when councils of stakeholders manage the cooperative use of resources.[83] Cooperation is fostered by ensuring access to environmental information and public participation in environmental decision-making.[84]

As Enrico Coen observes, "Cooperation also plays an essential role by allowing people to benefit from each other's skills. This both promotes achievements within groups and leads to further levels of competition among them. By bringing people and ideas together, cooperation also leads to an enormous number of combinatorial possibilities, creating a vast cultural space through which our species can move."[85] Enduring cooperation emerges when the bonds between humans and nature are acknowledged, accepting what Edward O. Wilson calls "biophilia."[86]

6. The principle of biophilia

Instinctively prone to cooperate, humans can likewise enhance the instincts to care for nature by explicitly recognizing a legal principle of biophilia. Humans already enact laws implicitly based on biophilia, as

---

[81] See the Copenhagen Accord, UN Framework Convention on Climate Change, Decision 2/CP.15 (18 December 2009), at: www.unfccc.int/meetings/copenhagen-dec-2009/6295.php (last accessed June 3, 2013).

[82] Elinor Ostrom, *Governing the Commons: The Evolution of Institutions for Collective Action* (Cambridge University Press, 1999).

[83] See, e.g., in England and Wales through the Commons Act of 2006. Comparable regimes exist in the Adirondack Mountains of New York through the Adirondack Park Agency Act in 1972, available at: www.apa.ny.gov/Documents/Laws_Regs/APAACT.PDF (last accessed June 3, 2013), and the earlier establishment of the Forest Preserve of the State in 1894, Article XIV of the New York State Constitution, around which conservationists, recreationalists, property owners, and mining and timber interests all gather to engage in decisions on land stewardship.

[84] Principle 10 of the Declaration of Rio de Janeiro on Environment and Development 1992, later codified in the Aarhus Convention, available at: www.unece.org/env/pp (last accessed June 3, 2013).

[85] Enrico Coen, "The Crucible of Culture," in *Cells to Civilizations* (2012 edn), 264.

[86] Edward O. Wilson, *Biophilia – The Human Bond with Other Species* (Cambridge, MA: Harvard University Press, 1984).

in creating parks, wilderness areas, wildlife refuges, endangered species Acts, and other nature conservation laws. Humans establish parklands not for economic growth, but for recreation and spiritual pleasure and ecological study. Natural resource laws, and fish and game laws, are based on what science learns about ecological conditions. On one level, these may be regarded as merely utilitarian, to ensure the sustained yields of renewable species for their annual harvest. But the rapid expansion of conservation laws worldwide reflects a regard for nature that is profound, not instrumental. Legal sanctions include criminal penalties, and other indicators of strong cooperation.

Humans delight in nature. As Gordon Burghardt explains, humans evolved to appreciate "play," and evolved norms for "fair play," as did their languages or arts.[87] Laws encourage play in nature by designating parks, protected areas, trails, and other places for recreation and nature appreciation. Laws protect marine habitats, expand terrestrial parks, order the planting of trees, establish walking paths, save habitats, and carve out space for animals conveniently to cohabit with humans in watersheds.[88] In doing so, humans reinforce their positive instincts about nature.

Biophilia is a human instinct. Stephen Kellert observes that "all our biophilic values emerged as universal tendencies hammered into our genes because they reflect adaptive functions that advanced our health, fitness, and well-being over the course of human evolution and development."[89] Much of nature conservation law grows out of this principle of biophilia. It has as much claim on the political discourse as does the right to life. Biophilia sustains the right to the environment, acknowledged in Supreme Court decisions in India,[90] the Philippines,[91] and elsewhere. It underpins the world's first legal wilderness, New York State's "forever wild" Forest Preserve.[92] Biophilia provides the foundation for every local, state, provincial, national, or transnational park worldwide. No international law mandates the establishment of parklands. Human nature does.

---

[87] Gordon Burghardt, *The Genesis of Animal Play – Testing the Limits* (Cambridge, MA: MIT Press, 2005).
[88] See Barbara Lausche, *Guidelines for Protected Area Legislation* (Gland: IUCN, EPL Paper 81, 2011), available at: www.iucn.org (last accessed June 3, 2013).
[89] Stephen R. Kellert, *Birthright – People and Nature in the Modern World* (New Haven: Yale University Press, 2012), 195.
[90] See M. C. Mehta, "Making the Law World for the Environment," 2:4 *Asia Pacific Journal of Environmental Law* (1997) 349.
[91] *Oposa v. Factoran*, GR 10 101083 (July 30, 1993).
[92] Established in 1894. See Article XIV of the New York State Constitution.

As Wilson observes:

> An enduring code of ethics is not created whole from absolute premises but inductively, in the manner of common law, with the aid of case histories, by feeling and consensus, through an expansion of knowledge and experience, influenced by the epigenetic rules of mental development, during which well-meaning and responsible people sift the opportunities and come to agree upon norms and directions.[93]

Nature conservation societies in every part of the world today join nations in the International Union for Conservation of Nature (IUCN), whose mission is to secure "A just world that values and conserves nature."[94] IUCN's Commission on Environmental Law persuaded the United Nations to adopt the World Charter for Nature and the Convention on Biological Diversity, among other laws.[95] Amidst losses of habitats and other challenges of the Anthropocene, humans will expand *ex situ* preservation of species in botanical gardens, zoological parks, and the Svalbard Global Seed Vault in Norway, which conserves the seeds and DNA of plants worldwide.[96] For *in situ* protection, humans consciously will expand wetlands, wildlife sanctuaries, and other habitats, reversing previous actions as sea levels rise.

Evolved norms of biophilia are found in religious stewardship of God's creation and reverence of life as theological themes.[97] Each great religion provides for respecting and loving God's creation in nature. This universal acceptance of a biophilic norm in religions is well presented in Mary Evelyn Tucker's studies.[98] Biophilia's religious foundations reflect evolved norms humans hold toward nature. Environmental ethics reflects this

---

[93] Wilson, *Biophilia* (Harvard University Press Reprint 1990 edn), 124.
[94] Martin Holdgate, *The Green Web – A Union for World Conservation* (London: Earthscan, 1999). IUCN was founded in 1948, and Wolfgang E. Burhenne founded IUCN's environmental law program in 1963.
[95] Barbara J. Lausche, *Weaving a Web of Environmental Law* (Berlin: Erich Schmidt Verlag, 2008).
[96] Tracey Heatherton, "From Ecocide to Genetic Rescue," in: G. M. Sodikoff, *The Anthropology of Extinction* (Bloomington: Indiana University Press, 2012), 50–3.
[97] Thomas Berry, *The Great Work* (New York: Bell Tower, 1999).
[98] See the studies of the Forum on Religion and Ecology, "World Religions and Ecology Series," published by the Harvard Divinity School Center for the Study of World Religions, studies on Indigenous Religions (J. Grimm), Hinduism (C. K. Chapple and M. E. Tucker), Jainism (C. K. Chapple), Buddhism (M. E. Tucker and D. R. Williams), Confucianism (M. E. Tucker and J. Berthrong), Daoism (N. J. Girardot, J. Miller and Liu Xiaogan), Judaism (H. Tirosh-Samuelson), Christianity (D. T. Hessel and R. R. Ruether), Islam (R. C. Foltz, F. M. Denny and A. Bahauddin). See http://fore.research.yale.edu/publications/books/book_series/cswr/index/html (last accessed June 3, 2013).

same search for a belief-based set of values about nature.[99] As Robert N. Bellah demonstrates, the instinct for religion is itself an evolved norm,[100] which reflects biophilia through treating life as sacred.

Evolution produced this capacity for nature appreciation. Wilson observes:

> we are human in good part because of the particular way we affiliate with other organisms. They are the matrix in which the human mind originated and is permanently rooted, and they offer the challenge and freedom innately sought ... The more the mind is fathomed in its own right, as an organ of survival, the greater will be the reverence for life for purely rational reasons ... The drive toward perpetual expansion – or personal freedom – is basic to the human spirit. But to sustain it we need the most delicate, knowing stewardship of the living world that can be devised.[101]

Practical applications of the biophilia principle are found in building codes[102] or in land-use planning.[103] Public health, veterinary science, and wildlife conservation each are concerned with zoonosis, and biophilia can foster use of foresight and adaptation to maintain resilient and healthy conditions in both human and animal domains.[104] Biophilia motivates conscientious nurturing of life, to enhance resilience and health.

7. The principle of resilience

Resilience is innately a trait of human nature. Implicit in biophilia is a will to stimulate strong cooperation among humans toward nature, in order to enhance capabilities of resilience. Capacities for resilience allow humans and nature alike to rebound from the disruptions of the Anthropocene. Society implicitly recognizes the values of resilience in environmental laws, such as those protecting wetlands or providing for coastal zone

---

[99] See, e.g., Ridley, "Ecology as Religion."
[100] Robert N. Bellah, *Religion in Human Evolution* (Cambridge, MA: Belknap Press of Harvard University Press, 2011), which also references Gordon Burghardt's insightful studies on the human capacity for play.
[101] Wilson, *Biophilia*, 139–40.
[102] Ian McHarg, *Design With Nature* (Garden City: Natural History Press for the American Museum of Natural History, 1969).
[103] Stephen R. Kellert, Judith H. Heerwagen and Martin L. Mador, *Biophilic Design: The Theory, Science, & Practice of Bringing Buildings to Life* (Hoboken: Wiley, 2008).
[104] See the twelve Manhattan Principles of the Wildlife Conservation Society's "One World, One Health" program, available at: www.wcs.org/conservation-challenges/wildlife-health/wildlife-humans-and-livestock/one-world-one-health.aspx (last accessed June 3, 2013), and also www.OneWorldOneHealth.org (last accessed June 3, 2013).

management.[105] Communities and countries can magnify their capacities' resilience through all socio-ecological systems.[106] Humans and nature alike will depend on robust resilience amidst the surprises and disruptions of the Anthropocene.[107]

Resilience is a human instinct. Maxims, such as "saving for a rainy day" or rules such as the Precautionary Principle enhance resilience. Physicians promote resilience in patients to enhance medical treatment. Ecologists study resilience in natural systems under disturbance.[108] The biological roots of resilience relate to capacities to adapt and evolve. In human communities and countries, laws foster resilience when designing redundancy in socio-economic activity, such as for environmental management systems or fire and other emergency services. Resilient laws identify risks and eschew practices that exacerbate risk-prone situations. Conserving renewable natural resources takes on added importance as it enhanced resilience and reduced risks.

The Resilience Principle operates through insurance laws, which provide financial compensation for disaster losses. However, most of the world lacks a system of casualty insurance to pay expenses associated with severe storm events. Insurance builds resilience by providing self-reliant foundation to sustain cooperation for helping humans to cope with setbacks. To enhance resilience, humans have long organized mutual aid insurance systems.[109] Establishing insurance, including micro-insurance for poor regions, promotes honest, transparent, affordable, and effective adaptation to casualties.

---

[105] See the Freshwater Wetlands Act and the Tidal Wetlands Act of the State of New York, Articles 24 and 25, Environmental Conservation Law, 17 1/2 McKinney's Consolidated Laws of New York.

[106] See the studies from different disciplines of the Resilience Centre at the University of Stockholm, Sweden. See, e.g., B. Nykvist, *Social Learning in the Anthropocene. Governance of Natural Resources in Human Dominated Systems* (Doctoral Thesis in Natural Resource Management, Stockholm University), available as one of the publications of the Stockholm Resilience Centre at: www.stockholmresilience.org (last accessed June 3, 2013).

[107] Resilience is required in and after responses to disasters. See Vikram Kolmannskog and Lisetta Trebbi, "Climate Change, Natural Disasters and Displacement: A Multi-track Approach to Filling Protection Gaps," *International Review of the Red Cross*, no. 879 (2010), available at: www.icrc.org/eng/resources/documents/article/review-2010 (last accessed June 3, 2013).

[108] See B. Walker and D. Salt, *Resilience Thinking* (Washington, DC: Island Press, 2006).

[109] Janet Wright, Virginia Wadsley and Janice Artandi, *The History of the National Association of Mutual Insurance Companies, A Century of Commitment, 1895–1995* (Indianapolis: National Association of Mutual Insurance Companies, 1994).

Resilience is evident in great cities, whose roots predate the nations in which they are found today. Cities compare and adapt by adopting each other's successful attributes. Resilient systems learn how to practice adaptation. Encouraging a collective memory is a part of being resilient. Societies forget at their peril. In Fukushima, Japan in 1611, humans raised one-meter-high stone tablets to warn about tsunami wave heights, but in the twentieth century the tablets were ignored when developments were built behind the false security of man-made sea walls.[110] The year 2011 witnessed the Fukushima Daiichi disaster, with earthquakes, a tsunami, breach of sea walls, and destruction of a nuclear power plant. Laws for resilience compensate for human tendencies toward such complacency.

Laws can magnify resilience by requiring all societal planning to take measures that enhance resilience. Resilience laws build redundancy and buffers to facilitate recover from disruptions. Deployment of programs based on the Resilience Principle relies on foresight, which is also an evolved trait of human nature.[111] The conservation leader Theodore Roosevelt recognized foresight as a "distinguishing" characteristic of humans, and led his nation in enacting biophilic laws.[112] Recognizing a duty to enhance resilience whenever possible would strengthen observance of the Precautionary Principle[113] and the Principle of Environmental Impact Assessment (EIA).[114]

There are other evolved norms that deserve study, and would have promising roles if enacted as legal principles. For example, evolved norms for foresight can also motivate sharing and caring. Darwin notes, "When a man risk his life to save that of a fellow-creature, it seems also more correct to say that he acts for the general good, rather than for the general happiness of mankind."[115] Matt Ridley observes, "There is no other animal that exploits the law of comparative advantage between groups."[116]

---

[110] Martin Fackler, "Tsumani Warnings, Written in Stone," *NY Times*, April 20, 2011. It has been suggested that the capacity of humans to forget unpleasant times or events is an evolved instinct, but humans also have capacities to remember and fashion ways to counteract forgetfulness.

[111] Charles Darwin, *The Variation of Animals and Plants Under Domestication* (London: John Murray, 1868).

[112] Theodore Roosevelt, Address by the President, Proceedings of the Conference of Governors of the United States, The White House, May 13–15, 1908 (Printed by Act of Congress, 1908), 8.

[113] Rio de Janeiro Declaration on Environment and Development (1992), Principle 15.

[114] Ibid., Principle 17.

[115] Darwin, *The Descent of Man*, 2nd edn, 136.

[116] Ridley, *The Origins of Virtue*, 209–10.

Thomas Princen recognizes how humans can measure what is sufficient to meet needs, while sharing so that others can do the same; humans can magnify their capacity to share once sufficiency is satisfied.[117] Norms about sufficiency focus on human instincts for attaining a "sufficient" return, while avoiding "over-consumption," which is pilloried as the sin of gluttony. The 1992 Earth Summit agreed to end "unsustainable patterns of consumption and production."[118] Princen observes: "The science of ecological rationality – complexity theory – is one that leads to very unscientific notions like humility and caution, much as the experiential knowledge of long-standing resources users does."[119]

Without a principle for sharing or sufficiency, humans are apt to take imprudent risks, jeopardizing resilience in nature and humans alike. As Enrico Coen observes, "From an evolutionary point of view, it doesn't pay to be satisfied. It is better to continually search for actions that might increase the chance of survival and reproduction."[120] Survival in the Anthropocene is advantaged through understanding sufficiency. Stephen R. Kellert terms over-consumption "an inordinate fondness of materialism."[121] Sufficiency reflects evolved norms about fairness and equity. Compassion, empathy, and caring are traits of human nature, also codified in concepts of justice.

8. Justice for humans and nature

Principles based on evolved norms are appearing worldwide under the rubric of environmental rights. This is not surprising, since the thirst for justice itself is an evolved norm. The emergence of environmental rights, such as guaranteeing public participation in environmental decision-making,[122] illustrates how humans are adapting concepts of justice to the conditions of the Anthropocene. Courts in most nations are essential for the effectiveness of environmental law,[123] and more than fifty nations

---

[117] Thomas Princen, *The Logic of Sufficiency* (Cambridge, MA: MIT Press, 1995).
[118] Paragraphs 4.3 and 4.26, Agenda 21 (1992), UN Doc A/CONF. 151/4 (1992).
[119] Princen, *The Logic of Sufficiency*, 44–5, citing with favor political theorist John S. Dryzek, *Rational Ecology: Environment and Political Economy* (Oxford: Blackwell, 1987).
[120] Coen, *Cells to Civilizations*, 268.
[121] Kellert, *Birthright*, 63.
[122] Principle 10 of the Rio de Janeiro Declaration on Environment and Development (1992).
[123] These experiences are analyzed by Louis J. Kotzé and Alexander R. Paterson in *The Role of the Judiciary in Environmental Governance – Comparative Perspectives* (Alphen

have established some 400 environmental courts and tribunals to adjudicate environmental rights.[124] These courts are designing new remedies to restore nature's resilience and vindicate environmental rights.[125] Judges apply evolved norms, such as biophilia, in legal contexts and courts articulate legal environmental principles.[126]

Environmental rights are often grounded in constitutions.[127] For example, New York's highest court[128] enforced a constitutional right of nature to be "kept as forever wild forest land."[129] Courts enforce and extend the public trust doctrine to protect nature[130] in rulings from courts from Australia[131] to India.[132] Ecuador's constitution provides a Right of Nature, coequal to Human Rights,[133] in addition to ensuring an environmental

---

aan den Rijn: Wolters Kluwer, 2009), which examines the strengths and weaknesses of environmental adjudication in nineteen nations.

[124] George Pring and Catherine Pring, *Greening Justice: Creating and Improving Environmental Courts and Tribunals* (Washington, DC: The Access Initiative, housed within the World Resources Institute, 2009).

[125] The first scholarly commentaries about the substantive and procedural aspects of environmental judicial adjudications appear in 3:1 *Journal of Court Innovation* (2010) available at www.courts.state.ny.us/court-innovation/Winter-2010/JCI_Winter10a.pdf (last accessed June 3, 2013). See also the symposium on "Environmental Courts and Tribunals: Improving Access to Justice and Protection of the Environment Around the World," 29:2 *Pace Environmental Law Review* (Winter 2012) 363, available at digitalcommons.pace.edu/pelr/vol29/iss2 (last accessed June 3, 2013).

[126] Justice Brian Preston, Chief Judge of the Environment Court of New South Wales (Australia), has summarized these as falling under five topics: (a) substantive justice, (b) procedural justice, (c) distributive justice, (d) restorative justice, and (e) therapeutic justice. "Benefits of Judicial Specialization in Environmental Law: The Land and Envrironment Court of New South Wales as a Case Study", 29:2 *Pace Environmental Law Review* (2012) 396–440 at 435, available at: http://digitalcommons.pace.edu/pelr/vol29/iss2.

[127] Boyd, *The Environmental Rights Revolution*.

[128] *The Association for the Protection of the Adirondacks and Another v. Alexander Macdonald, Conservation Commissioner of the State of New York and Another*, 228 AD 73, 239 NYS 31 (App. Div 1930), affirmed 253 NY 234.

[129] Article XIV, Constitution of the State of New York.

[130] See Katherine R. Leisch, "A Trusting Public: How the Public Trust Doctrine Can Save the New York Forest Preserve" (2010), online at digitalcommons.pace.edu (last accessed June 3, 2013).

[131] *Willoughby City Council v. Minister Administering the National Parks & Wildlife Act* (1992), 78 LGRA 18 (Australia).

[132] *M.C. Mehta v. Kamal Nath and others* (1977), SCC 388 (India).

[133] Article 71 of the Constitution of 2008 provides: "Nature or *Pachamama*, where life is reproduced and exists, has the right to exist, persist, maintain and regenerate its vital cycles, structure, functions and its processes in evolution. Every person, people, community or nationality, will be able to demand the recognitions of rights for Nature before the public organs."

right for humans;[134] Ecuador's courts have recognized nature's right to have humans respect a river's ecosystem integrity.[135] The Supreme Court of the Philippines in *Oposa v. Factoran*[136] enforced the Constitution's provision for "balanced and healthful ecology in accord with the rhythm and harmony of nature"; the Court's rules provide that when any person seeks a Writ of Nature (*Kalikasan*), a court promptly must enjoin the alleged behavior and require the responding party to demonstrate its compliance with all applicable environmental laws.[137] India has adopted its Green Tribunals Act, and has established its first regional environmental courts. China has more than sixty environmental chambers in fourteen courts in Provinces, for hearing citizen complaints against polluters.

These independent, yet congruent legal innovations illustrate how humans marshal comparable environmental principles of law to guide behavior in favor of resilience and sustaining human health and ecosystems. Legal principles based on evolved norms "ring true." They can be applied in local neighborhoods and small communities, as well as on the scale of countries and regions. In observing principles based on evolved norms, individuals need not wait for governments to act, since each person instinctively responds to the same evolved capacity to act.

Cognitive science has much to learn yet about how humans will adapt to radical environmental change. Juridical studies of sociobiology have just begun. As Darwin put it, "We are not here concerned with hopes or fears, only with the truth as far as our reason allows us to discover it."[138] Throughout the Holocene, communities and countries cooperated to fashion many different governing systems. In the future, human nature will prompt new adaptations in law and governance. Evolved norms

---

[134] Article 397 of the Constitution of 2009 provides "To permit any natural person or legal entity, human community or group, to file legal proceedings and resort to judicial and administrative bodies without detriment to their direct interest, to obtain from them effective custody in environmental matters, including the possibility of requesting precautionary measures ... The burden of proof regarding the absence of potential or real danger shall lie with the operator of the activity or the defendant."

[135] Erin Daly, "Ecuadoran Court Recognizes Constitutional Rights to Nature," Widener Law School blog, available at: http://blogs.law.widener.edu/envirolawblog/2011/07/12/ecuadorian-court-recognizes-constitutional-right-to-nature (last accessed June 3, 2013). See *Arco Iris v. Ecuador Mineral Institute* (1993), and *R.F. Wheeler and E.G. Huddle v. Attorney General of the State of Loja* (2011).

[136] GR 10 101083 (July 30, 1993).

[137] Rules of Procedure for Environmental Cases, AM No. 09–6-8-SC (effective April 29, 2010), available at www.lawphil.net/courts/supreme/am/am_09-6-8-sc_2010.html (last accessed June 3, 2013).

[138] Darwin, *The Descent of Man*, 2nd edn, Chapter XXI, 644.

provide the capacity for this quest. Human social and cultural decisions will codify the norms as environmental rights, elements of justice.

By magnifying evolved norms selected to be legal principles, humans can help one another, and all of nature. The evidence of sociobiology affirms that humans can shape a new rule of law for nature. Any canon useful for the life of the law will grow out of the kinship that humans and nature share. The three legal principles here may provide humanity's compass by which to navigate its – *our* – intergenerational travels through the Anthropocene.

PART II

A rule of law for nature: theories and reflections

4

Grounding the rule of law

KLAUS BOSSELMANN

In memory of Staffan Westerlund (1942–2012)

1. Grounding the rule of law in a time of crisis

The rule of law means that no one is above the law. But if the law itself is ill-conceived, its rule may not do anyone a service. A case in point would be a legal obligation to willingly and systematically destroy the natural environment. Only someone blinded by ignorance would insist on respecting a law that calls for our collective demise.

The conventional understanding of the rule of law finds the solution in the democratic process. In a democracy, a proposal to destroy our collective living conditions is highly unlikely to make it into law. And if it does, such law can be repealed by the courts or by a new parliamentary majority. If this does not happen, individuals can exercise their right to civil disobedience. The rule of law principle is not affected.

What happens, however, if the life-destroying character of law remains unnoticed? Aside from individual resistance (of a few enlightened people) and possible survival of some self-contained elements of society, the collective will have to bear the consequences of its ignorance and may eventually perish. Such ecocide might be viewed as a tragedy, but again not as a failure of the rule of law. A theoretical alternative could be to perceive the rule of law not as an absolute, but as context-bound and grounded in further requirements about its own validity. As a consequence, not *any* law qualifies for the rule of law, but only law that meets some basic requirements.

The current global crisis should never have happened. Finance, austerity, poverty, food, water, energy, climate, biodiversity – they are all related and mere aspects of one big crisis called the sustainability crisis. It should never have happened, but could we have prevented it? Could some better grounding of the rule of law have prevented it? Assuming that explainable socio-economic patterns and phenomena aggravate the crisis, we should ask what role our social institutions such as governments and laws have in this process. Have they been complicit, and if so in what way?

The thesis of this chapter is that the law has been complicit in a sense of legitimizing and legalizing excessive growth and environmental destruction. It is further argued that domestic and international law have been widely ignorant of ecological realities. Both share this ignorance with their creator, that is modern Western society moulded in certain beliefs and values. On the other hand, as we are seeing dramatic global change, fuelled not just by corporatism and politics, but also by social activism (with new ways of communication and networking), we can also realize the importance of law in this context. The law can be either an accomplice of the status quo or a facilitator of change. And if the rule of law has been oblivious of some ecological preconditions of its own and society's continued existence, this omission can, and should, be overcome.

Relating the rule of law to the ecological challenge is very timely. The theme of this book reflects on twenty-five years since the Brundtland Report and twenty years since the Rio Earth Summit, both setting out the sustainable development agenda. Have governments and their laws responded? Arguably very little, but this immediately raises the issue of leadership. If the profound change that the Brundtland Report had called for and the intentions that states had expressed at the 1992 Rio Summit never materialized in law, then what does this say about the ability of states and governments to lead? Rio+20 would have offered the opportunity for stocktaking and critical self-reflection. While many civil society events at Rio+20 criticized states for being complicit with economic globalization and neo-liberalism, participating states themselves remained remarkably immune in the face of such criticism. Instead, they merely reaffirmed old promises.

The Rio+20 outcome document 'The Future We Want'[1] does little more than list voluntary measures that countries can accept or ignore. There are some good ideas such as partnerships, green consumption, other indicators, civil society participation and institutional reform, but none of these are revolutionary. The 2012 Rio document contains the same failed pledges and empty goals as the 1992 Rio documents. It is ignorant of the fact that the world today is less sustainable than ever before, it fails to

---

[1] UN A/CONF.216/L.1.

address the root causes, does not define sustainable development, has no parameters for measuring progress and is not legally binding.

This lack of leadership at state level is no excuse for the citizens of these states, the *demos*. To the contrary, democracy rests on continuously generated leadership at all levels. Typically, leadership requires charting the unchartered and inspiring others to follow. For environmental law scholars this could well mean revisiting the concept of the rule of law and its grounding in ecological realities.

This challenge can be summarized in two steps. The first step is to recognize the reality of planetary boundaries. Of the nine boundaries identified thus far,[2] three have already been exceeded (atmospheric greenhouse gas concentrations, rate of biodiversity loss and nitrogen cycle). The recognition of planetary boundaries sets a non-negotiable bottom line for all human activities. More particularly, it suggests a hierarchical order for the elements of sustainable development: the environment takes precedence, with humans second and the economy third. Accepting this understanding of sustainable development ('strong sustainability') is the first step.

The second step is to reflect this hierarchical order in the design and interpretation of laws governing human behaviour. The rule of law is the most basic tool for ensuring control and accountability of governments. It demands that governmental decisions are bound by law and implies that all citizens are subject to the law. But not any law can count for the true meaning of the rule of law. A purely 'formal' or 'thin'[3] recognition of the rule of law, deprived of any values and content, permits any law to find legitimate application. Such formalism is not what I have in mind here and is surely not good enough for nations that describe themselves as civilized and supportive of the virtues of citizenry.

How far can we realistically go with this notion? John Finnis once described the rule of law as '[t]he name commonly given to the state of affairs in which a given legal system is legally in good shape'.[4] Applying this substantive definition, we can only conclude that more than forty years of environmental law have not made much of a difference to the state of affairs or to the legal system. Both are in bad shape.

Even if we do not follow Finnis' definition, the rule of law has certain positive qualities associated with a modern democratic state. Western

---

[2] J. Rockström *et al.*, 'Planetary Boundaries: Exploring the Safe Operating Space for Humanity', 14:2 *Ecology and Society* (2009), 32.
[3] B. Tamanaha, *On the Rule of Law: History, Politics, Theory* (Cambridge University Press, 2004).
[4] J. Finnis, *Natural Law and Natural Rights* (Oxford University Press, 1980), 270.

legal systems usually refer to the rule of law as one of their core characteristics along with democracy, justice and human rights. The rule of law may not be clearly defined – some see it as a highly contested concept[5] or even meaningless[6] – but no one would deny its fundamental importance. Our attitude to the rule of law may in fact be similar to justice and sustainability: we do not always agree on what they mean, but nevertheless we insist on their validity.

This is not to say that we do not need further clarification of what the title of this book entails. Quite the contrary. Much of what brings the contributors together is their shared desire to reconcile democracy, justice, human rights and the rule of law with humankind's responsibility for nature.

In this chapter we will first chart the rule of law (section 2), second, describe the 'uncharted', the context of nature (section 3), then define sustainability as a law-of-rule grounding principle (or grundnorm) (section 4), and finally sketch some implications for further environmental law research (section 5).

2. About the rule of law

The rule of law as a concept lacks a decisive definition and as such it is important to take the time to chart the various understandings, in an effort to find a core meaning from which to proceed.

The concept has its origins in the ancient Greek and Roman philosophers, although the rule of law as it is understood today did not take root until more than 1,000 years after the height of the Athenian empire.[7] The English conception materialized at the end of the seventeenth century with the glorious revolution of 1688, resulting in the move from the idea of *Rex Lex* ('The King is Law') to *Lex Rex* ('The Law is King'). The classic English expression, however, is found in Andrew Venn Dicey's 1885 work *Introduction to the Study of Law of the Constitution*.[8] While Dicey does not precisely define 'rule of law', he expounds three meanings, which arguably amount only to a description of the political and constitutional state of affairs in England at the time.[9] The first meaning is that a man

---

[5] J. Faundez et al., 'Editorial', 1 *Hague Journal on the Rule of Law* (2009), 1.
[6] J. Raz, 'The Rule of Law and its Virtue', in: J. Raz, *The Authority of Law: Essays on Law and Morality* (Oxford University Press, 1979), 210.
[7] Tamanaha, *On The Rule of Law*, 7.
[8] M. Neumann, *The Rule of Law: Politicizing Ethics* (Aldershot: Ashgate Publishing Ltd, 2002), 1.
[9] Ibid., 15.

can only be punished if he has broken an existing law, and not merely at the whim of those in power. Second, those in power are equally liable to punishment under the law as an ordinary man. Finally, Dicey viewed the constitution as akin to ordinary law, such that rights could not be entrenched in a constitution, but instead flowed from the English common law.[10] Dicey's rule of law is confined to the English legal system, and is of little value in universal application, save perhaps for his first meaning, which may be viewed as the core of the understanding of the rule of law internationally.[11]

Beyond Dicey, the rule of law has had attached to it various meanings that can helpfully be grouped into 'moralized' and 'non-moralized' conceptions. Philosophers such as Hayek, Raz and Rawls have all included threads of morality within their rule of law conceptions, some to a greater extent than others.[12] Hayek speaks of the 'inalienable right of the individual'.[13] Rawls includes the need for natural justice in the form of fairness, openness and impartiality in his rule of law conception, which is fundamentally based on the assumption that those to whom the law applies are rational beings.[14] Meanwhile, Raz also declares natural justice to be a requirement and suggests that there is a 'correct' way in which the law should apply.[15] All these writers seem to imply that the rule of law needs to be conceived of in a way that ensures conduct is not simply guided, but that it is guided in a *good* way.[16]

There are then the non-moralized conceptions of the rule of law, which seek to strip the notion down to its basic core, effectively eliminating the rights discourse. Hobbes, Jennings and even Dicey are proponents of this view. Dicey seemingly rejects rights supremacy in his third 'meaning' of the rule of law,[17] where he states that constitutional laws are no different to ordinary laws. Rights therefore do not hold a position of guarantee, as they are simply another creation of law. Hobbes' conception of the rule of law is shaped by his primitive state of nature theory, where individuals were less concerned with ensuring their rights were upheld and more

---

[10] A. V. Dicey, *Introduction to the Study of the Law of the Constitution* (London: Macmillan, 1960), 203.
[11] Neumann, *The Rule of Law*, 15.
[12] Ibid., 2.
[13] F. A. Hayek, *The Road to Serfdom* (London: Routledge, 1944), 58.
[14] J. Rawls, *A Theory of Justice* (Cambridge, MA: Harvard University Press, 1971), 238.
[15] Raz, 'The Rule of Law and its Virtue', 216.
[16] Neumann, *The Rule of Law*, 12.
[17] Ibid., 17.

preoccupied with surviving and living in peace.[18] Jennings' basic notion of the rule of law is in similar vein to Hobbes', though he expands it to the international stage, speaking of the relationship *between* states rather than *within* them. Jennings speaks of international society as being lawless, with the rule of law existing to settle disputes and maintain peace.[19] These non-moralized conceptions are based on the simple idea that there can be no time for moral niceties until a rule of law providing peace and stability has been established.

This is not to say, however, that moral ideals cannot follow. While there is no consensus on one perfect moral theory, there is no reason why we cannot use the normative rule of law concept as a foundation for moral guidance.[20] Indeed, one could argue that as society has progressed from Hobbes' experience of civil war to modern democracy, it would make little sense to return to a shallow 'state of nature' conception of the rule of law. Rather, this basic rule of law idea should have added to it qualifiers to ensure that not just *any* law should be followed.

Having focused on the English expressions of the rule of law, it is prudent to turn now to look at some of the European conceptions. European legal systems do not refer to the 'rule of law'; instead they speak of *rätt staat* (Danish/Swedish/Norwegian) and *Rechtsstaat* (German/Dutch) or *Rechtsstaatprinzip* and *Rechtsstaatlichkeit* (German). The literal translation of 'rule of law' (e.g., *Herrschaft des Rechts*) would be far too limiting to capture the system of principles and values associated with the concept of the rule of law. One obvious difference is that virtually all Continental European countries relate the idea of law (*Recht, Rätt, droit, derecho, diritto*) to the idea of the state (*staat, état, estado, stato*). Both ideas are intertwined and describe the expectation that a government gains legitimacy and legality only through adherence to predefined standards and principles.

What counts for such standards and principles may vary widely. One German scholar lists twenty-four principles as constituting the *Rechtsstaat* including, for example, the principle of the constitutional state based on fundamental rights, the supremacy of the constitution and the principle of proportionality.[21] It is typical for the Romano-Germanic legal tradition

---

[18] T. Hobbes, *Leviathan* (Harmondsworth: Penguin Books, 1968), 187ff.
[19] I. Jennings, *The Law and the Constitution* (University of London Press, 1959), 42ff.
[20] Neumann *The Rule of Law*, 109.
[21] K. Sobota, *Das Prinzip Rechtsstaat. Verfassungs- und verwaltungsrechtliche Aspekte* (Tübingen: Mohr Siebeck 1997).

to derive the content of the rule of law from an entire system of mutually reinforcing and limiting principles. Depending on what principles are invoked and how they are defined, it is possible to give the *Rechtsstaat* certain flavour and shape in the form, for example, of *Umweltstaat*[22] ('environment state') or *ökologischer Rechtsstaat*[23] ('eco-constitutional state'). This contextual aspect of the rule of law will be explored further below.

It may be interesting at this point to note the findings of the World Justice Project Rule of Law Index 2011.[24] Sweden is found to be the world's most respected country in terms of government accountability, absence of corruption, clear and stable laws, open government, regulatory enforcement, access to justice and protection of fundamental rights. Second on average is Norway, third New Zealand, fourth the Netherlands and fifth Germany. The United Kingdom features at ninth place and the United States at eighteenth behind Poland, but the point to be made here is that – with the exception of New Zealand – the top ranked countries do not even refer to the 'rule of law' in their respective jurisdictions.

Certainly the lack of a settled definition can be seen equally as a weakness and a strength. It is a weakness because it leaves the concept vulnerable to penetration by unrestrained government power, while its strength lies in the absence of formality, allowing it to be moulded and applied to different concepts, in our case through the establishment of an environmental grundnorm.[25] Preventing the exercise of arbitrary power by government and safeguarding individual rights is the core of the rule of law and represents a consensus that is perhaps shared all around the world today. Beyond that, however, there is no international terminological consensus.

A recent report for the European Commission[26] acknowledges a variety of meanings of the rule of law, but specifically identifies some core elements across legal cultures and expressed in numerous international documents: (1) independence and impartiality of the judiciary, (2) legal

---

[22] M. Kloepfer (ed.), *Umweltstaat als Zukunft* (Bonn: Economica, 1994); C. Callies, *Rechtsstaat und Umweltstaat* (Tübingen: Mohr Siebeck, 2001).
[23] K. Bosselmann, *Im Namen der Natur – Der Weg zum ökologischen Rechtsstaat* (Munich: Scherz, 1992) and *When Two Worlds Collide* (Auckland: RSVP, 1995); R. Steinberg, *Der Ökologische Verfassungsstaat* (Frankfurt: Suhrkamp, 1998).
[24] M. Agrast, J. Botero and A. Ponce, *WJP Rule of Law Index 2011* (Washington, DC: The World Justice Project, 2011).
[25] G. Walker, *The Rule of Law: Foundation of Constitutional Democracy* (Melbourne University Press, 1988), 3.
[26] F. Ehm, *The Rule of Law: Concept, Guiding Principle and Framework*, CDL-UDT(2010)022 (Strasbourg: Council of Europe, December 6, 2010).

certainty, (3) non-discrimination and equality before the law, (4) respect for human rights, (5) separation of powers, (6) the principle that the state is bound by law, and (7) the substantive coherence of the legal framework.[27] The report concludes by stating that it can be deduced that there exists a rule in customary international law that demands that the rule of law operates in a state as a precondition for membership of international organizations.[28]

The international dimension is perhaps the most significant feature in the contemporary understanding of the rule of law principle. If adherence to the rule of law is a characteristic of the modern state and its recognition in international law, then any grounding of it in nature – in whatever shape or form – would have ramifications for the contents of domestic and international law. Given the cross-boundary nature of environmental problems, such globalization of the rule of law opens new opportunities for overcoming the outdated dichotomy between domestic and international law systems. Notions around 'global law' have already entered the legal vocabulary, suggesting the existence of norms common to all people.[29]

3. The context of nature

How then can the rule of law be related to the environmental problematique?

Starting with the rather obvious proposition that nature is not adequately recognized in current legal systems, this needs only the briefest of overviews.

With its cultural and socio-economic context, modern Western law is merely part of the enclosure of nature. Environmental law was never intended to turn this process around; its purpose is rather more modest. Nature as a whole has of course never been on the radar of legal systems; rather 'natural resources' and discrete environmental media (soil, water,

---

[27] Ibid., 7.   [28] Ibid., 16.
[29] T. C. Halliday and P. Osinsky, 'Globalization of Law', 32 *Annual Review of Sociology* (2006), 447–70; C. Harlow, 'Global Administrative Law: The Quest for Principles and Values', 17 *The European Journal of International Law* (2006), 187–214; K. Jayasuriya, 'The Rule of Law in the Era of Globalization: Globalization, Law and the Transformation of Sovereignty: The Emergence of Global Regulatory Governance', 6 *Indiana Journal of Global Legal Studies* (1999), 425–56; D. Held, A. McGrew, D. Goldblatt and J. Perraton, *Global Transformations: Politics, Economics and Culture* (Stanford University Press, 1999), 32–86.

air, plants and so on) is how nature has found representation in the legal system. More crucially, the utilitarian approach of modern Western law perceives the natural environment primarily as a commodity, setting environmental objectives into competition with economic and social objectives. In our commodified world this means that no number of environmental laws will ever be enough to override those laws supporting economic growth, private property and state sovereignty.

These (and other[30]) characteristics can be summarized as environmental reductionism with which legal systems are currently beset.[31] Among its manifestations are compartmentalization, fragmentation and anthropocentrism.[32] Environmental reductionism needs to be replaced with ecological expansionism. By this we mean a process that starts with a fundamental normative commitment and aims for its implementation at all levels of law-making.

3.1 Environmental grundnorm

In legal terms, this new commitment can be described as a basic environmental rule or grundnorm.[33] Such a grundnorm would underpin and guide the interpretation of existing law and the creation of new laws.

For our purpose, we can define a grundnorm as a basic norm to bind governmental power in the same sense as the rule of law is generally perceived as a basic norm to bind governmental power. This understanding differs from Kelsen's definition[34] and is closer to Kant's argument that any positive law must be grounded in a 'natural' norm of general acceptance and reasonableness (*Vernunft*) to prevent pure arbitrariness (*blosse Willkür*).[35] The existence of an environmental grundnorm, therefore, rests on the assumption that respecting the planet's ecological boundaries is a

---

[30] See, e.g., B. Pardy, 'The Hand is Invisible, Nature Knows Best, and Justice is Blind: Markets, Ecosystems, Legal Instrumentalism and the Natural Law of Systems', 44 *Tulsa Law Review* (2009), 67–92.

[31] K. Bosselmann, 'Losing the Forest for the Trees: Environmental Reductionism in the Law', 2:8 *Sustainability* (2010), 2424–48, available at: www.mdpi.com/2071-1050/2/8/2424 (last accessed 4 June 2013).

[32] Ibid., 2431–3.

[33] L. Godden, 'Book Review: The Principle of Sustainability', 47 *Osgoode Hall Law Journal* (2009), 807–16 at 808; see also B. Pardy, 'In Search of the Holy Grail: A Rule to Solve the Problem', 1 *International Journal of Sustainable Development Law* (2005), 29.

[34] Referring to the source (*Grund*) of the validity of positive law. According to Kelsen's pure legal theory, the validity of positive law is conditional to the acceptance of a (not predefined) *Grundnorm*.

[35] I. Kant, *Die Metaphysik der Sitten*, vol. VI (Berlin: Akademieausgabe, 1907).

dictate of reason (*Gebot der Vernunft*) and general acceptance (*allgemeine Gültigkeit*).

It is important to note, however, that any reasoning for an environmental grundnorm is ethical in nature and grounded in natural law. This does not in any way weaken its legal relevance, but needs perhaps some justification. The notorious rivalry between positivism and natural law has never been particularly helpful. As argued elsewhere,[36] natural law should primarily be seen as a rejection of the dichotomy between morality and legality of which positivism has been guilty. Morality – good or bad – manifests itself in any type and content of law. While the extent of codified morality may be contentious, its existence is not – or rather should not be – in doubt. Only crude positivists may find this suspicious. Put another way: natural law is only ever suspicious to those who find nothing unsuspicious in existing positive law.[37]

This leads us to the question of content. If the strategy is to overcome environmental reductionism through promoting an environmental grundnorm, we need to describe its content positively. It is here where natural law reasoning can help us further.

3.2 Natural law

Environmental law has its roots in natural law as Sean Coyle, Karen Morrow[38] and others[39] have shown, but the same is true for human rights law. Human rights are based on the assertion that humans are born free and equal and should be protected accordingly. There is no scientific evidence behind this assertion. By contrast, it could be argued, environmental protection is justified as a matter of scientific proof. As humans are entangled in ecological interdependencies, we cannot escape nature and hence should organize our cultural norms accordingly. However, no amount of scientific evidence has so far convinced Western societies and governments to actually do that. Current law does not assume an absolute of ecological interdependencies.

---

[36] Bosselmann, *When Two Worlds Collide*, 359–63.
[37] Ibid., 362.
[38] S. Coyle and K. Morrow, *The Philosophical Foundation for Environmental Law* (Oxford: Hart Publishing, 2004), 9–58.
[39] D. Nolan (ed.), *Environmental and Resource Management Law*, 3rd edn (Wellington: LexisNexis, 2005), 92; Bosselmann, 'Losing the Forest for the Trees', 2029.

3.3 The human and natural sphere

The rejection of such an absolute is not due to a lack of scientific evidence, but rests rather on anthropological assumptions. The Western experience has been that our dependence on nature is not absolute, but only partial. As 'natural beings' we humans are no different from other natural beings. However, the argument goes, as 'cultural beings' humans are creating their own world that does not necessarily follow the same laws as the natural world. Everything that humans have ever created and developed are cultural achievements, and this includes the way in which we organize our lives in relation to our environment. This also means, however, cultural achievements can be advanced any time and in any way we want.

The entire environmental debate since the late 1960s centres on the question of whether or not existing cultural achievements will see us through the ecological crisis. Some believe that the human mind has no limits and will prevail over any limitations of the physical world. Others insist on the validity of laws of thermodynamics and other physical limitations that no amount of cultural achievements can change. So, who is right?

As already mentioned, science itself cannot give us the answer; however, this is not due to a lack of certainty. It is for principle reasons that we cannot rely on science alone. The debate is actually about perceptions, not reality. After all, ever since Immanuel Kant we cannot access objective reality directly, but only through (mind-controlled) perception. It is therefore quite appropriate to speak of clashing belief systems or myths. We can also speak of conflicting myths. A myth is a mental model or paradigm to interpret reality and respond to it. Our age of industrial capitalism is full of myths. Here is but a selection:

- the myth of unlimited resources;
- the myth of human superiority;
- the myth of primacy of the individual;
- the myth of rational behaviour;
- the myth of universal property rights;
- the myth of the invisible hand;
- the myth of almighty monetary value;
- the myth of environment as commodity;

- the myth of objective economics;
- the myth of objective science.[40]

All these and many more myths feed into each other and can be summarized as the Western political-economic worldview. Its counterpart can then be described as the global political-ecological worldview. Each of the various myths just mentioned has a logical counterpart. And while we cannot go into further detail here, it should be clear that there is, in fact, an alternative. Arguably, more and more people believe that:

- resources are limited;
- humans are not superior;
- no individual lives in isolation from others;
- behaviour is not purely rational;
- property rights are not universal; and so on.

While it may be true that humans can only ever create and develop cultural achievements, this does not tell us anything about the usefulness of these achievements for long-term sustainability. Some may have been useful, others undoubtedly not.

The situation that the world finds itself in today speaks for itself. We are experiencing a rapid decline of ecological systems that support us and an ever-increasing gap between rich and poor. At the same time, we are still waiting for governments to steer development into a more sustainable direction. These are measurable facts and put the dominant worldview (of more is better) into question. We must ask, therefore, what new cultural achievements are required.

3.4   Culture of self-constraint

Assuming that the rule of law, the idea of human rights and democratic governance are all valuable cultural achievements not to be sacrificed, we can aim for complementing or underpinning them with an environmental grundnorm, perhaps most usefully described as the principle of sustainability. The preservation of ecological integrity, as an overarching requirement for the way we govern ourselves, would counter a number of the myths of the Western political-economic worldview. It would set limits to the use of resources, constrain humans from seeking ultimate superiority, require cooperation instead of competition, add emotion to

---

[40] J. Peet, *Energy and the Ecological Economics of Sustainability* (Washington, DC: Island Press, 1992).

rationality, put property rights into a wider perspective and dismiss as empty fantasies the ideas of the invisible hand, almighty monetary value and objectivity. In short, the idea of sustainability can help shift the outdated Western economic rationality toward global ecological rationality. Essentially, ecological rationality describes a culture of self-constraint.

The culture of self-constraint is grounded in natural law, of course, but so is the dominant growth-culture. The case for sustainability is, however, a strong one and can be traced back to all the many cultures (and countercultures) that have shown their wisdom in the past and today. I find it crucial to identify sustainability as part of European history and as a counterpart to the Western development that has created this modern ecological crisis in the first place. European history is richer than just a history of destruction. In addition to the rule of law, human rights and democracy, we should be confident enough to add sustainability to our Western heritage.

4. Sustainability as a foundational principle

If we trace the historical and philosophical foundations of sustainability from their beginnings and relate them to the corresponding developments of legal theory and practice,[41] we can see an ever-increasing gap between individual entitlement and common responsibility. This can be observed, for example, in the way John Locke defined the idea of property rights and how the modern concept of private property isolated itself from any responsibilities for the commons.[42] The domination of property rights appears to be the greatest obstacle in our search for law based on sustainability.

4.1 Short history of sustainability

On the other hand, there is a wealth of sustainability wisdom in the history of all cultures,[43] and European culture is no exception. The experience of pre-industrial Europe is well worth noting. By the mid 1800s

---

[41] Ibid., 10–26.
[42] K. Bosselmann, 'Property Rights and Sustainability: Can they be Reconciled?', in: D. Grinlinton and P. Taylor (eds.), *Property Rights and Sustainability: The Evolution of Property Rights to Meet Ecological Challenges* (Amsterdam: Martinus Nijhoff, 2011), 23–42.
[43] See e.g. J. Diamond, *Collapse: How Societies Choose to Fail or Succeed* (New York: Viking Books, 2005) and K. Bosselmann, *The Principle of Sustainability* (Aldershot: Ashgate

Europe's forests had all but gone. Deforestation had reached a degree that threatened the entire economy of Europe.[44] This opened up two possibilities. One was to look for a new energy source (i.e. coal) to refuel the economy, the other to restore and maintain renewable energy (i.e. timber) in a sustainable manner.

In opposition to the emerging fossil fuels economy in England, forest management scholars in Germany proclaimed the wisdom of replacing every tree felled by planting a new one. They cited the medieval land-use system (*Allmende*) as the mother of sustainable economies. The *Allmende* system recognized public ownership of the land in guiding any form of private land use. That way the substance of the land could be protected from overuse, thereby preserved for future generations. This effect was termed *Nachhaltigkeit* by German economist Hans Carl von Carlowitz 300 years ago.[45] The first modern statute based on the sustainability principle was the Weimar Forestry Statute of 1775. The term and concept eventually dominated forest economic theory and were exported, for example, to the French Forest Academy where, in 1837, its director Adolphe Parade translated it to *soutenir* (showing its Latin roots: *sustinere* = to keep, preserve, sustain). From there it reached the English translation of sustainability. By the mid 1800s the notion 'living from the yield, not from the substance' was widespread among forest academies and indeed science faculties throughout Europe. It was state-of-the-art knowledge, yet contrary to the philosophical assumptions of the new industrial age.

The fact that the Industrial Revolution ignored this knowledge does not render it useless, obviously. It only meant that the idea of sustainability did not fit the pervasive idea of progress.

When we look back over the history of human cultures – including European culture – we can conclude that sustainability is part of the common heritage of humanity. It may be a forgotten part, but nevertheless an

---

Publishing, 2008), 3 with respect to J. Weeramantry's Separate Opinion in the ICJ *Gabčikovo-Nagymaros* case of 1997.

[44] See J. Radkau, *Natur und Macht – Eine Weltgeschichte der Umwelt* (Munich: Beck, 2000), 245; published in English as *Nature and Power: A Global History of the Environment* (Cambridge University Press, 2008).

[45] H. C. von Carlowitz, *Sylvicultura Oeconomica, Anweisung zur Wilden Baum Zucht* [*Forest Economy or Guide to Tree Cultivation Conforming with Nature*] (Freiburg: TU Bergakademie Freiburg und Akademische Buchhandlung, 2000 [1713]). See also U. Grober, *Sustainability: A Cultural History* (Totnes: Green Books, 2012), 76–89; U. Grober, *Deep Roots: A Conceptual History of Sustainable Development (Nachhaltigkeit)* (Berlin: Wissenschaftszentrum Berlin für Sozialforschung, 2007).

existing part that did not need to be newly invented in the late twentieth century.

4.2 Ecological core of sustainable development

The modern discourse of sustainable development did not start from scratch (in the form of the Brundtland Report). Rather it was informed by the widely felt notion of the 1970s and early 1980s that there cannot be infinite growth in a finite world. The Brundtland Commission seemed to be quite clear about this, at least initially. The inaugural meeting of the Commission in October 1984 called for 'a future which is more prosperous, more just, and more secure because it rests on policies and practices that serve to expand and sustain the ecological basis of development'.[46] In many passages the Report emphasized that we are borrowing the environmental capital from future generations and that economic growth must be constrained to preserve the Earth's ecological integrity.[47] It should also be noted that the Brundtland Commission was able to draw from the 1980 World Conservation Strategy that provided clear guidance of what kind of development could be considered to be sustainable:

> This is the kind of development that provides real improvements in the quality of human life and at the same time conserves the vitality and diversity of the Earth. The goal is development that will be sustainable. Today it may seem visionary but it is attainable. To more and more people it also appears our only rational option.[48]

Hans Christian Bugge, a personal advisor to Prime Minister Gro Harlem Brundtland in her role as chair of the Commission, is well aware of this context of sustainable development. Together with Christina Voigt he edited the book *Sustainable Development in International and National Law*[49] to mark the twentieth anniversary of the Brundtland Report. The

---

[46] World Commission on Environment and Development, *Our Common Future* (Oxford University Press, 1987), 356.
[47] For example: 'We borrow environmental capital from future generations with no intention or prospect of repaying. They may damn us for our spendthrift ways, but they can never collect on our debt to them. We act as we do because we can get away with it: future generations do not vote; they have no political or financial power; they cannot challenge our decisions.' Ibid. 'From One Earth to One World', para. 25.
[48] 1980 World Conservation Strategy (IUCN, UNEP, WWF), available at: http://data.iucn.org/dbtw-wpd/edocs/WCS-004.pdf (last accessed 4 June 2013).
[49] H. C. Bugge and C. Voigt (eds.), *Sustainable Development in International and National Law* (Groningen: Europa Law Publishing, 2008).

book's contributors widely share the view that the Report's concept of 'sustainable development' assumed ecological sustainability at its core. Consequently, if preservation of the Earth's ecological integrity is a prerequisite for any cultural achievements (as defined above), it sets limits to both economic and social development.[50] Further, if we accept that the integrity of the Earth's ecosystems cannot be sliced up into pieces that fit into areas inside and outside national boundaries, then states need to accept fundamental fiduciary environmental duties.[51]

From an ecological perspective, the difference between natural systems and human-made systems is not categorical and should not be overstated. The two are neither equal nor can they be balanced against each other. Humans depend on natural systems – like all other species – and any hopes for sustainable development need to respect this dependency.

The case for sustainability as a foundational principle (grundnorm) is ethically strong, historically evidenced and scientifically sound. It provides the grounding of the rule of law that we are looking for.

4.3   Ecological approach to the rule of law

In broader jurisprudential terms, this grounding calls for the greening of the entire system of law and governance as, for example, captured in the notion of the eco-constitutional state (*ökologischer Rechtsstaat*). The eco-constitutional state differs significantly from a state merely committed to the rule of law (*Rechtsstaat*) on the one hand, and environmental protection (*Umweltstaat*) on the other. Rather, both must be seen as mutually reinforcing and together defining the state. Such an integrating view is in stark contrast to the traditional liberal idea of the state (perceived to be 'neutral').

Most strikingly, the liberal concept of the rule of law/*Rechtsstaat* has its focus on the well-being of humans, whereas the ecological concept of the rule of law/*Rechtsstaat* has its focus on the well-being of humans and nature. The difference between both models is not merely gradual, but paradigmatic as we have seen, although commonalities and overlaps in practical law-making are possible.

---

[50] See K. Bosselmann, 'Strong and Weak Sustainable Development: Making the Difference in the Design of Law', 13 *South African Journal of Environmental Law and Policy* (2007), 14–23.
[51] Bosselmann, *The Principle of Sustainability*, 173.

5. Conclusion: implications for environmental law research

This book is devoted to exploring the rule of law for nature. As its contributors aim to expand the rule of law, most would not be satisfied simply with more environmental laws or better enforcement of existing laws. Instead, they seem to be concerned with better *content* reflective of ecological realities.

Professor Staffan Westerlund, one of the pioneers of environmental law, has left a very important legacy with his work on the methodology of environmental law. Recently, he made this revealing observation: 'Environmental Law as an academic discipline has not really achieved anything of significance for ecological sustainability.'[52] How true! We may thank forty years of environmental legislation for a steady increase of protected areas, for better management of natural resources, for improved air and water quality, for increased recycling, more energy efficiency and so forth. But the shift towards sustainable development remains a distant goal – as if environmental law never really existed.

5.1 A new era of environmental legal research

In this situation, the best we can do is to reconsider some basics. Westerlund has shown us the direction. He called for a new era of environmental legal research characterized as *proactive* (instead of reactive), informed by *system theory* and geared towards a *'theory of sustainable development'*, which he summed up in this way: 'The core problem lies in achieving and maintaining ecological sustainability as the necessary foundation for sustainable development.'[53] This is a call on every scholar in the environmental law community.

If we follow a proactive, system-theoretical and sustainability-focused approach to legal research, it will be broader in scope, greater in depth and a lot more promising than much of what we have done in the past. There

---

[52] S. Westerlund, 'Theory for Sustainable Development: Towards or Against?' in: H. C. Bugge and C. Voigt (eds.), *Sustainable Development in International and National Law* (Groningen: Europa Law Publishing, 2008), 48–65.

[53] Ibid., 64; see further S. Westerlund, 'Law and Mankind's Ecological Dilemma', in: M. Führ, R. Wahl and P. von Wilmowsky (eds.), *Umweltrecht und Umweltwissenschaft. Festschrift für Eckart Rehbinder* (Berlin: Erich Schmidt Verlag, 2007). See also the excellent analysis by A. Johannsdottir, *The Significance of the Default: A Study in Environmental Law Methodology with Emphasis on Ecological Sustainability and International Biodiversity Law* (Uppsala University, 2009).

is enormous potential for environmental law scholars to be the vanguards for transforming the entire legal system. If it is true, as many commentators have suggested, that the biggest challenges of the twenty-first century will centre on human rights and the environment, then environmental lawyers have a very important role to play.

The following ten subject areas have found significant attention in recent years and deserve further investigation. They all concern legal principles and instruments seen from the sustainability perspective:

1. Justice: how can our understanding of justice be broadened to include intragenerational justice, intergenerational justice and interspecies justice ('ecological justice', 'global justice')?
2. Human rights: how can human rights be strengthened and advanced to include responsibilities for nature ('ecological human rights', 'rights of nature')?
3. Private property: how can concepts of property be enhanced to include responsibilities for the commons ('enclosure of the commons')?
4. State: how can the state be enabled to function as a guardian or trustee for the natural environment ('territorial sovereignty vs. environmental trusteeship')?
5. Liability: how can corporations be held liable for environmental crimes ('ecocide')?
6. Multilevel governance: how to solve the scale problem of governance with regard to sustainability as a universal principle ('governance for sustainability')?
7. Democracy: how can democracy be restored and, at the same time, advanced as a transboundary and value-based concept of governance ('ecological citizenship', 'Earth democracy')?
8. Normative frameworks: importance of the Earth Charter and other civil society documents for multilevel governance ('third pillar of UN system')?
9. Institutions: how can institutions of trusteeship for the global commons be designed and promoted ('World Environment Organization', 'UN Trusteeship Council')?
10. Constitutionalism: trends towards constitutionalizing ecological values and principles ('eco-constitutionalism', 'eco-constitutional state').

The list can be expanded, of course, but should illustrate the wide spectrum of issues we need to explore for an ecological grounding of the rule of law (*Rechtsstaat*). This exploration may well be open-ended as we are entering largely unchartered territory.

However, the imperative of ecological sustainability provides clear guidance. In the words of Aldo Leopold, one of the founders of modern environmentalism: 'A thing is right when it tends to preserve the integrity, stability, and beauty of the biotic community. It is wrong when it tends otherwise.'[54] This ecological imperative is not very far from Kant's categorical imperative[55] and hence quite close to the traditional sociological grounding of the rule of law.

The grounding of the rule of law, as envisaged here, merely reflects the reality that social relationships are embedded in ecological relationships. Its core is respect and care for the community of life[56] (not just human life). This surely stands in the tradition of the Age of Reason that began 250 years ago.[57]

---

[54] A. Leopold, *A Sand County Almanac* (Oxford University Press, 1949).

[55] 'Act only according to that maxim whereby you can, at the same time, will that it should become a universal law.' *Grundlegung zur Metaphysik der Sitten* (Berlin: Akademie-Ausgabe, 1782), vol. IV, p. 420; English translation by J. W. Ellington, *Grounding for the Metaphysics of Morals*, 3rd edn (London: Hackett Publishing, 1993), 30.

[56] Earth Charter, first main principle, available at: www.earthcharterinaction.org/invent/images/uploads/echarter_english.pdf (last accessed 4 June 2013).

[57] Kant's verdict that 'a revolution may well put an end to autocratic despotism ... or power-seeking oppression, but it will never produce a true reform in ways of thinking' – 'Beantwortung der Frage: Was ist Aufklärung?' [Answering the Question: What is Enlightenment?], *Berlinische Monatshefte* 1784 – is a reminder that changed thinking is at the heart of any genuine change.

5

The rule of Nature's law

CORMAC CULLINAN

1. Introduction

This is an opportune time to reflect on the state of environmental law globally. In 2012 the United Nations Conference on Sustainable Development convened in Rio de Janeiro, twenty years after the famous 'Earth Summit', thirty years after the United Nations World Charter for Nature and forty years after the Stockholm Declaration. In the intervening years there has been an unprecedented increase in public awareness of environmental issues, huge numbers of environmental treaties have been agreed and thousands of regional, national, provincial and local environmental laws have been passed.

There have been important successes, for example in relation to the protection of the ozone layer and the conservation of some species of whales, such as the Southern population of Right Whales that visit the shores of South Africa to calve in greater numbers each year. However, global biodiversity, the health of major ecosystems, climate change and the state of the world's forests, freshwater systems and marine ecosystems are, with few exceptions, in a dramatically worse state than they were in at the time of the 1992 Earth Summit.[1] Human impacts on the planet far exceed what is ecologically sustainable. These facts have been

---

[1] The United Nations Environment Programme (UNEP) has published five *Global Environmental Outlook Reports* between 1997 and 2012, which together chronicle the progressively worsening consequences of exploiting Earth far beyond ecologically sustainable levels. The *Fourth Global Environmental Outlook Report* published in 2007 (GEO-4) was prepared by about 390 experts and reviewed by more than 1,000 others across the world. It warns explicitly that 21.9 hectares of land is required on average to support each human being, but at current population levels only 15.7 hectares per person is available. Even this may understate the problem by assuming that the Earth's 'resources' are available for humans to appropriate for their exclusive use. Optimizing the health and functioning of the community of life as a whole would require even greater reductions in the ecological footprint of humanity.

repeatedly confirmed by many authoritative studies, including the series of *Global Environmental Outlook* reports published by the United Nations Environment Programme (UNEP) and the 2005 Millennium Ecosystem Assessment (MA) report.[2]

The MA report concluded that approximately 60 per cent (15 out of 24) of the ecosystem services that it examined are being degraded or used unsustainably, including: fresh water, capture fisheries, air and water purification, and the regulation of regional and local climate, natural hazards, and pests. This means that Earth's capacity to sustain human life (and many other living organisms) has already been very significantly compromised and that human activities are continuing to worsen the situation. Since the deterioration is continuing (and in many cases accelerating), the situation today is substantially worse than recorded in the MA report.

2. A failure of governance

It is now painfully clear that human governance systems at both the international and national levels have failed, and continue to fail, to prevent human activities undermining the integrity, vitality, health and functioning of the natural communities of the planet.

Ten years ago, in 2002 on the eve of the Rio+10 World Summit on Sustainable Development in Johannesburg, I attended an international environmental law conference in Pietermaritzburg in South Africa. Everyone at that conference was already aware that environmental destruction was accelerating despite an explosion of environmental laws during the previous decade. However, the response of the majority of the environmental lawyers present was 'there is nothing wrong with environmental law, the problem is that it isn't being enforced'. Based on this diagnosis of the problem, the remedy was, of course, to improve enforcement. Better enforcement is always a good idea, but now, ten years later, we cannot honestly continue pretending that better enforcement is anywhere near enough to alter the unsustainable development path of contemporary industrial civilizations and prevent their eventual collapse.

---

[2] The Millennium Ecosystem Assessment was conducted between 2001 and 2005 by more than 1,360 experts worldwide. The MA was a state-of-the-art scientific appraisal of the condition and trends in the world's ecosystems and the services they provide to humanity (such as clean water, food, forest products, flood control and natural resources) and the options to restore, conserve or enhance the sustainable use of ecosystems.

Unpalatable as this may be, particularly to those of us who have devoted much of our professional lives to developing environmental law, it is very important that we acknowledge that making incremental improvements in environmental law has not been sufficient to reverse these destructive trends, and there is no reasonable prospect of that changing. In order to achieve the rapid and fundamental changes that are required to address the challenges that now face us, we will have to make a quantum leap in governance.[3]

In any event, incremental change is likely to be too slow. There is now far more greenhouse gas in the atmosphere, poison in the soils, soils in the sea, salinity in the fresh water and species heading for extinction than twenty years ago.[4] In most cases the forces that are driving this deterioration are either undiminished or gaining strength, and degradation is accelerating as cumulative and systemic impacts multiply.[5] This means that there is real risk of pushing ecosystems over 'tipping points' beyond which we will be powerless to prevent them changing to new states unfavourable to human well-being.[6] Indeed, whether or not the

---

[3] This conclusion is supported by the finding of the *Fifth Global Environmental Outlook Report* (GEO-5), published by UNEP in 2012. The principal findings are recorded in *GEO-5: Summary for Policy Makers* (which was negotiated and endorsed on 31 January 2012). A key finding was that: 'Each region found, however, that even were such apparently successful policies more widely implemented, there is little confidence that some of the current global environmentally adverse trends would be reversed – innovative approaches are definitely needed.' Ibid., 15.

[4] The deteriorating 'state of the environment' is described in many authoritative studies including the five *Global Environmental Outlook Reports* published by UNEP and the 2005 Millennium Ecosystem Assessment report.

[5] For example, the 2005 Millennium Ecosystem Assessment report states that: 'Nonlinear (accelerating or abrupt) changes have been previously identified by a number of individual studies of ecosystems. The MA is the first assessment to conclude that ecosystem changes are increasing the likelihood of nonlinear changes in ecosystems and the first to note the important consequences of this finding for human well-being. Examples of such changes include disease emergence, abrupt alterations in water quality, the creation of "dead zones" in coastal waters, the collapse of fisheries, and shifts in regional climate.' *Millennium Ecosystem Assessment, Ecosystems and Human Well-being: Synthesis* (Washington, DC: Island Press, 2005).

[6] The dangers associated with these critical thresholds is emphasised in the *GEO-5: Summary for Policy Makers*, which states that: 'The currently observed changes to the Earth System are unprecedented in human history. Efforts to slow the rate or extent of change – including enhanced resource efficiency and mitigation measures – have resulted in moderate successes but have not succeeded in reversing adverse environmental changes. Neither the scope of these nor their speed has abated in the past five years … As human pressures on the Earth System accelerate, several critical global, regional and local thresholds are close or have been exceeded. Once these have been passed, abrupt and

relatively stable environmental conditions on which human civilization has depended for the past 10,000 years will continue beyond this century now depends on what action is taken (or not taken) during the next decade or two to prevent and reverse the degradation of ecosystems.⁷

The theme for the Rio+20 meeting was 'the future we want'. If we extrapolate the current trends in environmental destruction for a further twenty years to see the future we are heading for, it is apparent that in the unlikely event of a Rio+40 meeting being convened, it is likely to be more like a wake. If present trends continue, a Rio+40 will be mourning the extinction of tens of thousands of species and the deaths of millions if not billions of people, in a world racked with social upheaval and a deteriorating quality of life for almost everyone. The future we wanted in 2012 will be a distant dream and we will be facing a very, very bleak future indeed: a future dominated by runaway climate change and other dramatic alterations in our habitat, which by then we will have little or no ability to influence.

It is understandable that many people who are aware of the extent of this ecological damage feel depressed and hopeless. However, that saps the will to act and I believe that at this crucial time it is important to throw all our efforts behind an exciting new movement that is already starting to reconfigure global society and to reorient it towards the goal of living well in harmony with Nature. For lawyers it is particularly exciting because one of the fundamental goals of this movement is to transform the predominant concept of law. It is about expanding the conceptual framework and changing the purpose, not only of environmental law, but also of legal systems as whole, in order to create governance systems that provide an adequate legal framework within which to address the principal challenges of the twenty-first century. This is nothing less than the early stages of a new cultural Renaissance that will change our idea of what it means to be human, and reorient and restructure human societies throughout the world – what the great American

---

possibly irreversible changes to the life-support functions of the planet are likely to occur, with significant adverse implications for human well-being.' UNEP, GEO-5, 6).

[7] The *GEO-5: Summary for Policy Makers* states that: 'There are compelling reasons to consider policies and programmes that focus on the underlying drivers that contribute to increased pressure on environmental conditions, rather than concentrating only on reducing environmental pressures or symptoms. Drivers include, inter alia, the negative aspects of population growth, consumption and production, urbanization and globalization ... Often these drivers combine and interact.' UNEP, GEO-5, 14.

scholar and 'geologian' Father Thomas Berry referred to as the 'Great Work' of our time.[8]

This will require reconceptualizing the rule of law.

3. The rule of law

The concept of the rule of law is a highly contested one and there are many different understandings of what the rule of law and the related principle of legality should mean. In general, advocates of the rule of law would agree that at the heart of the concept is the idea that everyone, including the state, should be subject to predetermined legal rules that restrain the arbitrary exercise of power. In European jurisprudence the emergence of this concept has sometimes been characterized as the shift from 'the king is law' (*rex est lex*) to 'the law is king' (*lex est rex*).[9]

Professor Lon Fuller defined 'law' as 'the enterprise of subjecting human conduct to the governance of rules' and advanced eight 'principles of legality'. According to Fuller, law must meet the requirements of: generality, promulgation, non-retroactivity, clarity, non-contradiction, possibility of compliance, constancy through time and congruence between official action and declared rule.[10] Although legal systems in well-functioning democracies would usually reflect these principles of legality, in essence they define the elements that are necessary for law to function effectively rather than whether or not the legal system is just or moral.

For example, during the apartheid era in South Africa many (if not all) of Fuller's principles of legality were complied with (e.g., generality, promulgation, clarity, non-contradiction), but because the substantive content of many of those legal rules were discriminatory and oppressive, the end result was a consistently and predictably unjust system. In other words unjust and discriminatory law was applied predictably, consistently and effectively so that in effect the rule of law promoted injustice.

An adequate discussion of the nuances of the different approaches to the rule of law is beyond the scope of this chapter, but for present purposes two main points are relevant. First, the rule of bad law is not a good thing. Applying unjust laws effectively and in a manner that satisfies the principles of legality is worse than applying them ineffectively and is far

---

[8] T. Berry, *The Great Work: Our Way Into the Future* (New York: Bell Tower, 1999).
[9] See the chapter by Klaus Bosselmann in this book.
[10] L. L. Fuller, *The Morality of Law*, revised edition (New Haven: Yale University Press, 1969).

worse than applying good laws, even relatively ineffectively. If the law is king, then the normative content of the law makes the difference between being subject to a good ruler or a bad ruler. Second, it is important to be conscious of why we make law, because without being clear about the purpose that it is intended to serve, we cannot evaluate its effectiveness and whether or not it is fit for purpose.

4. The purpose of law

If law is indeed the enterprise of subjecting human conduct to the governance of rules, we need to ask ourselves: to what end? What is the purpose that we hope to achieve by doing so? The purpose is the yardstick for measuring the extent to which a law or a legal system is effective. If a legal system is ineffective in promoting the attainment of the desired purpose, then it is deficient, regardless of whether this failure is attributable to poor substantive rules or to a failure to comply with principles of legality.

The introduction of new legislation is usually justified on the basis that it is in the interests of the society as a whole, for example it promotes the public good or the national interest (even though in fact it may be intended to benefit a specific interest group that lobbied for its enactment). However, the purpose of the legal system as a whole is rarely considered or discussed. If pushed to provide an explanation of its purpose, lawyers and political scientists would probably point to the need to maintain social harmony and stability by providing predetermined rules for how decisions are to be made and power exercised and for resolving disputes justly, and mechanisms for protecting the rights of citizens. Certainly if a legal system is effective in promoting social harmony, stability and social justice, then it is undoubtedly making a major contribution to creating conditions favourable for the pursuit of human happiness and well-being.

If we assume that a 'good' legal system subjects human conduct to the governance of rules for the purpose of establishing conditions in which the members of a community can individually and collectively enhance their well-being and fulfil their human potential, then we have a yardstick (admittedly still imprecise) for beginning to assess actual legal systems.

Of course many societies that may agree on this meta-purpose have widely divergent view on the nature of the legal rules that should be used to promote it. For example, some put their faith in promoting the functioning of the market as a means of increasing human well-being while others favour strong authoritarian government to maintain social stability. However, contemporary legal systems in almost all countries focus on maintaining harmonious relationships between legal subjects (i.e., humans and juristic persons such as the state and corporations) and give minimal attention to the relationships between those legal subjects and other-than-human actors (often referred to collectively as 'Nature'). (One of the main reasons for this is that other-than-human-beings are legally defined as property rather than legal subjects.) The inadequate attention given by governance systems to fostering mutually beneficial and hence sustainable relationships between human and other-than-human beings is evident in the deterioration in the integrity, health and functioning of the natural communities that sustain life on Earth.

It is now abundantly clear that a legal system cannot provide the conditions necessary or conducive to social harmony and the enhancement of human potential unless it also prevents human beings from undermining the relationships that are necessary to maintaining the fundamental conditions required for human well-being. For example, upholding the human right to life depends on ensuring access to clean water, which in turn depends on protecting the functioning of the whole hydrological cycle, and in some cases the stability of the global climate. A legal system that fails to prevent people from destroying the functioning of ecosystems that provide the water that it requires also fails to create the conditions necessary for social harmony, enhanced well-being and human rights. In other words, it is deficient in that it is ineffective in achieving its desired purpose.

Perhaps the primary challenge facing humanity in the twenty-first century is how to establish governance systems that are effective in inducing people to pursue well-being by enhancing rather than undermining the health of ecological systems – a rule of law for Nature.

5. Domination or participation?

In my view, the main reason why contemporary legal systems give inadequate attention to maintaining harmonious relationships between humans and other-than-human beings is because they are based on an unexamined underlying assumption that there is a radical discontinuity between our species and 'Nature' or 'the environment'. Humans are, of course, different to other species, rivers and mountains. The problem is that we regard ourselves as exceptional, in the sense that we do not consider ourselves fully subject to the laws of Nature, and we regard ourselves as in some way separate from, and superior to Nature. We conceive of our role as managing, controlling and directing Nature to achieve our own ends, and consequently place ourselves and our societies in opposition to Nature.

This understanding of the role of the human permeates contemporary legal systems. The law defines all beings that are not humans or juristic persons as objects, or 'property' and 'natural resources' available for exploitation. This means that the legal character of the relations between humans or corporations on the one hand and the other-than-human natural world is the same as the relationship between a slave owner and a slave. The former is a subject with legal rights and the latter is an object incapable of having legal rights. The question of maintaining a harmonious relationship that balances the needs of both parties does not even arise because the 'other' is not perceived as a subject with interests of its own.

Contemporary legal systems have sought to address the most obviously problematic aspects of environmental degradation and the consequential impacts on human health and well-being by developing a specific branch of the legal system that concerns itself with protecting Nature, namely environmental law. In practice environmental laws tend to restrict the exercise of private rights (particularly land ownership) in the public interest, often by establishing a requirement to obtain an authorization or a permit from a public body before undertaking certain activities that have the potential to have a detrimental impact on the environment. Although the public perception of environmental law is often that it protects other species at the expense of humans, in fact almost all environmental law is deeply anthropocentric. It does not disturb the fundamental legal conception that only human beings and certain juristic persons (e.g., companies) are legal subjects with the capacity to hold legal rights, and that all of Nature is property that does not have legal subjectivity, and accordingly cannot have legal rights.

The main concern of environmental law is not to balance human interests against those of other beings in order to promote harmonious coexistence and the common good of the whole community (as is done between people), but to simply to keep the harm caused by exploitative activities within limits acceptable to human society at that time. Consequently, it seldom addresses the forces that drive the exploitative behaviour. For example, the international negotiations under the United Nations Framework Convention on Climate Change are not directed at addressing the structural causes of climate change (e.g., the economic, legal, political and societal incentives to pursue carbon-intensive, highly consumptive lifestyles) or at achieving optimal greenhouse gas concentrations in the atmosphere (i.e., pre-industrial levels). The negotiations are about how to ensure that catastrophic climate change does not derail the ongoing growth of industrial societies and about who must take responsibility for implementing the necessary measures. The greenhouse gas concentrations aimed at are not informed by what is best for the community of life on Earth but by what is politically acceptable.

The reality, of course, is that the human species is part of 'Nature' – we evolved in relationship with all that has come into being as part of Earth (other 'beings') and our well-being is derived entirely from our participation in this Earth community. This means that in order to maintain the fundamental physical conditions necessary for human well-being (e.g., access to food, water and shelter) as well as those necessary for our full intellectual and spiritual development (e.g., complexity, relatedness, beauty and reverence), we need to maintain harmonious relationships with the other beings within the Earth community. However, we have defined the class of legal subjects whose interests the law seeks to protect in a way that excludes all that is not human. Consequently, contemporary legal systems have failed to develop effective mechanisms for balancing human interests against those of other beings in a manner that is conducive to maintaining the health and integrity of the natural communities within which we exist. The pursuit of dominance has blinded us to the fact that if our species is to flourish and persist, we too must occupy an ecological niche, by providing for our needs in a way that also strengthens the web of relationships that create the ecological communities that sustain us all.

However, if we abandon the erroneous beliefs that we are separate from the Earth community and superior to all beings and instead wholeheartedly embrace our participation within the community of life, a vast vista of exciting new legal possibilities comes into view.

6. Reimagining the rule of law

The concept of the rule of law looks very different, for example, if one approaches it not from the narrow perspective of a human-only world but from the wider perspective that law must regulate humans within the context of the Earth community that enfolds them.

The first issue arising is what is the meaning of 'law' from the perspective of the Earth community? Traditional formulations of the rule of law require that all rules and powers must be derived from duly enacted or established laws – what is the equivalent from an Earth-centric rather than anthropocentric perspective? If one attempts to answer that question, it is immediately apparent that human legal systems do not arise in a context of complete chaos but within an ordered universe. The 'laws of Nature' (which encompass the laws of physics, chemistry, biology and ecology) interact to establish a system of order that precedes, encompasses and prevails over human legal systems. As Father Thomas Berry put it, 'The Universe is the primary law maker'.[11]

The self-ordering of the universe can be understood as a 'Great Jurisprudence',[12] which can be discovered by inductive reasoning based on close observation and experience of Nature. This Great Jurisprudence can be used to inform and guide the development of human jurisprudence ('Earth jurisprudences') that may in turn inform the development of laws that give effect to them ('wild laws'). For example, the stupendous biological diversity that surrounds us is an indication that the universe has an inherent tendency to diversify. This suggests that we should be wary about enacting laws that seek to impose unnecessary homogeneity because we may well be working against the fundamental principles of the system of which we are part.

Interestingly, the 'laws of Nature' would be consistent with many of the principles of legality identified by Fuller (e.g., generality, non-retroactivity, constancy through time), except that there is little congruency between the rules declared by Nature and the 'official action' taken by states and no means of reviewing and setting aside human actions that are inconsistent with the laws of Nature. Fuller, of course, did not formulate these principles of legality to apply to the laws of Nature, but they nevertheless provide an interesting metaphor for the problems that arise when official action is inconsistent with predetermined rules and there is no corrective mechanism.

For example, most governments today accept that a range of human activities are generating such high levels of greenhouse gas emissions that the limits established by Nature for the maintenance of climatic stability on Earth have been violated. These actions jeopardize the survival of other species and undermine the health, integrity and functioning of the Earth community. From an Earth community perspective such behaviour is contrary to the interests of the community as a whole and profoundly anti-social, and Earth is in the process of responding

---

[11] Thomas Berry and Mary Evelyn Tucker, *The Sacred Universe: Earth, Spirituality, and Religion in the Twenty-first Century* (New York: Columbia University Press, 2009).

[12] The concept of a 'Great Jurisprudence' is introduced and explored in C. Cullinan, *Wild Law. A Manifesto for Earth Justice* (Dartington: Green Books, 2003, first published by Siberink, Cape Town, 2002).

to this conduct through phenomena such as climate change. Believing that we can escape the consequences of violating natural limits or laws is a potentially fatal mistake founded on the illusion of human exceptionalism. If we are to avoid being 'sanctioned' by Nature, we must align our legal systems with the laws of Nature and establish mechanisms for reviewing and invalidating decisions that contravene fundamental 'Earth laws'. Applying the rule of law in this way would mean, for example, that a court could set aside a decision authorizing the construction of a new coal-fired power station on the basis that the decision-maker does not have the power to authorize activities that violate the functioning of vital natural systems by exacerbating climate change. Put differently, it is unlawful for a decision-maker to impose liabilities on others (including future generations) by allowing natural limits to be transgressed.

This may seem a fanciful way of extrapolating essentially human concerns about 'lawfulness' to the larger Earth community that is unconcerned by legal niceties. However, if we are to expand the ambit of concern of legal systems so that they regulate human behaviour within the context of the Earth community, then it is necessary to expand our legal language and concepts to embrace our relationships with all aspects of that community. One of the ways of doing this is to recognize that all beings have certain fundamental legal rights, notably the right to exist and play their roles within the Earth community, in order to create corresponding legal duties on humans to respect those rights. For example, if the law recognizes a river as a legal person with fundamental rights to exist and play its ecological role, it means that the law must protect the rights of the river to flow, to alter its course within its floodplain and to be free of pollution. This means that the legal system must impose and enforce correlative duties on human beings not to infringe these rights of the river.

The rights of different beings will sometimes conflict with one another, however, and no rights can be absolute. This means that an infringement by humans of the rights of a river may be justifiable in certain circumstances but not in others. For example, it may be justifiable to interfere to a limited extent with a river's right to flow if this is necessary to protect a fundamental human right such as the right to life. However, the decision as to whether the rights of humans prevail over those of the river or vice versa would be determined not on the basis of human rights being inherently superior, but by balancing their respective rights to produce an outcome that best promotes the health, integrity and functioning of the

Earth community to which both parties belong.[13] This would require the establishment of publically funded institutions to represent the interests of other-than-human beings and new courts or other institutions with the necessary knowledge and understanding to adjudicate between the competing interests of humans and other members of the Earth community in order to promote the greater good of the whole community.

7. The transformation of law

The idea that legal systems should recognize aspects of Nature as legal subjects with rights sounds strange and even nonsensical to many lawyers training in legal traditions that define all Nature as property. Professor Christopher Stone's suggestion that 'natural objects' should be given legal standing was widely ridiculed by the lawyers in the 1970s when he first proposed it.[14] However, these ideas have persisted, and in the 1990s the cultural and religious historian and philosopher Father Thomas Berry proposed that a new jurisprudence should be developed based on the following core principles (among others):

> The universe is a communion of subjects, not a collection of objects. As subjects the component members of the universe are capable of having rights.
> The natural world on the planet Earth gets its rights from the same source that humans get their rights, from the universe that brought them into being.
> Every component of the Earth Community has three rights: the right to be, the right to habitat, and the right to fulfill its role in the ever-renewing processes of the Earth Community.[15]

---

[13] Article 1 paragraph 7 of the Universal Declaration of the Rights of Mother Earth states that: 'The rights of each being are limited by the rights of other beings and any conflict between their rights must be resolved in a way that maintains the integrity, balance and health of Mother Earth.'

[14] Christopher D. Stone, 'Should Trees Have Standing? Towards Legal Rights for Natural Objects', 45 *Southern California Law Review* (1972), 450. Stone's article motivated the famous dissenting judgment by Justice Douglas in the case of *Sierra Club* v. *Morton*, 405 US 727, 741–42 (1972) in which he stated that: 'The critical question of "standing" would be simplified and also put neatly into focus if we fashioned a federal rule that allowed environmental issues to be litigated before federal agencies or federal courts in the name of the inanimate object about to be despoiled, defaced or invaded by roads and bulldozers and where injury is the subject of public outrage. Contemporary public concerns for protecting nature's ecological equilibrium should lead to the conferral of standing upon environmental objects to sue for their own preservation.'

[15] Berry, *The Great Work*, 161.

Ten years ago when I wrote 'Wild Law',[16] which builds on the work of scholars such as Thomas Berry and outlines what a new 'Earth jurisprudence' could look like, the prospects of actually developing and implementing 'wild laws' that reflected that perspective seemed fanciful to many people. I certainly was not confident that it would happen on a wide enough scale or fast enough to make enough of a difference. I was simply pointing out that I thought that if our species is to flourish on this planet, then I think that the conclusion that we must align our governance systems with the laws of Nature is inescapable.

However, the events of the past four years have given me great hope that we will see very fundamental and unprecedented changes in legal systems during the next few decades, although it remains to be seen whether those changes will have a sufficient global impact to change the future of species for the better. Four years ago the philosophy of Earth Jurisprudence and the idea of recognizing that Nature has rights were invisible on the international stage, and even within the environmental law community only a few people had even heard of this approach. Since then there has been a rapid acceleration in the uptake of these ideas.

Perhaps the most significant milestone to date occurred in September 2008. Ecuadorians voted overwhelmingly in a referendum to adopt a constitution that explicitly recognized that Nature has rights and imposed positive obligations on the state and citizens to protect those rights. These provisions have already been invoked successfully in court to protect Nature. For example, on 30 March 2011 the Provincial Court of Justice of Loja granted a constitutional injunction in favour of the Vilcabamba River, against the Provincial Government of Loja. During the widening of the Vilcabamba–Quinara road large quantities of rock and excavation material had been dumped in the Vilcabamba River, disfiguring the banks of the river, destroying riverside land and increasing the risk of severe flooding. The Court applied the precautionary principle and found that the Provincial Government of Loja had to prove that widening the road would not harm the environment, rather than the plaintiffs having to prove that damage had occurred. The Court also rejected the Provincial Government's defence that the road-widening was necessary to meet people's needs on the basis that the case concerned enforcing respect for the constitutional rights of nature and not preventing the widening of the Vilcabamba–Quinara road, and consequently there was no infringement of the constitutional rights of the people.

---

[16] Cullinan, *Wild Law*.

Furthermore, on 30 August 2012 the New Zealand government signed a preliminary agreement with the Whanganui Maori tribe (iwi) that will result in the Whanganui River being recognized as a legal person called 'Te Awa Tupua' whose interests will be protected by two guardians, one from the Crown and one from a Whanganui River iwi.[17]

On 22 April 2010 a Universal Declaration of the Rights of Mother Earth was proclaimed by a People's World Conference on Climate Change and the Rights of Mother Earth in Cochabamba, Bolivia that was attended by 35,000 people (and many governments). I was privileged to lead the drafting of the Universal Declaration of the Rights of Mother Earth, which is intended to complement and contextualize the 1948 Universal Declaration of Human Rights. I believe that one of the most significant aspects of it is that it is a people's document that was shaped directly by the people who participated in the People's World Conference in Cochabamba and does not depend for its legitimacy on adoption by the United Nations or any country (although that would be welcomed).

Despite opposition from many countries, this approach is becoming more visible, even within the United Nations. In April 2011 Dr Vandana Shiva of India and I had the privilege of addressing the United Nations General Assembly on these issues during an interactive dialogue on living in harmony with Nature. References to the rights of Nature were also included in both the final declaration of the Rio+20 World Summit on Sustainable Development in Rio de Janeiro, Brazil in June 2012[18] and in the final declaration of the People's Summit at Rio+20. Although the rights of Nature language in the official Rio+20 declaration was substantially weaker than that proposed in earlier drafts and does not explicitly endorse this approach, it is significant that this approach has now entered official United Nations discourse. More importantly, social movements

---

[17] See www.wrmtb.co.nz/new_updates/TuutohuWhakatupuaFinalSigned.pdf (accessed 15 February 2013).

[18] The language originally proposed was substantially watered down and the final political outcomes document of the Rio+20 Conference entitled 'The Future We Want' contained the following statements: '39. We recognize that planet Earth and its ecosystems are our home and that "Mother Earth" is a common expression in a number of countries and regions, and we note that some countries recognize the rights of nature in the context of the promotion of sustainable development. We are convinced that in order to achieve a just balance among the economic, social and environmental needs of present and future generations, it is necessary to promote harmony with nature. 40. We call for holistic and integrated approaches to sustainable development that will guide humanity to live in harmony with nature and lead to efforts to restore the health and integrity of the Earth's ecosystem.'

throughout the world are beginning to advocate recognizing the rights of Nature as a means of countering the increased commodification of Nature on which the reconceptualized 'Green Economy' approach being promoted at Rio+20 is based.[19]

For lawyers this approach opens up exciting new opportunities. It will require interdisciplinary collaboration between lawyers, scientists and indigenous and local communities that have a deep understanding of ecosystems, to enhance our understanding of the fundamental laws of the universe. It will require creative thinking and debate to clarify how traditional legal concepts such as 'unlawfulness' and 'justice' can be adapted to apply to laws that do not originate from legislatures and practical innovations to establish institutions that are competent to give effect to this approach. In short, it will require rethinking everything!

8. Conclusions

The significant governance challenges facing us in the twenty-first century cannot be solved simply by strengthening the application of the rule of law in relation to environmental law. The crucial question is not how to use the rule of law to protect the environment but how to align legal systems with Earth's laws. The challenge is to develop legal theories, laws and practices that conform to the rule of Nature's laws. This means changing and restructuring industrial societies and changing the purpose of law so that instead of facilitating and legitimizing domination and exploitation, they promote ecological and social integrity and health. This is the most significant and urgent challenge we now face. It is also an exciting opportunity to contribute to an evolutionary leap in law and governance.

---

[19] The Final Declaration of the People's Summit in Rio+20 rejected what it referred to as the so-called 'green economy' and the commodification of life on which it is based, and supported the rights-based approach stating that: 'The defense of the commons is guaranteed by a series of human rights and the nature, solidarity and respect for different worldviews and beliefs of peoples, for example, the defense of "Living Well" as a way to exist in harmony with nature, which presupposes a just transition to be built with workers/and the people.' For a critical analysis of the concept of 'Green Economy' see the chapter by Rebecca Bratspies in this book.

PART III

Designing a rule of law for nature:
new dimensions and ideas

6

Ecological proportionality

An emerging principle of law for nature?

GERD WINTER

1. Introduction

Approaches to give nature a more important place within the law governing human societies have often constructed nature to have subjective rights in relation to human beings. An outstanding example is the vision to acknowledge nature to have a right of standing in court proceedings,[1] another the construct of a *contrat naturel* that shall complement the *contrat social*.[2] The difficulty of these suggestions is that while in the real world the weighing of conflicting rights and the striking of deals is necessary, the concept of subjective rights does not provide guidance on how to do this. On the other hand, sustainable development is much en vogue as an objective (i.e., not rights-based) principle to promote the role of the protection of nature. However, the principle has widely been rendered toothless because it was understood as enabling any balancing of economic, social and natural concerns, which mostly comes out favouring economic interests.[3] Another objective concept is the analysis of economic costs and environmental benefits of environmental policies.[4] But insofar as the concept insists on using common denominators, its method of monetarization of qualitative values has not been convincing, and if it contents itself with qualitative balancing, it is once again without criteria

---

[1] See C. Stone, *Should Trees Have Standing? Law, Morality, and the Environment*, 3rd edn (Oxford University Press, 2010).
[2] M. Serres, *Le Contrat Naturel* (Paris: Flammarion, 1992).
[3] See G. Winter, 'A Fundament and Two Pillars: The Concept of Sustainable Development 20 Years after the Brundtland Report', in H. C. Bugge and C. Voigt (eds.), *Sustainable Development in International and National Law* (Groningen: Europa Law Publishing, 2008), 25–45, at 26ff.
[4] For an overview of the state of the art see B. C. Field and K. C. Field, *Environmental Economics*, 5th edn (New York: McGraw-Hill, 2009), 44ff., 118ff., 137ff.

for how to reach acceptable results. My suggestion is to try proportionality as a principle promoting the role of nature in law and providing adequate criteria of balancing. This principle has emerged as a quite sophisticated means of restriction of power within human society. I suggest also using it as a means of restriction of power of man over nature.

2. From sociological to ecological proportionality

2.1 The tradition of proportionality

Proportionality is a widely accepted principle of the rule of law. It was developed to structure relationships between governmental power and the citizen and was designed to ensure that public power when intruding into the rights of citizens in pursuit of public interests shall do so only under certain preconditions. These are the following:

- the objective pursued by the government shall be justifiable (1);
- the measure taken shall be
  - effective, i.e., capable of serving the public interest (2),
  - necessary, i.e., not replaceable by an alternative that is equally effective but less intrusive on individual rights (3), and
  - balanced, i.e., not excessively intrusive on individual rights in view of the importance of the public interest (4).

The principle can be represented as indicated in Figure 6.1. The arrows indicate that the measure taken will in one way or other cut across individual rights when aiming at an objective. The dotted arrow, representing alternative B, would be more burdensome than alternative A and is therefore to be rejected.

Proportionality (*Verhältnismäßigkeit*) has diverse legal–cultural origins of which the German has possibly been the most influential. In Germany the principle originated in the police law of the nineteenth century when courts developed the doctrine that the police, when taking measures to securing public order, are not allowed to interfere with individual rights more than maintaining public order necessitates.[5] This implied two tests: that the least intrusive measure must be chosen, and that the measure may not be out of proportion with the problem to be solved. Gradually, the principle became more differentiated and was developed into a general

---

[5] V. Götz, *Allgemeines Polizei- und Ordnungsrecht*, 11th edn (Göttingen: Vandenhoeck & Ruprecht, 1993), 130ff.

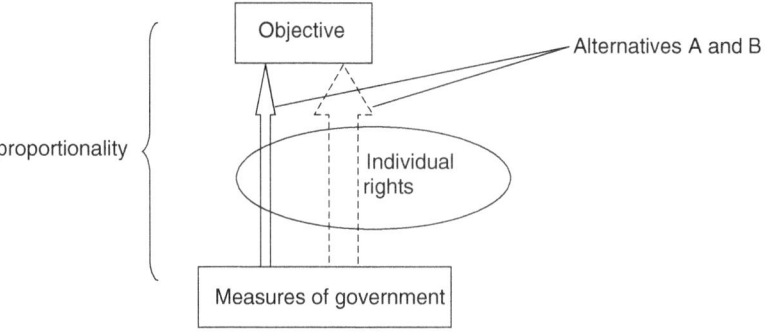

Figure 6.1 The traditional proportionality principle

check of discretionary administrative action and even into a constitutional principle controlling the legislature when a law was to intervene into basic rights.[6] In French administrative law a similar development took place, although more attached to sectoral administrative law.[7]

The foundation in both the German and French legal systems eased the way of proportionality to the European level. There it could also be married with the principle of reasonableness that stems from English common law as a standard of checking administrative discretion, but which is more procedural and less systematic than the proportionality test.[8] The European Court of Justice (ECJ) adopted it in its early jurisprudence on European basic rights as a means to restrict encroachments that are in principle legitimate,[9] applied it to the fine-tuning of Member State restrictions of the EC/EU basic freedoms and also subjected to it

---

[6] P. Lerche, *Übermaß und Verfassungsrecht. Zur Bindung des Gesetzgebers an die Grundsätze der Verhältnismäßigkeit und Erforderlichkeit* (Cologne: C. Heymanns Verlag, 1961), 29ff.

[7] Police law provided the learning field for the least intrusion test and expropriation law, that of the weighing of private and public interests, called *bilan coût-avantages*. See G. Dupuis, M.-J. Guédon and P. Crétien, *Droit Administratif*, 12th edn (Paris: Dalloz, 2011), 841.

[8] H. W. R. Wade, *Administrative Law*, 5th edn (Oxford: Clarendon Press, 1982), Chapter 12. It has been suggested that proportionality should also be adopted as a common law principle: see C. Harlow and R. Rawlings, *Law and Administration* (Cambridge University Press, 1997, reprinted 2006), 118, citing J. Jowell and A. Lester, 'Proportionality: Neither Novel nor Dangerous', in J. Jowell and D. Oliver (eds.), *New Directions in Judicial Review* (London: Stevens, 1988).

[9] ECJ judgment of 17 December 1970, Case 11/70 (*Internationale Handelsgesellschaft*), paragraphs 12 and 14.

any discretionary administrative decisions of the European organs, and in particular of the Commission.[10]

Thus, proportionality has become a wide-ranging principle of domesticating governmental powers when encroaching on individual rights or competence realms of lower ranged governance levels.

2.2 Suggesting an analogy

What I wish to suggest is that the principle should not only be applied to governmental activities that intrude on citizens' rights but also to those citizens' activities that intrude on nature. This analogy is justifiable because the two areas of application have a common denominator, that is the limitation of power. In the first case it is state power over society (or the collective over the individuals) that must be tamed; in the second it is societal power over nature that must be tamed. Proportionality in the second sense would be a requirement of justifying uses of nature by society. "Society" would include individual persons and enterprises, but also governmental bodies in their capacity not as regulators but as direct users of nature.

For the sake of clear terminology I shall refer to the two kinds of proportionality as sociological and ecological. While sociological proportionality (or in short socio-proportionality) shall primarily protect basic rights of citizens against governmental intrusions, ecological proportionality (or eco-proportionality) shall protect nature against intrusions by society (including nature-consuming governments) (see Figure 6.2).

The reason for this new targeting of the principle is the increasing scarcity of natural resources that are available for modern societies, be it biodiversity, water, clean air or a liveable climate. The implication is that societal actors are not primarily constructed as right holders but rather as bearers of obligations (although this does not exclude rights-based action against those who do not fulfil their obligations). The crucial point is thus that human society is required to justify its interests in view of nature. Nature is no longer the "environment" of mankind, which is protected by physically limiting human encroachments. Rather it is a resource that must be spared unless there is good reason to consume it.

---

[10] While the principle has been developed for situations where basic rights of individuals are encroached upon, it has been extended to check intrusions by higher governance levels into competence realms of lower levels. See, e.g., Art. 5(4) Treaty on the Functioning of the European Union (TFEU) where it functions as part of the subsidiarity principle. It even figures as a self-standing general principle of checking EU powers.

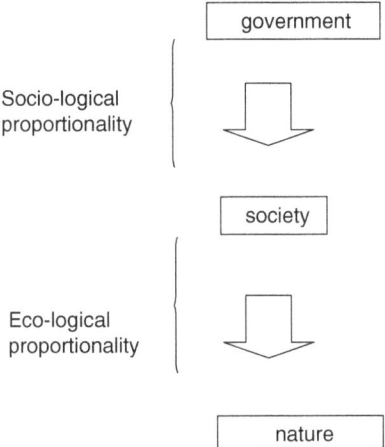

Figure 6.2   Two versions of proportionality

2.3   Designing ecological proportionality

Eco-proportionality would entail the following fourfold test: If an activity encroaches on natural resources:

- the actor must pursue a justifiable societal objective (1); and
- the activity shall prospectively be
  - effective, i.e., capable of serving the objective (2);
  - necessary, i.e., not replaceable by an alternative that is less intrusive on natural resources (3); and
  - balanced, i.e., not excessively intrusive on natural resources in view of the importance of the societal objective (4).

The principle can be represented as set out in Figure 6.3.

In more detail an ambitious version of the test would require the following four demands:

1. While in socio-proportionality the objective pursued by the individual is conceived as free choice, it is now subjected to a duty to give reasons. This is a veritable skandalon of the concept, but it is understandable in view of the ever growing scarcity of natural resources. It is not justifiable, for instance, to use agricultural products for biofuel where they are needed for human consumption, or to capture rare animals for keeping them as pets. Unlawful uses are also not justifiable.

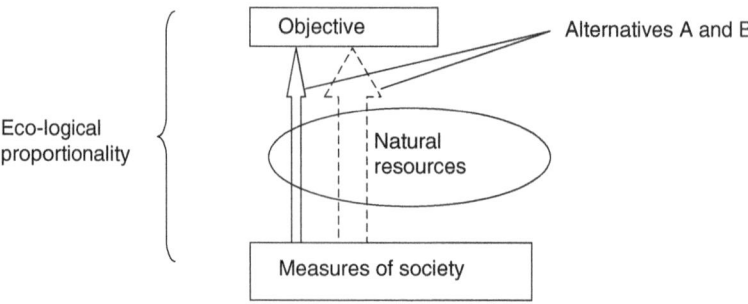

Figure 6.3   Eco-proportionality

2. If an objective is justifiable, the means taken should be fit to serve it. For instance, if a dam for hydropower generation is to be built, it needs to be proved that the river will feed sufficient water into the reservoir.
3. The most important element of eco-proportionality is the testing of alternative means. The alternative that causes the least adverse effects on natural resources should be preferred. However, as not all alternatives will serve the objective in exactly the same way, some deviation from the full realization of the objective should be accepted.
4. Assuming an objective is justified and the means is also as effective as necessary, then the means should nevertheless be rejected if its adverse effects on nature are excessive if weighed against the importance of the goal. For instance, if the extension of a highway can only be done by crossing a nature reserve due to geographical factors, but this would increase its transportation capacity by only 5 per cent, the adverse effect may be found excessive in relation to the objective.

Admittedly, it is overly ambitious to suggest introducing this scheme for all areas of utilization of scarce natural resources. It would, however, be a great step forward if at least the consideration of alternatives became a general requirement, even if the objective of an activity remained completely at the actor's discretion. The range of concretization of the two most important elements – a reasonable objective and the test of alternatives – shall be further explained.

As for the requirement of a reasonable objective, the range of possible justification reaches from personal pleasure and economic profit to the use value of a product or service up to a public interest. A public interest would have to be required, when it is unavoidable that highly valuable environmental assets are sacrificed for the objective, such as if a rare natural habitat is destroyed for the sake of a better transportation infrastructure. The more serious the damage or risk of damage, the more weighty the benefit must be if the adverse effect is to be accepted. As the objective is an appropriate guide for determining the scope of alternatives that should be considered, it should be noted that the more the objective is formulated in general terms, the broader the scope of alternatives becomes. For instance, if the objective is defined to facilitate transportation between two agglomerations, roads and railways are two options to be considered. If the definition is less generally defined to facilitate individual transportation, only different kinds and lines of roads would be included. Finally, if the objective is very specifically determined so that a six-lane highway is to be built in a precisely delimited corridor, only small geographical deviations can be discussed. An appropriate arrangement would be for the decisions in the first and second cases to be taken at a higher and lower administrative level, respectively, while the third case should not be accepted at all for not adequately distinguishing between goals and means.

Concerning the role of alternatives, the choice of options can be left subjectively to the developer, or it can follow from objective criteria. For instance, Directive 2011/92/EU on environmental impact assessment of projects confines the test to "the main alternatives studied by the developer".[11] By contrast, Directive 2001/42 on environmental impact assessment of plans speaks of "reasonable alternatives".[12] This objective language is less inclined to misuse by developers. As for the scope of alternatives that are to be checked, as already mentioned the (private or public) objective of the use of nature should serve as a criterion. In addition, it must be clarified if measures compensating any damage caused by an alternative are to be counted as reducing its negative impact. This should depend on the kind of natural resource at stake. For instance, the removal of living resources may be treated differently from chemical pollution, because the damage can be made good more easily in the first than in the second case. A last problem is related to the fact that alternatives may differ in their degree of attaining the objective, and they may involve different financial costs. For instance, the tunnelling of a biotope is of course more

---

[11] Directive 2011/92/EU of the European Parliament and of the Council on the assessment of the effects of certain public and private projects on the environment, OJ 2012 L 26/1, Annex IV Sec. 2.
[12] Directive 2001/42/EC of the European Parliament and of the Council of 27 June 2001 on the assessment of the effects of certain plans and programmes on the environment, OJ 2011 L 197/30, Art. 5(1).

costly than cross-cutting on the surface. It appears that such questions of goal attainment and financial side-effects must be solved by appropriate weighing of interests. Significant costs and curtailment of objectives may be a reason for accepting an alternative that is second-best in environmental terms.

3. Legal status

The examples given already indicate that ecological proportionality is not alien to legal codification. Nonetheless, the principle should first of all be conceived as a social norm, not as a legal norm.[13] More than socio-proportionality, which encourages acting egoistically unless the state sets limits, eco-proportionality is particularly appropriate for adoption as a social norm because it explicitly aims at a societal self-commitment on how society should utilize natural resources. In addition, it may also be framed as a requirement of state-based law.

We will explore in the following to what extent the principle has already entered the realm of both social and legal norms.

3.1 A social norm

In respect of social norms we will ask if individuals, enterprises and governmental bodies, when utilizing natural resources, reflect on whether the activity serves a justifiable objective, whether the objective can be reached by less intrusive means and whether the residual encroachment is outweighed by the importance of the objective.

In the social world proportionality has indeed spread widely in what is called environmental consumption. For instance, more and more consumers compare products and services not only in terms of price and functionality but also in terms of environmental impact of their manufacture, operation and disposal. Not only are least intrusive alternatives considered, but even the objectives of consumption are put into question. The use of bicycles is one example: in comparison with the car, in many situations the bicycle is not only the less intrusive alternative but also a

---

[13] On the emergence and role of social norms ("conventions") as distinct from legal norms, see as a classical text Max Weber, *Rechtssoziologie*, J. Winckelmann (ed.) (Neuwied: Luchterhand, 1960), 63ff. For a rich empirical study on "folkways", see W. G. Sumner, *Folkways. A Study of the Sociological Importance of Usages, Manners, Customs, Mores and Morals* (New York: Ginn and Company, 1906).

better justifiable objective because it is faster in inner cities and healthier for the rider.

In the economic world, codes of conduct of enterprises and enterprise networks sometimes contain recommendations reflecting elements of ecological proportionality.[14] While many multinational corporations only commit themselves to vague goals of sustainable economic behaviour,[15] there are others that strive for minimization of environmental impact and are even prepared to reflect on the benefits of their products. For instance, the Swiss chemical company Novartis has until recently counted the following among its principles of its 'Policy on Corporate Citizenship' concerning health, safety and environmental (HSE) performance:[16]

> We strive to make efficient use of natural resources and minimize the environmental impacts of our activities and our products over their life cycle. We assess HSE implications to ensure that the benefits of new products, processes and technologies outweigh remaining risks.

The minimization clause can be seen as a testing of alternatives and the efficiency requirement as a form of effectiveness test. Most significantly the corporation is prepared to weigh the benefits of the products with the remaining environmental risks.

A more modest example can be found in the Organisation for Economic Co-Operation and Development (OECD) guidelines on multinationals. Although they derive from a state-based international organization, they

---

[14] Industrial self-regulation has since long introduced technical standards, domestically and regionally (H. Schepel, *The Constitution of Private Governance. Product Standards of Integrating Markets* (Oxford: Hart Publishing, 2005), 101–76) and more recently also globally (O. Dilling, 'Proactive Compliance? Repercussions of National Regulation in Standards of Transnational Business Networks', in O. Dilling, M. Herberg and G. Winter (eds.), *Responsible Business. Self-Governance and Law in Transnational Economic Transactions* (Oxford: Hart Publishing, 2008), 96–8). Such standards (as well as more ambitious schemes such as Standard 14000 of the International Organization for Standardization (ISO) on environmental management are elements of an emerging environmental law of the firm. Eco-proportionality would go beyond this because it demands putting production goals into question and searching for product alternatives.

[15] See for instance the websites of the multinational chemicals corporations BASF and Bayer.

[16] This wording appeared until March 2013 on the Novartis website, but has since been replaced by a less ambitious formula that focuses on emission reduction, leaving out the balancing of benefits from products with environmental costs. See www.novartis.com/corporate-responsibility/responsible-business-practices/protecting-the-environment/index.shtml (last visited 24 June 2013).

can be regarded as a self-commitment standard shared by progressive industries. They posit among other things:[17]

> [Enterprises should:]
>
> 6. Continually seek to improve corporate environmental performance, at the level of the enterprise and, where appropriate, of its supply chain, by encouraging such activities as:
> (a) adoption of technologies and operating procedures in all parts of the enterprise that reflect standards concerning environmental performance in the best performing part of the enterprise;
> (b) development and provision of products or services that have no undue environmental impacts; are safe in their intended use; reduce greenhouse gas emissions; are efficient in their consumption of energy and natural resources; can be reused, recycled, or disposed of safely.

The guidelines claim that technologies should reflect the standards that have no undue environmental impacts; are safe in their intended use; reduce greenhouse gas emissions; and are efficient in their consumption up to the standard of the best performing factory of the entire concern. Although this does not yet entail a comparison with the best technologies worldwide, it does trigger the consideration of alternatives and the orientation towards the multinational's obligation to reach best standards. Likewise, when choosing the kind of product or service provided, the enterprise should respect quite ambitious yardsticks such as "no undue environmental impacts", safe use, greenhouse gas reduction, energy and resource efficiency, and the reuse, recycling and safe disposal of waste.

Of course, such guidelines are recommendations and self-commitments, not binding rules, and they are framed in adhortative, not in obliging language. They are nevertheless examples of social norms. The more they are concrete and supported by organizational infrastructure such as specialized environmental officers, reporting commitments, management plans, internal auditing mechanisms and so on, the more they will be considered as self-obligatory.[18]

---

[17] OECD (2011), *OECD Guidelines for Multinational Enterprises*, OECD Publishing, Chapter VI No. 6, available at: http://dx.doi.org/10.1787/9789264115415-en (last visited 5 June 2013).

[18] M. Herberg, 'Global Legal Pluralism and Interlegality: Environmental Self-Regulation in Multinational Enterprises as Global Law-Making', in O. Dilling, M. Herberg and G. Winter (eds.), *Responsible Business. Self-Governance and Law in Transnational Economic Transactions* (Oxford: Hart Publishing, 2008), 30–2.

3.2 A legal norm

In conclusion, the principle of eco-proportionality is indeed emerging as a social norm. It is important as a source of societal self-regulation, especially in those areas where the law has not yet intervened. Eco-proportionality is, however, also suitable as the content of state-based binding legislation. Of course, state-based legislation can also formulate basic rules that society should respect when utilizing natural resources. In fact, given the present-day urgent need for bolder steps towards environmental protection, it may serve as an appropriate instrument for guiding society towards showing better respect for nature. This is all the more so if it can be shown that the principle is not entirely new but can already be traced in some legal contexts. Examples given before as well as additional ones may show that this is indeed the case. They concentrate on the EU and Germany as far as national or regional cases are concerned, but also include cases of international agreement.

One elaborate example is a set of criteria established for the protection of the European Network of Protected Areas called Natura 2000. If a project that causes significant adverse effects on a Natura 2000 site is to be realized, it can exceptionally be authorized if there are no alternative solutions that have no or fewer adverse effects and the adverse effects are outweighed by an overriding public interest. In such a case compensatory measures shall be taken that reduce the impact (Art. 6(4)(1) Directive 1992/43/EC). The provision reads:

> If, in spite of a negative assessment of the implications for the site and in the *absence of alternative solutions*, a plan or project must nevertheless be carried out for imperative reasons of *overriding public interest*, including those of a social or economic nature, the Member State shall take all *compensatory measures* necessary to ensure that the overall coherence of Natura 2000 is protected [emphasis added].

A similarly sophisticated example is provided by the German Federal Nature Protection Law (Bundesnaturschutzgesetz, BNatSchG).[19] Section 15 BNatSchG establishes that whenever a project causes a significant alteration of nature and landscape (*Eingriff in Natur und Landschaft*), the following criteria must be fulfilled. First, it has to be assessed whether any adverse effects of the project can be avoided. Here, project variants

---

[19] Section 15 Federal Act on Nature Protection (Bundesnaturschutzgesetz – BNatSchG).

are sought that intrude less into nature.[20] As a second step, any adverse effects that are found to be unavoidable must be compensated for either by remediation near to the spot (*Ausgleichsmaßnahme*) or by restitution, possibly further away (*Ersatzmaßnahme*). As a third step, the remaining damage must be weighed against the importance of the project; if it is weightier than the project, the latter is impermissible. If it is less grave, some monetary compensation must be paid.

Further examples are given below in summary versions. A short comment in square brackets indicates which elements of eco-proportionality are represented.

- A derogation from the obligations to protect endangered bird species is permissible for reasons of interests of public health and safety, air safety and prevention of serious damage to crops, "where there is no other satisfactory solution" (Art. 9 Directive 2009/147/EC) [objective to be justified, alternatives to be tested].
- Member States may derogate from the obligation to ensure good surface water quality if the environmental and socio-economic needs served by water uses cannot be achieved by a significantly better environmental option not entailing disproportionate costs (Art. 4(5) Directive 2000/60/EC) [alternatives to be tested, objective to be considered].
- New plant protection products that contain certain immanently dangerous substances may not be approved if for the envisaged uses an authorized plant protection product, or a non-chemical control or prevention method, already exists that is safer for the environment (Art. 50(1)(a) Regulation (EC) 1107/09) [alternatives to be tested].
- The production and marketing of certain immanently dangerous chemicals can only be authorized if either their health or environmental risk is adequately controlled or outweighed by socio-economic benefits and if there are no suitable alternative substances or technologies (see Art. 60(2) t. 60 Regulation(EC) 1907/06) [alternatives to be tested, solution to be weighed against objective].
- An environmental impact assessment (EIA) must show what alternatives to the proposed project were tested and why they were rejected (Art. 5(3) Directive 2011/92/EU; Art. 5 Directive 2001/42/EC) [alternatives to be tested].

---

[20] The project can, however, not be put into question *in toto* at this stage, and the scope of alternatives is confined to those at the same location.

- An operator of a dangerous installation must apply best available techniques, which are defined to be techniques aiming at environmental protection that are most effective, advanced and practically suitable, but also economically viable and considering the costs and advantages (Art. 2 no. 10 Directive 2010/75/EU) [alternatives to be tested; costs to be weighed against environmental advantages].

A number of international agreements have also adopted elements of the eco-proportionality principle.

- According to the Convention on Persistent Organic Pollutants (POPs), "when considering proposals to construct new facilities or significantly modify existing facilities using processes that release chemicals listed in this Annex, priority consideration should be given to alternative processes, techniques or practices that have similar usefulness but which avoid the formation and release of such chemicals" [alternatives to be tested].
- The Convention on Environmental Impact Assessment in a Transboundary Context provides that the EIA contains "a description, where appropriate, of reasonable alternatives (for example, locational or technological) to the proposed activity and also the no-action alternative"[21] [alternatives to be tested].
- According to the Protocol on Strategic Environmental Assessment (SEA), the environmental report shall "identify, describe and evaluate the likely significant environmental, including health, effects of implementing the plan or programme and its reasonable alternatives"[22] [alternatives to be tested].
- The Convention for the Protection of the Ozone Layer suggests an exchange between contracting parties of technical information on:
  - The availability and cost of chemical substitutes and of alternative technologies to reduce the emissions of ozone-modifying substances and related planned and ongoing research;
  - The limitations and any risks involved in using chemical or other substitutes and alternative technologies, as well as socio-economic

---

[21] Espoo Convention on Environmental Impact Assessment in a Transboundary Context of 1991, Art. 4 with Appendix II (b).
[22] Protocol on Strategic Environmental Assessment to the Convention on Environmental Impact Assessment in a Transboundary Context of 2003, Art. 7(2). Disappointingly, a survey of strategic environmental reports in Germany showed that alternatives were considered only in a third of all cases. See R. Wulfhorst, 'Die Untersuchung von Alternativen im Rahmen der Strategischen Umweltprüfung', *NVwZ* (2011), 1099.

information on, among others, "The costs, risks and benefits of human activities which may indirectly modify the ozone layer and of the impacts of regulatory actions taken or being considered to control these activities"[23] [alternatives to be tested, objective ("benefits") to be considered].

In conclusion, it appears that eco-proportionality has been adopted by a number of national, EU and international legal acts in different forms, and sometimes in a rather comprehensive version. There seems to be some rationale behind the choice of design. It appears that the more ambitious the test, the greater the value the concerned natural resource is considered to have, or the more serious the adverse effect. Thus, the particularly strict version of Natura 2000 is explained by the rarity status of the protected resources. By contrast, the lenient version required for an EIA may follow from the fact that the EIA covers many effects and the environment as a whole, not just particularly serious effects or particularly endangered resources.

3.3 Social and legal norms combined

Often the law does not conclusively regulate a problem. In such cases the principle of eco-proportionality may instead guide actors as a social norm that complements the legal norm. Three situations may be highlighted in which such complementary function is most promising: when the law is widely absent, structurally unambitious or rather vague.

3.3.1 Unregulated areas

Multinational enterprises often invest in countries that do not operate adequate environmental standards. According to customary international law, their rules of their home country do not apply in the foreign country.[24] As already indicated, these enterprises nevertheless sometimes do not exploit this regulatory gap, but strive for some kind of self-regulation. If they go further than the applicable law requires, this is often motivated by economic calculus such as the image of their product in consumer countries or economies of scale for pollution abatement technology. However, the ambition could also be based on respect for nature and a sense of need

---

[23] Vienna Convention for the Protection of the Ozone Layer of 1985, Annex II Nos. 4 and 5.

[24] P. Birnie, A. Boyle and C. Redgwell, *International Law and the Environment*, 3rd edn (Oxford University Press, 2009), 788.

to justify its utilization. Eco-proportionality as a social norm would suggest itself as a principle in that situation, at least in the form of alternatives testing. The OECD guidelines have already been cited as an example that could be further elaborated.

3.3.2 Undercutting thresholds

Environmental standards setting quality objectives for air, water, soil, biodiversity and so on are often based on insufficient knowledge about the appropriate protective level. As a safety device, some regulations such as that on dangerous installations require the application of best available techniques even if the environmental standard is not exceeded.[25] But in other areas such requirement does not apply. In the emissions trading concept in climate protection law it is even rejected. Although the capping of emissions in the Kyoto Protocol system has obviously been too lenient, emitters are nevertheless not required to do more by using best emission reduction techniques, but are allowed and even stimulated to sell non-used allowances derived from the fixed quota.[26] Eco-proportionality would provide a ground for going further out of respect for nature.

Eco-proportionality could also provide a foundation for the precautionary principle. While precaution is constructed to mean that most thresholds rest on uncertain knowledge, the fact is that threshold-setting is a political struggle between economic and ecological interests that often disregards scientific knowledge. Precaution is therefore a fall-back position of those who lost the game. Resting it on the presumption for nature would at least acknowledge that precaution is a matter of politics rather than of cognition. The requirement that best available technologies must be applied is then a yardstick, not to cope with uncertainty but to pay tribute to the growing scarcity of natural resources. It would suggest that natural resources should not be consumed if the consumption can be avoided.

3.3.3 References by formal law

Sometimes the law explicitly refers to social norms. This is true, for instance, for the standard of due diligence in tort law, duties of care in environmental law, good practices in the law of agriculture and so on. In

---

[25] See section 3.2 above.
[26] For this observation see in more detail G. Winter, 'The Climate Is No Commodity: Taking Stock of the Emissions Trading System', 22:2 *Journal of Environmental Law* (2010), 1–25, at 16.

such cases eco-proportionality can serve as guidance for adopting more elaborate rules.

Often the law is not explicitly referring to social norms but implicitly relies on them because the problem at stake escapes precise regulation. For instance, living natural resources such as plants, animals and their ecosystems have the capacity of reproduction and recovery from damage. The capacity is limited because lost species cannot be revived, destroyed habitats are slow in recovery, toxic substances may persist for thousands of years and human settlements can hardly be removed. But before these limits are reached, there is leeway to shape nature and thus a need for management. For this reason protection standards are often formulated in very broad terms. For instance, when transportation and energy networks are built, they unavoidably cost living nature. How should it be determined whether that is to be tolerated or not? Once again, eco-proportionality would help here as a frame of balancing interests, even where it has not been introduced as a legal standard.

4. Overlapping proportionalities in environmental law

Eco- and socio-logical proportionality appear to be overlapping in the realm of environmental law. In environmental law many rules already establish basic obligations of society vis-à-vis nature, asking for respect for it and obviously also requiring proportionality of means and ends, including alternatives testing. For instance, the German Federal Law on Protection from Emissions (Bundesimmissionsschutzgesetz – BImSchG) empowers the competent authority to order the operator of a dangerous installation to improve its environmental performance unless this causes unproportional costs. The relevant provision, Article 17, reads:

(1) In order to perform the obligations resulting from this Act or from any ordinance issued hereunder, orders may be issued following the granting of the licence or an alteration notified pursuant to Article 15(1). If after the issue of such a licence or after an alteration notified pursuant to Article 15(1), the protection of the general public or the neighbourhood against any harmful effects on the environment or any other hazards, significant disadvantages and significant nuisances turns out to be inadequate, the competent authority shall issue subsequent orders.

(2) The competent authority shall not issue any subsequent order if such order would lack *proportionality*, above all if the effort needed to

comply with an initial order is not commensurate with the *desired effect*; in this respect, special attention shall be paid to the nature, volume and hazardousness of the emissions originating from the installation and the immissions released by it as well as to the *useful life* and the characteristic *technical features* of the installation [emphasis added].

Proportionality in this sense is also an important principle in international law. For instance, Article 2.2 of the Agreement on Technical Barriers to Trade (TBT Agreement) requires that a measure aiming at a public interest such as health or environmental protection shall not be more trade-restrictive than necessary. The Appellate Body has established a rather sophisticated methodology of how to apply the test, requiring consideration of the following:

(i) the degree of contribution made by the measure to the legitimate objective at issue;
(ii) the trade-restrictiveness of the measure; and
(iii) the nature of the risks at issue and the gravity of consequences that would arise from non-fulfilment of the objective(s) pursued by the Member through the measure. In most cases, a comparison of the challenged measure and possible alternative measures should be undertaken. In particular, it may be relevant for the purpose of this comparison to consider whether the proposed alternative is less trade restrictive, whether it would make an equivalent contribution to the relevant legitimate objective, taking account of the risks non-fulfilment would create, and whether it is reasonably available.[27]

However, this kind of proportionality, although dealing with environmental protection, is still characterized by the logic of minimizing encroachments on societal interests, as is familiar from its application in state-citizen relationships. Environmental protection appears here as a public interest. The means serving it must be limited in order to protect individual rights. In contrast, eco-proportionality would reverse the question and demand that societal interests are limited in view of the protection of nature. Socio-proportionality, even in the realm of environmental protection policy, starts with a presumption for societal interests, while eco-proportionality departs from a presumption for the protection of nature. In the first vision mankind appears as master and nature as

---

[27] AB Tuna WT/DS381/AB/R, No. 322.

Table 6.1. *Socio-proportionality and eco-proportionality compared*

	Socio-proportionality	Eco-proportionality
Objective justifiable?	Justify protection of nature	Justify social benefits
Means effective?	Exclude options that entail a superfluous burden on society	Exclude options that entail a superfluous burden on nature
Means necessary?	Choose the option that entails least burdens on society while being equally effective	Choose the option that entails least burdens on nature while being equally effective
Means balanced?	Sacrifice nature if the burden for society is excessive	Sacrifice social benefit if burden for nature is excessive

servant; in the second nature is seen as the source without which humankind cannot survive.

The distinction between socio-proportionality in the realm of environmental policy and ecological proportionality may appear academic, because in both concepts societal interests are weighed against the interests of nature. But as the relevant law is often indeterminate, basic starting points and orientations do make a difference.[28] For instance, a major distinct feature of eco-proportionality is that it puts individual and social welfare interests more radically into question than does socio-proportionality. In traditional environmental law these interests remain largely unquestioned. For instance, in the cited Article 17 BImSchG, only "the useful life and characteristic features of the installation" are considered on the side of societal interest, and in the equally cited Article 2.2 TBT Agreement only free international trade is considered. No question is raised as to whether the installation and international trade, respectively, provide a service for society. By contrast, eco-proportionality would ask more fundamentally for reflection on goals and giving reasons for them.

---

[28] The author feels that this difference has not been elaborated sufficiently in his chapter 'Balancing Environmental Risks and Socio-Economic Benefits of Alternatives: A General Principle and its Application in Natura 2000', in I. L. Backer, O. K. Fauchald and C. Voigt (eds.), *Pro Natura – Festskrift til Hans Christian Bugge* (Oslo: Universitetsforlaget, 2012), 585–601.

Table 6.1 is an attempt to structure the difference between the two proportionalities by varying the answers to the four tests.

5. Conclusion

Eco-proportionality is proposed as a possibile structure for the balancing of interests of exploitation and protection of nature, thus fettering the discretion built into concepts such as nature rights, the *contrat naturel*, sustainability and cost–benefit analysis. Eco-proportionality is an analogy to the well-established principle of proportionality, here called socio-proportionality. Both principles have a common denominator in that they make a check on power, power of the state over society and of society (as individual and collective) over nature, respectively. As in socio-proportionality, eco-proportionality requires four tests, namely a justifiable objective of action and the effectiveness, necessity and weighing of means. It has been shown that the principle is already present both as a social and legal norm. There is reason to suggest that it should enter into more spheres of societal practice and legal order, at the same time taking a more differentiated and ambitious shape.

7

Sustainable development and the rule of law for nature

A constitutional reading

LOUIS J. KOTZÉ

1. Introduction

Sustainable development has been at the centre of the global environmental law, policy and governance architecture for the greater part of the twentieth century, and in many ways it has been and continues to function as the guiding principle for many socio-legal and political interventions and reforms that seek to govern the human–environment interface.[1] A generous interpretation of the concept suggests that sustainable development does not aim for a 'singular "steady state", but rather the best possible dynamic for dwelling in the world taking into account the needs of [the] economy, society and environment'.[2] While some have (correctly in my view) labelled sustainable development an ideological palliative,[3] and while others have called for stronger forms of sustainable development as opposed to weak manifestations that only entrench the impoverished sustained human development rhetoric,[4] it remains the most widely accepted conceptual aid to guide global society through the, often politically messy, growth-versus-limits labyrinth.[5] To be sure, it is an 'abstract

---

[1] See generally, Ulrich Beyerlin and Thilo Marauhn, *International Environmental Law* (Oxford: Hart Publishing, 2011), 73–84.
[2] Robin Libby and Steffen Will, 'History for the Anthropocene', 5:5 *History Compass* (2007) 1694–1719, at 1695.
[3] Benjamin J. Richardson, 'A Damp Squib: Environmental Law from a Human Evolutionary Perspective', *Osgoode CLPE Research Paper 08/2011*, Osgoode CLPE Research Paper Series Vol. 07(3), available at http://ssrn.com/abstract=1760043 (last accessed 13 August 2012).
[4] See generally, Klaus Bosselmann, *The Principle of Sustainability: Transforming Law and Governance* (Aldershot: Ashgate, 2008).
[5] Reinhard Steurer and Rita Trattnigg, 'Nachhaltigkeit regieren: Eine Einleitung im Wissenschaft-Praxis Dialog', in Reinhard Steurer and Rita Trattnigg (eds.), *Nachhaltigkeit regieren: Eine Bilanz zu Governance-Prinzipien und -Praktiken* (Munich: Oekom Verlag, 2010), 15.

political value' that 'has become the worldwide dominating leitmotif for shaping international environmental and development relations'.[6] While sustainable development is neither an innovative approach to environmental protection, nor a particularly successful intervention to promote environmental protection, politics and neo-liberal anthropocentrism dominate reality and in the absence of any other politically acceptable construct that does not offend prevailing anthropocentric demands, weak sustainable development will probably prevail for the near future. Accepting the foregoing inevitability, this chapter poses a central question: does sustainable development still have any decisive role to play in upholding the rule of law for nature? In this chapter I suggest that it does when considered through a constitutional lens.

There are some examples of domestic legal regimes that have constitutionally entrenched sustainable development. In South Africa, for example, sustainable development has been an integral part of the legal order since the advent of democracy and transition to a constitutional state in 1994. Following decades of oppression and racial discrimination under apartheid, the broader political and socio-economic changes in the country were accompanied by sweeping reforms of, among others, the environmental governance regime. The country enshrined an environmental right in the Constitution of the Republic of South Africa 1996 (Constitution), and adopted a comprehensive body of environmental legislation to give effect to its broader policies and the myriad constitutional objectives of the new environmental right.[7] By means of this entrenchment, sustainable development has thus become a constitutional issue or concern in the country. Is it possible to determine whether sustainable development in constitutional guise has what it takes to uphold the rule of law for nature in South Africa? The courts are uniquely situated to engage with sustainability conflicts that arise in the constitutional setting by exercising their day-to-day adjudicative functions that are aimed at resolving conflicts in law and society.[8] For present purposes, such an appraisal will therefore require an investigation of how the courts, as guardians of the Constitution and the rule of law, have engaged with sustainable development in the context of the Constitution.

---

[6] Beyerlin and Marauhn, *International Environmental Law*, 76.
[7] See generally Michael A. Kidd, *Environmental Law*, 2nd edn (Cape Town: Juta, 2011).
[8] Louis J. Kotzé and Anél Du Plessis, 'Some Brief Observations on Fifteen Years of Environmental Rights Jurisprudence in South Africa', 3:1 *Journal of Court Innovation* (2011) 101–20.

Returning to the central research question, this chapter seeks to investigate whether the 'tired' concept of sustainable development could be 'resuscitated' by clothing it in constitutional terms and whether sustainable development as a feature of environmental constitutionalism could contribute to upholding the rule of law for nature in South Africa as determined by the manner in which the South African judiciary has engaged with sustainable development. Section 2 of the chapter examines the meaning of the rule of law in South Africa, with section 3 situating this meaning in the environmental context. Section 4 then reflects on sustainable development as a constitutional concern that is closely connected to the rule of law for nature in South Africa and concludes with section 5, which appraises the manner in which the South African courts have engaged with sustainable development to date.

2. The rule of law

In general terms, the rule of law has been described as 'the glory of the Western legal tradition',[9] and while there are many different interpretations of this doctrine, it is generally understood to require of government 'to act in accordance with pre-announced, clear and general rules that are enforced by impartial courts in accordance with fair procedures'.[10] In doing so, the rule of law makes it incumbent on government to obey the law and it prohibits government from exercising any power unless that power is mandated by law.[11] The law must also be publicly promulgated, prospective in effect (as opposed to being retrospective), understandable, consistent, non-contradictory and relatively stable.[12] Other views explain that the rule of law contains procedural elements based on the principle of legality, which requires decision-making to be made in terms of generally known principles of law;[13] it entails that no one is above the law; and the law binds all those involved in exercising government authority.[14] Notably, these characteristics are mostly procedural in nature; they do not relate

---

[9] Dan A. Tarlock, 'The Future of Environmental "Rule of Law" Litigation', 17:2 *Pace Environmental Law Review* (2000) 237–72, at 247.

[10] Ian Currie and Johan De Waal, *The Bill of Rights Handbook*, 5th edn (Cape Town: Juta, 2010), 10.

[11] Tarlock, 'The Future of Environmental "Rule of Law" Litigation', 248.

[12] Jaco Barnard Naudé, 'The Post-Apartheid Legal Order', in Tracy Humby, Louis J. Kotzé and Anél A. Du Plessis (eds.), *Introduction to Law and Legal Skills in South Africa* (Oxford University Press, 2012), 27.

[13] Currie and De Waal, *The Bill of Rights Handbook*, 11.

[14] Tarlock, 'The Future of Environmental "Rule of Law" Litigation', 248.

to the *substance* of the law, but rather provide 'procedural guidelines' for conducting legislative and administrative processes in a country.[15]

In the South African context, the rule of law also has a substantive element that must be understood in terms of the country's post-apartheid constitutional dispensation. Whereas the procedural elements of the rule of law have always been part of South African law (ironically in the past to uphold the rule of apartheid law), the rule of constitutional law specifically relates to the substantive content and objectives of the law including, for example, the protection of human rights and advancement of freedom and democracy. As Dyzenhaus[16] points out:

> The commitment in new-order South Africa to the supremacy of the constitution [sic] and the rule of law does not, in itself, mark a departure from the past. The apartheid legal order implemented a racist ideology through law but was formally no less committed than the new order to both the supremacy of the constitution [sic] and the rule of law.

What makes the 'new-order' rule of law different from the apartheid era rule of law, is that the Constitution and its provisions collectively seek to break from a past political and legal dispensation that was in every way directly opposed to constitutionalism: 'what marks the difference is the fact that the Constitution also guarantees a list of rights and liberties, and utterly rejects the discriminatory ideology of the previous order.'[17]

There are now various principles that underlie the constitutional order, including: constitutionalism, democracy, accountability, separation of powers, checks and balances, devolution of powers and the rule of law.[18] To be sure, the rule of law is more than a constitutional principle; it is considered a constitutional value along with other values upon which South Africa is founded, including human dignity, the achievement of equality and the advancement of human rights and freedoms, non-racialism and non-sexism, and constitutional supremacy.[19] These constitutional values and principles are not mere statements of fact; they set out ambitious transformative objectives that are cast in 'higher' or supreme constitutional language and they must be purposefully and actively fulfilled, achieved and advanced. Reiterating the purposive obligation on

---

[15] Naudé, 'The Post-Apartheid Legal Order', 27.
[16] David Dyzenhaus, 'The Pasts and Future of the Rule of Law in South Africa', *South African Law Journal* 124:4 (2008) 734–61, at 735.
[17] Ibid., 736.
[18] Currie and De Waal, *The Bill of Rights Handbook*, 7.
[19] Section 1 of the Constitution.

government to fulfil, achieve and advance constitutional values, the Constitution also requires government to 'respect, protect, promote and fulfil the rights in the Bill of Rights',[20] including the environmental right and all its elements. Moreover, the rule of law is justiciable to the extent that any law or conduct inconsistent with it may be declared unconstitutional and invalid.[21]

Importantly, in tandem with the other constitutional principles, the rule of law:

> tie[s] the provisions of the Constitution together and shape[s] them into a framework that defines the new constitutional order. *The basic principles therefore influence the interpretation of many other provisions of the Constitution, including the provisions of the Bill of Rights which must be interpreted consistently with them.* The Constitution, in turn, shapes the ordinary law and must inform the way legislation is drafted by the legislature and interpreted by the courts.[22]

The rule of law thus provides a standard of constitutionality in terms of which other law and conduct must be measured; it very directly provides an interpretative framework for constitutional provisions; it indirectly provides an interpretative framework for all other laws; and because it contains procedural and substantive elements, it has the potential to strengthen commitments to legality.[23] The rule of law protects against abuse of government power and arbitrary decision-making by requiring that all law and government conduct be rationally related to a legitimate government purpose and it requires government to protect the individual's basic fundamental rights.[24] It elevates constitutional law by subjecting everyone and all actions to the authority and to the rule of constitutional law; and because it provides a measure and standard for constitutional interpretation to the courts, it automatically elevates the courts to the status of supreme guardians of the rule of law.

3. Extending the rule of law to nature

What does the rule of law mean in the environmental context (or the rule of law for nature)? There are various possible manifestations of the rule

---

[20] Section 7(2) of the Constitution.
[21] Currie and De Waal, *The Bill of Rights Handbook*, 7.
[22] Ibid., 7–8 (emphasis added).
[23] Dyzenhaus, 'The Pasts and Future of the Rule of Law', 738.
[24] Currie and De Waal, *The Bill of Rights Handbook*, 11–12.

of law for nature. In the United Sates during the 1960s, a 'rule of law litigation' strategy was used to serve as a 'counter-pressure to the inevitable swings in legislative and executive enthusiasm for environmental protection'.[25] It created the possibility to satisfy environmental interests by using the orthodox manifestation of the rule of law through litigation, namely to keep in check the executive and legislature acting 'outside', or abusing the law, and to force these authorities to comply with environmental obligations. As a consequence, courts were able to step forward as environmental champions to keep these abuses in check and thereby to uphold the rule of law.[26] The rule of law for nature has also been described as a strategy to make environmental laws more effective, and as a strategy that aims to ensure better environmental law compliance and enforcement.[27] Another view posits the rule of law for nature as meaning better administrative decision-making and compliance with administrative justice and the associated practice of good environmental governance.[28] In this respect it has been shown by one empirical study that the 'rule of law raises governance capacity, which directly improves environmental policy and economic development'.[29] These manifestations all satisfy the procedural characteristics of the rule of law's traditional incarnation. In the environmental context it would entail: the need for government to be subjected to the general law and, more specifically, to environmental laws; the need for government to only act in accordance with the law; the ability of the courts to oversee government actions, including their administrative and legislative functions that are relevant to environmental issues; the need for government to be accountable and to exercise just administrative action and general good environmental governance practices; and the process to make good environmental laws.

The substantive dimension of the rule of law for nature is the extent to which it could be used to create, maintain, improve and/or protect the substantive 'goodness' of environmental laws and thus environmental interests. In this sense, the rule of law for nature must be understood in

---

[25] Tarlock, 'The Future of Environmental "Rule of Law" Litigation', 244.
[26] Ibid., 241.
[27] Richard J. Ferris and Zhang Hongjun, 'Reaching Out to the Rule of Law: China's Continuing Efforts to Develop a More Effective Environmental Law Regime', 11 *William and Mary Bill of Rights Journal* (2003) 570–602.
[28] David S. Tatel, 'The Administrative Process and the Rule of Environmental Law', 34 *Harvard Environmental Law Review* (2010) 1–8.
[29] Meng-jieu Chen, *Rule of Law and Environmental Policy Stringency*, Institute for the Study of Aspects of International Competition (ISIAC Working Paper 10–3), available at: http://web.uri.edu/isiac/files/wp10-3.pdf (last accessed 14 June 2013).

terms of the broader issue of environmental constitutionalism, which is a value-laden concept that exudes numerous characteristics that could legitimize, dignify and improve a legal order.[30] Being a part of environmental constitutionalism, the rule of law for nature, among others, provides the opportunity and the means by which to reform environmental governance and laws; it prioritizes environmental care by equating it at the higher constitutional level to fundamental rights, ethics and universal moral values; it provides a legitimate foundation and means for creating and enforcing environmental rights, values and other sources of ecological obligation; it provides the means to dictate the content of laws; and it establishes moral and ethical obligations with respect to the environment and a justificatory basis for, and authority to require, proper performance of these obligations.[31]

4. Sustainable development and the rule of law for nature

Unlike the rule of law, sustainable development is not mentioned in any of the founding provisions of the Constitution. On its own, sustainable development therefore does not constitute a constitutional value or explicit constitutional principle, as is the case with the rule of law. Yet sustainable development is a constitutional issue and it is constitutionally entrenched in South Africa in various ways.

First, sustainable development is *indirectly* implied by the constitutional context and constitutional values, including human dignity, equality and freedom. People could presumably only lead a dignified life and enjoy equal access to social benefits, economic opportunities and environmental resources if these are available in equal measure to all. At the same time, the improvement of people's quality of life will necessarily encompass all sustainability considerations including social, economic and ecological conditions. Put differently, the broader constitutional ideals, and the specific objectives of human dignity, equality and human rights protection, can only be achieved if 'development' in its broadest sense is also socially, economically and ecologically sustainable. Moreover, while the aspect of 'freedom' as a constitutional value is not elaborated in the Constitution, South Africa's oppressive history, the context of

---

[30] Anne Peters, *The Constitutionalist Reconstruction of International Law: Pros and Cons* (NCCR International Trade Working Paper No. 11 (07–2006), at 3.
[31] Louis J. Kotzé, 'Arguing Global Environmental Constitutionalism', 1 *Transnational Environmental Law* (2012) 199–233, at 210.

constitutional reform and the objectives of the Constitution collectively suggest that people should not only be free from political oppression, but also free from social oppression, economic hardship and deleterious ecological impacts that could impact freedom. In this way sustainable development is indirectly implied and required by the Constitution, and the 'new' constitutional dispensation will only prevail if it occurs within a sustainability paradigm.

Second, a central (if not *the* central) component of the Constitution is the Bill of Rights, which, in the words of the Constitution itself, is considered the 'cornerstone of democracy in South Africa'.[32] The Bill of Rights 'enshrines the rights of all people ... and affirms the democratic values of human dignity, equality and freedom'.[33] Like other jurisdictions in the world,[34] the South African Constitution provides an environmental right that states that:

> Everyone has the right:
> (a) To an environment that is not harmful to their health or well-being; and
> (b) *To have the environment protected, for the benefit of present and future generations*, through reasonable legislative and other measures that:
>   (i) Prevent pollution and ecological degradation;
>   (ii) Promote conservation; and
>   (iii) *Secure ecologically sustainable development and use of natural resources while promoting justifiable economic and social development.*[35]

The wording of this section suggests that sustainable development is an explicit constitutional objective to the extent that it is inherent to the environmental right. This means that government must achieve, advance, respect, protect and promote the sustainable development objectives of the right. The right clearly contains the inter- and intragenerational characteristics typically associated with sustainable development and it articulates the constitutional objective to create a balance between ecological, social and economic considerations.

The National Environmental Management Act 107 of 1998 (NEMA) is South Africa's central environmental framework Act and is considered to give effect to the environmental right and the loftier constitutional ideals

---

[32] Section 7(1).   [33] Ibid.
[34] See generally, David R. Boyd, *The Environmental Rights Revolution: A Global Study of Constitutions, Human Rights, and the Environment* (Vancouver: UBC Press, 2012).
[35] Section 24 (emphasis added).

related to the right.[36] NEMA defines sustainable development as 'the integration of social, economic and environmental factors into planning, implementation and decision-making so as to ensure that development serves present and future generations'.[37] The Act understands sustainable development to be a process and balancing measure that seeks to consider social, economic and ecological factors when engaged with governing development in its broadest sense, with the objective of ensuring inter- and intragenerational equity.

Third, despite the strong language in favour of sustainable development, nothing in the right, or elsewhere in the Constitution, suggests that people have a 'right to sustainable development'. People only have a right to demand environmental protection, which in turn must be accomplished by means of legislative and 'other' measures that must secure sustainable development. The right nevertheless obliges the government to achieve sustainable development through legislative and other measures that must protect the environment, also in temporal terms, by regulating pollution, promoting conservation and securing a balance between ecological, social and economic considerations.

In sum, sustainable development, as an element of environmental constitutionalism in South Africa, assumes some of the procedural and substantive characteristics of the rule of law for nature. As a constitutional issue, sustainable development is therefore directly related to the rule of law for nature. It incorporates the procedural aspects of the rule of law for nature to the extent that it provides a standard for the creation and execution of reasonable legislative and other administrative measures that must aim to protect the environment for the present and future generations. It does so by using the content and the objectives of the environmental right as the prevailing standard or baseline for the rule of law for nature. Additionally, all legislative and administrative measures must achieve certain substantive objectives such as environmental protection. Thus, if a government agency fails to promulgate legislation that does not correspond to these procedural and substantive requirements, that legislation could very well militate against the rule of law for nature. Or where an administrative decision is taken in terms of legislation, for example to allow mining in an ecologically sensitive area, and where that decision does not properly consider the impacts on present and future generations, it could similarly breach the rule of law for nature. Importantly, in those instances where deviations from the rule of law for nature are evident,

---

[36] See the Preamble to NEMA.   [37] Section 1.

it would be possible to declare legislation and administrative decisions unconstitutional and invalid.[38]

5. A judicial appraisal

To what extent has sustainable development contributed to upholding the rule of law for nature in South Africa? In the landmark decision of *BP Southern Africa* v. *MEC for Agriculture, Conservation, Environment and Land Affairs* (*BP Southern Africa*),[39] the applicant (the petroleum company BP Southern Africa) applied to the government (the environmental authority and respondent) for an environmental authorization to establish and operate a filling station that would have been closely situated next to other filling stations. The environmental authority refused the authorization because, among other reasons, there already existed two filling stations in close proximity to the proposed development and the authority considered that this would have had adverse environmental *and* socio-economic impacts. BP argued that the environmental authority did not have the mandate to decide on socio-economic issues and that its mandate only included environmental issues. BP stated that:

> the department's refusal of its application had been its desire to regulate the economy so as to protect the commercial interests of existing filling stations. Such commercial interests … were a socio-economic consideration which were unrelated to and had no significant relationship to the environment and which the department had therefore not been entitled to take into account in reaching its decision.[40]

The High Court disagreed with BP and found that the environmental authority's mandate also included an assessment of socio-economic considerations when it had to evaluate environmental impacts:

> environmental rights requirements should be part and parcel of the factors to be considered without any *a priori* grading of the rights. It will require a balancing of rights where competing interests and norms are concerned. This is in line with the injunction in s 24*(b)*(iii) that *ecologically sustainable development and the use of natural resources are to be promoted jointly with justifiable economic and social development*. The balancing of environmental interests with justifiable economic and social development is to be conceptualised well beyond the interests of the present living generation. This must be correct since s 24*(b)* requires

---

[38] See the discussion above in section 2.
[39] 2004 (5) SA 124 (W).   [40] Paras. C–D at p. 125.

the environment to be protected for the benefit of 'present and future generations'.[41]

Sustainable development, in the Court's view, entailed a consideration of many factors including: the need to preserve natural systems for the benefit of future generations; the aim of exploiting natural resources in a manner that is equitable, sustainable, prudent, rational, wise and appropriate; and the need to ensure that environmental considerations are incorporated into economic and other development considerations.[42] This interpretation corresponds with the constitutional scope, content and meaning of sustainable development and it led the Court to conclude that:

> It has been held that the goal of attaining sustainable development is likely to play a major role in determining important environmental disputes in the future. This is so because sustainable development constitutes an integral part of modern international law and will balance the competing demands of development and environmental protection. *The concept of 'sustainable development' is the fundamental building block around which environmental legal norms have been fashioned, both internationally and in South Africa,* and is reflected in s 24(b)(iii) of the Constitution. Pure economic principles will no longer determine, in an unbridled fashion, whether a development is acceptable. Development, which may be regarded as economically and financially sound, will, in future, be balanced by its environmental impact, taking coherent cognisance of the principle of intergenerational equity and sustainable use of resources in order to arrive at an *integrated management of the environment, sustainable development and socio-economic concerns.*[43]

More recently, the Constitutional Court utilized sustainable development in an even more profound manner in *Fuel Retailers Association of Southern Africa v. Director General: Environmental Management, Department of Agriculture, Conservation and Environment, Mpumalanga Province* (*Fuel Retailers*).[44] Like the *BP Southern Africa* judgment, *Fuel Retailers* dealt with the nature and scope of the obligations of environmental authorities when they make decisions that could affect the environment. More particularly, it was concerned with 'the interaction between social and economic development and the protection of the environment'[45] during decision-making. As in *BP Southern Africa*, a developer applied for an environmental authorization to construct a filling station. The environmental

---

[41] Paras. C–D at p. 143 (emphasis added).
[42] Paras. G–I at p. 143.
[43] Paras. A–D at p. 144 (emphasis added).
[44] 2007 (6) SA 4 (CC). [45] Para. A at p. 8.

authority (the respondent) granted the authorization, but this decision was appealed by the applicant (the Fuel Retailers Association). One of the grounds of appeal was that the need, desirability and sustainability of the proposed filling station had not been considered by the authority and, similar to *BP Southern Africa*, that the proposed filling station would be closely situated to other filling stations that already adequately served the needs of the community. The applicant applied to the Constitutional Court for a review of the authority's decision to allow the filling station, based on the contention that the environmental authority did *not* consider the socio-economic impacts of the filling station, while it was clearly under a statutory obligation to do so. The authority, however, was of the opinion that it was not necessary for it to do so since another environmental authority involved in the authorization process (the municipality) had already considered the 'need and desirability' of the proposed filling station. This, they argued, was similar to socio-economic considerations that have already been considered. The Constitutional Court ultimately found that the environmental authority had misconstrued the nature of its obligations under NEMA, and as a consequence had failed to apply its mind to the socio-economic impact of the proposed filling station.

In its decision, the Court confirmed that NEMA provides for sustainable development that 'requires environmental authorities to consider the social, economic and environmental impact of a proposed activity including its disadvantages and benefits'.[46] Importantly, it also confirmed that sustainable development is a constitutional issue:

> This case raises an important question concerning the obligation of State organs when making decisions that may have a substantial impact on the environment ... The need to protect the environment cannot be gainsaid. So, too, is the need for social and economic development. How these two compelling needs interact, their impact on decisions affecting the environment and the obligations of environmental authorities in this regard, are *important constitutional questions*.[47]

This illustrates the remarkable appreciation of the Constitutional Court for sustainable development in the constitutional context; it recognizes that sustainable development is a 'superior' constitutional issue, not merely a policy matter or statutory measure; the obligation to ensure sustainable development cannot merely be assumed, some deliberate governance intervention is required and sustainable development therefore

---

[46] Para. D at p. 9.
[47] Para. I at p. 20 to para. A at p. 21 (emphasis added).

creates governance obligations; and at the core of these obligations is the duty to consider and balance social, economic and ecological interests.

The Court then launched into an interrogation of sustainable development and found that:[48]

> development cannot subsist upon a deteriorating environmental base. Unlimited development is detrimental to the environment and the destruction of the environment is detrimental to development. Promotion of development requires the protection of the environment. Yet the environment cannot be protected if development does not pay attention to the costs of environmental destruction. The environment and development are thus inexorably linked.[49]

Quoting from the Brundtland Commission Report, the Court acknowledged that '[E]conomy is not just about the production of wealth, and ecology is not just about the protection of nature; they are both equally relevant for improving the lot of humankind'.[50] It added that:

> The idea that development and environmental protection must be reconciled is central to the concept of sustainable development. At the core of this Principle [sic] is the principle of integration of environmental protection and socio-economic development ... The practical significance of the integration of the environmental and developmental considerations is that environmental considerations will now increasingly be a feature of economic and development policy.[51]

Here the Court clearly recognizes that socio-economic development cannot be divorced from ecological considerations. In this sense sustainable development is not only a constitutional objective, it is also a 'mediating principle' and approach to resolve the conflict that inevitably arises between competing social, economic and ecological considerations. In the words of the Court, the integration principle 'implies the need to reconcile and accommodate these three pillars of sustainable development', and '[s]ustainable development provides a framework for reconciling socio-economic development and environmental protection'.[52]

---

[48] Para. C at p. 21.
[49] Paras. E–H at p. 21. This view was reaffirmed by J. Sachs in his dissenting judgment at para. I at p. 2 to paras. A–B at p. 45.
[50] Paras. A–B at p. 22 and Report of the World Commission on Environment and Development, Chapter 1, para. 42.
[51] Paras. A, F–G at p. 24.   [52] Paras. E–F at p. 25.

6. Conclusion

The foregoing analysis suggests that sustainable development can play a meaningful role in upholding the rule of law for nature in South Africa. First, sustainable development has clearly been characterized by the courts as a constitutional objective that, in tandem with the loftier ideals of constitutionalism and the rule of law, should strive to fulfil the objectives of the environmental right and environmental protection more generally. Through a constitutional lens, sustainable development is part of: law that transcends all other law; fundamental law that is onerous to amend or to repeal; law that curtails political power and state authority; law that reflects the living law of the people, deriving its legitimacy from a social contract and its authority from the sovereignty of the people; and law that exudes an ethical core in the form of universal fundamental rights and 'higher' constitutional values.[53]

Second, 'development' must be approached by the government in terms of its three-pillared manifestation. Thus, where the government must authorize a proposed development, it will have to consider the social, economic and ecological aspects of that development; this requirement is of a 'mandatory nature and the materiality of the requirement is manifest'.[54] In this way, a measure of respect for the rule of law for nature will be maintained. Nevertheless, in any sustainability assessment by authorities and the courts, there are no, and neither can there be any, absolutes. While it may very well be that no development will have some ecological benefits, where appropriate, socio-economic development must also be allowed if it is justifiable:[55]

> Sustainable development does not require the cessation of socio-economic development but seeks to regulate the manner in which it takes place. It recognises that socio-economic development invariably brings risk of environmental damage as it puts pressure on environmental resources. It envisages that decision-makers guided by the concept of sustainable development will ensure that socio-economic developments remain firmly attached to their ecological roots and that these roots are protected and nurtured so that they may support future socio-economic developments.[56]

---

[53] Kotzé, 'Arguing Global Environmental Constitutionalism', 205.
[54] *Fuel Retailers*, para. D at p. 36.
[55] See section 24 of the Constitution, which sets 'justifiability' as a requirement for sustainable development.
[56] *Fuel Retailers*, paras. C–D at p. 26.

Third, if the rule of law for nature also means protecting environmental interests at the expense of socio-economic interests, then sustainable development has played a meaningful role in providing the balancing measure to the courts in their efforts to uphold the rule of law for nature. But the obligation on the authorities and the courts does not stop there. Equally important would be the obligation on authorities and the courts to consider the temporal aspects of a development that are couched in terms of equity, both in an intra- and intergenerational sense:

> The very idea of sustainability implies continuity. It reflects a concern for social and developmental equity between generations, a concern that must logically be extended to equity within each generation. This concern is reflected in the principles of inter-generational and intra-generational equity which are embodied in both s 24 of the Constitution and the principles of environmental management contained in NEMA.[57]

More specifically, '[E]nvironmental concerns do not commence and end once the proposed development is approved. It is a continuing concern … environmental legislation imposes a continuing, and thus necessarily evolving, obligation to ensure the sustainability of the development.'[58] Authorities and courts will therefore have to take a long-term view of the impacts, costs and benefits of a development when using sustainable development as a mediating or reconciliatory approach in governance and dispute resolution.

Fourth, the fact that the courts are willing to step forward as the guardians of the rule of law for nature through their generous interpretation of sustainable development is encouraging and it harks back to the idea of 'rule of law litigation' in the USA, as explained above. The Constitutional Court confirmed in *Fuel Retailers* with reference to the Johannesburg Principles adopted at the Global Judges' Symposium during the World Summit on Sustainable Development in 2002:

> The role of the courts is especially important in the context of the protection of the environment and giving effect to the principle of sustainable development. The importance of the protection of the environment cannot be gainsaid. Its protection is vital to the enjoyment of the other rights contained in the Bill of Rights; indeed, it is vital to life itself. It must therefore be protected for the benefit of the present and future generations. The present generation holds the earth in trust for the next generation. This trusteeship position carries with it the responsibility to look after the

---

[57] Ibid., paras. D–E at p. 32.   [58] Ibid., para. E at p. 33.

environment. It is the duty of the Court to ensure that this responsibility is carried out.[59]

This oversight role bodes well for a constitutional environmental governance dispensation that should seek to promote the procedural and substantive aspects of the rule of law for nature.

---

[59] Ibid., at paras. H–I at p. 39.

8

The principle of sustainable development

Integration and ecological integrity

CHRISTINA VOIGT

1. Introduction

On 26 April 2012 it was twenty-five years since the Brundtland Report *Our Common Future*[1] was published. Twenty-five years have passed since the concept of sustainable development gained currency in international affairs – and law; twenty-five years that it has been repeated in thousands of legally binding and non-binding documents. Has the world become more sustainable in this quarter of a century? The answer is a qualified 'no'.

In 2002, at the advent of the Johannesburg Summit, former UN General Secretary Kofi Annan had already issued the following warning: 'Unsustainable practices are woven deeply into the fabric of modern life. Some say we should rip up that fabric.' In Johannesburg, sustainability was not just adopted as one of the Millennium Development Goals. It was recognized, as Annan clearly stated, as 'a *prerequisite* for reaching *all* of the others'.[2]

In 2012, the 'Zero Draft' for the Rio+20 conference intended for heads of state and government to note that 'unsustainable development has increased the stress on earth's limited natural resources and on the carrying capacity of ecosystems'.[3] In the final version, this was changed to: 'We recognize that urgent action on unsustainable patterns of production and consumption where they occur remains fundamental in addressing environmental sustainability and promoting conservation and sustainable use

---

[1] World Commission on Environment and Development (WCED), *Our Common Future* (Oxford University Press, 1987).
[2] Statement by Secretary-General Kofi A. Annan, Johannesburg, South Africa, 3 September 2002. UN Press Release, SG/SM/8358, AFR/468, ENV/DEV/693.
[3] Zero Draft, 'The Future We Want', January 2012, available at: www.uncsd2012.org/thefuturewewant.html (last accessed 18 February 2013).

of biodiversity and ecosystems, regeneration of natural resources and the promotion of sustained, inclusive and equitable global growth.'[4] Right before Rio+20, the Global Environmental Outlook 5 provided proof of the deterioration of a large number of essential ecosystem services and cautioned that 'if humanity does not urgently change its ways, several critical thresholds may be exceeded, beyond which abrupt and generally irreversible changes to the life-support functions of the planet could occur'.[5] Apparently, not much has happened. Twenty-five years of the concept of sustainable development has certainly not made much of a difference.

There are many reasons for this state of affairs: states' immediate economic self-interest, the absence of political willingness and power to change the world towards sustainability and the clashing of a plurality of 'equally important' objectives and interests, to mention some.

There are, however, also reasons *inherent* in the conceptualization of sustainable development. One key aspect of sustainable development is the *integration* of environmental, economic and social objectives.[6] Integration is often understood as a merely procedural requirement. In the worst case it is perceived as meaning simply taking note of environmental aspects ('green washing'), while pushing the agenda of unconstrained economic development and cost-effectiveness. At best, it is understood as implying the balancing of three seemingly equally important elements.[7] Both conceptions are wrong. Integration understood in these ways is nothing more than a dangerous game; almost certainly leading to unsustainable results. Integration without a goal or purpose is simply meaningless. Integration needs to happen within a proper framework for decision-making and pertain to an overarching goal.

Sustainable development can only be achieved in the context of the rule of law, requiring fair, effective and transparent international and national governance arrangements and clear and implementable environmental laws. In particular the latter aspect of the rule of law demands a delimitation of the framework for integration. This chapter suggests that

---

[4] *The Future We Want*, FN Doc. A/CONF.216/L.1, 19 June 2012, para. 61.
[5] UNEP, Global Environment Outlook 5, Press release: *World Remains on Unsustainable Track Despite Hundreds of Internationally Agreed Goals and Objectives*, 6 June 2012, available at: www.unep.org/geo/geo5.asp (last accessed 18 February 2013).
[6] ILA, Committee on International Law on Sustainable Development, Resolution 07/12, and ILA Resolution 3/2002, annex as published as UN Doc. A/57/329, *New Delhi Declaration of Principles of International Law Relating to Sustainable Development*, available at: www.ila-hq.org (last accessed 18 February 2013).
[7] See *The Future We Want*, talking about 'the *balanced* integration of the three dimensions of sustainable development', paras. 76, 83, 87, 100 (emphasis added).

integration has to be made subject to the ultimate goal of ecological integrity – or ecosystem integrity – in order to be meaningful.

At Rio+20 heads of state and government recognized in this regard that:

> planet Earth and its ecosystems are our home ... and we note that some countries recognize the rights of nature in the context of the promotion of sustainable development. We are convinced that in order to achieve a just balance among the economic, social and environmental needs of present and future generations, it is necessary to promote harmony with nature.[8]

In this context, they called for 'holistic and integrated approaches to sustainable development that will guide humanity to live in harmony with nature and lead to efforts to restore the health and integrity of the Earth's ecosystem'.[9]

In the following, we will explore what integration means and what the purpose of integration is. This brings us to the question of limits. At the same time, it will reveal to us (one of) the reason(s) for the failure of sustainable development – so far – in guiding the development, implementation and interpretation of law in a truly sustainable way. Finally, we attempt to develop some ideas of how to remedy this situation.

2. What does integration mean?

Integration is the process of 'mak[ing] whole or becoming complete; bring[ing] (parts) together into a whole ... remov[ing] barriers imposing segregation'.[10] Integration in the context of sustainable development is process, but it is also substance.

The International Law Association (ILA) Committee on International Law on Sustainable Development defined the principle of integration as the key feature of its work. The Committee noted that '[i]ntegration is pivotal to the promotion of sustainable development. It is the principle of integration that both brings together the many challenges confronting the international community and, at the same time, provides the most realistic chance of their solution'.[11] In other words, the principle of integration 'forms the backbone of sustainable development'.[12]

---

[8] Ibid., para. 31.   [9] Ibid., para. 40.
[10] *Webster's New World Dictionary and Thesaurus* (2004), 354.
[11] See ILA, Committee on International Law on Sustainable Development Seventy-First Report, Berlin Conference 2004, 13.
[12] 1995 Report of the CSD Expert Group on Identification of Principles of International Law for Sustainable Development, Paper No. 3, para. 15.

At the legislative, administrative and judicial level, the integration of sustainable development's multitude of elements usually refers to the need to take all aspects into account, that is, states must ensure that economic and social interests, where they are represented, do not disregard environmental considerations. Similarly, when measures are undertaken for purposes of environmental protection, their economic or social implications need to be taken into account. What does that mean? Can sustainable development really 'be defined as a concept which attempts to integrate environmental considerations into economic and other development and which takes into account other than environmental needs while formulating the principles of environmental protection'[13] – and still make sense? This sounds like the hotchpotch of environmental, social and economic issues that Klaus Bosselmann is so critical of in his chapter in this book.[14] Such an approach does not tell us anything about the purpose of integration or its direction. Balancing without a goal is an empty exercise – and it is part of the reason for the current state of affairs.

An illustrative example of this situation comes from Norwegian domestic law. The Norwegian Nature Diversity Act 2009 notes as its purpose the following: 'The purpose of this Act is to protect biological, geological and landscape diversity and ecological processes through conservation and sustainable use, and in such a way that the environment provides a basis for human activity, culture, health and well-being, now and in the future, including a basis for Sami culture.'[15] Following this provision are principles for decision-making, such as the requirement that decision-making shall be based on sound science, the precautionary principle, an ecosystem approach and an assessment of the cumulative environmental effects on the ecosystem now or in the future.[16] While all this is very positive, there is a major drawback later in the Act. Section 14, titled 'Other important public interests', deals with balancing of diverse interests by simply stating: 'Measures under this Act shall be weighed against other important public interests.'[17]

Such weighing, as prescribed under section 14, includes economic, social and cultural interests, as well as effective resource management.

---

[13] M. Fitzmaurice, *Recueil des Cours*, vol. 293 (Leiden: Brill, 2001), 47.
[14] See Chapter 4 by Klaus Bosselmann in this book.
[15] *Naturmangfoldloven*, LOV-2009-06-19-100, Section 1 (purpose of the Act).
[16] Ibid., Chapter II.
[17] Ibid., Chapter II, Section 14.

Measures to protect nature diversity must be proportional to the consequences of these measures for other sectors of society, local communities and individuals.[18]

What do we see here? A legal requirement of balancing ('weighing against') that does not say much about its purpose or direction. If other interests are considered to be 'important' enough, then 'protecting biological, geological and landscape diversity and ecological processes' can simply be 'balanced away'. The text leaves a wide margin of discretion for decision-making by municipalities, both in determining what the other public interests are, the importance of these other interests (relative to what?) and the final setting of priorities. As a result of such wide margin of appreciation, in most countries the substance of the decision cannot be reviewed by a court. This means that once the decision has been taken, it is final.

The standard view is to accord the divergent elements equal importance. As a result, integration is perceived as a balancing act with supposedly unavoidable trade-offs – often on the environmental side.[19] In fact, trade-offs are the very essence of 'balancing'. However, some trade-offs cannot be made without rendering the outcome unsustainable.

If integration, as defined above, really is the process of 'making whole or becoming complete; bringing together into a whole', then certainly something more has to be in place than just the art of arbitrary juggling with different objectives of indeterminate importance. While there is no doubt that balancing environmental, economic and social factors is pivotal for sustainable development, it does not necessarily mean treating all three (or more) in the same manner. Equal treatment can be no more than an illusory or idealized goal in the absence of conceptual clarity.

The challenge is therefore to *delimit* the frame for the 'balancing process'. Integration in the context of sustainable development raises the fundamental question of whether economic, social and environmental interests are of equal importance or whether their obvious interconnectedness needs to be brought into some sort of systematic relationship in order to give the concept meaning.

---

[18] I. L. Backer, *Naturmangfoldloven Kommentarutgave* (Oslo: Universitetsforlaget, 2010), 117–18.

[19] Why trade-offs often occur to the detriment of environmental interests is explained in the excellent chapter (Chapter 1) by Hans Christian Bugge in this book.

3. The purpose of integration

As said above: Integration is 'mak[ing] whole or becoming complete; bring[ing] (parts) together into a whole'. The desired outcome of this process is integrity – generally defined as completeness, wholeness or unimpaired condition. In the context of sustainable development it is *environmental* integrity. Or more accurately: human development that (at a minimum) sustains important biophysical processes that support plant, animal and human life and that must be allowed to continue without significant change. The objective is to assure the continued health of the essential life support systems of nature, including air, water and soil, by protecting the resilience, diversity and purity of ecosystems.[20]

The priority of protecting ecosystem services does not per se derive from the concept of integration, but from the purpose of sustainable development to which it pertains. Sustainable development implies that ecological functions exist that are indispensable for a durable and equitable human society. Scientists use the term 'ecological' or 'ecosystem' services when referring to the conditions and processes through which natural ecosystems sustain and fulfil human life.[21]

Natural ecosystems provide the critical basis for all human societies. For a long time the fact has remained uncontested that societies derive a wide array of important life-support and economic benefits from the ecosystems in which they exit.[22] In later years an understanding across various disciplines has crystallized the idea, that human development, security, peace – humanity per se – depends on healthy ecological functions and conditions.[23] Sustainable development requires nations to set out and implement concrete

---

[20] For a description of ecosystem health, see Chapter 9 by Froukje M. Platjouw in this book.

[21] Ecosystem services are thus the functions carried out by ecosystems, including the benefits people obtain. The 2005 Millennium Ecosystem Assessment systemizes them into provisioning services such as food, water, timber and fibre; regulating services that affect climate, floods, disease, wastes, and water quality; cultural services that provide recreational, aesthetic and spiritual benefits; and supporting services such as soil formation, photosynthesis and nutrient-cycling. Millennium Ecosystem Assessment: *Living Beyond Our Means*, 2005, 3. See also G. D. Daily, *Nature's Services: Societal Dependence on Natural Ecosystems* (Washington, DC: Island Press, 1997).

[22] An ecosystem is a dynamic complex of plant, animal and microorganism communities and the non-living environment interacting as a functional unit.

[23] The ecological fundament of sustainable development can be based on arguments from various disciplines. On economic arguments, see, e.g., *OECD Environmental Outlook to 2050: The Consequences of Inaction* (Paris: OECD, 2012); Millennium Ecosystem Assessment, *Living Beyond Our Means* (Washington, DC: Millennium Ecosystem

goals that submit all other activities under the protection of those essential natural conditions on which human societies depend.[24]

This was something the World Commission called for, and it is essential still. 'At a minimum,' the Commission stated, 'sustainable development must not endanger the natural systems that support life on Earth,' adding that there were objective limits to what nature could bear.[25]

Integration in the context of sustainable development thus means to respect these functions as an absolute priority. They are irreplaceable on a global and temporal scale: neither knowledge, nor technology, nor economic wealth could provide any substitute.[26]

4. The 'inconvenient truth' of ecological integrity: limits

The discourse on sustainable development is almost clinically void of a discussion of limits. But this is part and parcel of the problem.

Assessment, 2005); N. Stern, *Stern Review – Report on the Economics of Climate Change* (Cambridge University Press, 2006); or The Economics of Ecosystems and Biodiversity (TEEB), *Ecological and Economic Foundations* (Washington, DC: Earthscan, 2010). On human rights-based arguments, see, e.g., Analytical Study on the Relationship between Human Rights and the Environment, Report of the United Nations High Commissioner on Human Rights (UN Doc. A/HRC/19/34, 16 December 2011), Report of the Office of the United Nations High Commissioner for Human Rights (UN Doc. A/HRC/10/61, 15 January 2009) as well as several Human Right Council Resolutions: 10/4, Human Rights and Climate Change (UN Doc. A/HRC/L, 25 March 2009), and 19/10, Human Rights and the Environment (UN Doc. A/HRC/19/19, 22 March 2012). On moral arguments, see, e.g., K. Bosselmann, 'The Concept of Sustainable Development', in K. Bosselmann and D. Grinlinton (eds.), *Environmental Law for a Sustainable Society* (Auckland: New Zealand Centre for Environmental Law, 2002), 81–96; H. C. Bugge, 'The Ethics of Sustainable Development – a Challenge to the Legal System', in E. M. Basse (ed.), *Bæredyktighed – en retsteoretisk begrepsanalyse* (Copenhagen: GradJura, 1995), 27–38; Edith Brown Weiss, *In Fairness to Future Generations: International Law, Common Patrimony and Intergenerational Equity* (New York: Transnational Publishers, 1989); E. B. Weiss, 'Intergenerational Equity in International Law' (1987) 81 *ASIL Procs* 126–33; E. B. Weiss, 'The Planetary Trust: Conservation and Intergenerational Equity' (1984) 11 *Ecology Law Quarterly* 495. And on ecological argument, see Daily, *Nature's Services*.

[24] Unnerstall notes accordingly: 'Der Vorrang des Umweltschutzes ergibt sich nicht per se aus dem Integrationsansatz ... sondern aus dem Ziel "nachhaltiger Entwicklung", auf das er gerichtet ist.' H. Unnerstall 'Nachhaltige Entwicklung und intergenerationelle Gerechtigkeit im Europarecht', in M. Bobbert, M. Düwell and K. Jax (eds.), *Umwelt, Ethik, Recht* (Tübingen: Francke Verlag, 2003), 146.

[25] WCED, *Our Common Future*, 44–5.

[26] See Daily, *Nature's Services*. A preliminary estimation of the economic value of the services provided to humans by ecological systems and the global natural capital stock that produces them ranges them at a price-level of US$54 trillion annually, compared to a

The Brundtland Report had already warned: 'But ultimate limits there are.'[27]

Integration in the context of sustainable development with the purpose of securing environmental integrity demands that ultimate ecological thresholds are respected. These thresholds define the ecological constraints for human activities and development, without which development cannot be sustainable.

These ecological limits – or planetary boundaries – are not unknown. There is a wealth of scientific data and knowledge.[28] These limits, defined on a planetary scale, need to be broken down to state level as obligations under international law and further defined at sub-state levels, such as regional, municipal, local, city, village even individual levels. There is no hocus-pocus in that. Science has the answers. What is missing, however, is the willingness of states and sub-state actors to act accordingly. The current state of the environment is not caused by failure or accident. It is wanted.

In the context of integration – as in the context of environmental lawmaking in general – the discussion of ecological limits has to be revived, and these limits need to be defined and included in the legal framework by clear, comprehensive, implementable and reviewable rules, for example such as air, soil, biodiversity or water quality standards. Ecological limits as a determining factor of the substance of legal rules is perhaps as close as we get to a rule of law for nature.

Once it is clear that some interests are more essential than others, it should also be clear that integration as a principle of sustainable development does not and cannot (necessarily and under all circumstances) mean giving equal weight to all concerns. Integration is eventually about making compromises. But these compromises have to be sustainable and – even more crucially – the *sum* of the compromises has to be sustainable, because it will be the *sum* of all measures that gives an indication of their sustainability.

By constituting these essential ecological conditions as a *de minimis* requirement of sustainable development, the concept inhabits a non-derogable ecological core. At this core lie the 'unchanging and universal

---

gross global product of US$18 trillion annually. See R. Constanza *et al.*, 'The Value of the World's Ecosystem Services and Natural Capital' 387 *Nature* (1997) 253–60.

[27] WCED, *Our Common Future*, 45.

[28] See, e.g., Millennium Ecosystem Assessment *Living Beyond Our Means*; J. Rockström *et al.*, 'Planetary Boundaries: Exploring the Safe Operating Space for Humanity' 14:2 *Ecology and Society* (2009) 32.

laws of nature' with which human activities need to be brought into and kept in harmony.[29] This core must be used as a point of departure and a 'principled priority' guide on how otherwise widely divergent priorities relate to each other. Thus, when integrating the components of sustainable development, priority must be given to protecting fundamental, natural life-supporting systems in principle and in practice. This aspect of sustainable development is the most fundamental – the one without which the concept becomes indeterminate and eventually meaningless.

5. Sustainable development as a general principle of law

What is sustainable development, then? Is it an objective, a concept, a process, a principle, or all of those things?[30] My argument is that it is a general principle of law. Its normative force, broad scope and support in the international community are indicative of its principled character and make it difficult to argue otherwise.[31]

Sustainable development has a normative content that is defined by the reconciliation of present and future economic, social and environmental interests within the limits set by certain essential ecological functions. Sustainable development has been recognized widely both by international and national legislatures and jurisprudential practice. This general recognition of its normative content can be understood as forming an *opinio juris communis*. The classification of sustainable development as a general principle of law according to Article 38.1(c) of the Statute of the International Court of Justice is thus legitimized by its widespread use in many national legal systems and in international law – signifying a common conscience – and the jurisprudence of international courts and tribunals, as well as by its moral necessity.

---

[29] This is what the WCED had already noted on: 'Human laws must be reformulated to keep human activities in harmony with the unchanging and universal laws of nature.' WCED, *Our Common Future*, 330. It can be claimed that, eventually, the concept is about values. See also *Outcome of Rio+20*, footnote 4 above. The ILA's International Committee on International Law on Sustainable Development recognizes that in order to acknowledge the concept's underlying challenges and tensions, it 'requires a renewed interest in the ethical dimensions of sustainable development'. International Law Association, *Report of the ILA International Committee on International Law on Sustainable Development*, Berlin Conference, 2004, 6.

[30] P. Sands, *Principles of International Environmental Law* (Oxford University Press, 1994), 305.

[31] C. Voigt, *Sustainable Development as a Principle of International Law* (Leiden: Martinus Nijhoff Publishers, 2009).

As a general principle, sustainable development – in particular its key aspect of integration – plays an important role in the application and enforcement of international and national law, especially in the solution of legal disputes. General principles play a normative role not only with regard to determining state conduct or the design of a policy measure, guiding legislative or regulatory action. Principles also have a normative function if they are perceived as influencing directly or indirectly the outcome of judicial decisions.[32]

The normative force of sustainable development can be exercised in a dispute settlement context. In this respect there is agreement that in the hands of judges, the principle 'could operate as some sort of "intervening principle" mediating between potentially conflicting rules or principles'.[33] Legal principles are 'correctives' to the written law.[34] They help bridge the gap between the 'law as it is' to the 'law as it ought to be' by introducing a communal sense of justice and dynamism where it is lacking in the respective norms.

6. Rule of law and the environment

The *rule of law* is pre-eminent to the achievement of sustainable development. Sustainable development needs to be promoted through a variety of media and channels, that is education, political decision-making, ethics, research and so on – but also through law. In this context legal scholars and practitioners, in particular 'judges being such an important part

---

[32] Koskenniemi recognizes a normative role of principles even in their indirect effect on the substance of the decisions through a court's background theory, that is 'when they provide knowledge of the values and goals of the legal order. Hereby they set limiting conditions for the construction of the background theory. They characterize the legal order in a very general fashion allowing the Court to perceive it in a meaningful way." M. Koskenniemi, *From Apology to Utopia: the Structure of International Legal Argument* (reprinted by Cambridge University Press, 2006), 381.

[33] See A. B. M. Marong, 'From Rio to Johannesburg: Reflections on the Role of International Legal Norms in Sustainable Development' 16:1 *Georgetown International Environmental Law Review* (2003) 21–76, at 45.

[34] See in this context T. Franck, 'Non-Treaty Law-Making: When, Where and How?', in R. Wolfrum and V. Röben (eds.), *Developments of International Law in Treaty Making* (Berlin: Springer, 2005), 417–35, noting at 435: 'Where a matter is referred to an international tribunal with jurisdiction to decide cases in accordance not only with treaty law and custom but also with "general principles of law" the option to enrich the law by ascertaining and employing general principles affords an opportunity for keeping the law from becoming unduly rigid. This is particularly important because the international law-making system as yet offers only a few, and usually cumbersome, processes for rectification.'

of the legal establishment – must necessarily be involved in this – and sensitively involved'.[35] Judges and arbitrators can, under certain circumstances, better defend long-term, common and global interests against the short-sighted sovereign (and often economic) interests often pursued by states in treaty negotiations.

The legal profession in general assumes a particular responsibility to ensure a balance of powerful and not so powerful or even voiceless (and powerless) interests, that is where the interests of generations unborn, ecological systems or the poor are involved. The principle of sustainable development can in these cases be a working tool for transforming and reforming the legal system. In this sense, sustainable development as a legal principle awaits the craftsmanship of concerned and serious legal scholars, practitioners and judges to shape it into a practical means of balancing conflicting interests in a sustainable manner, not derogating from its ecological core.

Legal scholars and practitioners can elevate the standing of the principle 'by moving it up the hierarchy of legal norms and principles, thus preventing it from being lightly brushed aside by political, commercial or other interests that seek to advance "development" whatever the cost'.[36]

There is still much work to be done on questions of doctrinal construction. The application of the principle might take a number of forms, from filling 'white spots' in the applicable law, enabling treaty interpretations that take account of this development in international, national and transnational law and, as Lowe suggested, to 'rewrit[ing], rather than strik[ing] down, a bargain struck by the parties that is shown to lead to unsustainable development'.[37]

It is this function of the principle of sustainable development that makes it one of the most vibrant elements of both international and domestic law. It is crucial to harness the potential of the sustainable development principle. This can only be done by recognizing its ecological core. Otherwise it becomes pointless. It is, however, important to note that the ecological core says nothing about the distribution of affluence among human societies. Respecting ecological limits is thus a necessary, but not sufficient, condition for sustainable development.

---

[35] C. G. Weeramantry and M. C. Cordonier-Segger (eds.), *Sustainable Justice: Reconciling Economic, Social and Environmental Law* (Leiden: Martinus Nijhoff, 2005), 444.

[36] Ibid., 445.

[37] V. Lowe, 'Sustainable Development and Unsustainable Arguments', in A. Boyle and D. Freestone (eds.), *International Law and Sustainable Development: Past Achievements and Future Challenges* (Oxford University Press, 1999), 39.

Hundreds of lawyers, chief justices, heads of jurisdiction, attorneys general, auditors general, chief prosecutors and other high-ranking representatives of the judicial, legal and auditing professions gathered in Rio from 17 to 20 June 2012 for the World Congress on Justice, Governance and Law for Environmental Sustainability. They stated clearly that 'Environmental sustainability can only be achieved in the context of fair, effective and transparent governance arrangements and rule of law'.[38] Also noteworthy is the new focus on the rule of law and the environment at the level of UN institutions. A UN High-Level Meeting on the 'Rule of Law and the Environment' took place on 17 February 2013 at the UN Office in Nairobi, Kenya, on the eve of the 27th session of the Governing Council/Global Ministerial Environment Forum of the UN Environment Programme (UNEP). The aim of the meeting was to provide a platform for participants to discuss important recent developments and new opportunities regarding the rule of law in the field of the environment, and to consider how the rule of law can be promoted for greater effect in the quest for environmental sustainability, sustainable development and social justice.[39] Legal scholars, lawmakers, judges, civil servants – all have a responsibility: not to neglect, but to stress sustainable development's ecological meaning, in particular in the process of integration of diverse, and often colliding, interests.

'Human laws must be reformulated to keep human activities in harmony with the unchanging and universal laws of nature.'[40] This is what the Brundtland Report demanded a quarter of a century ago. A coherent, normative theory of sustainable development that links the substantive, normative content of laws to the thresholds of fundamental ecological functions could elicit the role of lawyers as key figures in this transformation of the legal system.

---

[38] *Rio+20 Declaration on Justice, Governance and Law for Environmental Sustainability*, available at: www.unep.org/rio20/Portals/24180/Rio20_Declaration_on_Justice_Gov_n_Law_4_Env_Sustainability.pdf (last accessed 18 February 2013). The jurists gathered at Rio+20 also noted: 'Environmental sustainability can only be achieved if there exist effective legal regimes, coupled with effective implementation and accessible legal procedures, including on *locus standi* and collective access to justice, and a supporting legal and institutional framework and applicable principles from all world legal traditions.' Ibid.
[39] GC27/GME. For a summary see: IISD, 'Briefing note on the High-Level Meeting on the Rule of Law and the Environment', available at: www.iisd.ca/unepgc/27unepgc/hlmrle/brief/brief_hlmrle.html (last accessed 18 February 2013).
[40] WCED, *Our Common Future*, 330.

9

The need to recognize a coherent legal system as an important element of the ecosystem approach

FROUKJE MARIA PLATJOUW

1. Ecosystem degradation and the ecosystem approach

Today, many of our ecosystems around the world are threatened. Their degradation has become one of the major concerns particularly since the 1990s.[1] In order to halt the degradation of ecosystems and to ensure the provision of ecosystem services to mankind, an ecosystem approach in environmental governance has now been widely endorsed in legal and political instruments at the international and European, as well as national, level.[2]

Simply put, the ecosystem approach requires a governance approach that is based on the ecological boundaries of the ecosystem rather than jurisdictional boundaries, with the objective of combining the conservation of the structure and functioning of ecosystems, also described as the maintenance of ecosystem integrity, with efforts to meet social needs and the sustainable use of ecosystem services for human purposes. This dual objective of the ecosystem approach is endorsed in a variety of definitions, as well as in the Malawi principles that were adopted by the fifth conference of the parties to the Convention on Biological Diversity in 2000 to make the ecosystem approach more concrete. How exactly to reconcile the two objectives of both sustainable use and the maintenance of ecosystem integrity has been one of the major challenges of the ecosystem approach ever since its inception.

---

[1] The Millennium Ecosystem Assessment Report of 2005 as well as the more recent Global Biodiversity Outlook of 2010 concluded that human behaviour has led to the degradation of the world's ecosystems and their capacity to provide ecosystem services.

[2] See, amongst others, the 1972 Stockholm Declaration on the Human Environment, the 1992 Rio Declaration, Principle 7 (Agenda 21, Chapter 17), the CBD-COP-5 Decision V/6 and VII/11, the European Integrated Maritime Policy, the Marine Strategy Framework Directive and Norway's Nature Diversity Act of 2009.

Although flexibility in the legal system has been addressed as an important prerequisite to facilitate this integration, this chapter instead emphasizes the importance of a strong rule of law and a coherent legal system in order to ensure that ecosystem structure and functioning is conserved and that the maintenance of ecosystem integrity is ensured. Notwithstanding the dual objective of the ecosystem approach, the fifth Malawi principle made it clear that the 'conservation of ecosystem structure and functioning, in order to maintain ecosystem services, should be a priority target of the ecosystem approach'. Respecting this principle requires a legal framework that sets coherent rules and constraints under which balancing exercises take place.

The hypothesis of this chapter is that fragmentation of environmental law and the existence of broad discretion to weigh and balance diverging values/objectives significantly complicate an ecosystem approach. The chapter first shows that the ecosystem approach contains three interrelated dimensions of integration, including the integration and coherence of legal acts. The second part of the chapter will present some obstacles to coherence, such as fragmentation, discretion and the use of principles in environmental law. The final section will assess in more depth why a wide margin of appreciation in law will impede coherence in law and governance and the realization of an ecosystem approach.

2. Three dimensions of integration under the ecosystem approach

2.1 *The integration of governance interests: conservation vs. utilization*

As stated above, the ecosystem approach serves a dual objective. This entails satisfying human needs in a way that does not compromise the integrity of ecosystems.[3] This integration of different objectives is certainly imperative; however, the realization of this is also difficult. In a meeting of experts on the ecosystem approach in 2003, the experts concluded that with regard to the principle on finding the appropriate balance between conservation and use of biological diversity, 'The problem still remains one of identifying the limits to ecosystem functioning, within

---

[3] A. Trouwborst, 'The Precautionary Principle and the Ecosystem Approach in International Law: Differences, Similarities, and Linkages' 18:1 *Review of European Community and International Environmental Law* (2009) 26–37, at 28.

which to achieve "balance between" and "integration of" conservation and sustainable use.'4

It has been recognized that one of the tools to facilitate this type of integration is the participation of all kinds of stakeholders and decision-makers from all relevant administrative sectors.[5] The Conference of the Parties to the Convention on Biological Diversity (CBD-COP) reasoned that inter-sectoral cooperation between different aspects of public policy, for example nature conservation, agriculture, forestry and fisheries, and indeed other public policy areas such as land-use planning and economic development, will ensure that conservation interests are represented and integrated with utilization interests.[6]

2.2 The integration of governance sectors

The emphasis on inter-sectoral cooperation has resulted from the recognition that a sectoral approach to planning and management is generally insufficient to deal with complex interrelationships and diverse stakeholder priorities that exist in the world.[7] The COP explained in its rationale to the principle on inter-sectoral cooperation that:

> Intersectoral cooperation was prioritized because different sectors of society view ecosystems in terms of their own economic, cultural and societal needs ... Management of natural resources, according to the ecosystem approach, calls for increased intersectoral communication and cooperation at a range of levels (government ministries, management agencies, etc.).[8]

The need for inter-sectoral cooperation was emphasized not only within the context of the CBD, but also under the Law of the Sea.[9] Implementation of the ecosystem approach could be achieved through, inter alia, 'sectoral approaches and integrated management and planning on a

---

[4] CBD 2003, 'Review of the principles of the ecosystem approach and suggestions for refinement: a framework for discussion', UNEP/CBD/EM-EA/1/3, 8.

[5] As mentioned as one of the five points of operational guidance and one of the Malawi Principles on the operationalisation of the ecosystem approach. See UNEP/CBD/COP/4/Inf.9.

[6] See decision V/6 adopted by COP 5 in 2000.

[7] S. Kidd, A. Plater and C. Frid, *The Ecosystem Approach to Marine Planning and Management* (London: Earthscan, 2011), 1.

[8] See further UNEP/CBD/COP/4/Inf.9.

[9] See the Report on the Seventh Meeting of the United Nations Open-ended Informal Consultative Process on Oceans and the Law of the Sea (UNICPOLOS 2006).

variety of levels, including across boundaries';[10] and 'effective integrated management across sectors'.[11]

It appears that, under the ecosystem approach, the principle of cross-sectoral cooperation or integration has been rather difficult to achieve. This is so because sectors are different and they are subject to their own policies and administrations. In addition, governance structures are still very fragmented, where different sectors govern different elements of the same ecosystem, complying with different legal instruments through the use of diverging decision-making tools and traditions.

2.3 The integration of regulatory subject-matters and regulatory frameworks

Progress on inter-sectoral cooperation will be affected by the architecture and nature of the legal system. Today environmental law is extensive, diverse and fragmented. In the words of Borg:

> Even though the need for an ecosystem approach requires horizontal regulation that cuts across species, maritime zones, legal systems and political interests; regulation is assumed to be most effective if it is specialized and tailor made for the particular species and zones involved.[12]

With regard to the governance of one particular ecosystem, various legal acts may be applicable at the same time either directly or indirectly. Different acts may be aimed at the protection of different elements of the ecosystem, such as the water, the land and particular species; or they aim to regulate different activities within that ecosystem, such as shipping, building, aquaculture and fishing; or they may have an unintended effect on the ecosystem such as the adverse effects from industry, trade and transport.

The difficulty arising from the legal system not yet being ecosystem-based, but instead regulating different components of ecosystems, is complicated by the fact that the legal acts provide a certain margin of appreciation to decision-makers. This margin of appreciation is to be found particularly within rules with more abstract and discretionary wording and within environmental principles. Both fragmentation and

---

[10] Ibid., para. 7(j).
[11] Ibid., para. 7(k).
[12] S. Borg, *Conservation on the High Seas. Harmonizing International Regimes for the Sustainable Use of Living Resources* (Cheltenham: Edward Elgar Publishing, 2012), 278–9.

discretion certainly complicate cross-sectoral cooperation and the implementation of the ecosystem approach.

A coherent legal system needs to be recognized as an important element of the ecosystem approach. In fact, it could perhaps be argued that without a coherent legal system in place, an ecosystem approach in environmental governance will be difficult to implement; since inconsistency in law complicates cooperation across sectors, which in turn impedes the integration of the objectives of the ecosystem approach.

Under the discussions on the ecosystem approach, the integration of regulatory frameworks has not yet been given the attention it deserves, despite the fact that the problem of inconsistent laws was briefly mentioned in a 2004 workshop on the ecosystem approach in Europe.[13] Indeed, during the workshop several obstacles for the implementation of the ecosystem approach were found. These included inter-sectoral aspects, the problem of outdated and inconsistent laws, and the conflict between long-term ecological and short-term social and economic aims.[14]

Coherence in a legal system requires that the various fragments of law hang or fit together, that they are mutually supportive, and that they flow from or express a single unified viewpoint.[15] In the light of the ecosystem approach, legal coherence more specifically requires that the different legal acts that apply to one and the same ecosystem serve the overarching objective of the ecosystem approach. This requires consistency among legal acts with regard to balancing mechanisms, rules and principles. The following section will consider three obstacles to coherence in environmental law.

3. Obstacles to legal coherence

As indicated above, the establishment of a coherent legal system is complicated by the architecture and nature of environmental law. Three issues will be discussed more thoroughly. These are the fragmentation

---

[13] In 2004 an international workshop, 'Ways to promote ideas behind the CBD's ecosystem approach in Central and Eastern Europe', brought together twenty-six experts from ten European countries from 5 to 9 May.

[14] H. Korn, R. Schliep and J. Stadler, 'Report of the International Workshop on "Ways to Promote the Ideas behind the CBD's Ecosystem Approach in Central and Eastern Europe"', BFN Federal Agency for Nature Conservation, 120 *Skripten* (2004) 5–6.

[15] K. Kress, 'Coherence' in: D. Patterson (ed.), *Companion to Philosophy of Law and Legal Theory* (Cambridge: Blackwell Publishing, 2010), 521–39.

of environmental law, the presence of discretionary environmental rules and the use of environmental principles.

3.1 Fragmentation of environmental law

Ecosystems are currently affected by a large number of legal acts. There are not only a great number of legal acts that have the protection of the environment as their main objective, but there are also an even greater number of legal instruments regulating activities that indirectly have a significant impact on the environment. Overall, environmental law within most nation states has become rather extensive, diverse and fragmented.[16] The fragmentation of environmental law is not merely a national phenomenon. At the European level as well, a considerable amount of legal instruments exist that can have an impact on the environment. Examples are the directive establishing a greenhouse gas emissions trading scheme[17], a Waste Framework Directive[18] and a directive on integrated pollution prevention and control (IPPC).[19] Even though more recent directives have emerged that contain a more integrated approach within their respective fields, coordination or harmonization between these directives has been difficult. More specifically, the 2000 EU Water Framework Directive adopted a holistic approach to water that is reflected in the river basin approach.[20] Then the 2008 EU Marine Strategy Framework Directive (MSFD) adopted an ecosystem-based perspective for maintaining healthy ecosystems in marine waters.[21] Since the two directives both apply within the coastal zone up to one nautical mile, some degree of harmonization between the directives is required. However, not only do the directives differ in their application of the ecosystem approach,[22] there are also inconsistencies in

---

[16] For example, in Norway as well as in the Netherlands more than twelve different national legal acts apply to their respective national parts of the North Sea ecosystem.
[17] Directive 2003/87/EC of 13 October 2003 establishing a scheme for greenhouse gas emission allowance trading within the Community and amending Council Directive 96/61/EC.
[18] Directive 2008/98/EC of 19 November 2008 on waste and repealing certain directives.
[19] Directive 2008/1/EC of 15 January 2008 concerning integrated pollution prevention and control.
[20] Directive 2000/60/EC of 23 October 2000 establishing a framework for community action in the field of water policy (Water Framework Directive).
[21] Directive 2008/56/EC of 17 June 2008 establishing a framework for community action in the field of marine environmental policy (Marine Strategy Framework Directive).
[22] The ecosystem approach in the Water Framework Directive has been described as a 'deconstructing, structural approach', whereas the MSFD takes a 'holistic, functional approach'. See further Borja *et al.* (2010), 'Marine Management – Towards an Integrated

terms of concepts, terminology and time frames. Although the adoption of the MSFD in 2008 created an opportunity for a merged approach enabling a harmonized, seamless transition from catchment through transitional waters and coast to an open marine system, it has turned out to be rather difficult to achieve consistency between the two directives.[23]

The fragmentation of international environmental law has also been studied at an international level. One example that might illustrate this fragmentation is the amount of norms that have emerged from international treaties and international customary law to regulate the sustainable use of living resources on the high seas.[24] Another example is the fragmentation between different areas of international law. In particular, the interplay between international climate change law and world trade law has been discussed intensively.[25]

The challenge of fragmentation may become more apparent when environmental law is applied to particular cases or situations. Environmental law consists of both legal rules and principles. The following two sections aim to explain the role of principles, particularly when faced with more generally formulated rules. The sections will show that even though the principles provide some direction, most principles allow for a varying range of interpretations. This, in combination with the fragmentation of environmental law, may increase inconsistency in environmental law and governance.

3.2 Discretionary rules in environmental law

As a result of the fragmentation of environmental law, the legal rules of environmental law are numerous. As to every activity with a potential effect on the environment, different legal rules apply. The rules of environmental law are not homogenous in character. They may vary from being more abstract to being more concrete. In particular, rules that fall

---

Implementation of the European Marine Strategy Framework and the Water Framework Directives' 60 *Marine Pollution Bulletin* (2010) 2175–86.

[23] Ibid., 2184.
[24] Borg, *Conservation on the High Seas*.
[25] See C. Voigt, *Sustainable Development as a Principle of International Law: Resolving Conflicts between Climate Measures and WTO Law* (Leiden: Martinus Nijhoff Publishers, 2009), who explores the intersection between climate change law and world trade law. Yet another example may be H. van Asselt, 'Managing the Fragmentation of International Environmental Law: Forests at the Intersection of the Climate and the Biodiversity Regimes' (2011) *Journal of International Law and Politics*, available at: http://ssrn.com/abstract=1703186.

under the command-and-control type of regulation and market-based regulation may at times be rather specific. For instance, the environmental quality objectives in the Water Framework Directive are regulated quite concisely. A different example might be the directive on ambient air quality for Europe, which sets standards for fine particle pollution in the European Union.[26] The standards that are set in these two directives have been formulated specifically.

A considerable amount of legal rules are, however, formulated in an open form; they contain a degree of discretion. One good example might be the term 'disproportionate costs' used in the Water Framework Directive.[27] Another example can be found in the Norwegian Nature Diversity Act of 2009, which states that:

> The objective [of this Act] is also to maintain ecosystem structure, functioning and productivity *to the extent this is considered to be reasonable*.[28]

The key section in the Pollution Control Act states that when deciding on an application for a pollution permit, the authority must 'consider the effects of the pollution together with other inconveniences and benefits of the activity'.[29] The key provision in the Energy Act[30] simply states that the production or transmission of energy requires a permit,[31] and the objective of the act is to ensure energy production that is 'rational' for society.[32]

The degree of discretion and flexibility differs from legal act to legal act; the legal rules vary from being highly concrete and specific to being more abstract and vague. Even though concrete legal rules may be found, a certain degree of discretion may, however, often be present. When legal rules are formulated openly, and decisions need to be taken that involve conflicting concerns, recourse may be had to the environmental principles.

---

[26] Directive 2008/50/EC of 21 May 2008 on ambient air quality and cleaner air for Europe.
[27] Article 4(7)d of the Water Framework Directive.
[28] Norway's Act of 19 June 2009 No. 100 Relating to the Management of Biological, Geological and Landscape Diversity (emphasis added).
[29] Section 11 of Act No. 6 of 13 March 1981 concerning protection against pollution and concerning waste.
[30] Act No. 50 of 29 June 1990 relating to the generation, conversion, transmission, trading, distribution and use of energy, etc.
[31] Ibid., section 3–1.
[32] See further H. C. Bugge, 'Environmental Law's Fragmentation and Discretionary Decision-making. A Critical Reflection on the Case of Norway', in: E. Røsæg, B. Schafer and E. Stavang (eds.), *Law and Economics. Essays in Honour of Erling Eide* (Oslo: Cappelen, 2010), 55–75.

More concretely, when the precise content of the legal rule is unclear, the legal rules may be applied in the light of relevant environmental principles that have shaped the legal act, or that have been explicitly included in the legal act.[33] As the next section will show, the environmental principles, unfortunately, do not often provide a straightforward answer as to how to apply the legal rules.

3.3   The use of environmental principles

The development of environmental principles that now form an important part of environmental law has been influenced by the concept of sustainable development that really became popular in 1987 through the publication of *Our Common Future*.[34] Many environmental principles that now play an important role in international and national environmental law and policy can be seen as an effort to make the rather abstract ideal of sustainable development more concrete.[35] Examples are the integration principle, the precautionary principle and the principle of public participation.

Among the principles of environmental law, there are principles of a more substantive nature and procedural principles. Substantive principles, such as the precautionary principle and the 'polluter pays' principle, are more abstract and will help us to discover the foundations for decisions to be taken and judgements to be made. Procedural principles are less abstract, more like rules. An example of the latter may be that impact assessments shall be undertaken for proposed activities that are likely to have a significant adverse effect on the environment. Other examples are the principles on the access to information, participation in decision-making and access to justice.

The principles of environmental law could actually serve to overcome the problems of fragmentation and broad discretionary power, provided that they are understood and applied consistently by the various authorities. However, most principles do not aspire to denoting or determining exactly the outcome of the decision-making. Instead they may imply a

---

[33] See further J. M. Verschuuren, 'Sustainable Development and the Nature of Environmental Legal Principles' 9:1 *Potchefstroom Electronic Law Journal* (2006) 1–57, at 18–19 and 35–8.
[34] World Commission on Environment and Development, *Our Common Future* (Oxford University Press, 1987).
[35] Verschuuren, 'Sustainable Development', 11.

certain normative direction and indicate different possible factors that may be taken into account and weighed against each other.[36] Even within the normative direction, a variety of interpretations seem possible.[37] The application of legal rules in the light of these principles seems, therefore, not to result in predictable outcomes.

3.4   To sum up

Thus far it has been indicated that due to the fragmentation of environmental law and governance and the use of discretionary rules and principles, an ecosystem approach may be difficult to realize. The reason behind this supposition is that the architecture and nature of the legal system may hinder attempts at cooperation across governmental sectors. With regard to the issue of fragmentation and discretion in the context of the ecosystem approach, there exists, however, a more fundamental dilemma, namely that discretion in law requires value judgements to be performed on ecosystems. As will be shown in the final section, this is often a very arbitrary exercise. In addition, fragmentation entails that these arbitrary value judgements are performed ad hoc on different parts of the same ecosystem. This may very well contradict the ideology behind the ecosystem approach and the objective of maintaining ecosystem integrity.

4.   Challenges of a wide margin of appreciation

This final section will explain why a too wide margin of appreciation for decision-makers may pose challenges to the governance of our ecosystems. This postulation builds on three aspects. These are related to the difficulty and controversiality of executing value judgements on our ecosystems, the problem of uncertainty surrounding human behaviour and ecosystem functioning, and the fact that our ecosystems provide certain life-supporting systems upon which we depend for our sustenance.

---

[36] J. Ebbesson, 'The Rule of Law in Governance of Complex Socio-ecological Changes' 20:3 *Global Environmental Change* (2010) 414–22, at 418–19.
[37] A. D. Tarlock, 'Is There a There There in Environmental Law?', 19:2 *Journal of Land Use & Environmental Law* (2004) 213–54, at 239–40.

4.1 Incommensurable and incomparable values

When the governance of an ecosystem is regulated by a set of legal instruments that contain a degree of discretion, the responsibility for ensuring the maintenance of ecosystem integrity has been left to decision-makers. Decision-making in relation to ecosystems is, however, not an easy task; it is not only difficult to place a value on ecosystem services, but it is also difficult to compare these values with other competing values that are at stake in the decision process. Two approaches may be distinguished for carrying out value judgements on (parts of) ecosystems. This section will show that under both approaches there is a chance that the worth of the ecosystem may be conceived differently or inconsistently throughout decisions.

The first approach is based on the idea of commensurability of the value of ecosystem services, and applies a cost–benefit analysis (CBA) to weigh and balance diverging values.[38] Under the CBA, these diverging values need to be expressed as a monetary unit. The idea that diverging values need to be expressed by a common denominator has boosted the development of valuation methods to enable the value of ecosystem services to be expressed in monetary terms. A variety of valuation methods are currently being applied. Even though these valuation methods will not be explained in depth here, it could be said that each of them is subject to technical difficulties that complicate the identification of the real value of the ecosystem service.

In addition to the technical difficulties embedded in the valuation methods, these methods have been criticized for being unable to reveal the real value of the ecosystem services because of the so-called 'water–diamond paradox'.[39] The Economics of Ecosystems and Biodiversity (TEEB) 2010 report also recognized this problem and highlighted that the degradation of ecosystems could be significantly slowed or reversed if the

---

[38] CBA is an economic institution that is used extensively in decision-making procedures. The mechanism offers a way to compare the diverse benefits and costs associated with changes to ecosystem services by attempting to measure them and expressing them as a common denominator.

[39] This paradox, as was described by Adam Smith in a passage in the *Wealth of Nations*, means that the market price of an item does not reflect its true value. The market price of a diamond is much higher than the price of water, even though water is, in contrast to diamonds, of immeasurable value to human survival. Adam Smith, *An Inquiry into the Nature and Causes of the Wealth of Nations*, Chapter 4, Book I (1776), available at: www.econlib.org/library/Smith/smWN1.html (last accessed 24 June 2013).

full economic value of the services were taken into account in decision-making.[40]

The second approach is based on the idea that rational choices are possible without setting a monetary price on environmental values. This approach rejects the commensurability of the value of ecosystem services (and many other ecological and social values) and uses instead multiple criteria, such as monetary terms and quantitative[41] or qualitative[42] indicators.[43]

To facilitate the decision-making process, these criteria are often integrated in a multi-criteria decision analysis, which is concerned with structuring and solving decision and planning problems that involve multiple criteria.[44] The weighing of the conflicting interests consists of a ranking of preferences. Agreement on the ranking of preferences and the formulation of a single 'compromise' rank order are, however, often difficult to achieve due to the fact that stakeholders and decision-makers often have different goals, preferences and interests.[45]

Both approaches are used in decision-making on the environment. However, both of them are also subject to technical challenges that will complicate their use. In the context of the ecosystem approach, an important concern is that the worth of the ecosystem may be conceived differently or inconsistently throughout decisions. When the value of the ecosystem is to be expressed through monetary terms, its calculated value depends on a relatively high number of variables, such as the particular services that are monetized, the particular valuation methods that are applied, the discount rate used, the availability of scientific knowledge on the ecosystem services, the capability of the economist to take into

---

[40] See TEEB, 'The Economics of Ecosystems and Biodiversity: Mainstreaming the Economics of Nature: A Synthesis of the Approach, Conclusions and Recommendations of TEEB' (2010), available at: www.teebweb.org/publications/teeb-study-reports/synthesis (last accessed 6 June 2013).
[41] Quantitative analysis would directly measure the change in ecosystem services resulting from the change in land use (for instance, frequency/volume of estimated increase in flood risk/carbon dioxide emissions).
[42] Qualitative analysis would simply describe the potential scale of impacts (for instance, increased flood risk) and the decision-maker would have to make a judgement as to their importance relative to any financial costs and benefits.
[43] See further, for example, J. O'Neill, A. Holland and A. Light, *Environmental Values* (London: Routledge, 2008), 23.
[44] See for instance M. Getzner, C. L. Spash and S. Stagl, *Alternatives for Environmental Valuation* (London: Routledge, 2005).
[45] G. A. Mendoza and H. Martins, 'Multicriteria Decision Analysis in Natural Resource Management' 230:1–3 *Forest Ecology and Management* (2006) 1–22, at 14.

account this scientific knowledge, and so forth. The number of variables and the difficulties surrounding some of them means that the ecosystem may be valued differently under each decision.

Likewise under multi-criteria decision analysis, there is also a considerable risk that the worth of the ecosystem is valued differently each time a decision needs to be made. This is because the facts of the case may be different and there may be different competing interests at stake in the attempt to reach a compromise. Moreover, the preferences of stakeholders and decision-makers are often subjective and contextualized to the facts of the case and the other interests at stake.

In sum, both approaches to value judgements on ecosystems may lead to arbitrary outcomes, where the same ecosystem may be valued differently each time a decision is made. This is an important aspect to consider while striving toward an ecosystem approach in environmental governance. Because of this contradiction, a considerable degree of discretion for decision-makers when carrying out value judgements on ecosystems may be inappropriate.

4.2 Uncertainty about the functioning of the ecological system

Another aspect that needs to be considered when examining the appropriateness of a wide margin of appreciation within environmental law is the issue of uncertainty over the value of certain ecosystems and their services and the uncertainty about the potential effects of certain policies and projects on the functioning of ecosystems.

An important reason behind this uncertainty is that the functioning of ecosystems is often complex and poorly understood. As Chavas stated:

> Ecosystems change over time in complex ways. First, ecosystems involve many ecological variables that interact with each other. Second, ecosystem dynamics can be highly nonlinear, meaning that knowing the path of a system in some particular situations may not tell us much about its behavior under alternative scenarios ... Third, ecosystems are subject to unpredictable effects of variables that are not anticipated by decision-makers. These unpredictable effects generate uncertainty due to lack of knowledge and/or lack of information. The best available scientific information typically is incomplete and uncertain for most decision-makers.[46]

---

[46] J. P. Chavas, 'Ecosystem Valuation under Uncertainty and Irreversibility' 3 *Ecosystems* (2000) 11–15, at 11–12. See also Kidd, *The Ecosystem Approach to Marine Planning*, 21.

This uncertainty makes it difficult to decide the best way to manage ecosystems. Lack of consensus on environmental decisions among citizens and scientific disciplines, as well as experts, is common. Imprecise knowledge about ecosystems contributes to this situation because different parties often have different information about the state of the environment.[47] Related to the problem of uncertainty is the risk of irreversibility. Irreversibility occurs when the ecosystem cannot escape from a particular state no matter what action is taken. A good example of irreversibility is the extinction of species: species that become extinct cannot feasibly be brought back into any ecosystem.[48]

If the value of the ecosystem is currently unclear but may become better known in the future, then preserving it now allows the 'destroy or conserve' issue to be revisited at a time when decision-makers are better informed; whereas destroying the ecosystem forces a permanent choice without the benefit of better knowledge.[49] Making decisions on ecosystems under conditions of uncertainty and irreversibility clearly poses additional problems and risks. This is particularly obvious is the case of ecosystems that provide certain life-supporting systems.

4.3 The importance of life-supporting systems

Value judgments on diverging values become tricky particularly when our life-supporting systems are affected. In fact, a too-wide margin of appreciation in law may validate and justify decisions that (tacitly) allow the degradation of the essential ecological systems upon which we depend for our sustenance. For this reason, certain ecosystems should be protected and conserved through regulation without leaving these issues to the arbitrariness of decision-making processes.

On the same matter, but within the context of sustainable development, Lafferty argues that:

> The challenge of sustainable development involves *the prospect of irreversible damage to life-support systems*. This implies that there will be at least *some* environmental/ecological objectives that simply cannot be 'balanced' with political goals that challenge the basis for such life-support

---

[47] Chavas, 'Ecosystem Valuation', 11.
[48] See also N. Hanley and E. B. Barbier, *Pricing Nature. Cost Benefit Analysis and Environmental Policy* (Cheltenham: Edward Elgar Publishing, 2009), 210.
[49] National Research Council, *Valuing Ecosystem Services. Toward Better Environmental Decision-making* (Washington, DC: The National Academies Press, 2005), 219.

systems ... Vital environmental concerns must – when 'push comes to shove' in policy and budgetary conflicts – be seen as principal.[50]

Likewise, Voigt states that the integration of environmental, social and economic considerations in the context of sustainable development entails setting limits. Certain ecological limits simply need to be respected:

> The framework within which sustainable development and the integration of all aspects of society need to be viewed derives ultimately from fundamental, universal, and indispensable ecological functions on which they depend. To respect these functions is an absolute priority.[51]

5. Moving forward

This chapter has shown that the integration of legal acts, or the existence of a coherent legal system, ought to be recognized as an important element of the ecosystem approach. Several obstacles to legal coherence have been identified, such as the fragmentation of environmental law, a degree of discretion given to decision-makers to weigh and balance diverging values/objectives, and the use of environmental principles that do not denote a particular outcome in case of a conflict between objectives and interests.

Due to the fragmentation of environmental law and governance, the margin of appreciation is used in diverging manners across governmental sectors. This is so because governmental sectors have developed their own sectoral approaches to the governance of 'their' part of the ecosystem with their own tools, mechanisms and traditions. Furthermore, due to the difficulties related to the execution of value judgements on ecosystems, it could be argued that even within the various involved sectors the value of an ecosystem may be conceived differently under various decisions. This may impede the realization of the ecosystem approach.

For this reason and in order to stimulate further progress on the implementation of the ecosystem approach, a coherent legal system ought to be in place. An ecosystem approach requires environmental law first of all to harmonize the legal acts that apply to the same ecosystem. Second, the overarching objective of that legal system, such as to maintain the integrity

---

[50] W. Lafferty, 'From Environmental Protection to Sustainable Development: the Challenge of Decoupling through Sectoral Integration', in: W. Lafferty (ed.), *Governance for Sustainable Development* (Cheltenham: Edward Elgar Publishing, 2004), 203 (emphasis added).

[51] Voigt, *Sustainable Development as a Principle of International Law*, 52.

of that ecosystem, should be codified. Third, discretionary principles and rules should be interpreted and applied in accordance with that overarching objective. Fourth, environmental law should decrease dependency on and arbitrariness in value judgements on ecosystems by creating rules on the conditions for their use, the execution of value judgements and the implications of value judgements for the outcome of final decisions.

It would also be desirable to unravel the exercise of value judgements into two distinct steps. The first step would be the valuation of the ecosystem; the second step would be the balancing and weighing of this ecosystem value against other conflicting values. Determining the value of the ecosystem is a rather controversial and difficult exercise and it would be advisable to withdraw this exercise from the sectoral authorities. Instead, this exercise could be carried out in a different arena overarching the various sectors, so that the value of the ecosystem is clear, stable and common. This value may then be integrated in the balancing exercises that take place in the various sectors.

This weighing and balancing exercise could apropos also be subject to more clear and coherent rules or guidelines. How to weigh the various interests and values? Certain overriding ecological concerns cannot simply be traded off, and the protection of these concerns needs, therefore, to be ensured by law. Moreover, there is a need for rules on the implications of value judgements for the final decision. Are they legally binding, is a contrary decision allowed? Suppose that, in a particular case, the value of ecosystem services is estimated to be higher that the benefits of proposed building activities, what happens when the building activities are preferred and executed anyway? These kinds of questions need to be regulated clearly and consistently across legal instruments.

Finally, minor legislative changes may significantly increase coherence in environmental law and governance. For instance, legal acts that apply to one and the same ecosystem could contain similar terminology across acts. Often a variety of definitions across legal acts refer to the same idea, such as 'environmentally responsible', 'environmentally defensible' or 'environmentally justifiable'. In addition, commonly used discretionary terms and principles need to be interpreted consistently by the various governmental sectors that are involved in the governance of that particular ecosystem. For instance, the precautionary principle should have the same implications under the various legal acts. Likewise, the meaning of proportionality, rationality and reasonableness should be clear and consistent.

In sum, in order to ensure the conservation of ecosystem structure and functioning, and to ensure a healthy level of provision of ecosystem services to future generations, the importance of a strong and coherent legal system should not be underestimated. Therefore, the existence of a coherent legal system needs to be recognized as an important element of the ecosystem approach.

10

An emerging legal principle to restore large-scale ecoscapes

ANASTASIA TELESETSKY

1. Introduction

Today, even though we realize that we are a part of nature, our actions are having potentially irreversible impacts on the environment.[1] As we dam rivers, saturate waterways with nitrogen, and alter the composition of the atmosphere, our wild success as a species has implications not just for other species but also for ourselves.[2] In response to these threats, we have developed a "rule of humanity in nature," trying through the concept of sustainable development to restore a disrupted balance between humanity and nature.[3] But as scholars in law and ecology have noted, there is no balance point in nature.[4] The lack of a balance point is particularly pronounced in the recent debate over the dawn of the Anthropocene Era, where human impacts may now be altering geophysical processes.[5]

Collectively as an international society, we are recognizing that in repeatedly privileging human economic interests over non-human concerns (e.g. adequate habitat), we have inextricably altered the fabric of life. If we have duties to future generations,[6] it becomes important that today's

---

[1] Erle C. Ellis, Kees Klein Goldewijk, Stefan Siebert, Deborah Lightman, and Navin Ramankutty, "Anthropogenic Transformation of the Biomes, 1700 to 2000," 19 *Global Ecology and Biogeography* (September 2010), 589–606.
[2] Johan Rockström *et al.*, "A Safe Operating Space for Humanity," 461 *Nature* (September 23, 2009), 472–5.
[3] "The Future We Want," 24 UN General Assembly A/66/L.56, para. 39 (2012).
[4] Jonathan B. Weiner, "Beyond the Balance of Nature," 7 *Duke Environmental Law and Policy Forum* (1996), 1–24, at 7.
[5] Paul Crutzen and Eugene Stoermer, "The Anthropocene," 41 *International Geosphere-Biosphere Newsletter* (2000), 17–18. See also Chapter 3 by Nicholas Robinson in this book.
[6] Edith Brown Weiss, "The Planetary Trust: Conservation and Intergenerational Equity," 11 *Ecology L.Q.* (1984), 495–582.

population takes responsibility for both contemporary and historical processes of environmental degradation[7] and to ask whether there is a possibility of creating a "rule of law for nature."

Is it possible to collectively shift our focus to a "rule of law for nature"? After Hurricane Katrina, Cyclone Nargis, and Superstorm Sandy, it becomes apparent that "nature," defined here to include our human activities, is not a static object but has become a dynamic force that must be better understood if humans and the ecosystems that we depend upon are to survive as part of nature. The "rule of law for nature" is no longer simply a matter of concern for environmentalists. It has become a matter of concern for economists. In 2013 the World Economic Forum released its global risks report that included a direct acknowledgment of the need for economic law to factor in the limitations of the environment and for environmental law to acknowledge its reliance on a functioning economy.[8]

We can shift to a "rule of law for nature" if global and regional landscape and seascape restoration efforts that cross national boundaries form the foundation for such a rule. As this chapter will argue, even though restoration has been on the global agenda primarily as a remedial strategy,[9] the largely national approach to restoration in practice has been too piecemeal, disconnected, and remedial. What is needed instead, in order to build resilience into our economic and environmental systems, is a more robust legal approach to restoration that focuses on a state's duty to restore landscapes in order to provide self-sustaining ecological functions and structures for nature.

---

[7] One question is why should this generation be responsible for environmental impacts that were not the making of this generation? One answer is that we are "paying" collective reparations for the actions of generations that came before us. See generally Federico Lenzerini, *Reparations for Indigenous Peoples: International and Comparative Perspectives* (Oxford University Press, 2008).

[8] World Economic Forum, Global Risks Report (2013) 11, available at: www3.weforum.org/docs/WEF_GlobalRisks_Report_2013.pdf (last accessed June 6, 2013).

[9] See e.g. Convention on Biological Diversity (Article 8(f): Parties shall "[r]ehabilitate and restore degraded ecosystems"), Law of the Sea (Article 61: "[Conservation and management measures] shall also be designed to maintain or restore populations of harvested species"), and the United Nations Convention on the Law of Non-Navigational Uses of International Watercourses (Article 27: "Watercourse States shall … take all appropriate measures to … mitigate conditions related to an international watercourse that may be harmful to other watercourse States, whether resulting from natural causes or human conduct") (not in force) that all provide an obligation to restore.

2. *Lex lata* principle of environmental restoration as remedial mitigation

There is an existing rule of law related to environmental restoration. It is largely a reactive law that operates as either functional mitigation for expected environmental harms[10] or as a political response to disaster.[11] In both cases, the restorative response is reactive to environmental degradation. Legally mandated restoration work is often piecemeal and focused on human-centered project objectives such as reducing storm surge or decontaminating lands toxic to humans. In terms of metrics of success, projects are considered complete once a certain density of trees has been planted or a certain amount of toxic material removed. In some instances, measurements are based on indices such as the Habitat Suitability Index, which "may inadequately represent ecosystem function and process."[12] Short-term mitigation projects without adequate long-term monitoring may jeopardize not just the quality of existing restoration efforts but also the future of new restoration projects.[13]

Restoration is also implicated in the duty for states to assess substantial environmental impacts.[14] If environmental harms are identified, the existing principle of environmental restoration as mitigation provides the opportunity to proceed on the proposed project by delaying the remediation of environmental impacts of the project to some future date. For example, in large-scale mining it is uncommon for a government entity to deny a permit rather than to condition the permit on post-use restoration

---

[10] See e.g. Council on Environmental Quality, "Final Guidance for Federal Departments and Agencies on the Appropriate Use of Mitigation and Monitoring and Clarifying the Appropriate Use of Mitigated Findings of No Significant Impact," January 14, 2011, available at: http://ceq.hss.doe.gov/ceq_regulations/guidance.html (last accessed June 6, 2013).

[11] Resources and Ecosystems Sustainability, Tourist Opportunities, and Revived Economies of the Gulf Coast States Act of 2012 ("RESTORE"), *Public Law* (2012), 112–41.

[12] S. Kyle McKay *et al.*, "Metric Development for Environmental Benefits Analysis," EBA Technical Notes Collection. ERDC TN-EMRRP-EBA-4 (Vicksburg, MS: US Army Engineer Research and Development Center), available at: http://el.erdc.usace.army.mil/elpubs/pdf/eba04.pdf (last accessed June 6, 2013).

[13] R. M. Thom, 'Adaptive Management of Coastal Ecosystem Projects', 15 *Ecological Engineering* (2000), 365–72, at 366: "[Compensatory mitigation] projects are often carried out under major time and cost constraints, which can result in reduced planning time, poor site selection, and lack of understanding of conditions of the restoration site, causing further uncertainties about the performance of the project and ultimately reducing the success of the project."

[14] *Argentina–Uruguay* (*Pulp Mills* case), ICJ Reports 2010, 14, 83 para. 204.

of the site. The problem is, again, one of the environmental quality of the restoration effort. For example, in the United Kingdom there is great enthusiasm for converting former rock quarries into lakes in order to create habitats.[15] From the point of ecology, should a novel ecosystem such as the post-quarry lake ecosystems be sufficient compensation for a lost heath ecosystem or a forest ecosystem?

Finally, the principle of environmental restoration is triggered when a state causes environmental harm. Where the duty to prevent environmental harm has been breached, there may be an obligation to provide reparations. The first form of reparation available to injured states is restitution, which requires parties to "re-establish the situation which existed before the wrongful act was committed, provided and to the extent that restitution: (a) is not materially impossible; (b) does not involve a burden out of all proportion to the benefit deriving from restitution instead of compensation."[16] Arguably if environmental restoration is not impossible or excessively burdensome, then it may constitute a form of material restitution in the case of a transboundary dispute. But to what extent must a state undertake restoration? One can imagine a transboundary water dispute such as that on the Mekong River involving upstream damming leading to downstream fishery damage. If there was to be state responsibility, the possibility of restoration as a form of reparation raises the same questions of ecological quality that are raised by implementing obligations related to sustainable development and environmental impact assessment. Would restoration require the removal of the dam or would it be sufficient to fund downstream aquaculture projects?

Reading the existing principle of environmental restoration as an offshoot of the existing principles and obligations of sustainable development, environmental impact assessments, and state responsibility suggests that environmental restoration is simply another application of the "rule of humanity in nature." Restoration becomes part of a balancing game of numbers. As a result, governmental entities pursue an array of projects that include everything from promises of nationwide reforestation to requirements for wetland acreage replacement with the success

---

[15] "Old quarries 'should be turned into nature reserves to support wildlife'," *The Telegraph* (April 12, 2010); Cemex Regenerating and Restoring Local Communities, available at: www.cemex.co.uk/su/su_re.asp (last accessed June 6, 2013) (see Branton Nature Conservation Area, Berkswell Quarry, and Amswell Quarry transforming former drylands to marshlands).

[16] International Law Commission, Draft Articles on State Responsibility for Internationally Wrongful Acts (2001), Article 35.

of these projects measured by increases in acreage rather than underlying ecological integrity.[17] Some of the environmental systems that are "restored" under the current principle of restoration are incapable of functioning independently due to limited size, while other systems have been restored to functions that never existed in the area. Recognizing that many of the restoration projects have failed to restore needed ecosystem functions and structures, we need a different principle of restoration based on the active implementation of the principles of non-regression and ecological integrity to replace the current principle of case-by-case uncoordinated environmental restoration.

3. *Lex ferenda* principle of restoring large landscapes/seascapes (ecoscapes)

Restoration is generally associated with compensation, mitigation, and post-disaster relief. As described above, the various projects required in response to an environmental assessment or in response to an environmental restoration order issued by an executive agency or a judiciary are largely emergency responses. Yet pigeonholing restoration as an "*ex post*" response limits the potential of restoration to become one of the most important social and economic activities in the Anthropocene. Restoration as an "*ex ante*" measure provides us with the opportunity to collectively seek to redefine our relationship with the environment based on our new understandings of the limitations of nature to recover from rapid change. Described below is a proposed new principle of restoration that is based on reviving ecosystem-wide functions and structures at the landscape/seascape (ecoscape)[18] level rather than on mitigating for the loss of certain species. To revive ecosystem functions at such levels may frequently require transnational responses that might be characterized as transecological responses because they span different habitat units that have been politically defined to include only areas

---

[17] Richard Ambrose, John Callaway, and Steve Lee, *An Evaluation of Compensatory Mitigation Projects Permitted Under Clean Water Act Section 401 by the California State Water Quality Control Board, 1991–2002* (Los Angeles: California State Water Resources Board, 2006), 252–4.

[18] "Ecoscape" is used in this chapter to refer to large landscapes and seascapes with self-sustaining ecological functions and structures. As a term, it is useful in focusing attention on promoting governance opportunities for restoration by emphasizing communities' physical and emotional relationship with the lands and waters that they consider their homelands.

of protection.[19] Existing and emerging duties of international law provide a basis for this proposed new obligation for states to cooperate on large ecoscape restoration.

3.1 Restoration science and ecoscapes

Understanding that restoration must play a central role in national and international environmental policy, scientists use a number of working definitions to describe what restoration entails. The Society for Ecological Restoration International defines "ecological restoration" as "the process of assisting the recovery of an ecosystem that has been degraded, damaged, or destroyed."[20] The Society of Wetland Scientists describes restoration as "actions taken ... that result in the reestablishment of ecological processes, functions, and biotic/abiotic linkages that lead to a persistent, resilient system integrated within its landscape."[21] One of the earliest advocates of ecological restoration defines restoration as "getting the system back on track, not only in an ecological, but ideally even in an evolutionary sense."[22] In all of these definitions the emphasis is not on a specific end product but on a process of reversing certain types of human impact from poor land-use choices to over-exploitation of resources.

Many of the current large-scale environmental restoration efforts undertaken by states have two primary limitations: the projects are not undertaken for the primary goal of restoring ecological processes or the projects are too narrowly focused on "hotspot" restoration efforts that fail to restore fundamental ecological processes.[23]

Scientific experiments on a 1,000 square kilometer site Brazil have provided valuable evidence that single large-scale tracts are better for conservation than multiple smaller reserves. In the 1970s ecologists created the "Minimal Critical Size of Ecosystem Project" that explored the impact

---

[19] For example, the 1.3 million square kilometer Yellowstone to Yukon Conservation Initiative is a transecological project because it transcends numerous habitats to address the protection of the region as a whole ecological landscape greater than the sum of the part of the various ecosystems characterized within US, Canadian, federal state, and provincial political boundaries. See generally www.y2y.net (last accessed June 6, 2013).
[20] Society of Ecological Restoration, www.ser.org.
[21] Society of Wetland Scientists, www.sws.org.
[22] William Jordan III, *The Sunflower Forest* (Berkeley: University of California Press, 2003), 21–2.
[23] Peter Kareiva and Michelle Marvier, "Conserving Biodiversity Coldspots," 91 *American Scientist* (2003), 344–51. ("The hotspot approach would result in high levels of protection for a few species-rich areas to the neglect of many others.")

of fragmentation on species and concluded that larger areas support healthier ecosystem processes.[24] Scale matters since "the bigger an ecosystem is, the more complete it is ecologically, and the more likely it is to be more or less self-sustaining."[25] Responding to existing legal mitigation requirements and relying on extremely limited funding, most restoration ecologists have only focused on small reserve projects. There is, however, the potential for greater ecological success by envisioning and executing much larger projects. As Jordan, an experienced restoration ecologist, suggests, "[S]caling up may lead to certain technical difficulties, [but] if these difficulties can be overcome, the work is likely to become easier as elements are added, subsystems kick in, and the system begins to come to life, pulling itself along, taking over more and more of the work, and to some extent directing its own development."[26]

What becomes clear from the ecological science is that self-sustaining ecoscape restoration cannot simply be a process of *ex post* mitigation at small scales. There needs to be a new legal paradigm that moves beyond the existing unsuccessful piecemeal efforts. States' restoration efforts must be *ex ante* planned responses conducted at physical scales large enough to be capable of restoring ecosystem functions and processes.

3.2 Ecoscape restoration and state practice

A future legal principle for proactive ecoscape restoration is not simply an academic idea. There are several practical examples of states and regions responding to needs for large ecoscape restoration. While these examples do not yet rise to the level of creating any customary legal obligation, they are informative of a trend in practice for a wide array of states, including both developed and developing nations. These current efforts are both national and transnational. For example, regarding national programs for landscape level restoration, in the United States there are efforts under the Estuary Restoration Act to support a nationwide estuary habitat restoration strategy, which includes government technical and financial assistance[27] for activities that result in "improving

---

[24] Richard Bierregaard, *Lessons from Amazonia: The Ecology and Conservation of a Fragmented Forest* (New Haven: Yale University Press, 2001).
[25] Jordan, *The Sunflower Forest*, 109.
[26] Ibid., 110.
[27] The Estuary Restoration Act (Title I of United States Public Law 106–457, The Estuaries and Clean Waters Act of 2000). Amended by Section 5017 of the Water Resources Development Act of 2007, Public Law 110–114. Sec. 109.

degraded estuaries or estuary habitat or creating estuary habitat (including both physical and functional restoration), with the goal of attaining a self-sustaining system integrated into the surrounding landscape."[28] For the purposes of this statute, restoration is intended to be proactive and not reactive.[29]

Regarding regional programs, across the globe there are numerous transboundary programs underway to govern large marine ecosystems (LMEs) that have been delineated on the basis of ecological criteria rather than political boundaries.[30] Each of the sixty-four LMEs is expected, as appropriate, to address as an ecological unit how to "recover depleted fish stocks, restore degraded habitats, and reduce and control coastal pollution and nutrient over-enrichment."[31] There have been a number of successful large-scale multi-state restoration efforts including the restoration of wetlands along the Danube River and the Black Sea in order to reduce nitrogen pollution in the Black Sea LME.[32]

Also across the globe are national projects responding to regional deforestation concerns that are contributing to global targets agreed upon by the Global Partnership on Forest Landscape Restoration. In 2011 states committed as part of the Bonn Challenge to restore 150 million hectares of deforested and degraded lands by 2020.[33] As of December 2012, Costa Rica, El Salvador, Brazil, the United States, and Rwanda have committed to restoring 20 million hectares with India proposing to restore 10 million hectares.[34] In countries such as El Salvador and Rwanda, the restoration commitments are nationwide large landscape commitments.[35]

---

[28] Ibid., Section 103(4)(A).   [29] Ibid., Section 103(4)(C).

[30] The Large Marine Ecosystem Approach to the Assessment and Management of Coastal Ocean Waters: Introduction to the LME Portal, available at: www.lme.noaa.gov (last accessed June 6, 2013).

[31] Ibid.

[32] Alfred Duda, "GEF Support for the Global Movement toward the Improved Assessment and Management of Large Marine Ecosystems," in Kenneth Sherman *et al.* (eds.), *Sustaining the World's Large Marine Ecosystems* (Gland: IUCN, 2009), 6.

[33] IUCN, "Leaders Define Pathway to Restoring 150 Million Hectares of Lost Forests" (September 2, 2011), available at: www.iucn.org/?uNewsID=8147 (last accessed June 6, 2013).

[34] IUCN, "Landscape Restoration Movement Approaches 50 Million Hectares with El Salvador and Costa Rica Commitments" (December 6, 2012) www.iucn.org/?uNewsID=11607 (last accessed June 6, 2013).

[35] Ibid. (El Salvador's commitment represents half of its land mass); IUCN, "Rwanda Moving Forward on Ambitious Landscape Restoration Plan" (May 12, 2011), available at: www.iucn.org/?uNewsID=7476 (last accessed June 6, 2013).

Could these existing national laws and international strategies evolve into a broader legal principle to require states to engage in proactive engagement in large-scale restoration of ecosystem processes? While current legal developments only seem to require environmental restoration as ex post responses to restore a resource, rehabilitate a site, or provide legal restitution, the emergence of multilaterally supported global restoration initiatives such as the Large Marine Ecosystems and the Global Partnership on Forest Landscape Restoration suggest new trends for emerging global responsibilities related to restoration efforts. This chapter argues for the emergence of a new ecoscape-based restoration principle based on an *ex ante* obligation to conduct restoration projects with an objective of restoring large-scale ecosystem processes.

3.3 An emerging legal principle of ecoscape restoration?

A global commitment to restore proactively at the ecoscape level has not yet been realized, with current practice promoting transboundary restoration efforts reflecting a patchwork of commitments. Yet continued political support and funding for large marine ecosystem programs and the global reforestation partnership efforts suggest an emerging trend beyond simple voluntarism. States participate in ecoscape-level projects not simply because they make ecological sense but also because these projects satisfy existing and emerging state obligations.

The emerging derivative principle of ecoscape restoration is an extension of existing obligations to restore under the Convention on Biological Diversity and to cooperate regionally. It also provides a practical demonstration of two emerging principles: the principle of non-regression and the principle of ecological integrity. If states have a duty to cooperate and to restore degraded ecosystems because of an internal obligation not to retrogress in terms of environmental protection and to ensure environmental security for its citizens, then this furthers the legal basis upon which to position a new principle of international law requiring states to restore ecological processes within ecoscapes either unilaterally or cooperatively. The following sections detail the legal foundation for a proposed principle of ecoscape restoration.

3.3.1 Duty to rehabilitate and restore degraded ecosystems

The Convention on Biological Diversity (CBD) has 193 parties and includes key language on restoration that has been widely adopted. Article 8(f) requires that "Each Contracting Party shall, as far as possible and as appropriate: ... (f) Rehabilitate and restore degraded ecosystems."[36] Many states, in light of their legal requirements for environmental mitigation after mining or timber projects, would argue that they are in compliance with this CBD obligation. By the letter of the law, they might be in compliance with routine reforestation projects that create novel ecosystems,[37] but if the spirit of the law is in part the "conservation of biological diversity" at the ecosystem level,[38] then states have further work to do if the sustainability of biological diversity actually depends on the conservation of ecosystem processes at sufficiently large ecoscape scales to absorb disruptions to the ecological system.

The CBD parties recognize this additional commitment through their twelve management principles defining the ecosystem approach. Principle 7, recommending that the ecosystem approach "be undertaken at the appropriate spatial and temporal scale",[39] is particularly significant evidence of a multilateral commitment to restoring large-scale ecological processes. The CBD does not explicitly assign an appropriate spatial scale for states, but if science is a benchmark for what is an appropriate scale, then the scientific evidence suggests that states should be making efforts to restore ecosystem processes over large areas. While states already have a duty to restore, this duty must be extended to ecoscape level restoration for the duty to have substance. There is no indication from the CBD that Article 8(f) is a procedural obligation and not a substantive obligation. The proposed principle of ecoscape restoration codifies ecologically necessary contours for implementation of the existing duty to restore under the CBD.

3.3.2   Duty for transboundary cooperation

A key aspect of an ecoscape principle of restoration is a duty to cooperate in order to prevent irreversible harm to ecosystem processes. While this may not require a multilateral response, it will definitely require bilateral and regional responses especially where states' territories are small and the shared ecosystem processes are dispersed. Cooperation is the fundamental driver for most transboundary environmental

---

[36] Convention on Biological Diversity, 31 ILM 818 (1992) (adopted June 5, 1992) (entry into force December 29, 1993).
[37] Richard Hobbs et al., "Novel Ecosystems: Theoretical and Management Aspects of the New Ecological World Order?", 15 *Global Ecology and Biogeography* (2006), 1–7, at 2.
[38] Convention on Biological Diversity, Article 1.
[39] Conference of the Parties Summary, available at: www.cbd.int/gbo1/chap-03.shtml (last accessed June 6, 2013).

obligations. States already have an obligation to use, manage, and conserve shared natural resources.[40] Principle 7 of the 1992 Rio Declaration provides an excellent summary of the existing obligation to cooperate whereby state parties agreed that they "shall cooperate in a spirit of global partnership to conserve, protect and restore the health and integrity of the Earth's ecosystem."[41] Embodied within these pre-existing obligations to cooperate is also the obligation to cooperate particularly for transboundary restoration efforts, but also in global restoration efforts where some states may require additional human and financial resources to be able to responsibly undertake ecoscape level restoration projects.

3.3.3 Principle of non-regression

A principle of restoring ecoscapes might also be grounded in the emerging principle of non-regression.[42] Borrowed from the field of international human rights law and incorporated into national human rights legislation particularly in civil law countries, the principle of non-regression is an international environmental legal principle strongly advocated for by the legal academy and non-governmental organizations.[43] As applied to environmental legislation, a general non-regression principle argues that existing environmental law must not be modified to the detriment of environmental protection. The emergence of the principle is based on pre-existing principles including the duty to prevent harm, public participation, intergenerational equity, and precaution.[44] The idea is that certain types of legislation that serve social protection functions, such as human rights and environmental law, must be progressive rather than regressive.

---

[40] United Nations Environmental Program, Principles on Conservation and Harmonious Utilization of Natural Resources Shared by Two or More States, 17 ILM (1978) 1094; Declaration of the UN Conference on Environment and Development, UN Doc. A/CONF151/26/Rev.1, Report of the UNCED, vol. 1 (New York).

[41] Declaration of the UN Conference on Environment and Development.

[42] Michael Prieur, *De L'urgente Nécessité De Reconnaître Le Principe De "Non Régression" En Droit De L'Environnement*, IUCN Academy of Environmental Law, 2011(1) 26–40, available at: www.iucnael.org/en/component/docman/doc_download/663-de-lurgente-necessite-de-reconnaitre-le-principe-de-non-regression-en-droit-de-lenvironnement.html (last accessed June 6, 2013). (Also referring to non-regression as a "principle of standstill" or "status quo.")

[43] See e.g. International Centre of Comparative Law, Recommendations for Rio+20, available at: www.cidce.org/rio/pdf%20appel/Recommendations.pdf (last accessed June 6, 2013).

[44] Prieur, *De L'urgente Nécessité*, 31–2.

Whether such a principle exists as a general international principle remains to be seen. The European Parliament on September 29, 2011 supported the recognition of the principle of non-regression for environmental protection.[45] Yet at the United Nations Conference on Sustainable Development in June 2012, member states could only agree to "not backtrack from our commitment to the outcome of the United Nations Conference on Environment and Development."[46]

For the ecoscape restoration principle to emerge as a legal principle does not inherently depend on the recognition of non-regression as a general principle, but its long-term success does. Where corridors and reserves are necessary in order to ensure self-sustaining ecological processes, these physical areas cannot become negotiable when a new government assumes power in a state that has different economic development priorities. In addition to protecting large ecosystem boundaries, states cannot use the law to substitute management systems that might undermine the integrity of an ecosystem.

3.3.4 Principle of ecological integrity of territory as an extension of human environmental security

Finally, a principle of ecoscape restoration might emerge on the basis of an emerging necessity for a state to meet its population's environmental security needs in order to satisfy either a state's domestic legal obligations or an international customary right for a healthy environment. In around 177 states out of 192, there is a explicit recognition in state constitutions, court decisions, or multilateral agreements that citizens have a legally cognizable right to a clean or healthy environment.[47] For the ninety-two states with recognized constitutional rights for a clean or healthy environment, states have a responsibility to actively restore ecologically degraded

---

[45] European Parliament resolution of September 29, 2011 on developing a common EU position ahead of the United Nations Conference on Sustainable Development, P7_TA(2011)0430.

[46] "The Future We Want," 20.

[47] David R. Boyd, "The Constitutional Right to a Healthy Environment, Environment: Science and Policy for Sustainable Development," *Environment* (July–August 2012), available at: www.environmentmagazine.org/Archives/Back%20Issues/2012/July-August%202012/constitutional-rights-full.html (last accessed June 6, 2013). Countries that have failed to adopt this right include the United States, Canada, Japan, Australia, New Zealand, China, Oman, Afghanistan, Kuwait, Brunei Darussalam, Lebanon, Laos, Myanmar, North Korea, Malaysia, and Cambodia.

territory in order to ensure some degree of basic environmental security for its population.[48]

What about a duty to restore for states that have not codified a right for their population to have a clean or healthy environment? Are there legal arguments that these states might also have obligations to engage in state-administered or state-funded restoration? Based on the practice of ninety-two states with constitutional right-based provisions, there is emerging customary international law that citizens of a state are entitled to some level of protection of the domestic environment by the state.[49] What the level of protection might be remains open to debate. An argument for customary international law is never easy, yet here the argument that a customary right to a healthy environment triggers a restoration duty on the part of the state goes straight to the heart of one of the core characteristics for statehood.

Why must states have actual territory in order to be considered eligible for recognition as a state? One reason is that states must have some assembly of natural resources available to the people of the state in order to sustain the population that resides within the state from generation to generation. Where territory ceases to have any self-sustaining ecological functions, it arguably ceases to be functional territory for the purposes of statehood because it cannot deliver needed resources for its population. While some depleted resources may be able to be substituted by using the channels of trade, other natural resources such as a reliable source of fresh water are essential to the stability of a state, since trade in these fundamental resources can also raise issues related to human rights and sustenance resources.[50] This argument for a customary obligation to restore ecosystems that no longer function for human subsistence purposes is supported by political obligations that states have already undertaken as

---

[48] Narottam Gaan, *Environmental Security: Concepts and Dimensions* (New Delhi: Kalpaz Publications, 2004), xvi.

[49] Particularly noteworthy among the Constitutions for its articulation of environmental rights is the 2008 Ecuador Constitution, where Title II, Chapter Seven, Article 72 provides: "Nature is entitled to restoration. This restoration is independent of the obligation of the State and persons or companies to compensate individuals and groups that depend on affected natural systems. In cases of severe or permanent environmental impact, including those linked to the exploitation of nonrenewable natural resources, the State shall establish the most effective mechanisms to achieve the restoration, and take appropriate measures to eliminate or mitigate adverse environmental consequences." (Translation available in Donald Anton and Dinah Shelton, *Environmental Protection and Human Rights* (Cambridge University Press, 2011), 125).

[50] See e.g. the provision of water and wastewater services between Israel and Palestine, which has raised numerous fundamental human rights concerns.

civil rights. Each of the 141 states that have accepted the International Covenant on Civil and Political Rights must have some ecologically functioning land in order to ensure that a state's population is not deprived "of its own means of subsistence."[51] The concept that a state must protect the integrity of its own territory for vital renewable resources such as functioning land and water is further bolstered by Principle 3 of the Stockholm Declaration, indicating that the "capacity of the earth to produce vital renewable resources must be maintained and, wherever practicable, restored or improved."[52] For many states, the lack of ecologically functional land might reduce a state to a virtual entity incapable of ensuring its population a means of subsistence and therefore impact a population's ability to exercise rights of self-determination.[53]

What does this discussion of territory and self-sustenance for citizens mean for a new principle of restoration of ecological functions? This extension of the state's responsibility to protect the environment as part of the promotion of human rights seems a natural progression of the concept of the "responsibility to protect" (R2P). While the R2P concept has been largely used as a concept to explain state interventions in the matters of another state (e.g. NATO involvement in Libya),[54] the same type of argument can be extended in that states owe a responsibility to protect their own citizens from chronic environmental degradation since, as the Secretary-General noted, "The responsibility to protect, first and foremost, is a matter of State responsibility, because prevention begins at home and the protection of populations is a defining attribute of sovereignty and statehood in the twenty-first century."[55]

Even though the United Nations has not extended the "responsibility to protect" to the case of ecological intervention, there is no reason to believe that the "responsibility to protect" cannot apply domestically. In

---

[51] International Covenant on Civil and Political Rights (in force March 23, 1976), Article 1(2).
[52] Stockholm Declaration on the Human Environment, UN Doc.A/CONF.48/14/Rev.1, 11 ILM 1416 (1972).
[53] See e.g. Carl N. McDaniel and John M. Gowdy, *Paradise for Sale: A Parable of Nature* (Berkeley: University of California Press, 2000), explaining how the mining of phosphate on the Pacific island of Nauru without restoration of the land has led to a situation where the small population is now unable to sustain itself on the remaining land and is dependent on foreign imports for sustenance goods.
[54] United Nations Secretary-General's Report on Implementing the Responsibility to Protect (January 12, 2009), A/63/677, 4 (R2P is focused on preventing genocide, war crimes, ethnic cleansing, and crimes against humanity).
[55] Ibid., para. 14.

fact, if we rely on the United Nations Secretary-General's statement that "responsibility to protect ... begins at home," then R2P becomes a reliable legal basis on which to guarantee environmental security for a domestic population.[56] While it may not be widely accepted by states that they have a responsibility to restore ecosystems on behalf of their populations, it is now axiomatic among multilateral agencies that environmental degradation should be regarded as a threat to international security.[57]

States that do not address the ongoing degradation of ecosystems may be at risk of failure as a state by creating a cycle of insecurity that results in the state failing to protect citizen's basic environmentally-based human rights. Failure to unilaterally restore degraded landscapes or seascapes may trigger sovereign failure, resulting in possible population migrations to neighboring states or conditions of instability and violence.[58] Populations that flee environmental degradation frequently contribute to environmental degradation in their struggle to survive.[59] To protect a population's human right to a clean and healthy environment, states have an *ex ante* obligation to ensure restoration of ecological processes within landscapes and seascapes to a level that can deliver some self-sustaining ecosystem services and goods for its citizens.

4. Concluding thoughts

If one accepts that there is a legal basis for ecoscape restoration and that such a principle should be implemented, what difference would it make in a global context? In the current situation of case-by-case application of the principle of environmental restoration, states end up with a variety of often unconnected places that meet fixed criteria, such as quantity of ground cover or background toxin levels. There is little synergy between

---

[56] See generally Simon Dalby, "Environmental Dimensions of Human Security," in Rita Floyd and Richard Matthew (eds.), *Environmental Security: Approaches and Issues* (Abingdon: Routledge, 2013), 121–38.

[57] Klaus Toepfer, "Foreword", in Felix Dodds and Tim Pippard (eds.), *Human and Environmental Security: An Agenda for Change* (London: Earthscan, 2006), xvii.

[58] Crisis States Research Centre, "Crisis, Fragile and Failed State Definitions," 2006, available at: www2.lse.ac.uk/internationalDevelopment/research/crisisStates/download/drc/FailedState.pdf (last accessed June 6, 2013) (The London School of Economics' Crisis States Research Centre definition of a "failed state" as a state that is collapsing because it can no longer perform its basic security and development functions and has no effective control over its territory and borders.)

[59] Roger Zetter, "Are Refugees an Economic Burden or Benefit?" 41 *Forced Migration Review* (December 2012), 51.

the restoration sites. The principle of ecoscape restoration would address this challenge because it would not be a reactionary principle relying on restitution, compensation, or disaster to trigger the principle, but could rather function as a guideline principle for national development strategies. Articulating a principle of ecosystem restoration also has the potential to define a new awareness around restoration in much the same way that awareness was defined around the human right to a clean environment before this right was widely adopted.[60]

Like other general international principles, the ecoscape restoration principle is flexible in its application. In practice, the principle can be implemented in a multitude of ways depending on the degradation of a given region. Some ecosystem processes such as rebuilding self-sustaining marine fisheries may respond to largely passive restoration. Others will require more active restoration. For example, in the case of forests there may be a need to establish "stepping stone" forests in patchwork lands or create habitat corridors.

The road from principle to practice will not be straightforward. It will require scientific experimentation, political will, and a flexible application of a rule of law for nature. Whether we call it a greenprint or a blueprint, we need systematic and long-term restorative responses to our ongoing impact on vulnerable ecological processes. To achieve the "restoration of the ecosystem at the planetary scale" called for by ecologists,[61] one might start by acknowledging a new global legal principle of ecoscape restoration in order to advance the rule of law for nature.

---

[60] Kristin Shrader-Frechette, *Environmental Ethics* (Pacific Grove: Boxwood Press, 1981), 96.

[61] Thomas Lovejoy and Ralph Ashton, "Stepping Up the Ambition for Carbon Management: a Vision for Carbon-rich, Cross-continental Biodiversity Corridors," 2:2 *Carbon Management* (2011), 101–3.

11

Traditional norms and environmental law

The sub-Saharan African case study

CHIZOBA CHINWEZE, CHUKWUEMEKA JIDEANI AND
GWEN Z. ABIOLA-OLOKE

1. Introduction

Nature has immense spiritual and traditional values for the indigenous people of the sub-Saharan African region. More than anywhere else in the world, the people of the sub-Saharan African region rely on environmental resources for their sustenance. The ecosystem serves as a safety net for these people. This dependence and relationship with nature has helped the people acquire skills over the years to manage profitable natural resources. Therefore, through their cultural norms and traditional knowledge, which is a law at the local setting, they protect their environment and natural resources along the generational linage. These laws, though not acknowledged by national or international regimes, are what protect the environment and sustain development. It is worthy to note that international environmental agreements are implemented at the domestic level by the rural people. Therefore, for effective global environmental governance, an adequate legal framework, well understood by the people, must exist. This chapter therefore endorses the bottom-up approach in environmental governance, which makes for a successful implementation of international treaties.

This chapter seeks to highlight the link between traditional norms and environmental governance and suggest ways to strengthen such environmental laws at sub-national, national and international levels.

2. Peoples, forests, values

The people of sub-Saharan Africa have a predominantly rural background with similar historic characteristics. The natural environment – land, water, trees, forests and atmosphere – all have immense spiritual and cultural significance for the people. As the people are mainly rural, they are very close to nature and actually depend on nature for sustenance. It is estimated that over 300 million families live in or near tropical forests and about 1.6 billion people around the globe depend on forests for their sustenance. In the sub-Saharan African culture, the Earth is referred to as 'mother' or 'womb' or Mother Earth and is held sacred. It is considered to be a deity and there are priests – Earth priests – who exercise spiritual control over the land. These Earth priests carry out rituals and scarifies on the land prior to planting and after harvest. In matters of land disputes these priests administer land oaths to the parties involved.

Traditional knowledge is deeply rooted in religious belief systems, customs, land-use practices and community-level decision-making. The Sun, Moon and stars feature in the myths and belief systems of the sub-Saharan Africans.

Trees and forests have significant cultural, religious and spiritual values for the sub-Saharan Africans. Forests serve as a link between the spiritual world and the people. For instance, in eastern Nigeria – as in most other West African countries – when a girl child is born, a tree (*Ogbu chi*) is planted for her, and the issues of her life are synonymous with the life of the tree. This makes for cultural trees and sacred forests. In this region the traditional leaders play an important role in the management of these valuable high biodiversity factors. They also regulate village life, control access to land and settle disputes. Indigenous forestry is widespread in the region with some tree species having spiritual significance for healing, ritual sacrifices, taboos and so on. These forest areas have been managed sustainably over hundreds of years through traditional knowledge and culture handed down the generations, through oral tradition and first-hand observation. This includes a set of empirical observations about the local environment and a system of self-management that governs resource use.[1] Ecological aspects are closely tied to social and spiritual aspects of the knowledge system.[2]

Although there exists a relationship between the spiritual life of the indigenous people of the sub-Saharan Africa and Mother Earth, the majority of the people hold land under customary law, but their rights

[1] International Association for Impact Assessment, *Respecting Indigenous Peoples and Traditional Knowledge: International Best Practice Principles*. Special Publication Series No. 9 (2012).
[2] Dene Cultural Institute, *Traditional Knowledge and Environmental Assessment* (submission to BHP Diamond Mine Environmental Assessment, Canada), 1995.

are almost never recognized under existing natural laws.[3] In Nigerian laws, for instance, as in many sub-Saharan African countries, land vests in the state and indigenous title to land is usually overruled on the basis of overriding state/public interest.[4] State land in Africa springs from several European legal traditions that came into force during the colonial era and that take legal precedence over customary principles, even though most landholding and transfer in rural Africa have continued to be arbitrated by customary authorities.

Although land tenure is legally vested with the state, indigenous people apply varied approaches in their legal argumentations,[5] which have been met with strong resistance from the state. One such step is accepting the sovereignty of the state, while arguing for rights within the framework of international and regional instruments and procedure. Article 17 of the UN Universal Declaration of Human Rights (UDHR) posits that everyone has the right to own property alone as well as in association with others; and that no one shall be arbitrarily deprived of their rights.[6] The UN Committee on Economic, Social and Cultural Rights (CESCR) has highlighted state obligations to recognize and respect indigenous peoples' law and resource rights under the International Covenant in Economic, Social and Cultural Rights. Other instruments concerned with environment and development have incorporated indigenous peoples' rights and issues. These include the Convention on Biological Diversity (CBD) Articles 8(j) and 10(c), and the Rio Declaration and Agenda 21 Principle 22. The UN Declaration on the Rights of Indigenous Peoples builds upon existing standards and attempts to redefine prevailing political, economic and cultural relations between indigenous people and the state.

However, many of the gains made on paper are yet to be fully practised, as the laws of many states remain substandard in relation to the international regime. Failure of many states' legal status of and jurisdiction over indigenous peoples' ownership, use and occupancy of land has been widely reported in sub-Saharan Africa;[7] and this has lead to conflicts,

---

[3] FAO, *A Survey of Indigenous Land Tenure in sub-Saharan Africa*, available at: www.fao.org/docrep/007/y5407t/y5407t0d.htm#bm13 (last accessed 27 June 2013).

[4] Section 1 Land Use Act 1978 Cap 202. LFN 1990, Section 44(1) 1999 Constitution.

[5] S. J. Anaya, 'Introduction', in S. J. Anaya, *International Law and Indigenous People* (Aldershot: Ashgate Publishing, 2003), xii–xxi at xii–xiv.

[6] UN Universal Declaration of Human Rights, available at: www.un.org/en/documents/udhr/index.shtml (last accessed 24 January 2013).

[7] Forest Peoples Programme, *Land Rights and the Forest Peoples of Africa: Historical, Legal and Anthropological Perspectives*, 2009, available at: www.forestpeoples.org/sites/fpp/files/publication/2010/05/overviewlandrightsstudy09eng.pdf (last accessed 24 January 2013).

displacements, deforestation, environmental degradation and resource depletion.

Cultural forests are among the oldest protected areas in the world, although they are not recognized by the WDPA (World Database on Protected Areas) and MDG (Millennium Development Goals) analysis that excluded indigenous peoples' and community conserved areas, as further explained below. The protected areas cover 12.7 per cent of the world's terrestrial area and 1.6 per cent of the global ocean area.[8] For a sustainable Earth, Target 11 of the CBD's Aichi Biodiversity Targets calls for at least 17 per cent of the world's terrestrial and inland water areas and 10 per cent of marine areas to be equitably managed and conserved by 2020. It will be recalled that the CBD requires parties to establish protected areas to conserve biodiversity. Thus in 2004, the CBD parties adopted the Programme of Work on Protected Areas (PoWPA). Most of the coverage statistics are derived either from CBD-mandated WDPA or the MDG analysis conducted in early 2011. The MDG analysis excludes those indigenous peoples' and community conserved areas and other area-based conservation measures that do not meet the International Union for Conservation of Nature (IUCN) definition of protected areas and are therefore not included in the WDPA. Furthermore, funding by the Global Environment Facility (GEF) for protected areas from 1991 to 1995 was roughly US$270 million with a plan to spend US$700 million for the period 2011–2014.[9] All these exclude the indigenous peoples' and community conserved areas. Even the Payment for Environmental Services (PES) and REDD-plus[10] exclude many of the poor that inhabit and control much of the ecologically sensitive land due to stringent requirements, criteria and technical complexities of participation. For Target 11 to be achieved in a world with a population of 7 billion in 2013 – projected to rise to over 9 billion by 2050 – coupled with climate change stresses, there is an urgent need for a strong inclusive partnership with the indigenous people who are custodians of natural resources. This entails recognizing and integrating traditional sacred sites and cultural values as part of sus-

---

[8] B. Bertzky, C. Corrigan, J. Kemsey, S. Kenney, C. Ravillous, C. Besançon and N. Burgess, *Protected Planet Report 2012: Tracking Progress towards Global Targets for Protected Areas* (IUCN and UNEP-WCMC, 2012).

[9] GEF online project database: www.thegef.org (last accessed 4 October 2012).

[10] REDD stands for reducing emissions from deforestation and forest degradation, while the '-plus' in REDD-plus widens the scope of the mechanism to include activities to conserve, sustainably manage and enhance forest carbon stock.

tainable development strategies as they have the potential to adequately safeguard protected areas.

3. Meeting the global objectives in environmental governance

Despite around 900 environmental treaties coming into force during the last forty years, human-induced environmental change is pushing the Earth system towards a critical tipping point, which damage may be irreversible unless urgent practical steps are taken to avert the danger. Climate science usually describes the issue as limiting the warming to 2°C above pre-industrial levels. For a global sustainable future, national and international institutions and governance mechanisms must be restructured and reoriented. But it is argued by many scholars that there is a political disconnect among countries engaged in international negotiations on climate change, which perhaps is the most challenging environmental issue of our time.[11] This fact is buttressed by the failure of the UNFCC COP 15 and COP 17 meetings to adopt a replacement treaty for the Kyoto Protocol, and the limited progress on this at COP 18, despite countries coming to a consensus on many issues. The International Institute for Sustainable Development (IISD) reported that the negotiations at Durban resulted in neither victory nor defeat,[12] and the World Resource Institute reported that at Doha only incremental progress was made and there was a lack of political will.[13] The political will to create, implement and adequately enforce effective regulatory mechanisms is crucial for global environmental governance, especially in challenging issues such as climate change. Thus global politics needs to be translated into domestic policy for the international treaty to be effectively implemented at the domestic level. It is worthy to note that most environmental problems are local in scope and as such decisions made at that level are most likely to match citizens' desires and aspirations, and therefore have greater legitimacy. International goals can only be met at the domestic level.

---

[11] B. Hudson, 'Federal Constitutions and Global Governance: The Case of Climate Change' 87:4 *Indiana Law Journal* (2012), 1455–515.
[12] J. Boyle, *Assessing the Outcome of COP 17. In Pursuit of a Binding Climate Agreement: Negotiators Expand the Mitigation Tent but Reinforced the Ambition Gap.* IISD Report, December 2011, available at: www.iisd.org (last accessed 24 March 2012).
[13] J. Morgan, *Reflections on COP18 in Doha: Negotiations Made only Incremental Progress* (WRI, 2012), available at: http://insights.wri.org/news/2012/12/reflections-cop-18-doha-negotiators-made-only-incremental-progress (last accessed 25 February 2013).

4. The traditional norms in sub-Saharan Africa

In sub-Saharan Africa two systems of governance exist: the modern system and the traditional system. Modern governance claims authority based on democracy and constitutional legality, much of which is inherited from the colonial period, despite the fact that colonialism itself was anti-democratic. The traditional leaders claim legitimacy based on history and religion that pre-dates the colonial period. They seem to represent true African values and authority.[14] For many people in the region, the traditional structure is more legitimate as many live according to their traditional status, norms and rules. This is also because the state is often weak and unable to improve the peoples' lives.[15] The traditional leadership represents indigenous African values and authority that have links with the divine – gods, spirits and ancestors. The king is seen as the intermediary between the departed ancestors, the living and the unborn, and the people have immense confidence in this institution. The legitimacy of the traditional institutions precedes the current post-colonial state based on political legitimacy. It should be noted that a form of authority has legitimacy only when people obey its law because they are convinced that they are in agreement as to how they should be ruled.

In sub-Saharan Africa the majority of the citizenry live in the rural areas, and the people are under the governance of traditional norms. Here, social control revolves around the dynamics of clanship, with the normative scheme being entrenched in a well-established rule of conduct enforced by the head of clans, chiefs and the supportive arms – the council of elders and advisors. Examples are the Tallensi of Northern Gahanna, the Sukuma of Tanzania, the Nuer of Southern Sudan, the Ibos of Nigeria and the Kikuya of Kenya. The community-level pattern of governance, which has a socio-political hierarchical structure, not only oversees social cohesion in giving guidance, direction, development, settlement of disputes, allocation of land and financial support, but also natural resource

---

[14] P. Jackson and H. Marquette. *The Interaction between Traditional Systems and Local Government Systems in sub-Saharan Africa: Annotated Bibliography* (International Development Department, University of Birmingham, 2010), available at: http://info.worldbank.org/etools/docs/library/136160/tslg/pdf/interaction.pdf (last accessed 29 April 2012).

[15] L. Georg and L. Wolf, *Traditional Structures in Local Governance for Local Development* (Institute of Political Science, University of Berne, May 2004), available at: www.georglutz.ch/docs/trad_struct_engl.pdf (last accessed 27 June 2013).

management for the benefit of the community.[16] The elders' forum, which comprises the king, emir or head chief and the heads of households or clans, oversees the affairs of the community, from the home unit to the community level. The youth leaders and advisors are answerable to the elders with the king at the head of affairs, and they enforce compliance with the traditional norms.

The African traditional system and rule of law provides checks and balances in the political structure for the benefit of the society. In countries such as Sudan, Somalia and East Timor, traditional structures are the only remaining and functional form of social organization after many years of civil war. The system seeks to preserve and control access to the natural resources. The locals are the managers, planners and harvesters of the natural resources; thus they are the determiners of the ways in which those resources are used. This environmental governance at the local level is what sustains the Earth systems. Although growing demands for food, feed, fuel and raw materials from land-based resources pose a considerable threat to the ecosystem,[17] with alarming rates of deforestation in Africa resulting in an annual loss of 3.4 million hectares between 2000 and 2010,[18] most traditional sacred rural forests still stand. The reasons for this are not far-fetched, as the people own allegiance to the traditional institutions. In African societies there are social structures that are hierarchical, which is essential for community life and progress. The normative scheme consists of elaborate bodies of well-established rules of conduct usually enforced by the elders, heads of clans, families and village mercenaries. For instance, there are set times and seasons for hunting and harvesting of forest resources, such as timber extraction, logging and to a lesser extent commercial firewood collection and charcoal production. The forest acts as a safety net for the people.

Pressure on natural systems at the local level arises primarily from agricultural activities, resource extraction and very low infrastructural expansion. Rural agriculture in sub-Saharan Africa involves shifting cultivation, pockets of plantation agriculture and cattle ranching. These traditional systems have households manage farms of mixed land uses with shorter fallow periods as production is for both subsistence and sale

---

[16] O. Otumfuo, *Traditional Systems of Government and the Modern State*. Keynote Address at the Fourth African Development Forum, Addis Ababa, 12 October 2004, available at: www.houseofnationalities.org/asantehene_king.asp (last accessed 28 April 2012).

[17] Millennium Ecosystem Assessment (MA), *Ecosystems and Human Well-being: Synthesis*, 2005.

[18] FAO, 'Global Forest Resources Assessment', *Forestry Papers*, Rome, 2010.

at markets. In contrast to the traditional frontier, the state engages large landowners to operate market-integrated systems and infrastructural development for economic strategy over environmental sustainability.

The global food, energy, environmental and financial crises of 2007/8 stirred up tension among national governments and prompted the current wave of complexes in land use. The assumption that biofuels are a viable long-term solution to current energy and ecological challenges, combined with a decline in land allocated to agriculture in developed countries, have pushed many institutions and corporations from various sectors to scramble for large tracts of land in developing countries. Large land grabs in sub-Saharan Africa by foreign countries and corporate entities have been widely reported.[19] The International Food Policy Research Institute reported that, in Madagascar, negotiations with Daewoo Logistic Corporation to lease 1.3 million hectares (which represents half of the country's farming land) for maize and palm oil production played a role in the political conflict that led to the overthrow of the government in 2009.[20] The Swedish-based companies Biomassive and Sekab are already growing crops in Mozambique and Tanzania for biofuel production. Sekab has already planted 20,000 hectares in Tanzania's coastal region and has plans to expand this to 400,000 hectares. The volume of ethanol from this project is expected to be enough to replace all petrol and diesel used by cars in Sweden and Norway. From 2008 to 2009 the Republic of Korea acquired 690,000 hectares of land in Sudan, and China was reported to have signed a land deal with Zimbabwe in March 2008 for over 100,000 hectares. European corporations, universities from the United States and pension funds are also named among those purchasing huge tracts of land in sub-Saharan Africa.[21]

From the forgoing it is evident that large land deals made by state actors in the region are an integral part of deforestation, unlike the traditional system that rarely sells land to non-indigenes.

Resource extraction such as logging, mining and oil exploration is another source of permanent long-term land change, which is resisted where it negatively affects traditional values. For instance, in 2000 the Ghanaian government granted rights to prospect for gold in Nawdoli, Lawra and Jirapa districts in upper West Ghana. These rights encouraged

---

[19] The WorldWatch Institute, *State of the World Report*, 2011.
[20] J. Von Braun, and R. Meinzen-Dick, *'Land Grabbing' by Foreign Investors in Developing Countries: Risks and Opportunities*, IFPRI Policy Brief, 13 April 2009.
[21] C. Chinweze, G. Abiola-Oloke., C. Kennedy-Echetebu and C. Jideani, *Biofuels and Food Security: Green Economy in sub-Saharan Africa*, E-bulletin of the United Nations Research Institute for Social Development, 22 November 2011.

illegal gold prospecting from 2007, threatening the Tanchara's sacred groves – green clusters of indigenous trees and shrubs revered as sacred lands. Traditional regulation for the protection of the sacred groves was enforced by the Tingandem, the spiritual leaders who are regarded as the true owners of the land.[22]

5. Contribution of nature to livelihoods and poverty eradication

More than anywhere else on the globe, the sub-Saharan Africans have relied on nature for sustenance. Millions of families depend on natural resources as safety nets. The importance of nature, for instance the forested ecosystem, to human well-being cannot be overstated.[23] Ecosystem services are benefits of nature to households and the economics of a community; many such services cannot be quantified financially, as the relationship between man and nature is complex and often non-monetized.

5.1 Forests and culture

A protected area in the local context addresses sustainable livelihoods and ecosystem services for the people; it mitigates natural disasters and ensures food security, clean water, climate change resilience, mitigation and adaptation, and alleviates poverty. In an era of scarce and competing resources, it is imperative that the natural resource is equitably managed and conserved. In recent times forest governance has been decentralized and more local actors play major roles in communal tenure.

Indigenous Peoples and Local Community Conserved Territories and Areas (ICCAs), described by the CBD Secretariat as 'natural and/or modified ecosystems, containing significant biodiversity values, ecological benefits and cultural values, voluntarily conserved by indigenous peoples and local communities through customary laws and other effective means',[24] contribute meaningfully to the conservation of the ecosystem,

---

[22] B. G. Yangmaadome, D. B. Faabelangne, E. K Derbile, W. Hiemstra and B. Verschuuren, 'Sacred Groves versus Gold Mines: Biocultural Community Protocols in Ghana' 65 *Participatory Learning and Action* (2012), 121–30.

[23] J. Boyd and S. Banzhaf, 'What are Ecosystem Services? The Need for Standardized Environmental Accounting Units' 63:2–3 *Ecological Economics* (2007), 616–26.

[24] CBD Secretariat, *Recognizing and Supporting Territories and Areas Conserved by Indigenous Peoples and Local Communities: Global Overview and National Case Studies*, Secretariat of the Convention of Biological Diversity, ICCA Consortium, Technical Series

species and genetic diversity through traditional knowledge and cultural practices. In its 2012 report[25] the CBD Secretariat noted that ICCAs are the world's oldest conservation initiative, much older than the formally designated protected areas of modern times. They ranged from tiny patches of nature to tens of thousands of square kilometres of sacred sites, habitats of threatened or culturally important species and indigenous territories, which include community forests and others.[26] There is therefore a need to recognize the significant role ICCAs could play in meeting commitments under other global agreements such as the Strategic Plan for Biodiversity 2011–2020, particularly in achieving Aichi Targets 11 (on protected areas), 13 (on food security), 16 (on the Nagoya Protocol on Access and Benefit Sharing) and 18 (on traditional knowledge and customary sustainable use), the CBD Programme of Work on Protected Areas (PoWPA), the Millennium Development Goals and the UN Declaration on the Rights of Indigenous Peoples.[27] However, the recent decisions of the CBD Conference of Parties, specifically decisions X/31[28] and IX/18,[29] call for recognition and support to be provided for ICCAs taking cognizance of threats and challenges to them, which include inappropriate and unsustainable development and commercial projects, lack of official recognition, economic changes and political inequalities.

5.2 Application of traditional knowledge and norms in forest governance

The dependence of the locals of the sub-Saharan region on forest resource for their livelihoods cannot be overemphasized. Through years of experience they both manage the forest resources profitably and cope with changing climatic conditions.

In the Umuatulu-Umueri community of Nigeria, as in any other community setting in the sub-Saharan African region, the community forest that has contributed immensely to cash income and non-cash income generation for the locals has been standing for hundreds of years. The continued existence of the forest is due to the cultural rules and norms

---

no. 64, 2012, available at: www.cbd.int/doc/publications/cbd-ts-64-en.pdf (last accessed 22 January 2013).

[25] CBD Secretariat, *Report of the Colloquium on the Role of ICCAs in Achieving the Aichi Targets*, 13 October 2012.

[26] Ibid.   [27] Ibid.

[28] UNEP/CBD/COP/X/31.

[29] UNEP/CBD/COP/DEC/IX/18.

guiding the management and harvesting of the forest products. Avoidance of deforestation is also achieved by allotting times when it is a taboo to enter the forest or harvest anything from the forest, such as on the various festival days and Ōge ukwu – special market days that occur once in every eight days. This forest-related traditional knowledge, which is handed down the generations, is interwoven with culture, religious beliefs, practice and the community-based decision-making process, and has made for good forest management, conservation of ecosystem services, biological diversity and identification/preservation of forest genetic resources as it is understood in science and international climate policy regime.

Traditional forest-related knowledge should be documented in close partnership with holders and users of this knowledge system, using ethically appropriate best practices. It is not enough for the UN Framework Convention on Climate Change (UNFCCC) to provide guidance for national and regional programmes; it should further demand clear local inputs for national inventory. The local and indigenous people should be provided with adequate training and technical assistance to adapt their traditional land-use system to modern economic conditions, as the majority of them have a low level of education. Furthermore, there is the need to mainstream traditional forest-related knowledge into national forest action plans and programmes for effective forest management, as the main objective of community-based forestry is to contribute to the conservation of standing forests and promote rural livelihoods. Again, a legal system for the protection of traditional forest-related knowledge should be developed to prevent attempts to patent existing traditional knowledge and curb biopiracy.[30]

The people who are the custodians and managers of the local forest have extensive knowledge of the composition of species, their abundance, distribution, behaviour and factors that influence them, as they are in steady contact with their ecosystem. Such knowledge is specific to different families – a household gifted in traditional healing/medicine, for instance, has a good knowledge of forest genetic resources associated with healing: leaves, fruits, seeds, roots, tree barks and the seasonal variations that influence their abundance, distribution, identification and so on. The family of hunters knows the variety of animal species in the forest, their migration patterns, hideouts, management practices and so on. Women and youth are also armed with forest resources management know-how.

[30] E/CN.18/2011/9/Add.2.

Women are the custodians of their households and they rely on forest for fuelwood, fodder, nuts and vegetables. As they go to fetch fuelwood, they also pick snails, mushrooms, spices and other materials for their household consumption. As such they know the timing and season of availability of these resources. This knowledge arises from experience, practices and personal teachings handed down from father to son, from mother to daughter, from one generation to another. In the community each distinct group is able to contribute to the development of a best practice management methodology, which ensures sustainable use of the natural resources for the benefit of the community and the livelihoods of the people living there. Because this local knowledge is tied to spirits and the gods of the land, the application of it is vehemently adhered to.

Non-specialized knowledge is connected with coping with climatic changes. Most homes in the Umueri community, for instance, do not have a clock, but they can tell the time by the length of shadows. Virtually everybody, except for toddlers and babies, can predict weather patterns by the movement of the clouds, Sun, Moon, wind, changes in plant phenology and changes in animal behaviour. Such knowledge boasts environmental governance and the coping capacity of the natives relative to climatic variations.

Traditional knowledge can help to provide science with concrete accurate local climatic information as its relationship with nature is typically based on observation. Thus the locals have on-the-ground climatic history and baseline field data. Traditional knowledge complements scientific knowledge by providing local practical experience through continual interaction with the ecosystem and responding to ecosystem changes. The integration of local traditional knowledge with science is required if the international goals of combating climate change are to be met.

6. Forest governance and climate change

Forests have become significant in climate change negotiations and serve the important function of carbon sequestration as sinks of carbon dioxide. Global attention has been turned to forests following the recognition of capacity of forests to sequester carbon and as a sink that reduces the concentration of carbon dioxide in the atmosphere, thereby helping in the mitigation of climate change impacts. Currently forests cover about 31 per cent of the world's total land area and store more than 289 gigatonnes (GT) of carbon in the above-ground biomass. More than 75 per cent of total terrestrial carbon sink and over 40 per cent of soil organic carbon stock is found in the forest ecosystem.[31] The plant biomass in tropical forests stores 340Pg C compared to 57Pg C in the boreal ecosystem, while tropical forest soils store 213Pg C compared to 338Pg C in boreal forests.[32] At present forests absorb an estimated 30 per cent of all anthropogenic CO_2 emissions from fossil fuel-burning and deforestation. On the other hand it is estimated that 20–25 per cent of annual global emission results from the destruction and deforestation of tropical forests.[33] Deforestation accounts for 35 per cent of carbon emissions in developing countries and 65 per cent in least developed countries.[34] However, the global rates of annual forest loss have decreased from 16 million hectares in the 1990s to approximately 13 million hectares between 2000 and 2010.

Although the global rates show signs of reduction, the rate in Africa and South America remains alarmingly high. The forests still standing in Africa are probably those managed by the communities. The key to achieving internationally agreed goals with respect to reducing tropical forest loss is to address stakeholders' engagement in sustainable forest management; this is consistent in particular with the decisions of the United Nations Framework Convention on Climate Change Conference of the Parties 4/CP.15 and 1/CP.16. At the Copenhagen Conference in December 2009, at its fifteenth session (COP 15) the parties adopted decision 4/CP.15 on the 'Methodological guidance for activities relating to reducing emissions from deforestation and forest degradation and the role of conservation, sustainable management of forests and enhancement of forest carbon stocks in developing countries'. The decision recognizes the need for full and effective engagement of indigenous peoples and local communities in, and the potential contribution of their knowledge to, monitoring and reporting of activities relating to decision 1/CP.13, paragraph 1(b)(iii). Paragraph 3 of the decision encourages, as appropriate, the development of guidance for effective engagement of indigenous

---

[31] R. Jandl, M. Linder, L. Vesterdal, B. Bauwens, R. Baritz, F. Hagedorn, D. Johnson, K. Minkkines and K. A. Byrne, 'How Strongly Can Forest Management Influence Soil Carbon Sequestration?' 137 *Geoderma* (2007), 253–68.

[32] IPCC, *The Carbon Cycle and Atmosphere Carbon Dioxide, Climate Change 2001: The Scientific Basis* (Cambridge University Press, 2001), 183–237.

[33] IPCC, *Land Use, Land Use Change and Forestry* (Cambridge University Press, 2000); REDD-net, International Negotiations, available at: http://redd-net.org/themes/international-negotiations (last accessed 20 February 2013).

[34] J. I. McAlpine, 'Forests and Climate Change: Bridging the Gaps', Guest Article #16. International Institute for Sustainable Development IISD-Reporting Service, available at: http://climate-l.iisd.org/guest-articles/forests-and-climate-change-bridging-the-gaps/ (last accessed 25 April 2012).

peoples and local communities in monitoring and reporting.[35] Also at the Cancun Conference in December 2010, the sixteenth Conference of Parties (COP 16) adopted decision 1/CP.16 on 'The Cancun Agreements: Outcome of the Work of the Ad Hoc Working Group on Long-term Cooperative Action under the Convention'. This decision includes a text on Chapter III, which referred to two important appendices. Appendix I on 'Guidance and Safeguards for policy approaches and positive incentives on issues relating to reducing emissions from deforestation and forest degradation in developing countries, and the role of conservation, sustainable management of forests and enhancement of forest carbon stocks in developing countries', paragraph 2(c)(d) calls for respect for the knowledge and rights of indigenous peoples and members of local communities, by taking into account relevant international obligations, national circumstances and laws and noting that the United Nations General Assembly has adopted the United Nations Declaration on the Rights of Indigenous People; and for the full and effective participation of relevant stakeholders, in particular indigenous peoples and local communities, in the actions referred to in paragraphs 70 and 72 of the decision.[36]

The Stern Review of the economics of climate change identified forest carbon sequestration as one of the most cost-effective mechanisms for combating climate change.[37] The Review was discussed at the Conference of the Parties to the UNFCCC in 2006 and 2007. The thirteenth session of the Conference of Parties in Bali 2007 (2/CP.13[38]) and the sixteenth session at Cancun in 2010 (1/CP.16) also promoted forest carbon sequestration as a key climate change mitigation and adaptation strategy, which has given rise to monetary compensation for protecting the forest ecosystem under the initiative of reducing emissions from deforestation and forest degradation in developing countries and payment for ecosystem services (PES). Paragraph 72 and 2 of Appendix I of decision 1/CP.16 refers to safeguards that should be promoted and supported when undertaking such activities; it emphatically calls for 'ensuring the full and effective

---

[35] FCCC/CP/2009/11/Add.1 (2010), available at: http://unfccc.int/resource/docs/2009/cop15/eng/11a01.pdf#page=3 (last accessed 7 June 2013).
[36] FCCC/CP/2010/7/Add.1 (2011), available at: http://unfccc.int/resource/docs/2010/cop16/eng/07a01.pdf#page=2 (last accessed 7 June 2013).
[37] Stern Review: The Economics of Climate Change, http://siteresources.worldbank.org/INTINDONESIA/Resources/226271-1170911056314/3428109-1174614780539/SternReviewEng.pdf (last accessed 27 June 2013).
[38] FCCC/CP/2007/6/Add.1–2/CP.13, paragraph 1–12.

participation of relevant stakeholders, inter alia indigenous peoples and local communities'.

7. Conclusions

The global negotiations on environmental governance to save the Earth's ecosystems from reaching tipping points are primarily dependent on the input at local levels where nature is nurtured and highly valued. Although the concept of multiple forest values and the increasing role of indigenous peoples and local communities in forest management has gained global attention in the discussions on international climate change, with for instance the theme of the International Year of Forest (2011) being 'Forest for the People',[39] yet there are several constraints that block the full and effective involvement of the local communities and indigenous people in the global climate solution contrary to the aims of international agreements. For instance, REDD-plus is still bogged down with issues of benefit-sharing and disagreements over how to verify and validate emission reduction, although attention is beginning to be shifted towards landscape-based mechanisms, which also seem even more cumbersome to quantify. In sub-Saharan Africa there are still issues of land tenure rights (indigenous peoples' rights), forest governance and gender elimination. It should be noted that African access to and/or rights over land are predominantly based on ancestry, tradition, customs or culture and are not necessarily backed by domestic legislation. Often they lack enforceable status and/or the land is state-owned with rights to access for indigenous people never properly defined.[40] Land change dynamics are inseparable from social interactions and choices. For instance, the spiritual or cultural values of forests to indigenous communities have guided their behaviour, attitudes and decisions in forest management and preservation over centuries without monetary incentives, thereby enhancing the benefits of forests to local livelihoods and sustaining the Earth systems, and thus combating vulnerability to climate change impacts. This is

---

[39] UNFF, 'Under-Secretary-General Calls for "People-Centred" Approach to Manage Forest Lands as Forum begins Ninth Session at Headquarters', UN Economic and Social Council. Department of Public Information, News and Media Division, New York, ENV/DEV/1179, 24 January, 2011.

[40] A. Graham, S. Aubry, R. Kunnemann and S. M. Suurez – (FIAN), 'Land Grab Study: "Advancing African Agriculture" (AAA): The Impact of Europe's Policies and Practices on African Agriculture and Food Security'. CSO Monitoring 2009–2010.

contrary to the mistaken belief that local populations are the main cause of deforestation.

Interestingly from the international arena, the parties to the CBD recognize the role that territories and areas governed or managed by indigenous peoples and local communities can play in meeting its mandate. In response to Decision X/31, the CBD Secretariat produced the CBD Technical Series 64, titled 'Recognizing and Supporting Indigenous Peoples and Local Community Conserved Territories and Areas (ICCAs)'. In furtherance of this, a full-day colloquium was organized by CBD and its partners on the fringes of COP 11 of CBD in Hyderabad, India in October 2012, on the Role of Indigenous Peoples and Local Community Conserved Territories and Areas in Achieving the Aichi Targets. The study suggested that officially designated protected areas comprise about 13 per cent of the world's total area, and an equal, if not greater, area may be conserved in ICCAs. The participants noted that in order to maintain and enhance the value of ICCAs, indigenous peoples and local communities governing them need adequate and appropriate recognition and support.[23]

One key point for the law is the representation and inclusion of local communities' viewpoints in decision-making, both at local and international levels, with the intention of incorporating the most marginalized segments of the community – women and the very poor[41] – who may have the very knowledge required for solutions to climate change. National governments have a big role to play in this aspect. However, the challenge of this inclusion is the risk of elite capture[42] in representation as there are limited capacities among the local communities.

Recognizing the value of traditional norms and their role in environmental governance is one thing; translating them into international law and policy for implementation at national and local level is another. Positive change is possible when political will is aligned with strategies of change.

---

[41] E/CN.18/2011/4.
[42] J. C. Ribot, 'African Decentralization: Local Actors, Powers and Accountability', Democracy, Governance and Human Rights' Paper 8 (2002), United Nations Research Institute for Social Development (UNRISD).

PART IV

Nature's rights

12

Rules of law for use and nonuse of nature

JAN LAITOS

For centuries, humanity prospered by controlling, depleting, and polluting nature's resources. Welfare was served when forests were turned into farms, wetlands into cities, mountains into mines. Developing countries were deemed successful if their natural landscapes had been transformed from wild lands to utilitarian places where we could live, work, and create individual wealth. It seemed that three types of natural resources (stock, renewable commodity, and public environmental) had one primary purpose: to be used and exploited by one special planetary species – us.[1]

1. Rules of law to benefit humans, not nature

1.1 First-generation resource use laws

Initially, laws, and particularly the common law of contract and property, encouraged and protected this resource use. Contract law permitted one user to make enforceable, credible marketplace deals with other potential users of resources, particularly stock resources, so that the resource would wind up with the user most willing to pay for it (and who, in theory, would put it to the most efficient use).[2] Then property law allowed users to own the resource, and to exercise the right to control, develop, and exploit it to enhance the owner's selfish interests.[3]

---

[1] Mark Sagoff, *Price, Principle, and the Environment* (Cambridge University Press, 2004), 15.
[2] Karl Polanyi, *The Great Transformation: The Political and Economic Origins of Our Time* (Boston, MA: Beacon Press, 1957); Adam Smith, *An Inquiry Into the Nature and Causes of the Wealth of Nations*, K. Sutherland (ed.) (Oxford University Press, [1776] 1993).
[3] David Feeny, "The Development of Property Rights in Land: A Comparative Study," in: Robert Bates (ed.), *Toward a Political Economy of Development: A Rational Choice Perspective* (Berkeley: University of California Press, 1988), 272. Harold Demsetz, "Toward a Theory of Property Rights," 57 *American Economic Review* (1967) 347.

These "first-generation" resource-use laws, prevalent throughout much of the nineteenth and early twentieth centuries, reflected a judgment that endured for multiple centuries: Stock and renewable commodity resources should first be owned and then utilized by individuals. These owner-individuals would, in pursuit of selfish interests, transform, extract, use, or exchange resources in the relevant market. The working assumption was that laws furthering the operation of the economic market would then ensure that what was best for the individual resource owner would ultimately also be best for the society in which that owner lived.[4]

1.2 Second-generation conservation laws, for future resource use

Eventually, however, excessive use depleted stock and renewable commodity resources. Reliance on the economic market as a resource-regulating mechanism had failed, in large part because owners of private property had little incentive not to use their resource wealth.[5] Indeed, if they did not use their resources, they were often, by operation of law, deemed to have abandoned or forfeited their rights to their property. For example, the American General Mining Law of 1872 declared that mining claimants would lose their claim if they did not perform annual assessment work to maintain the claim.[6] Gradual resource exhaustion and depletion caused lawmakers to adopt another category of resource use laws, second-generation law, designed to slow unchecked resource extraction, and create a more sustainable resource base for future generations of resource use. In the USA the Taylor Grazing Act of 1934 put restrictions on previously open grazing norms on rangeland, in order to ensure that forage would not be overly depleted.[7]

By the middle of the twentieth century, both first- and second-generation resource use laws (those encouraging present use and those conserving for future use) had not prevented the depletion of the stock and renewable resource base. Moreover, such use had begun to pollute public environmental foods, such as the air, the water, and the soil. The dominant

---

[4] Ronald Findlay, "The Roots of Divergence: Western Economic History in Comparative Perspective," 82 *American Economic Review* (1992) 158; Douglas C. North and Robert B. Thomas, *The Rise of the Western World: A New Economic History* (Cambridge University Press, 1973).

[5] A. V. Kneese and Blair T. Bower, *Environmental Quality Analysis: Theory and Method in the Social Sciences* (Baltimore: Johns Hopkins Press for Resources for the Future, 1972), 1–6.

[6] General Mining Law of 1872, 30 U.S.C. § 328.

[7] Taylor Grazing Act of 1934, 43 U.S.C. § 315 et seq.

"use" component of natural uses was now threatening another facet of resources – the critical "nonuse" component.

1.3 Third-generation resource nonuse laws

Nonuse values prevail when natural resources are *not* used by humans, and when the resource is left alone in its natural state. When resources are not used by humans, the resources themselves are spared, but so too are humans bettered. Humans benefit in at least three ways when resources are not excessively exploited and polluted, or when resources remain in a natural state. First, natural resources, especially public environmental goods (such as air and water), are preconditions to human survival and existence when they are not used as pollution sinks.[8]

Second, undeveloped natural lands and locations have recreational value for those wishing to engage in low-impact play. In addition, certain natural objects, such as wild lands or wildlife species, have high "existence" value for humans in that their mere existence in an unused condition is important to us; we place a value on their place in nature, even though we do not intend to consume or own them as we do stock or renewable commodity resources.[9]

Third, some resources (such as wetlands, rain forests, and estuaries) have economic value for humans in their natural condition because they provide crucial ecological services to humans that markets fail to price. Unspoiled nature serves as "natural capital," providing long-term economic benefits that offset the short-term disadvantages that are involved in forgoing human development.[10]

Mid-twentieth-century resource depletion and pollution adversely affected these nonuse aspects components of resources.[11] Our response to this threat to nonuse benefits was (once again) to turn toward the law and legal institutions. Throughout the Western world, and especially in the United States, a series of statutes was enacted, and government policies adopted, that were designed to curb resource use not because we

---

[8] Bill McKibben, *The End of Nature* (New York: Random House, 1989).
[9] John K. Krutilla, "Conservation Reconsidered," 57 *American Economic Review* (1967) 787.
[10] See Gretchen C. Daily (ed.), *Nature's Services: Societal Dependence on Natural Ecosystems* (Washington, DC: Island Press, 1997).
[11] Gretchen C. Daily, Susan Alexander, Paul R. Ehrlich *et al.*, "Ecosystem Services: Benefits Supplied to Human Societies by Natural Ecosystems," *Ecology* (Spring 1997) 2; Graciela Chichilnisky and Geoffrey Heal, "Economic Returns From the Biosphere," 391 *Nature* (1998) 629.

wanted to conserve the resource for more future use, but to protect our very human, purely anthropocentric need for resource *nonuse* benefits.[12]

Third-generation antipollution laws used command-and-control rules to constrain the risks that one person can impose on another during the course of resource use (such as public environmental goods being overexploited as receptacles for our garbage). Preservation laws protected forests, landscapes, wild lands, and wildlife from resource extraction and development.[13] Laws that attempted to stimulate private markets to protect the environment were seeking economic efficiency.[14] Proposed laws that focused on restoration of natural capital and ecosystem goods sought to protect the capacity of nature to deliver environmental services to humans.[15]

Laws furthering these four goals of protection, preservation, efficiency, and restoration were constructed around limiting human "use" intrusions into nature. The assumption behind third-generation antipollution laws was that if use were restricted, there would be less human contamination of the necessary "nonuse" qualities of public environmental goods (e.g., a clean and healthful atmosphere). The assumption behind third-generation preservation laws was that use limits would protect natural objects such as wild places and living organisms for low-level recreation and existence value. The assumption behind market-based solutions was that these would be more effective and less administratively expensive than command-and-control rules. The assumption behind third-generation ecosystem services initiatives was that excessive human use had degraded the ability of natural systems to provide humans with economically essential, but largely undervalued, nature-based goods.

---

[12] See, e.g., Richard J. Lazarus, *The Making of Environmental Law* (University of Chicago Press, 2004); National Park Service Organic Act, 16 U.S.C. § 22; Multiple Use Sustained Act, 16 U.S.C. §§ 528–531; Federal Lands Policy Management Act, 43 U.S.C. § 1701; Jan G. Laitos and Rachael B. Reiss, "Recreation Wars for Our Natural Resources," 34 *Environmental Law* (2004) 1091; *Southern Utah Wilderness Alliance* v. *Norton*, 542 U.S. 55 (2004). Other laws were designed to provide aesthetic and health benefits when use prohibitions were imposed. See *Hoffman* v. *Deschutes County*, 240 P.3d 79 (Or. App. 2010) (upholding setback requirements from structures near surface mine operations).

[13] Sagoff, *Price, Principle and the Environment*, 12; Endangered Species Act, 16 U.S.C. § 1531(b).

[14] David Driesen, "The Economic Dynamics of Environmental Law: Cost Benefit Analysis, Emissions Trading, and Priority Setting," 31 *Boston College Environmental Affairs Law Review* (2004) 501.

[15] Eric S. Higgs, *Nature by Design: People, Natural Processes, Ecological Restoration* (Cambridge, MA: MIT Press, 2003).

Such laws shared an *anthropocentric* perspective, by focusing solely on the harmful effect resource use had on humans, rather than the effect on the resource itself and its surrounding environment.[16] Consequently, nature, nature's resources, and the environment were viewed as mere goods that serve to satisfy human needs. For example, even one of the most significant of all the American third-generation environmental protection laws – the National Environmental Policy Act of 1969 – announced that its purpose was to "maintain conditions under which man and nature exist [to] fulfill the … requirement of *future generations of* Americans."[17] The rule of law continued to be anthropocentric, and nature remained an instrumentalist tool for human welfare.

1.4 Fourth-generation publicly held resource nonuse laws

When environmental harms persisted, or even escalated,[18] attention turned to yet another anthropocentric approach to environmental degradation and natural resources exhaustion. This proposal, still reflecting third-generation values, advocated future legal systems that would create "public" rights to environmental quality while continuing to adopt human-centric goals.

Arguments in favor of extending human rights principles into the environmental realm proposed the creation of a right, found in both international and constitutional norms, that could provide a substantive claim for all people to a clean, healthy, and sustainable environment. This legally acknowledged right could be collectively or individually held, and it would afford humans a priority to environmental nonuse values when resource use demands are being asserted.[19] For example, the Global "Rio

---

[16] Leonard Zobler, "An Economic–Historical View of Natural Resource Use and Conservation," 38 *Economic Geography* (1962) 190.

[17] National Environmental Policy Act, 42 U.S.C. § 4331(a) (emphasis added).

[18] Steve Newman, "Nearly the Hottest," *Boulder Daily Camera*, December 24, 2010, 4B; Neela Banerjee, "Climate Scientists Go Public," *Denver Post*, November 8, 2010, 5A; Hagit Affek, "What We Know About the Climate," *Yale Alumni Magazine* (July/August 2010), 28; Mark Lynas, *Six Degrees: Our Future on a Hotter Planet* (London: Fourth Estate, 2007).

[19] Gunther Handl, "Human Rights and the Protection of the Environment," in: A. Eide, C. Krause, and A. Roseas (eds.), *Economic, Social and Cultural Rights* (Leiden: Martinus Nijhoff Publishers, 2001), 1; Neil A. Popovic, "Pursuing Environmental Justice with International Human Rights and State Constitutions," 15 *Stanford Environmental Law Journal* (1996) 338.

Declaration" of 1992 was that "Human beings ... are entitled to a healthy and productive life in harmony with nature."[20]

The public's overriding human rights interest in private uses of land and resources could take one of two forms: (1) private property could be encumbered with the public's interest in ecological conservation,[21] or (2) government management of natural resources could be conditioned by a new duty to protect those resources consistent with a public trust obligation, where the government would serve as a trustee of nature for present and future generations.[22] Either approach would require private and government actions to give formal legal consideration of broader, future multigenerational ecological values other than near-term private consumptive and extractive use interests.[23]

The question then, of course, is whether second- and third-generation laws now in place, or even the addition of a new round of anthropomorphic fourth-generation human rights laws being contemplated, can prevent the environmental catastrophes that seem to characterize the twenty-first century.[24] Second-generation, use-regulating conservation laws simply slowed the inexorable exhaustion of stock and renewable resources. Third-generation nonuse laws, designed to protect humans from pollution and to preserve natural objects, have not been able to halt, and will not succeed in reversing, a natural planet-wide collapse.[25] Proposed fourth-generation laws continue to cling to anthropomorphism as a precondition to adoption, ignoring the intrinsic value of nature. As a result, we now face a combination of global climate change, natural systems destruction, species extinctions, and biomass depletion, which could compromise the integrity and survival of the Earth's biosphere.[26]

---

[20] Rio Declaration, UN Doc. A/CONF. 151/26; 31 ILM 874 (1992) – Principle #1.
[21] See, e.g., Eric T. Freyfogle, *The Land We Share: Private Property and the Public Good* (Washington, DC: Island Press, 2003).
[22] Mary Christina Wood, "Advancing the Sovereign Trust of Government to Safeguard the Environment for Present and Future Generations (Part I): Ecological Realism and the Need for a Paradigm Shift," 39 *Environmental Law* (2009) 43.
[23] Alyson C. Flournoy, 'The Case for the National Environmental Legacy Act,' in: A. Flournoy and D. Driesen (eds.), *Beyond Environmental Law* (Cambridge University Press, 2010), 3–25; Richard P. Hiskes, *The Human Right to a Green Future: Environmental Rights and Intergenerational Justice* (Cambridge University Press, 2009).
[24] Tyler Volk, CO_2 *Rising: The World's Greatest Environmental Challenge* (Cambridge, MA: MIT Press, 2008).
[25] James Gustove Speth, *The Bridge at the End of the World: Capitalism, the Environment, and Crossing From Crisis to Sustainability* (New Haven: Yale University Press, 2008).
[26] John M. Broder, "Climate Talks Yield Commitment to Ambitious, but Unclear, Actions," *New York Times International* (December 9, 2012), 11 (recognizing increasing frequency

2. A rule of law for nature legitimating non-anthropocentric nonuse values

Past and present laws do not seem to have protected the Earth's resources, which continue to be polluted, depleted, and adversely altered.[27] This persistent failure to preserve resource nonuse values suggests that an entirely new approach may be necessary. Perhaps a new rule of law is now in order, one where the benefits are not purely anthropocentric, but instead are ecocentric, and where the rights are not held by humans, but by nature.[28] In other words, *a rule of law for nature* should be considered.

2.1 Non-anthropocentric protection of natural resource nonuse values

If we are to enlist the rule of law to facilitate the greater cause of protecting and preserving resource nonuse values, then we must begin by recognizing: (1) the intrinsic, non-human-centric worth of nature and natural resources, and (2) the limits of an anthropocentric approach to environmental and resource-protective laws. Three issues are raised by a rule of law for nature that recognizes that natural resources and objects deserve a non-anthropocentric ability not to be used by humans. First, should such protection be manifested by imposing a *duty* on humans to preserve resources nonuse, or should resources be granted their own *right* of nonuse? Second, which components or manifestations of nature and the natural world should be protected? Third, if natural and environmental resources are to be protected as a matter of law for their own sake,[29]

---

of extreme weather events as well as drought and sea-level rise); Gautam Naik, "Polar Ice Melt is Accelerating," *Wall Street Journal* (November 30, 2012); Seth Borenstein, "Amount of Heat-Trapping Pollution the World Spewed Rose Again by 3 Percent," *The Denver Post* (December 3, 2012), 16A; W. Jeffrey Bolster, *The Mortal Sea* (Cambridge, MA: Harvard University Press, 2012); Ann Gibbons, "Are We in the Middle of a Sixth Mass Extinction?," *ScienceNow* (March 2, 2011); Robert Barr, "Carbon Output Forecast to Rise," *Denver Post* (January 20, 2011), 7B; Juliet Eilperin, "Study: Extinction Crisis Looms," *Denver Post* (October 27, 2010), 13A; Jonathan Leake, "Fish Stocks Eaten to Extinction by 2050," *Times* (July 11, 2010), 9; Justin Gillis, "Is It Global Warming? Probably, Scientists Say," *New York Times* (August 15, 2010), 19A.

[27] J. G. Laitos, *The Right of Nonuse* (Oxford University Press, 2012), 9–12.
[28] Susan Emmenegger and Alex Tschentscher, "Taking Nature's Right's Seriously: The Long Way to Biocentrism in Environmental Law," 6 *Georgetown International Environmental Law Review* (1994) 545.
[29] George Sessions (ed.), *Deep Ecology for the 21st Century: Readings on the Philosophy and Practice of the New Environmentalism* (Boston, MA: Shambhala Publications, Inc., 1995).

and not for their instrumental value to humans,[30] then such protection should be from what? And to what end?

2.1.1 A duty towards nature or a nature-held right of nonuse?

If non-anthropocentric legal nonuse rights are going to be provided to nature, one threshold inquiry is: Should positive law impose a duty on humans to not use natural resources in some circumstances, or should the law confer on nature its own right of nonuse? A rights-based approach permits the interests of the resource to be raised on behalf of the resource initially, while a duty to the resource puts the preliminary focus on humans, who would have to carry out that duty. A right of nonuse held by nature provides natural resources and environmental assets with legal legitimacy that is not derivative of a human duty, and should be preferred. However, such a right would have to possess sufficient legal clout to override purely utilitarian considerations regarding resources. And it would likely need to be enforceable without the need to show some harm to human interests.[31]

2.1.2 Which components of nature should have rights?

If policymakers are going to confer on natural resources, environmental goods, or ecological processes a legally enforceable "right" of nonuse, capable of sometimes resisting human use demands, then one important issue that needs to be resolved is this: What components of nature should be provided such a right? There appear to be three choices. First, a *biocentric* approach assumes that all living organisms are entitled to equal consideration under law, if not a right to fulfill their existence as evolutionary beings. Second, *deep ecology* transcends biocentrism and encompasses all natural entities and compounds, even non-living beings. Third, *ecological holism* presumes that all components of a natural system are important, living or not-living, and that the relevant natural entity is the interrelationship that emerges between nature's parts when humans do not interfere.[32]

Biocentrism acknowledges all living entities as inherently valuable, and that no living being (i.e., *homo sapiens*) is inherently superior to other living organisms. But a right based on biocentrism leaves out of its protection

---

[30] Timothy W. Luke, *Ecocritique: Contesting the Politics of Nature, Economy, and Culture* (Minneapolis: University of Minnesota Press, 1997).
[31] Robert Elliot, "Environmental Ethics," in: Peter Singer (ed.), *A Companion to Ethics* (Oxford: Basil Blackwell, 1993), 112.
[32] See, e.g., Aldo Leopold, *A Sand County Almanac* (Oxford University Press, 1949).

natural resources and environmental goods, such as the atmosphere and estuaries and even alpine mountain ranges, which are essential to life forms. Deep ecology extends the scope of the relevant natural environment to every natural entity that affects life, even though the object itself may not be alive. The waters of the world's oceans are not themselves living, but they are the home of most of the living organisms that inhabit this planet. The Earth's atmosphere is not living, but the gases in the air make life possible, and all terrestrial organisms, and most aquatic ones, require the presence of the gaseous envelope surrounding the earth. Deep ecology recognizes that it makes no sense to embrace a life-centered ethic (biocentrism) when life itself depends on non-living beings.

However, deep ecology does not necessarily extend to natural systems that exist between, and the interrelationships that form among, *all* natural beings – sentient and non-sentient animals, living trees and plants, non-living natural objects like rivers and mountains and air. The much broader concept of "ecological holism" captures the entire network of interrelations that exist between entities in nature, living or not, and the Earth. Should policymakers create a right of nonuse to protect resources from human use choices, perhaps the "right" should be an ecocentric one, transcending the anthropocentric and biocentric, and encompassing the interconnections of all beings.

2.1.3 What should be the purpose and content of the right?

Any right of nonuse afforded natural resources would have to set out under what circumstances the right could be triggered. The purpose and content of a right of nonuse would have to be articulated in order to decide when, and to what extent, the interests of natural resources would prevail over the countervailing rights of humans wishing to use or exploit those resources. It would be unprecedented to have nature's rights prevail over human rights, so the power of an ecocentric right of nonuse would have to be defined quite carefully.

Among the most basic rights that a natural resource might enjoy is the right to exist, especially when confronted with a human desire to destroy it for utilitarian ends. For example, the American Forest Service Act of 1897, which first set aside nationally owned forests to protect them from overharvesting, requires the Forest Service to "preserve the forests from destruction."[33] Another right, that is biocentric in nature, is the right to

---

[33] Forest Service Organic Administration Act of 1897, 16 U.S.C. § 551.

be able to continue to evolve as a species.[34] A right more consistent with ecological holism would prevent human use actions that either threaten ecosystems, or endanger natural resources that are "viable components of their ecosystems."[35] An even broader right is one that not only halts human use activities, but also seeks to preserve and restore "natural values" in an area.[36] Preservationist and restoration goals are prominent in wilderness acts[37] and in stream flow protection laws.[38]

If any of the above rights are triggered, would those nonuse rights, held by natural resources, actually *veto* a concomitant right, held by humans, to use the resources? In other words, is a right of nonuse an absolute right? It would be politically infeasible, and economically impractical, to provide nature with the means to halt human resource use activities whenever natural values or ecosystem health were threatened. Instead, if a right of nonuse is established, the right would need to be *considered* as part of the use calculus, along with the consequences for nature and natural systems if the right were ignored. Such a duty to consider ecocentric nonuse interests would be similar to the requirement embedded in the American National Environmental Policy Act that the "impacts" of resource use decisions be stated and considered before the action may proceed.[39]

2.2 Countries that provide for ecocentric resource nonuse protections

Various countries have already embraced the idea of providing nature and natural resources with a right *not* to be used by humans. In 2008 Ecuador was the first country to legislate rights for nature when its citizens voted their approval of a new constitution that expressly provides "nature … the right to exist, persist, maintain and regenerate its vital cycles, structure, functions and its processes in evolution."[40] The new constitution

---

[34] Endangered Species Act, 16 U.S.C. § 1532 (16); *Trout Unlimited* v. *Lohn*, 559 F. 3d 946, 950 (9th Cir. 2009); *South Yuba River Citizens League* v. *National Marine Fisheries Services*, 723 F. Supp. 2d 1247, 1251 (E.D. Cal. 2010).

[35] *Arizona Cattle Growers Ass'n* v. *Salazar*, 606 F. 3d 1160, 1166 (9th Cir. 2010); *Siskiyou Regional Education Project* v. *US Forest Service*, 565 F. 3d 545, 550–1 (9th Cir. 2009).

[36] *Pacific Coast Federation of Fishermen's Associations* v. *Gutierrez*, 606 F. Supp. 2d 1122 (E.D. 2008).

[37] 16 U.S.C. § 1133(c); *Wolf Recovery Foundation* v. *U.S. Forest Service*, 692 F. Supp. 2d 1264, 1267 (D. Idaho 2010).

[38] C.R.S. § 37-92-102 (3) [Colorado]; Or. Rev. Stat. § 537.348 (2) [Oregon].

[39] National Environmental Policy Act, 42 U.S.C. §4331(a).

[40] http://blogs.nature.com/news/thegreatbeyond/2008/09/ecuador (last accessed June 7, 2013).

also provided "every person, people, community" the ability "to demand the recognition of rights for nature before public bodies."[41] Not only does nature now have a right of nonuse, but also anyone, or any group of people, has standing to raise this right "before public bodies."

In 2013, Bolivia seems likely to pass a law granting all nature equal rights to humans. Nature's rights include the right to life and to exist, the right to continue vital cycles and processes free from human alteration, the right to pure water and clean air, and the right not to be polluted.[42] The underlying motive for them is that when resources are not used, they are "not polluted" by humans eager to use public environmental goods as waste sinks, and they can also perform natural services ("continue vital cycles and processes") that are necessary for planetary health. The Bolivian government is expected to establish a new "ministry of Mother Earth," and to appoint an Earth ombudsman.

Argentina's Congress has adopted legislation forbidding on its glaciers all "activities that may affect their natural condition or their function as a source of water."[43] The enforcement authority is the country's Secretary of Environment and Sustainable Development. These legal protections of glaciers are both non-anthropocentric (forbidding all human use activities that might "affect their natural condition") and human-centric (securing the function of glaciers as "a source of water," presumably for both humans and ecocentric systems).

2.3 Who may raise the rule of law for nature?

If the rule of law for nature creates a legal right of nonuse for, and held by, the natural resource, the final question is how, and by whom, the threatened natural resource may assert its own intrinsic value. In the United States, the judiciary, especially the federal judiciary, has demanded that rights, even an ecocentric right, cannot be adjudicated without the court

---

[41] Andrew C. Revkin, "Ecuador Constitution Grants Rights to Nature," *New York Times*, DOT Earth (September 29, 2008).
[42] Axis of Logic, "Bolivia Enacts Law of Mother Earth and GMO Ban" (November 5, 2012), available at: http://axisoflogic.com/artman/publish/Article_65111.shtml (last accessed June 27, 2013); Sara Shahriari, "Bolivia Enacts New Law for Mother Earth," *Indian Country* (October 26, 2012), available at: http://indiancountrytodaymedianetwork.com/gallery/photo/bolivia-enacts-new-law-for-mother-earth-141899 (last accessed June 27, 2013).
[43] Leonardo G. Rodriguez and Francisco A. Macias, "New Law on Minimum Standards for Protection of Glaciers," Marval, O'Farrell & Mairal Monthly Report (October 2010).

first being confronted with an injury that is experienced by a human.[44] This is the American law of "Standing to Sue." A better approach, adopted in other countries, is where an organization dedicated to the rule of law for nature is able to raise the rights and interests of the natural resource.

Under the doctrine of *actio popularis*, anyone could bring an action to defend the natural resource's rights, as long as the person could show actual or imminent injury to the resource's nonuse interests – to be free from human interference that prevents the operation of natural processes, or that pollutes/contaminates the resource, or that causes resource extinction. This group of representatives of nature's rights would include companies, individuals, or non-government organizations. However, permitting anyone to sue on behalf of the resources carries several risks. There is the potential that an insufficiently prepared representative would litigate the case, thus creating bad precedent and further harm the rights of the resources; some litigants could use the lawsuit to pursue their own agendas under the guise of protecting the rights of the resources. *Actio popularis* could also create a "race to the court" by various parties seeking to enforce the rights of the resources, and potentially create much litigation on the subject of who-is-able-to-bring-which-claims?[45]

While allowing the broadest possible vehicle for enforcing nature's rights, *actio popularis* could potentially create more harm than benefit to the resources. A concept discussed in the English case of *Regina v. HM Inspectorate of Pollution and Ministry of Agric., Fisheries and Food (Greenpeace)*[46] suggests that if the range of potential representatives eligible under *actio popularis* could somehow be linked to those with "sufficient interest" in the affected resource, then litigation raising the interests of resources would be more manageable. "Sufficient interest" refers to the interest and degree of responsibility a party takes in the particular resource or the environmental object that is worthy of a legal challenge asserting its rights.

In the *Greenpeace* case, Greenpeace, an environmental rights organization, sought a judicial review challenging the British Nuclear Fuels Company's application to discharge radioactive waste into the aquatic environment. The High Court granted Greenpeace standing, finding that it was "eminently respectable and responsible" and had a "genuine interest

---

[44] *Summers v. Earth Island Inst.*, 129 S. Ct. 1142, 1148 (2009).
[45] Michelle P. Bassi, 'La Naturalezza O Pacha Mama De Ecuador: What Doctrine Should Grant Trees Standing?' 11 *Oregon Review of International Law* (2009) 461–78.
[46] [1994] All E.R. 329 (QB).

in the issues raised." Borrowing from that concept, a proper representative for the rights of a natural resource would be an individual or an entity that: (1) has knowledge of the injured resource or ecosystem; (2) has a genuine interest, apart from its own interests, in protecting the resource; and (3) has adequate resources and expertise to adequately represent the resource in litigation. Well-established environmental organizations should easily be able to meet this standing requirement; however, it would be difficult, but not impossible, for individuals to establish standing, especially with regards to the last prong of this approach, which requires the representative to demonstrate sufficient resources to efficiently pursue the litigation.

3. Conclusion

During the past 150 years, many Western governments have deployed resource management laws that have one central theme: Each law assumes that the beneficiary of the government action should, ultimately, be the humans who use, or otherwise benefit from, the Earth's natural resources. First-generation resource use laws, second-generation conservation laws, third-generation resource nonuse laws, and fourth-generation publicly held resource nonuse laws all presume an anthropocentrism that is consistent with classic economics, where the ultimate test of a market decision is whether it maximizes the welfare of people. That standard for resource management decisions seems no longer to work for the planet and its biosphere. A new paradigm for resource decision-making should be considered, which is more ecocentric in nature, and which is equally concerned with the interests of the Earth, nature, natural resources, and the environment. These interests are not coterminous with the interests of humans. Instead of rules of law that are anthropogenic, rules of law for *nature alone* would legitimate a countervailing and largely heretofore overlooked value that should have a voice in future decisions about nature.

13

Realizing nature's rule of law through rights of waterways

LINDA SHEEHAN

1. Introduction

The iconic American author Mark Twain has been credited with the observation that 'whisky is for drinking; water is for fighting over'. This has never been a more fitting observation than today, when water laws worldwide allow the ongoing drying and contamination of rivers, streams, aquifers and estuaries.

This chapter uses water to examine the limits of current environmental protection laws to reverse degradation in the face of governance systems premised on unending growth and consumption of the natural world. It observes that 'nature's rule of law' – the overarching law set by the boundaries of the planet – demands we live within Earth's constraints. It further finds that recognition of the rights of nature to exist, thrive and evolve is essential to adherence to nature's rule of law, and that nature's rights originate from the same source as human rights: our shared existence on Earth.

Finally, the chapter illustrates application of these concepts in the context of the inherent rights of waterways to the sufficient, clean water necessary to protect ecosystem functions. The end goal of this exercise is the recognition that 'nature's rule of law' will lead us to planned, respectful sharing of the Earth, so that all needs are met, and people and planet flourish together.

2. Good intentions, flawed results

2.1 *Good intentions*

Many of the world's modern environmental laws arose out of our interactions with water: from fire hoses sagging mutely before a burning

Cuyahoga River in Ohio, to bewildered marine birds struggling to rid themselves of oil off Southern California, to the declaration of the death of Lake Erie, spanning the USA and Canada. The US Clean Water Act (CWA) 1972[1] flowed from these events, setting laudable goals including: achieving fishable and swimmable waters by 1983, eliminating the discharge of pollutants into navigable waters by 1985, and prohibiting the discharge of toxic pollutants in toxic amounts.[2]

The European Union's Water Framework Directive (WFD) 2000[3] similarly calls on Member States to achieve 'good ecological status' in rivers and lakes by 2015. The WFD provides a framework for member states to find solutions through management plans developed for identified River Basin Districts. It is complemented by the Urban Wastewater Treatment Directive and the Nitrates Directive, both of 1991.[4]

2.2 Flawed results

While progress has been made in clearing our waters of raw sewage and halting much of the dumping of toxic wastes, waterways remain far from healthy overall. Troubling water quality statistics include the following:

- Forty years after the Clean Water Act, over half of assessed US rivers and streams, and 67 per cent of lakes, reservoirs and ponds cannot meet one or more established beneficial uses, such as swimming, fishing and habitat.[5]
- The number of California wells contaminated with nitrates has increased from one-third of wells in the 1950s to nearly two-thirds in the 2000s,[6] with significant impacts.[7] This is a common pattern worldwide.

---

[1] 33 U.S.C. § 1251 et seq.
[2] 33 U.S.C. § 1251(a).
[3] Directive 2000/60/EC of the European Parliament and of the Council of 23 October 2000 Establishing a Framework for Community Action in the Field of Water Policy (EU Water Framework Directive).
[4] Council Directive 91/271/EEC of 21 May 1991 Concerning Urban Waste-water Treatment; Council Directive 91/676/EEC of 12 December 1991 Concerning the Protection of Waters against Pollution Caused by Nitrates from Agricultural Sources.
[5] US EPA, 'National Summary of Assessed Waters Report' (2010), available at: http://iaspub.epa.gov/waters10/attains_nation_cy.control (last accessed 27 June 2013).
[6] T. Harter, J. Lund et al., 'Addressing Nitrate in California's Drinking Water with a Focus on Tulare Lake Basin and Salinas Valley Groundwater' (University of California Davis, March 2012), 35, available at: http://groundwaternitrate.ucdavis.edu/files/138956.pdf (last accessed 27 June 2013) (UC Davis Report).
[7] Infants and children are particularly susceptible to illness from nitrate contamination. Ibid., 9.

- Despite huge investments resulting from the Wastewater Directive, European data indicate only a slight reduction in nitrate contamination of rivers and a large increase in aquifers. Organisation for Economic Co-operation and Development (OECD) data similarly demonstrate 'most major European rivers show no abatement of nitrates, and some have even grown worse'.[8]

Even where concentrations of contaminants are low and/or legal, they can combine to have a greater than expected toxic effect than when assessed individually.[9] Because many waterways fail current individual standards, such synergistic impacts bode ill for waterway and human health.

Water flows are also increasingly compromised, with water-dependent species disappearing as diversions increase. In California, the disappearance of once-abundant Chinook salmon and steelhead endangers the existence of their predators, including the mighty Southern Resident Killer Whale (*Orcinus orca*).[10] The impacts of over-diversion will escalate as climate change raises temperatures, thereby increasing evapotranspiration, desiccating soils and further pressuring waterways to give up more water than they can spare.

Similar patterns are emerging in Europe. By 2007 at least 11 per cent of Europe's population and 17 per cent of its territory had been affected by water scarcity. The European Commission expects further deterioration of Europe's water sources as climate changes drive temperatures upward.[11]

2.3 How did our good intentions fail us?

The failure of modern environmental laws to effectively reverse degradation forces introspection. The vision of the laws appeared solid: adopt

---

[8] E. Esteban and J. Albiac, 'Water Nonpoint Pollution Problems in Europe', GWF Discussion Paper No. 1224 (Global Water Forum, 3 July 2012), available at: www.globalwaterforum.org/wp-content/uploads/2012/04/Water-nonpoint-pollution-problems-in-Europe-GWF-1224.pdf (last accessed 27 June 2013).

[9] C. Laetz et al., 'The Synergistic Toxicity of Pesticide Mixtures: Implications for Risk Assessment and the Conservation of Endangered Pacific Salmon', 117:3 *Environmental Health Perspectives* (March 2009), 348–53.

[10] NOAA, 'NOAA Biological Opinion Finds California Water Projects Jeopardize Listed Species; Recommends Alternatives' (4 June 2009), available at: www.noaanews.noaa.gov/stories2009/20090604_biological.html (last accessed 10 June 2013).

[11] European Commission, 'Water Scarcity and Droughts in the European Union' (31 August 2012), available at: http://ec.europa.eu/environment/water/quantity/scarcity_en.htm (last accessed 10 June 2013).

clear goals and hold users accountable to them. The impact, however, has been to legalize pollution and extraction, with ongoing impacts.

For example, rather than eliminate the discharge of pollutants into navigable waters, the permit system set up under the CWA allows pollution as long as it does not have a 'reasonable potential' to violate water quality standards[12] – a far weaker goal. Similarly, the EU's WFD allows adoption of 'less stringent environmental objectives' or even exemptions from WFD provisions.[13]

The core flaw in current environmental statutes' ability to achieve a healthy natural world arises from their grounding in overarching, destructive governance systems that assume the environment is property to be used for human benefit, particularly to maximize individual monetary wealth. Because environmental statutes accept this larger paradigm as a given, they can only slow the pace of degradation, not reverse it. Without formal recognition in law of the inherent rights of the natural world to exist, thrive and evolve, we will continue to chip away at its health, to the detriment of our own.

2.4   Our future on this path

The long-term impacts of this flawed legal system are making themselves increasingly visible. For example, a 2011 Public Policy Institute of California report criticized the US Endangered Species Act for its lack of a 'provision for allowing species to go extinct', instead suggesting 'endangered species triage' as a new water management tool.[14] This 'God Squad' perspective will only spread without a pronounced shift from a 'humans over nature' world-view to one that recognizes nature as partner, not servant.

This shift in perspective is necessary for both environmental and human health. For example, clean water today bypasses many poorer communities, forcing families on limited budgets to buy bottled water to avoid illness and even death from the tap.[15] If we decide it is acceptable to select which waterways and species may have access to clean, sufficient

---

[12] 40 C.F.R. § 122.44(d).
[13] EU Water Framework Directive, paras. 31–32.
[14] E. Hanak, J. Lund et al., 'Managing California's Water: From Conflict to Reconciliation' (Public Policy Institute of California, February 2011), available at: www.ppic.org/main/publication.asp?i=944 (last accessed 10 June 2013).
[15] UC Davis Report, 47–51.

water, we set up an ethical structure that will deny clean water to humans as well.[16]

3. Changing course: recognizing nature's rights

Our current legal approach to interacting with the environment derives from the perspective that water, land, forests, air and wildlife are 'resources' or 'wealth' to be extracted, manipulated and controlled for human benefit. This perspective has not always been the case, however. For example, indigenous Californians understood their environment to have an intrinsic value of its own, one where '[n]ature was neither the enemy nor simply a means to an end or a commodity to be exploited for wealth or power'.[17] Water was essential to life, and it could not be bartered or sold.[18] Many of these beliefs and practices continue to this day.[19]

Systems theory, ecology and other scientific disciplines also demonstrate our deep connections with the world around us and caution us against actions that disrupt the harmonious functioning of those relationships. As observed by Einstein:

> A human being is part of a whole, called by us the 'Universe', a part limited in time and space. He experiences himself, his thoughts and feelings, as something separated from the rest – a kind of optical delusion of his consciousness. The striving to free oneself from this delusion ... is the way to reach the attainable measure of peace of mind.[20]

Our treatment of the environment as property rather than partner also conflicts with ethics, which calls for respect to be accorded to Earth's inhabitants based on our shared past, present and future. This is both a moral and utilitarian approach. It is moral because of our co-evolution with nature, and our integral relationship with it given our shared

---

[16] H. Bigas *et al.* (eds.), 'The Global Water Crisis: Addressing an Urgent Security Issue', Papers for the InterAction Council, 2011–2012 (Hamilton, Canada: UNU-INWEH, 2012), available at: www.inweh.unu.edu/WaterSecurity/documents/WaterSecurity_FINAL_Aug2012.pdf (last accessed 10 June 2013).
[17] N. Hundley, Jr, *The Great Thirst* (Berkeley: University of California Press, 2001), 1–2.
[18] Ibid., 25.
[19] Earthjustice, 'Judge Tosses Biological Opinion for Salmon and Steelhead in California' (16 April 2008) (quoting Winnemem Wintu Leader's observation that 'the salmon are our relatives, are sacred, and necessary for the continuation of life').
[20] A. Calaprice (ed.), *The New Quotable Einstein* (Princeton University Press, 2005), 206.

ancestry. It is utilitarian because if we humans divert all the water we feel we are 'entitled' to, we will simply drain the well dry.[21]

The operating assumption of nature as resource, rather than relative and partner with its own rights, has become so ingrained that we rarely notice, let alone challenge, it. But it was and is merely an assumption – one we can change through careful examination and thoughtful evolution.

3.1 Acknowledging the inherent rights of nature

In light of our integration with the natural world, we must evolve from fighting over its elements and learn to live with it wisely and respectfully. A governance system that recognizes our intimate relationships with nature will arise from an evolved understanding of the relative rights of both humans and the natural world. The international recognition of fundamental human rights helps provide a path forward for this task.

The Universal Declaration of Human Rights (UDHR), Article 1 recognizes that 'All human beings are born free and equal in dignity and rights'.[22] As articulated by the Declaration's Drafting Committee, 'the supreme value of the human person ... did not originate in the decision of a worldly power, *but rather in the fact of existing*'.[23] The UDHR protects numerous 'first-generation' human rights, or rights that serve to protect individuals from the excesses of the state. Such rights include the 'right to life, liberty and security of person' (Article 3) and the 'right to an effective remedy by the competent national tribunals' (Article 8).

Just as we protect humans' inherent rights from the excesses of potentially harmful governing bodies, so too should we protect our partners on Earth from the excesses of humans and human governance systems. Like our own value, the value of nature does not arise from our decisions on its worth but from its existence on this planet. This perspective is reflected in the 2010 Universal Declaration of the Rights of Mother Earth (UDRME), approved by an assembled delegation of over 35,000 people representing

---

[21] OECD, 'OECD Environmental Outlook to 2030' (2008) (by 2030, 47 per cent of the world's population will be living in areas of high water stress).

[22] Adopted by the UN General Assembly on 10 December 1948; available at: www.un.org/en/documents/udhr/history.shtml (last accessed 10 June 2013).

[23] Statement by Herman Santa Cruz, Chile. Available at: www.un.org/en/documents/udhr/history.shtml (last accessed 10 June 2013) (emphasis added).

140 countries in Cochabamba, Bolivia, who drew significantly from the UDHR for this purpose.[24]

With similar logic and ethics to the UDHR, the UDRME states that '[t]he inherent rights of Mother Earth are inalienable in that they arise from the same source as existence'.[25] Like the UDHR, the UDRME defends the rights-bearing entity (nature and its elements) from the excesses of governing authorities. These rights include the recognition that 'Mother Earth and all beings of which she is composed have ... the right to life and to exist' (Article 2, Section 1), and '[e]ach being has the right to a place and to play its role in Mother Earth for her harmonious functioning' (Article 2, Section 2). The UDRME specifically requires humans and their institutions to 'recognize and promote the full implementation and enforcement of the rights and obligations recognized in this Declaration' and requires 'damages caused by human violations of the inherent rights' to be 'rectified', with those responsible 'held accountable' (Article 3, Section 2).

The UDHR contains 'first-generation rights' (which protect individuals negatively from the excesses of the state) and 'second-generation rights' (which positively guarantee individuals equal conditions and treatment in fundamental areas). Nature's rights in the UDRME can be viewed as 'first generation-plus', in that they are necessary to protect the natural world negatively from the harmful impacts of both human governments and private human actions. As detailed above, our overarching legal and economic systems, and the environmental laws that accept those systems implicitly, are driving ongoing degradation of the natural world, which is treated as property with no rights of its own. Such harmful governance systems, and our actions consistent with them, must be altered to protect the fundamental rights of the natural world. Thus, rather than being conditioned on the availability of government resources, as with second-generation rights, recognition of nature's 'first-generation-plus' rights is deeply inherent to the life, liberty and security of the natural world. As fundamental rights, their implementation cannot be avoided through cost arguments, which themselves are generally based on the same flawed economic systems driving degradation.

Our failure to accept nature's inherent rights, which arise from its coexistence on our shared planet, is causing the devastation of the natural

---

[24] Available at: http://pwccc.wordpress.com/programa (last accessed 10 June 2013).
[25] UDRME, Art. 1(4).

world by our human laws and practices. Recognition of the rights of nature to exist, thrive and evolve will advance protection of the natural world from the excesses of human governance and private actions, which in turn will protect our own inherent, human rights to life, liberty and security of person.

3.2 Implementing nature's rights

Implementation of nature's inherent rights in our human law and economic systems can be guided by the UDRME, which observes that '[j]ust as human beings have human rights, all other beings also have rights which are specific to their species or kind and appropriate for their role and function within the communities within which they exist' (Article 1, Section 6). The UDRME further finds that '[t]he rights of each being are limited by the rights of other beings and any conflict between their rights must be resolved in a way that maintains the integrity, balance and health of Mother Earth' (Article 1, Section 7). Cultural historian Thomas Berry explains that 'Rivers have river rights. Birds have bird rights. Insects have insect rights. Humans have human rights. Difference in rights is qualitative, not quantitative. The rights of an insect would be of no value to a tree or a fish.'[26]

In other words, each element of the natural world holds subject-specific rights in order to fulfil its roles and evolutionary processes. Accordingly, nature's rights could be implemented via strategies specific to each rights-bearing entity. For example, waterways have waterway rights, such as the right to flow with water in an amount and quality necessary for the waterway and its dependent ecosystems and species to exist, thrive and evolve. Human rights to water, as recognized by the United Nations,[27] must be implemented consistent with these rights of waterways, lest we dry up the stream that nourishes us. Rather than rationalizing away the health of waterways, we can develop rights-based statutes that provide the requisite safeguards on government and private actions to ensure waterway (and human) well-being.

Implementation of nature's rights means we must provide the natural world with the ingredients it needs – habitat, nutrition, water – to

---

[26] T. Berry, *Evening Thoughts: Reflecting on Earth as Sacred Community* (San Francisco: Sierra Club Books, 2006), 149–50.
[27] UN Resolution 64/292, Human Right to Water and Sanitation (28 July 2010).

continue to positively exist and co-evolve with us. As famously observed by Gandhi, 'Earth provides enough to satisfy every man's need, but not every man's greed.'[28] By exploiting the natural world, we are violating its inherent rights and endangering ourselves.

The UDRME is an important first step in beginning to recognize the needs and rights of nature. Submitted to the United Nations shortly after its approval, the UDRME was also formally considered at the April 2011 UN Dialogue on Harmony with Nature.[29] In addition, it figured prominently at the June 2012 UN Conference on Sustainable Development (Rio+20), with the Final Declaration of the Rio+20 People's Summit calling on 'governments and people of the world to adopt and implement the Universal Declaration of the Rights of Mother Earth'.[30] While the final UN consensus document itself did not reference the UDRME, it specifically recognized the application of 'rights of nature' in the governing system of some of its member states as a strategy for achieving sustainable development.[31]

Since its adoption almost sixty-five years ago, the UDHR's commitment to basic rights and freedoms has been translated into constitutional, statutory and judge-made law through which human rights are expressed and guaranteed. The same can be done to reflect in law the rights of nature, and allow us to begin to reverse and repair environmental degradation and secure a flourishing future.

4. Acting for change: 'nature's rule of law'

4.1 *The rule of law is necessary to protect fundamental rights*

The rule of law is a system of governance that helps to ensure safe, prosperous societies. The UN describes the rule of law as:

> a principle of governance in which all persons, institutions and entities, public and private, including the State itself, are accountable to laws that

---

[28] Pyarelal, *Mahatma Gandhi – The Last Phase, Vol. 2* (Ahmedabad: Navajivan, 1958).
[29] UN, 'Interactive Dialogue on Harmony with Nature' (20 April 2011), available at: www.un.org/en/ga/president/65/initiatives/HarmonywithNature.html (last accessed 10 June 2013).
[30] Available at: http://cupuladospovos.org.br/wp-content/uploads/2012/07/FinalDeclaration-ENG.pdf (last accessed 10 June 2013).
[31] UN Resolution A/RES/66/288, 'The Future We Want', para. 39 (11 September 2012), available at: http://sustainabledevelopment.un.org/futurewewant.html (last accessed 10 June 2013).

are publicly promulgated, equally enforced and independently adjudicated, and which are consistent with international human rights norms and standards. It requires ... equality before the law, accountability to the law, fairness in the application of the law ... avoidance of arbitrariness and procedural and legal transparency.[32]

The Preamble of the UDHR describes application of the rule of law as 'essential' to the protection of human rights. The UN further finds adherence to the rule of law is necessary to achieve 'durable peace' and 'sustained economic progress and development'.[33]

Generally stated, the rule of law means no one is above the law. Norms, policies, institutions and processes that adhere to the rule of law create a society 'in which individuals feel safe and secure, where disputes are settled peacefully and effective redress is available for harm suffered, and where all who violate the law, including the State itself, are held to account'.[34]

Like the rule of law, environmental health is also essential to human well-being and security.[35] It is also critical to the protection of human rights in general; for example, the UN has recognized the human right to water as 'a pre-requisite to the realization of all other human rights'.[36] Accordingly, a number of existing international agreements and initiatives affecting the rule of law also include references to environmental health. For example, the United Nations Millennium Declaration, which supports the practical implementation of fundamental human rights, resolves to 'adopt in all our environmental actions a new ethic of conservation and stewardship', including halting the 'unsustainable exploitation of water resources'.[37] Despite such advances, however, we have yet to

---

[32] UN, 'Report of the Secretary-General on the Rule of Law and Transitional Justice in Conflict and Post-Conflict Societies' (23 August 2004), available at: www.unrol.org/files/2004%20report.pdf (last accessed 27 June 2013).

[33] UN, 'United Nations and the Rule of Law', webpage at: www.un.org/en/ruleoflaw/index.shtml (last accessed 10 June 2013).

[34] Ibid.

[35] US Office of the Director of National Intelligence, 'Intelligence Community Assessment on Global Water Security' (2 February 2012), iii, available at: www.state.gov/e/oes/water/ica/index.htm (last accessed 10 June 2013).

[36] UN Committee on Economic, Social and Cultural Rights, 'General Comment No. 15 (2002), The Right to Water' (E/C.12/2002/11, 20 January 2003), available at: www.un.org/waterforlifedecade/human_right_to_water.shtml (last accessed 10 June 2013).

[37] UN General Assembly, 'United Nations Millennium Declaration', A/RES/55/2 (18 September 2000), para. 23, available at: www.un.org/millennium/declaration/ares552e.pdf (last accessed 27 June 2013).

take the essential step of adopting governance systems based on a rule of law that protects the fundamental rights both of humans *and* the natural world.

4.2 *'The universe is the primary lawgiver'*

Because our current environmental laws rest on a rule of law that focuses on the well-being of human communities, they will fail to stem the ongoing tide of environmental degradation. Our flawed perspective of nature as property to feed unending economic growth falsely assumes we can take forever from a finite planet. In fact, we have overshot several planetary boundaries already[38] and will pass planetary tipping points[39] without a fundamental reordering of our perspective towards nature's laws. Despite these clear trends, we have yet to even begin meaningful implementation of the UN's direction to evolve human laws and activities to be in 'harmony with the universal laws of nature'.[40]

As recognized by the UN and described by Berry, 'the universe is the primary lawgiver'.[41] We need to evolve our laws, economic systems and other human institutions in humble acknowledgement of 'nature's rule of law', or risk our well-being and security on a global basis. We can and must expand our understanding and application of the rule of law to encompass the universe's ultimate ordering of our lives to achieve thriving human and environmental communities.

4.3 *Applying 'nature's rule of law'*

Evolving our governance principles to implement the rights of ecosystems and species through an expanded rule of law will allow us to begin the necessary process of recognizing nature's needs and limits in our daily lives. There is growing precedent for this path. In 2008 Ecuador adopted a constitutional provision endowing nature with inalienable, enforceable

---

[38] J. Rockström *et al.*, 'A Safe Operating Space for Humanity', 461 *Nature* (24 September 2009), 472–5. For a discussion on planetary boundaries, see Chapter 4 by Klaus Bosselmann in this book.

[39] A. Barnosky *et al.*, 'Approaching a State Shift in Earth's Biosphere', 468 *Nature* (7 June 2012), 52–8.

[40] World Commission on Environment and Development, 'Our Common Future' (UN A/42/427, 4 August 1987), para. 80, available at: www.un-documents.net/wced-ocf.htm (last accessed 10 June 2013).

[41] T. Berry, *The Great Work: Our Way into the Future* (New York: Bell Tower, 1999).

legal rights.[42] Its new Constitution declares the natural world has the right to exist, persist, maintain itself and regenerate its vital cycles, structure, functions and processes in evolution.[43] Further, the Constitution parallels the UDHR and UDRME by providing the natural world with a right to restoration independent of humans' right to compensation[44] and specifying a clear process for enforcement of the rights of nature before public bodies.[45]

These constitutional provisions were tested in a successful March 2011 case brought on behalf of the Vilcabamba River. The court found the river's constitutional right to flow had been violated by destructive road development practices and ordered the river to be fully restored to health.[46]

Protections of the rights of waterways are also being developed in New Zealand, through court agreements between Maori iwi and the Crown government. In August 2012 an agreement between the Whanganui iwi and the Crown granted to the Whanganui River rights and standing as a legal entity, with co-guardians to be assigned to protect those rights.[48] The agreement 'recognises the intrinsic interconnection between the Whanganui River and the people of the River (both iwi and the community generally)', and finds 'the health and wellbeing of the Whanganui River is intrinsically interconnected with the health and wellbeing of the people'.[49] This agreement is a promising start to a series of agreements that will complete the system of governance that protects the rights of the river and its watersheds.

---

[42] 'Rights of Nature', Constitución de la República del Ecuador, Title II, Ch. 7 (September 2008), available at: http://pdba.georgetown.edu/Constitutions/Ecuador/english08.html (last accessed 27 June 2013). See also the Preamble to the Constitution, recognizing human dependence on and interconnections with nature.

[43] Ibid., Art. 71. See also Art. 10, stating that nature is a subject of rights in the Constitution.

[44] Ibid., Art. 72.   [45] Ibid., Art. 71.

[46] *Vilcabamba River v. Provincial Government of Loja*, Provincial Justice Court of Loja, No. 11121–2011–10 (30 March 2011), available at: http://earthlawcenter.org/static/uploads/documents/Vilcambamba_River_Decision_3_31_11.pdf (last accessed 10 June 2013). See also summary in English at: http://therightsofnature.org/first-ron-case-ecuador/ (last accessed 10 June 2013).

[48] See, e.g., C. Finlayson, 'Whanganui River Agreement Signed' (30 August 2012), available at: www.beehive.govt.nz/release/whanganui-river-agreement-signed (last accessed 10 June 2013).

[49] 'Tūtohu Whakatupua Agreement between the Whanganui Iwi and the Crown' (30 August 2012), available at: http://earthlawcenter.org/static/uploads/documents/Whanganui_River_Agreement.pdf (last accessed 10 June 2013).

Finally, municipalities around the United States similarly are passing local laws that create enforceable rights for '[n]atural communities and ecosystems, including ... water systems ... to exist and flourish'.[50]

These and other rights-based environmental laws provide significant movement forward in developing governance systems consistent with nature's rule of law. The next step is to implement them widely, to ensure the rights they espouse bear fruit through the mechanism of application. Challenges will certainly arise, particularly around how wisely to protect the rights of people and the environment when they appear to be in conflict. Aldo Leopold opined eloquently on this decision-making challenge, offering that '[a] thing is right when it tends to preserve the integrity, stability, and beauty of the biotic community. It is wrong when it tends otherwise.'[51] The Wingspread statement on the precautionary principle adds to this substantive guideline an overlay of process consistent with the rule of law, stating that decision-making in uncertainty 'must be open, informed and democratic and must include potentially affected parties'.[52]

An evolving rule of law that incorporates and respects the laws of nature, and that includes transparent, equitable and effective processes of law and justice that advance those rights, will guide us toward lifestyles in harmony with each other and the planet. California's water challenges provide an opportunity to examine some of the practical actions we might take in achieving this vision.

5. Example: implementing waterway rights in California

Water management in California rests on a massive infrastructure that moves water primarily from the northern and eastern parts of the state to population centres and agricultural operations in the San Francisco area, Central Valley and Southern California. Despite the fragility of California's water-dependent ecosystems and its long dry spells, water governance over the last century and a half has been driven by a 'first in

---

[50] City of Pittsburgh Legislative Information Center (1 December 2010), available at: http://pittsburghpa.gov/lic/, and also at: earthlawcenter.org/static/uploads/documents/Marcellus_Shale_Ord_Pittsburgh_1.pdf (last accessed 10 June 2013). Santa Monica, Office of the City Clerk, 'An Ordinance of the City Council of the City of Santa Monica Establishing Sustainability Rights' (9 April 2013), available at: http://www.smgov.net/departments/council/agendas/2013/20130409/s20130409_07A1.htm (last accessed 29 July 2013).
[51] A. Leopold, *A Sand County Almanac* (Oxford University Press, 1949), 262.
[52] 'Wingspread Consensus Statement on the Precautionary Principle' (26 January 1998), available at: www.sehn.org/wing.html (last accessed 10 June 2013).

time, first in right' race that rarely accounts in practice for environmental needs. People may hold rights to divert water from waterways for human uses, but waterways have no equivalent rights to retain clean water sufficient to maintain their health, or the health of their dependent ecosystems and species. The result has been a dangerously well-trod path of use, overuse, environmental decline and hasty reaction.

This pattern can begin to be broken by granting waterways the right to be at the planning table from the beginning, rather than at the end when the damage is done. If water rights are the legal system by which water is allocated to humans, then the law must also recognize the inherent rights of rivers to flow, and the rights of fish to swim. Such laws would guide us to modify our behaviour to reflect the limits and rights of the waterways.

5.1 Modernizing the law to protect the rights of waterways and aquatic species

Changes to California's Constitution and Water Code can be made to implement nature's rule of law for waterways by, first, recognizing the fundamental rights of waterways to the sufficient clean water they need to thrive. Laws can also be clarified to identify equitable, accessible, accountable and efficient processes by which waterways' water rights will be upheld, implemented and enforced. Given the UN's recognition that human activities must be in harmony with the 'universal laws of nature', the minimum water needs of waterways must be given priority over other uses in recognition of our utter dependence on adequate waterway flows.

In addition to identifying in law the rights of waterways to clean, adequate flows, the legal changes would need to include processes for pairing those water rights with identified water sources, particularly in over-allocated water basins. Examples of strategies to 'harvest' environmental flows from existing uses include, but are not limited to, the following:

- Determinations as to whether the existing human water use is a 'waste and unreasonable use' pursuant to California Water Code Section 275 and California Constitution Article X; if so, the water could be freed for waterway use.
- Initiatives to convince existing water rights holders to give up their water rights, such as through a charitable giving process that allows tax breaks for donations.

- Increases in fees on water diversions to encourage voluntary release of unneeded rights.
- Formal adjudications of relative water rights in over-allocated water basins, where such adjudications include water rights for waterways to ensure their health.

In addition to freeing up and reallocating existing water rights, water for waterways can be found by assigning waterway rights associated with 'new' water sources, such as recycling/reuse, stormwater capture and storage, and conservation. Although ocean desalination currently is not 'sustainable' from an energy or greenhouse gas emission perspective, if desalination plants are built, they must be required to allocate a meaningful portion of the new water rights to waterways.

New and reallocated water rights should be assigned as needed to waterways in a public, transparent effort that considers the relative requirements of waterways and human populations for their fundamental needs. Equally transparent accounting will be essential to ensuring flows put back into a waterway stay in the waterway, rather than simply being removed downstream. Finally, water quality should be considered along with flow through heightened controls on discharges that require the discharger to show no harm, in recognition of the rights of the environment (and humans) to be free from contamination.

In all of these efforts, decisions should be made with a consideration of broader implications, to ensure that what benefits an area locally does not have larger-scale, injurious environmental repercussions. This is of particular concern in a state such as California, where much of the water is used far from its original source.

5.2 Defining 'healthy' waterways

The process for advancing waterways' fundamental rights to the water needed for their health and well-being can begin immediately with the compilation of data needed to define and maintain waterway health. The US Environmental Protection Agency's Healthy Watersheds Initiative and the California Water Quality Monitoring Council's 'Healthy Streams Partnership'[53] are developing holistic analytic processes that identify 'healthy' waterways. This contrasts with the CWA's focus on water quality

---

[53] Available at: www.mywaterquality.ca.gov/monitoring_council/healthy_stredms (last accessed 10 June 2013).

standard violation, which generally tracks decline rather than improvement of waterway well-being.[54]

Science-based flow standards[55] that identify 'healthy' flows are also being developed, as are assessments of fish and ecosystem water requirements that can further identify 'healthy' flows.[56] Compiled with water diversion data, this information can begin to build an overall picture of what a waterway 'right to health' would look like, and identify the strategies for achieving it.

Where the science of impacts is still in development, agency staff could defer permission for a new or modified use until more definitive science is presented at the appropriate level of proof by those who would so use the waterways. Passing this responsibility back to those on whom it rightfully belongs will begin to change the current destructive world-view of a servile environment that may be degraded for human profit, to an ethic of mutual respect and care.

5.3 Enforcing waterway rights

Understandable, transparent and effective enforcement mechanisms are essential to implementation of a successful water governance system that operates consistently with nature's rule of law. Waterway rights should be overseen and enforced by independent legal guardians or trusts, who would be given a clear fiduciary responsibility to fully protect and enforce the identified water rights as advocates for their waterway clients. Independent guardians could be appointed by a state authority and would report to the public on their activities. However, they must have full and primary responsibility for protecting the waterways to which they are assigned. By contrast, government agencies necessarily must consider the input of multiple stakeholders. While they could implement the overall water governance process in a manner consistent with the rule of law,

---

[54] 40 C.F.R. § 122.44(d)(1)(i).
[55] See SWRCB, 'Development of Flow Criteria for the Sacramento-San Joaquin Delta Ecosystem' (3 August 2010).
[56] See California Department of Fish and Wildlife instream flow reports at www.dfg.ca.gov/water/instream_flow_recommendations.html (last accessed 27 June 2013); State Water Board, 'AB 2121 Instream Flows Policy' and related documents at www.waterboards.ca.gov/waterrights/water_issues/programs/instream_flows (last accessed 10 June 2013); and California Ocean Protection Council instream flow analyses at www.opc.ca.gov/category/projectsbytopic (last accessed 10 June 2013).

they cannot serve as truly independent guardians for the waterways.[57] Independent and effective enforcement should also be bolstered with a citizen suit provision that allows the public to take action in court to protect the rights of waterways as needed.

Finally, a reliable source of funding is essential to ensuring programme success. Fees on water diversions, among other sources, could provide a regular funding stream.

6. Conclusions

It is relatively easy to get caught up in the minutiae of increasingly complex environmental challenges and miss the larger picture: a vision of ensuring a healthy, thriving environment that also supports human needs, advanced through tools such as laws that recognize the fundamental rights of ecosystems and species to exist, thrive and evolve. We must order our own governance systems consistently with 'nature's rule of law' in order to achieve this vision.

Our current human-focused rule of law fails to incorporate the natural world with which we share this planet, and so cannot achieve the fundamental human rights it is designed to protect. The rule of law must respect the fundamental rights of all of Earth's inhabitants in order to be a rule *of* law, rather than rule *by* law. As observed by the former Chief Justice of South Africa, the apartheid government's laws were clear, publicized and transparently enforced, but they utterly failed to protect the fundamental rights of all of South Africa's people, making the nation's rule of law merely 'an empty vessel into which any law could be poured'.[58]

All are harmed when human communities are separated and marginalized under the law. So too are we all harmed when we separate and marginalize the natural world in our laws. Expansion of the rule of law to

---

[57] For example, although a court agreement grants the US Forest Service legal rights to ensure minimum flows in the Scott River in Northern California to protect endangered fish, the Forest Service has failed to use these rights even where the river is drained essentially dry. *In the Matter of Determination of Rights of the Various Claimants to the Waters of Scott River Stream System*, Order No. 30662, 12–13 (Siskiyou Co. Sup. Ct., 16 January 1980), available at: http://klamathriverkeeper.org/Documents/Scott-River-Decree.pdf (last accessed 10 June 2013); Klamath Riverkeeper, 'Tell the Forest Service: Only You Can Prevent Extinction' (2012), available at: http://org2.democracyinaction.org/o/5834/p/dia/action/public/?action_KEY=11549 (last accessed 10 June 2013).

[58] M. Agrast et al., 'WJP Rule of Law Index 2012–13' (The World Justice Project, 2012–2013), 9, available at: http://worldjusticeproject.org/sites/default/files/WJP_Index_Report_2012.pdf (last accessed 10 June 2013).

recognize the overarching, universal laws of nature will guide us towards laws and institutions that best protect the fundamental rights of humans, ecosystems and species, and prompt us to develop clear, accountable, accessible and efficient processes to achieve those rights. In this way, we will achieve our vision of life in true and prosperous harmony with nature.

PART V

Procedural dimensions of a rule of law for nature

14

Towards a new instrument for promoting sustainability beyond the EIA and the SEA

The holistic impact assessment

MASSIMILIANO MONTINI

1. The need for a new regulatory model

The world is currently facing a deep global crisis, which, far from being purely financial or economic, is rather systemic. In fact, such a crisis is showing a reality that has more or less intentionally remained veiled so far: the impossibility of a limitless economic growth on a finite Earth. The present global crisis is witnessing the failure of the neo-classical economic model (neo-liberalism) that has characterized the last decades. Such a model is based on the gross domestic product growth as the major (if not unique) indicator of development and adopts a sectoral thinking that tends to separate the economic dimension from the environmental and social dimensions, while not paying the due attention to the latter and to their interactions and interconnections. In brief, it is a development model, *rectius* a 'model of growth', that is unsustainable for the Earth's ecosystem, neither in the short term nor in the long term.[1]

---

[1] The deep relationship between the economy and the environment, neglected by the neo-classical economy, is explained by the two fundamental laws of thermodynamics, which may be considered as an economic formulation of the physical relations. In fact, the Earth is a closed system with regard to 'matter', that is, a system in which there is neither increase nor decrease in material entropy. On the contrary, as it continuously receives energy from the sun, the Earth is an open system in regard to energy, although the reservoirs of fossil fuels are progressively being depleted. On these issues see C. J. Cleveland, 'Biophysical Economics: Historical Perspective and Current Research Trends', in R. Costanza, C. Perrings and C. J. Cleveland (eds.), *The Development of Ecological Economics* (Cheltenham: Edward Elgar, 1997) (originally published in 38 *Ecological Modelling* (1987) 47); N. Georgescu-Roegen, 'The Entropy Law and the Economic Problem', in R. Costanza, C. Cleveland and C. Perrings (eds.), *The Development of Ecological Economics*

It is therefore absolutely necessary to change the dominant economic model. To this effect, it would not be sufficient simply to adjust and revise the current development patterns based on the traditional neo-classical economic model, as proposed by the 'green economy' approach. Quite the contrary, a systemic shift of paradigm, grounded on a new reference economic model, should be pursued. The new paradigm ought to be based on the principle of sustainability.

The principle of sustainability, which predates the concept of sustainable development as enshrined in the Brundtland Report,[2] has been defined as 'the duty to protect and restore the integrity of the Earth's ecological systems'.[3] This definition of the principle is correctly grounded on the concept of 'ecological sustainability' and implies that economic development that ignores the inherent ecological limits of the Earth can never be sustainable.[4]

In the language used in the economic literature, the requested shift of paradigm should be accompanied by the shift from the so-called weak sustainability approach, which has so far influenced the application of the traditional neo-classical economic model, to the strong sustainability approach, promoted by so-called ecological economics. Such an approach analyses how ecosystems and economic activity interrelate, focusing more on the requirements of the system than on those of the individual.[5] In fact, in the 'ecological economics' rationale, the ecosystem contains the economy to which it supplies a throughput of matter/energy taken from *in natura* uses according to some rules of sustainable yield rather than according to individual willingness to pay.[6] Therefore, this approach seems to be better suited to taking into account the inherent ecological limits to development.

(Cheltenham: Edward Elgar, 1997) (originally published in H. E. Daly (ed.), *Economics, Ecology; Ethics: Essays Towards a Steady-State Economy* (San Francisco: W. H. Freeman & Co., 1980), Chapter 3).

[2] See K. Bosselmann, *The Principle of Sustainability* (Aldershot: Ashgate Publishing, 2008), 12.

[3] Ibid., 53.   [4] Ibid.

[5] M. Common and C. Perrings, 'Towards an Ecological Economics of Sustainability', in R. Costanza, C. Cleveland and C. Perrings (eds.), *The Development of Ecological Economics* (Cheltenham: Edward Elgar, 1997) (originally published in 6(1) *Ecological Economics* (1992), 7).

[6] H. E. Daly, 'Allocation, Distribution and Scale: Towards an Economics that is Efficient, Just and Sustainable', in R. Costanza, C. Cleveland and C. Perrings (eds.), *The Development of Ecological Economics* (Cheltenham: Edward Elgar, 1997).

The shift from weak to strong sustainability corresponds to the shift from a sectoral to a holistic approach.[7] This implies a reallocation of priorities calling not only for relevant environmental, social, economic and cultural changes, but also for legislative and policy innovations. In such a context, therefore, the role of law also has to be revised and restored, in opposition to the current deregulation and liberalization trends that have played, and are still playing, a crucial role in the present crisis. In particular, a rebalance between command and control and market-based instruments is needed and such an activity has to be informed by the strong sustainability paradigm, since weak sustainability aims at making our political and economic systems more environmentally sensitive, but without any fundamental institutional change.[8]

As a consequence, the new approach should be also reflected in the way traditional legal instruments for the protection of the environment and of the ecosystem are conceived and applied. For instance, a major effort of reorientation should be made in the field of the preventive assessment of negative impacts possibly caused by projects as well as by plans and programmes on the environment.

In such a context, the two main legal instruments presently existing, namely the environmental impact assessment (EIA) and the strategic impact assessment (SEA), have been in the recent past, and still represent, very useful tools for the prevention of possible negative impacts on the environment of a given territory. Their application, however, is affected by several shortcomings that undermine their effectiveness. On this premise, this chapter will focus on the analysis of the main features and the most relevant shortcomings of these two instruments, in particular within the European Union legal system, and then will consider the possibility of merging them into a new single instrument, in order to better coordinate and maximize their contribution to the promotion of sustainability.

---

[7] On the term 'holistic' and its meaning, see F. Capra, *The Turning Point* (New York: Simon & Schuster, 1982).

[8] B. J. Richardson and S. Wood, *Environmental Law for Sustainability* (Oxford: Hart Publishing, 2006), 14.

2. The shortcomings of the SEA and EIA in the light of sustainability

2.1 EIA: a critical appraisal

The environmental impact assessment (EIA) is a procedure aimed at assessing the likely impacts of a project on the environment before its implementation. Through the obligation imposed by EIAs, public authorities are required to gather information on the potential negative effects of a project on the environment and to integrate this into the decision-making process. In other words, it may be said that EIA's final goal is to try to make decisions more environmentally sensitive.[9]

EIA appeared as a requirement for public decision-making in the USA for the first time in 1969, under the National Environmental Policy Act (NEPA).[10] Since then, EIAs have been widely accepted at the global level. A vast number of domestic legal systems adopted national EIAs[11] and EIA obligations are today encompassed in several international treaties.[12] At the worldwide level, EIA has increasingly emerged as a fundamental element of a preventive approach towards environmental protection and sustainable development.[13] In the European Union context, EIA is regulated by Directive 11/92, which 'codified' the original EIA Directive 85/337 and its amendments in a single text.[14]

---

[9] M. Lee, *EU Environmental Law Challenges, Change and Decision-Making* (Oxford: Hart Publishing, 2005), 171.
[10] See National Environmental Policy Act of 1969, 42 U.S.C. §§ 4321–4370(f) (2000).
[11] N. Craik, *The International Law of Environmental Impact Assessment, Process, Substance and Integration* (Cambridge University Press, 2008), 23.
[12] Among them: the 1978 UNEP Principles on Conservation and Harmonious Utilization of Natural Resources Shared by Two or More States; the 1980 Protocol for the Protection of the Mediterranean Sea Against Pollution from Land-based Sources; the 1982 UN Convention of the Law of the Sea (Article 204); the 1991 Antarctic Environmental Protocol to the Antarctic Treaty; the 1991 UNECE Convention on Environmental Impact Assessment in a Transboundary Context (Espoo); the 1992 UN Convention on Biological Diversity (Article 14); the 1992 UN Framework Convention on Climate Change.
[13] The 1992 Rio Declaration on Environment and Development contributed greatly to elevating EIA among the mandatory requirements of this environmental preventive approach through Principle 17, which states that 'Environmental impact assessment, as a national instrument, shall be undertaken for proposed activities that are likely to have a significant adverse impact on the environment and are subject to a decision of a competent national authority'.
[14] In more detail, the original Directive 85/337/EC on the assessment of impacts of certain public and private projects was amended in 1997 by Directive 97/11/EC and in 2003 by Directive 2003/35/EC, which sought to align the provisions on public participation with

The EIA Directive applies both to public and private projects likely to have 'significant effects on the environment by virtue of their nature, size or location'.[15] The assessment shall encompass the direct and indirect effects of a project on human beings, fauna and flora; soil, water, air, climate and the landscape; material assets and the cultural heritage; as well as the interaction between the factors mentioned above.[16]

EIA can be integrated into the existing procedures for granting consent to projects in the Member States.[17] The main steps of the EIA process are as follows:

(1) a screening phase for the competent authority to determine whether the project is likely to have significant impacts on the environment (when not included in the list of projects for which an EIA is mandatory according to Annex I);
(2) a scoping phase during which the developers provide a description and all relevant information on the project;
(3) a consultation process with the general public and agencies with environmental responsibilities (where the project has transboundary implications, neighbouring Member States should also be consulted);
(4) a final decision to grant consent or not to the project, which should consider the EIA's findings.

The Directive lists in Annex I the types of projects for which an EIA is mandatory. In Annex II the types of projects for which it is up to each Member State to determine whether or not to make them subject to an EIA are enumerated. For the latter types of projects, Member States have a wide margin of discretion, which can be exercised on a case-by-case examination or on the basis of thresholds or criteria previously determined in general terms, taking into account the relevant selection criteria set out in Annex III.[18]

The EIA procedure set up by the Directive seems to be quite well articulated and efficient. However, it has some shortcomings, as highlighted also by the European Commission in its periodical Reports on the implementation of the Directive.

---

the Aarhus Convention. More recently, it was replaced by Directive 11/92/EU, which 'codified' the previous directives and its amendments into a single text without any significant change.

[15] Article 2(1), Directive 11/92.
[16] Article 3, Directive 11/92.
[17] Article 2(2), Directive 11/92.
[18] L. Krämer, *EU Environmental Law*, 7th edn (London: Sweet & Maxwell, 2011), 156.

For instance, the 2003 Report on the application and effectiveness of the EIA Directive showed inter alia a wide diversity of national approaches to project screening and to the setting of thresholds for determining whether to make projects subject to EIA or not, an often inadequate provision of information on the projects, a sometimes scarce consideration of the alternatives, a limited opportunity for public participation in some Member States resulting in difficulty in assessing its effective weight in the decisional process, and a widespread poor quality control of the EIA procedure. Moreover, it called for an effort to improve the judicial review on formal requirements and to better integrate other concerns, such as those related to human health and biodiversity, into the assessment.[19]

Furthermore, the subsequent 2009 Report on the application and effectiveness of the EIA Directive, while acknowledging that Member States' transposition and implementation of the EIA Directive is largely in line with its main objectives and requirements, found that some improvements and amendments are needed, insofar as the effective application of the Directive suffers from the sometimes inadequate quality of the information used in the EIA documentation and from an often poor overall quality of the EIA process.[20]

Some of the major shortcomings of the EIA Directive deserve a more detailed analysis. First, the practical implementation of the Directive's provisions is largely left to the Member States and has sometimes given rise to marked differences in its concrete application. For instance, a major difficulty lies in the uncertainty of determining which projects should be made subject to an EIA. In this case, as regards Annex I projects, the selection criterion based on a rigid list may sometimes have the consequence of narrowing down the potential field of application of the Directive. Moreover, the wide margin of discretion left to the Member States with regard to Annex II projects may lead to a too broad variety of approaches on whether to require an EIA or not in similar cases. In such a context, it should be noted that the European Court of Justice (ECJ), through its case law, has promoted a trend towards the limitation of the discretionary power left to the Member States by the Directive. In respect of

---

[19] European Commission, *Application and Effectiveness of the EIA Directive (Directive 85/337/EEC as Amended by Directive 97/11/EC): How Successful Are the Member States in Implementing the EIA Directive?* COM (2003) 334 final.

[20] European Commission, Report on the application and effectiveness of the EIA Directive (Directive 85/337/EEC, as amended by Directives 97/11/EC and 2003/35/EC), COM (2009) 378 final.

this, the ECJ affirmed that de facto the EIA procedure is necessary every time a project is likely to have significant effects on the environment.[21] Moreover, it limited the cases when exceptions to EIA can be granted,[22] it interpreted extensively what constitutes a 'project',[23] and it established that when deciding whether a project falling under Annex II should be submitted to EIA or not, the selection criteria included in Annex III are all binding and shall be adopted and integrated into the national legislation.[24] Unfortunately, as it has been correctly argued, daily practice demonstrates that this case law is often ignored.[25]

Second, the EIA Directive essentially lays down procedural requirements that ought to be followed by the Member States, but it neither establishes obligatory environmental standards for a correct assessment, nor imposes a legal obligation to follow the EIA findings. In fact, Article 8 of the Directive simply prescribes that the results of consultations and information gathered during the EIA procedure 'shall be taken into consideration in the development consent procedure'. In other words, there is no legal obligation to abide by the results and the recommendations of the EIA procedure in the development consent phase.[26] At the origin of this deficiency lies the idea that environmental impact assessment is not a procedure that should prohibit certain types of development capable of hindering the environmental integrity of a given land,[27] but rather should lead to a better-informed and more transparent decision-making process. In fact, there is just a presumption that the collection of information gathered during the EIA procedure will improve the environmental sensitivity of the final decisions, despite the fact that the development consent may be granted even when serious negative effects are expected.[28] Moreover, the

---

[21] See C-431/92 *Commission* v. *Germany* [1995] ECR I-2189; C-131/94 *Commission* v. *Belgium* [1996] ECR I-2323; C-392/96 *Commission* v. *Ireland* [1999] ECR I-5901.

[22] See C-142/07 *WWF* v. *Autonome Provinz* [1999] ECR I 5613, where the Court said that 'Only projects which mainly serve national defence purposes may therefore be excluded from the assessment obligation'.

[23] C-142/07 *Ecologistas en Acción-CODA* [2008] ECR I-6097; C-2/07 *Abraham et al.* [2008] ECR I-1197.

[24] C-156/07 *Aiello et al.* v. *Comune di Milano*.

[25] Krämer, *EU Environmental Law*, 156.

[26] Craik, *The International Law of Environmental Impact Assessment*, 150.

[27] P. G. G. Davis, *European Environmental Law, An Introduction to Key Selected Issues* (Aldershot: Ashgate Publishing, 2004), 156

[28] Krämer, *EU Environmental Law*, 157.

omission of the EIA procedure, when due, seems to be treated differently in the various Member States.[29]

Third, the EIA procedure, as it stands, seems not to be well-suited to achieving satisfactory coordination with other procedures and policies, such as with regard to biodiversity and climate change in particular, as well as with other types of assessments, such as the one required under the Habitats Directive. Moreover, the scope of the EIA procedure is limited to the assessment of projects likely to have 'significant effects on the environment'. This means that there is a limited possibility for considering the possible negative effects of a project on interests and values not directly linked to the environmental dimension, but rather pertaining to the social, economic and cultural spheres, which may be relevant for a certain territory.

Fourth, the implementation of the EIA Directive in the various Member States has shown a lack of harmonized practices for public participation. Despite increasing public participation in the decision-making process, there is in fact still no standard practice with regard to the scope and meaning of public participation within the EIA procedure. Too often the public participation requirement is perceived by the competent national authorities in the Member States as a merely 'procedural', rather than a 'substantial' requirement, whose contribution is not really able to influence the outcome of the final decisions.

2.2   SEA: a critical appraisal

The strategic environmental assessment (SEA), also known as strategic impact assessment (SIA) under international law, deals with the assessment of the likely negative effects of policies, plans and programmes on the environment. It was first introduced in the USA together with the EIA under the 1969 NEPA[30] and is closely connected to the EIA. In fact, the SEA replies to the objections raised with regard to the limited scope of the EIA evaluation, according to which, in many cases, projects follow policy decisions already taken in general plans and programmes. Therefore, the separation of the two types of environmental assessment from the

---

[29] In such a case, the situation is very different in each of the 27 Member States. For instance, some of them, such as the UK, oblige the developer to restart a new procedure, whereas others, like Germany, consider the omission as an administrative error irrelevant for planning consent.

[30] See above footnote 10.

broader policy setting can entail the risk that the environmental impacts of plans and programmes are not consistent with those of projects. In light of the principle of sustainability, it seems that environmental considerations should be better anticipated at an upper level and earlier stage of the decision-making process, as constitutive elements of the process itself.[31] Indeed, SEA aims at integrating environmental considerations with economic and social interests related to policies, plans and programmes, thus creating a reference framework for the correct evaluation of projects.

Similarly to EIA, SEA is nowadays an instrument adopted and widely used worldwide, both at the international and the domestic levels.[32] In the European context, SEA is mandated by Directive 2001/42.[33]

SEA should be coordinated with and complementary to EIA. This seems to be possible and advisable, since EIA applies at a lower level to projects, whereas SEA applies at an upper level to policies, plans and programmes.[34] In other words, EIA operates 'downstream' and SEA 'upstream'. In such a context, whilst EIA is meant to focus on the effects of a single project, SEA should analyse the cumulative impacts of the several activities included in a plan or programme.

Within the EU context, the SEA Directive applies to a wide range of public plans and programmes prepared at national, regional or local

---

[31] S. Marsden and J. De Mulder, 'Strategic Environmental Assessment and Sustainability in Europe: How Bright Is the Future?' in S. Marsden and T. Koivurova (eds.), *Transboundary Environmental Impact Assessment in the European Union, The ESPOO Convention and its Kiev Protocol on Strategic Environmental Assessment* (Abingdon: Earthscan, 2011). For a broader discussion on the necessity to have an integrated decision-making process in the field of sustainable development law, see J. Dernbach, 'Achieving Sustainable Development: the Centrality and Multiple Facets of Integrated Decision Making', 10 *Indiana Journal of Global Legal Studies* (2003), 247.

[32] For example, within the framework of the 1991 Espoo Convention, in 2003 the parties adopted the Kiev Protocol on strategic environmental assessment to the Convention on Environmental Impact Assessment in a Transboundary Context (adopted on 21 May 2003 and entered into force in 2010). The recognition of the importance of a strategic assessment integrated in the earlier phases of the decision-making process is also present in the Aarhus Convention, with regard to the public participation requirement for plans and programmes, and in Principle 4 of the Rio Declaration on Environment and Development (1992), which acknowledges that 'environmental protection shall constitute an integral part of the development process and cannot be considered in isolation from it'.

[33] Council Directive 2001/42/EC of 27 June 2001 on the Assessment of the Effects of Certain Plans and Programmes on the Environment.

[34] See for instance Article 2(7) Espoo Convention. See also Craik, *The International Law of Environmental Impact Assessment*, 155.

level and is required by legislative, regulatory or administrative provisions. The SEA Directive does not apply to mere policies, if not encompassed in official plans or programmes. Unlike the EIA Directive, the SEA Directive does not contain a list of specific plans/programmes to be made subject to the assessment, but establishes that SEA is mandatory for plans/programmes falling in the areas of agriculture, forestry, fisheries, energy, industry, transport, waste/water management, telecommunications, tourism, town and country planning or land use, and which set the framework for future development consent of projects listed in the EIA Directive or which have been determined to require an assessment under the Habitats Directive.[35]

For plans/programmes not included in the areas listed above, Member States have to carry out a screening procedure to determine whether such plans/programmes are likely to have significant environmental effects. If there are likely to be significant effects, an SEA must be carried out. The screening procedure is based on the criteria set out in Annex II of the Directive. For the SEA procedure, an environmental report is prepared in which the likely significant effects on the environment and the reasonable alternatives to the proposed plan or programme are identified, described and evaluated. The public and the concerned environmental authorities are informed and consulted on the draft plan or programme and the environmental report. As regards plans and programmes that are likely to have significant effects on the environment in another Member State, the Member State in whose territory the plan or programme is being prepared must consult the other Member State(s). The competent national authorities have the duty to take into account the environmental report and the results of the consultations before the final adoption of the plan or programme. Once the plan or programme is adopted, the concerned environmental authorities and the public have to be adequately informed. Moreover, Member States must monitor the significant environmental effects of plans and programmes, in order to identify at an early stage possible unforeseen adverse effects.

In 2009 the European Commission issued a Report on the application and effectiveness of the Directive on SEA,[36] in which it presented and evaluated the main critical issues regarding the application of the Directive and analysed its effectiveness. In such a context, the European

---

[35] Article 3(2), Directive 2001/42.
[36] Report on the Application and Effectiveness of the Directive on Strategic Environmental Assessment (Directive 2001/42/EC), COM (2009) 469 final.

Commission affirmed that Member States have shown some difficulties and the need for further guidance in relation to its implementation, in particular in the interpretation of certain key concepts of the Directive, such as those related to the screening criteria, as well as in the identification of alternatives, the coordination mechanisms and/or in the joint procedures for fulfilling the requirements for assessment under other Directives, such as the Habitats Directive.

However, the most relevant shortcoming related to the application of the SEA Directive seems to be the lack of coordination with the EIA procedure. The two procedures seem too often to proceed on two parallel tracks, without any common vision or approach. This may lead to different and inconsistent views on the activities conducted at upstream and downstream level, which are likely to have significant effects on a certain territory. Therefore, the lack of coordination between the two procedures seems to be the most urgent question to be addressed.

3. The way forward: the HIA (holistic impact assessment)

3.1 Is there a need for merging SEA and EIA?

From the analysis conducted above, it emerges that the SEA and EIA procedures represent very important tools for preventing possible negative impacts on the environment of a given land, which present many similarities, but lack coordination between them. How to determine, then, whether there is a need for merging them within a single framework?

The starting point in this respect ought to be the fact that the two instruments share a common aim. Indeed, although SEA and EIA are two separate instruments and apply to different types of *ex ante* evaluation, one being at the 'upstream' level of the plans and programmes, while the other referring to the 'downstream' level of the projects, they substantially have a common objective. Such objective consists in the prevention of the negative effects of certain plans and programmes (SEA) as well as of certain projects (EIA) on the environment.

The possibility of merging the two instruments together has in fact been considered at EU level.[37] The European Commission has recognized that there are different potential areas of overlap between the two Directives. This is the case, for instance, 'where large projects are made up of sub-projects; for projects that require changes to land use plans; for plans and

[37] See COM (2009) 378, 8; COM (2009) 469, 12.

programmes which set binding criteria for the subsequent development consent of projects; and for hierarchical linking between SEA and EIA ("tiering")'.[38] However, after having addressed this issue, the European Commission affirmed that the two instruments have their specificities and should not be merged.[39] To this effect, in particular, it argued that 'the objectives of the SEA are expressed in terms of sustainable development, whereas the aims of the EIA are purely environmental'.[40] Moreover, it added that the SEA, unlike the EIA, requires the competent authorities to be consulted at the screening stage, calls for an assessment of reasonable alternatives, has an explicit provision concerning the use of information from other sources and includes requirements on monitoring and quality control.[41]

In my opinion, the reasoning of the European Commission with regard to the allegedly different approach of the two legal instruments towards environmental protection and sustainable development is not convincing. In particular, the consideration that only the SEA Directive contains an explicit reference to sustainable development cannot be a decisive reason to conclude that the two Directives are too different to be merged.

Quite to the contrary, a careful analysis of the scope of the two Directives shows that they share a common objective, approach and rationale. This is demonstrated by the fact that SEA and EIA represent two very similar procedures, both promoting the preventive assessment of certain activities likely to have negative consequences on the environment. The major difference between them lies simply in the fact that the assessment required is conducted at different stages: in the case of SEA at the planning stage, whereas in the case of EIA at the project stage. Moreover, the fact that the EIA Directive does not contain an explicit reference to the concept of sustainable development does not exclude the possibility for interpreting and applying its provisions in the light of the principle of sustainability, with a view to promoting sustainable development.

My proposal is therefore that in order to give value to the explicit (SEA) and implicit (EIA) reference to sustainable development and achieve a better coordination between the two procedures, they should be merged into a new single instrument, based upon a holistic sustainability approach. The new instrument, which could be named holistic impact assessment (HIA), would represent the common framework for the assessment of all the activities likely to have significant adverse effects on a certain territory.

---

[38] See COM (2009) 378, 8.
[39] Ibid.   [40] Ibid.   [41] Ibid.

Within such a context, the two types of evaluations will continue to exist and be conducted separately, still dealing respectively with the upstream and downstream assessment, but will be placed under a single framework, inspired by a common approach, governed by the same rules and managed in a coordinated way.

3.2 HIA: a new single instrument to promote a holistic sustainability approach

The merging of the SEA and EIA procedures into a new single instrument, namely the HIA, would in my opinion represent the best solution to addressing the main open issues and tackle the major shortcomings presently affecting the two procedures, which are still shaped on a sectoral-based approach.

The main reasons to support the merging and establishing the new instrument may be summarized as follows.

First, the merging of the SEA and EIA into the HIA would promote a true vertical integration among the two procedures within a common reference framework, inspired by the same kind of holistic sustainability approach. This will realize an effective 'tiering' of the two upstream and downstream assessments (SEA and EIA) and reduce the observed lack of coordination presently existing between the two procedures. By so doing, the risk that the two procedures lead to different and inconsistent views on the activities conducted at upstream and downstream level, within the same territory, will be greatly reduced. Moreover, the merging of the SEA and EIA into a single instrument would also improve coordination with other procedures and policies, such as in particular with regard to biodiversity and climate change, as well as with other types of assessments, such as the one required under the Habitats Directive.

Second, the revised SEA and EIA procedures, operating as integrated instruments within the single HIA framework, would represent very valuable tools for promoting an improved spatial planning. In this sense, the two revised procedures, rather than limiting the upstream and downstream assessments to 'procedural' instruments only, with a limited role and limited effects on the decision-making related to the spatial development of a certain territory, could give a 'substantial' contribution to more accurate and effective land planning, inspired by a common sustainability rationale, as explained below.

Indeed, the HIA would promote a holistic approach to the upstream and downstream assessments, which will lead to a more comprehensive evaluation of the activities likely to have significant effects on a certain territory. Under such a holistic approach, the possible negative effects of the plans and programmes as well as of the projects will be assessed with regard to the specific features of the given territory. By so doing, it will be possible to better understand the local territorial context, including the environmental peculiarities, the relevant local traditions and the cultural vocation of the land where a certain initiative is to be located and thereby promote a more accurate and comprehensive assessment of its possible negative effects.

Third, the establishment of the HIA could promote the adoption of a common approach towards the definition of the plans and programmes as well as to the projects that ought to be subject to SEA and EIA evaluations. It is well known that the present EIA regime prescribes compulsory assessment for projects falling under the Annex I list, while Member States retain a wide margin of discretion with regard to Annex II projects. On the other hand, SEA assessment is mandatory for plans and programmes falling in certain given areas. However, the ECJ has affirmed, with specific regard to the EIA, that de facto the procedure is necessary every time that a project is likely to have significant effects on the environment. This reasoning may well also apply to the SEA assessment. For this reason, under the HIA framework the question could be solved along the lines indicated by the Court, by prescribing that SEA and EIA evaluations are mandatory every time that certain plans/programmes or projects are likely to have significant negative effects on a certain territory.

Fourth, the HIA could also promote a new and more progressive approach to the issue of the 'value' of SEA and EIA procedures with respect to the development consent phases. In fact, the present situation, whereby there is no legal obligation to abide by the results and the recommendations of the two procedures in the development consent phases, is clearly not satisfactory. For this reason, I think that under the new holistic approach promoted by the HIA, which is inspired by sustainability considerations, the findings of the assessment procedures should become fully binding upon the relevant policymakers and more specifically upon the authorities in charge of granting the development consent.

Finally, the HIA could also reinforce and improve the role of public participation, within both SEA and EIA procedures. In this sense, the existing provisions and their concrete application in the Member States should be carefully revised, in order to promote as far as possible a 'standard practice' for public participation within the EU territory. To this effect, the main guiding criterion should be to make public participation a more effective instrument that can substantially influence decision-making, rather than being (often) reduced to a mere 'procedural' requirement, whose results may be easily ignored or by-passed.

4. Conclusion

This chapter has presented and discussed the major shortcomings of the EIA and the SEA, which are the two main legal instruments existing for the preventive assessment of the possible negative impacts of projects as well as plans and programmes on the environment.

The analysis has focused in particular on the application of the EIA and the SEA in the European Union legal system. The experience gained at EU level with those instruments shows that they pursue a common aim, have a similar approach and present many similarities. However, the lack of coordination in their concrete application may lead to unsatisfactory and paradoxical results.

For this reason, I have argued that they should be merged into a new single instrument, based upon a holistic sustainability approach, namely the holistic impact assessment (HIA). The new instrument would represent the common framework for the assessment of all the activities likely to have significant adverse effects on a certain territory. Within such a context, therefore, the two types of evaluations (EIA and SEA) would continue to be conducted separately, still dealing respectively with the upstream and downstream assessment, but would be placed under a single framework, inspired by a common approach, governed by the same rules and managed in a coordinated way.

In my opinion, the merging of the EIA and SEA within the HIA would help in solving the major shortcomings presently affecting the application of the two procedures, thus promoting a true 'tiering' of the two upstream and downstream assessments; an improved, more accurate and effective land planning; a common approach towards the definition of the plans/programmes and the projects that ought to be subject to the EIA and SEA; a more progressive approach towards the recognition of a legal obligation to abide by the results of the procedures in the development consent phase; as well as an improved role for public participation in both the EIA and the SEA.

For all these reasons, the establishment of the HIA should be pursued, starting from the EU level, with a view to promoting a holistic sustainability approach to land planning and a more effective and coordinated prevention of all the possible negative impacts caused by either plans/programmes or projects on the environment of a given territory.

15

Enforcing environmental responsibilities

An environmental perspective on the rule of law
and administrative enforcement

ANNIKA K. NILSSON

1. Introduction

The focus of environmental law research is generally on reformulating the laws of man to harmonize with the laws of nature, in order to best further sustainable development.[1] A fundamental idea is that the laws of nature must be decisive in substantive regulation of what is allowed and what is not. This chapter investigates how procedural aspects of law can be reformulated to support regulation with due respect for nature. This directs attention to the interplay between the decisive character of ecological sustainability and the rule of law. A challenge is to formulate effective and relevant legal rules and processes that safeguard ecological sustainability, while at the same time safeguarding legal certainty and hindering abuse of public power.

A common focus of critical environmental law discourse is the wide discretion of regulatory authorities. Due to traditional perceptions of the rule of law and legal certainty, such discretion will benefit private interests rather than environmental concerns, described as public interests. In enforcement, moreover, the public regulator must show evidence of sufficient basis for its enforcement decisions and measures. This means that environmental interests will generally run the risk of being affected by lack of scientific certainty, or of sufficient information in general. That goes against the fundamentals of environmental law, and thus poses a threat to its integrity. The main function of procedural law is to provide

---

[1] Report of the World Commission for Environment and Development, *Our Common Future*, 1987 (Transmitted to the General Assembly as an Annex to document A/42/427 – Development and International Co-operation: Environment) (Oxford University Press, 1997), 330.

the means and safeguards for realization of the aim and purpose of substantive law, and protection of relevant rights and legitimate interests. It is therefore motivated to review procedural environmental law.

In this chapter fundamental aspects of the rule of law are analysed in the context of administrative regulation, specifically supervision and enforcement under environmental law. The chapter is written from a Swedish perspective, based on a *Rechtsstaat* tradition rather than a rule of law tradition. It nevertheless aims for a discussion of fundamental principles that are basically common to these traditions. Environmental challenges to the rule of law are investigated in the context of general development of such principles, departing from the formal rule of law, moving to development of a substantive *Rechtsstaat* concept, and finally the pluralistic reality of public authority today. These changes are paralleled with development of environmental law to provide appropriate protection of a wide and heterogenic scope of stakeholders and legitimate interests in administrative enforcement procedure. The developments are also discussed in context of fundamental rights and freedoms.

2. A formal rule of law at the core of the *Rechtsstaat*

2.1 *The rule of law and a formal concept of legal certainty*

Before developing an environmental perspective on the rule of law, some basics should be noted. *Rechtsstaat* doctrine is based on liberal legal discourse and civil and political rights. The *Rechtsstaat* is distinguished from a police state, which is free to act in accordance with legitimate discretion, based on instrumentalistic purposive aspects.[2] In essence, state authorities are entrusted to do whatever is needed to reach legitimate aims. A *Rechtsstaat* will instead rule through law, and be ruled by law; the individual has private autonomy in relation to the state and other individuals. Clear regulation of administrative authority is demanded in respect of the rights and freedom of the individual. In principle, limitation of exercise of state power provides protection against totalitarianism.[3] The rule

---

[2] K. Tuori, 'Har förvaltningsrätten en framtid?', *Förvaltningsrättslig tidskrift* (2003/4), 553–73, at 556–60.
[3] A. Peczenik, *Vad är rätt? Om demokrati, rättssäkerhet, etik och juridisk argumentation* (Stockholm: Norstedts förlag, Fritzes, 1995), 46; H. Sundberg, *Allmän förvaltningsrätt* (Stockholm: P. A. Norstedt & Söners Förlag, 1955), 112–13; K. Tuori, *Critical Legal Positivism* (Aldershot: Ashgate, 2002), 16; Tuori, 'Har förvaltningsrätten en framtid?', 555–7.

of law provides safeguards against abuse of state power. The principles and structures of administrative law are based in the vertical character of exercise of public authority over the citizen.[4] At the core of this lies the rule that the state (in practice public administration) may only intervene in the legal positions of individuals based on competence prescribed to it in law.[5]

Legal certainty is the citizen's perspective of the rule of law, and means that public power is to a high degree exercised under law, and not arbitrarily. Crucially, legal certainty demands foreseeability, and connects to the legitimacy of public authority. Foreseeability is safeguarded through clear and precise general rules, transparency and administrative responsibility for proper exercise of authority. It provides security for citizens so that they can plan their actions, make investments, and act responsibly and in accordance with law.[6] This is formal legal certainty at the core of the *Rechtsstaat*.[7]

2.2 Formal legal certainty in enforcement of environmental law

Formal legal certainty is central in administrative enforcement of environmental law, where public authorities regulate individual actors who cause environmental harm or risk thereof. Procedural safeguards protect the addressee of enforcement (the person causing or risking environmental harm) against unlawful or excessive exercise of public authority. Such safeguards are expressed as enforcer responsibilities for due procedure, sufficient decision-making materials and evidence. This focus on protection of the addressee under the rule of law has been criticized in environmental law discourse, with arguments of plurality of interests challenging the concept of legal certainty in the context of environmental governance. Despite the fundamental legitimacy of protecting the individual against arbitrary or excessive exercise of public authority, such apprehension

---

[4] Sundberg, *Allmän förvaltningsrätt*, 53–4; Tuori, 'Har förvaltningsrätten en framtid?', 559.
[5] Peczenik, *Vad är rätt?*, 50; Tuori, 'Har förvaltningsrätten en framtid?', 557.
[6] Peczenik, *Vad är rätt?*, 50–1 and 89–90; H. Sundberg, 'Förvaltningen och rättssäkerheten', *Svensk Juristtidning* (1935), 321–35, 322.
[7] A. Peczenik, 'Rätt och moral i olika juristroller', in F. Sterzel (ed.), *Rättsstaten – rätt, politik och moral*, Rättsfondens skriftserie 31 (Uppsala: Iustus förlag, 1996), 42–54, at 42–3 and 53; E. M. Basse, 'Retssikkerhed i miljøretten – hvilke begreber kan anvendes?', in E. M. Basse (ed.), *Miljørettens grundspørgsmål. Bidrag til en nordisk forskeruddannelse* (Copenhagen: Gad, 1994), 121–43, at 122.

must be supplemented with concerns for substantive legal certainty of other affected interests and individuals.[8]

The criticism can be illustrated with an enforcement case concerning nuisance, for example potential contamination of a neighbour's fresh water resource from private sewerage. Rules of proper procedure protect the addressee of the enforcement. The individual causing risk or harm is thus protected against arbitrary or excessive exercise of administrative authority. The authority must ensure sufficient grounds for any demands for precautionary measures, for example the status of the neighbour's fresh water, the health and environmental effects thereof, and causality between the contamination and the addressee's sewerage. The authority must also ensure that demands are precise and proportionate, for example showing in detail what measures the addressee must take, and that there is no cheaper or less intrusive method. If challenged, it must provide evidence of these grounds. Unclear or poor grounds for public intrusion into the freedom of the individual are thus detrimental to the regulator. Nevertheless, this means that the stakeholders whose interests are protected by public authorities carry the risk of uncertainties inherent to preventive and precautionary regulation – to the benefit of the polluter. From an environmental perspective one could ask why the actor addressed with the enforcement action enjoys more legal certainty than the neighbour suffering the harm. Why should the addressee be given the benefit of the doubt when decision-making materials are insufficient?[9] Such safeguards contradict the fundamental principle of precaution.

The focus of legal certainty discussed paints a simplified picture of the exercise of public authority, with the individual addressee as victim of intrusive and onerous manifestation of public power infringing on his fundamental autonomy. Many individual rights and interest are legitimately concerned in environmental regulation, including future generations and nature itself, with its intrinsic value.[10] Where enforcement measures are taken, or indeed not taken, every decision will be beneficial or onerous, respectively, to opposing stakeholders. A beneficial decision for the actor causing environmental risks intrudes into other legitimate individual and public interests. Prioritizing one party over the

---

[8] Basse, 'Retssikkerhed i miljøretten', 122–3.
[9] Compare: A. Nilsson, 'Något om JO:s syn på miljöskydd och rättssäkerhet', in G. Michanek and U. Björkman (eds.), *Miljörätten i förändring – en antologi*, Rättsfondens skriftserie 36 (Uppsala: Iustus förlag, 2003), 57–78, at 63–4.
[10] SOU 1966:65, 195–202; A. B. Christophersen, *På vei mot en grønn ret? Miljørettens utvikling i lys av den økologiske erkjennelse* (Oslo: Ad Notam Gyldendal, 1997), 42.

other seems unfair. Overemphasis on protecting the addressee can lead to environmental interests not being given the protection prescribed by law, and thus put the whole purpose of environmental regulation at risk. Under-implementation of environmental law may thus be ascribed to fundamental principles of the rule of law.[11] A specific environmental concept of legal certainty has therefore been argued, suggesting a wider scope of protected interests and parties.[12] However, fundamental principles of the *Rechtsstaat* have also advanced beyond a formal principle of rule of law. This development will be described next.

3. The rule of law and legal certainty in a substantive perspective

3.1 State responsibilities for protecting legitimate interests

Rechtsstaat ideals can also be discussed from a substantive perspective, in which the state should protect individual and collective interests of the public,[13] and public authorities have a fundamental task of realizing public policy. The administration will consequently protect legitimate public interests, and individual rights, as their public task requires – not only upholding the law against offenders, but also actively and proactively furthering political aims implemented into law. That calls for effective administrative authority and powers to realize democratically based policy.[14]

The substantive rule of law and legal certainty relate to protection of legitimate rights and interests.[15] Hence, not only is the addressee of an administrative decision protected with a wider sense of legal certainty, but other concerned parties and interests are also so protected.[16] Exercise of power must be legitimately based both in law and in the public interest, and the individual should be able to trust the state to realize policy and protect rights and expectations stated in law. This calls for fair and appropriate exercise of authority, safeguarded by ideals of purposiveness,

---

[11] Nilsson, 'Något om JO:s syn på miljöskydd och rättssäkerhet', 57–8.
[12] Basse, 'Retssikkerhed i miljøretten', 129–33, 139.
[13] Peczenik, *Vad är rätt?*, 46–7.
[14] Compare: Sundberg, *Allmän förvaltningsrätt*, 112 and 'Förvaltningen och rättssäkerheten', 321.
[15] Peczenik, *Vad är rätt?*, 60–3; Tuori, 'Har förvaltningsrätten en framtid?', 560–5.
[16] Basse, 'Retssikkerhed i miljøretten', 122–3 and 131; K. J. de Graaf, J. H. Jans, A. T. Marseille and J. de Ridder, 'Administrative Decision-making and Legal Quality: An Introduction', in K. J. de Graaf, J. H. Jans, A. T. Marseille and J. de Ridder (eds.), *Quality of Decision-Making in Public Law* (Groningen: Europa Law Publishing, 2007), 1–10, at 3.

equality and reasonableness. Openness, foreseeability and clear communication in the exercise of power will also manifest appropriate use of legitimate power.[17]

The rule of law and legal certainty thus involve much more than limiting exercise of state powers. The public task entails finding an appropriate balance between formal legal certainty and a more substantive sense of justice that protects legitimate rights and interests. This illustrates the delicate balance between effective exercise of public authority and safeguards against abuse of state powers.[18]

3.2 Substantive legal certainty and protection of environmental interests

In the context of environmental law, a substantive environmental perspective on the rule of law and legal certainty is realized through environmental responsibilities. The state has responsibilities to realize environmental goals,[19] to prevent environmental harm and to implement sustainable development and fundamental principles of environmental law, for example the polluter pays principle (PPP) and the precautionary approach. Environmental responsibilities and sometimes rights are stated in many national constitutions,[20] providing a counterweight to rights and freedoms of the individual causing environmental risk or harm. The Swedish constitution prescribes public responsibility to further sustainable development and a good environment for present and future generations.[21] These responsibilities are further prescribed in environmental statutes and instructions to public bodies, demanding that the authorities take measures to promote and protect environmental interests. Poor

---

[17] Peczenik, *Vad är rätt?*, 47–50; Sundberg, 'Förvaltningen och rättssäkerheten'.
[18] Peczenik, *Vad är rätt?*, 62–63; Sundberg, 'Förvaltningen och rättssäkerheten', 322. See also: L. Vahlne Westerhäll, 'Statlig och kommunal styrning av social trygghet – försörjningsbehov som en rättssäkerhetsfråga', in L. Vahlne Westerhäll (ed.), *Rättssäkerhetsfrågor inom socialrätten* (Stockholm: Norstedts juridik, 2002), 22–47.
[19] Declaration of the UN Conference on the Human Environment, Stockholm, 5–16 June 1972 (Stockholm Declaration), Principle 1–11; Declaration of the UN Conference on Environment and Development, Rio de Janeiro, 3–14 June 1992 (Declaration), Principle 3, 7–8; Agenda 21 stating what must be done in the twenty-first century. See also: M. Decleris, *The Law on Sustainable Development. General Principles*, Report for the European Commission, Environmental Directorate-General (Luxembourg: Office for Official Publications of the European Communities, 2000), 17.
[20] E.g. Constitution of Finland Section 20; Constitution of Namibia Art. 95; Constitution of the Russian Federation, Art. 42.
[21] Instrument of Government (1974:152) Chapter 1 Section 2.

functioning of this system is argued to entail implementation deficits and as such failure by the state to resolve environmental problems and effectively carry out its responsibilities.[22]

Manifestation of state responsibility can be seen in administrative duties to supervise, handle complaints and take enforcement action against individuals in order to control compliance with environmental law.[23] An enforcement authority must deliver an administrative decision in response to a complaint so that concerned parties have the opportunity to appeal.[24] Such procedural functions reflect protection of a wider range of legitimate interests. Environmental interests are thus protected under the rule of law.

The substantive result is another matter, however. Public duties and tasks under environmental law are often formulated in general terms, providing the competent authority with wide discretionary powers that are difficult to review effectively, at least if such review is based on a formal view of legality. A more substantive view on public responsibility and legal certainty calls for similarly substantive steering and control of public administration. Substantive administrative or judicial review is necessary in order to control the exercise of administrative discretion in relation to the responsibilities of the authorities, the environmental interests that they are to protect and the environmental objectives that they are to promote. Commonly, control of purposive, appropriate and effective exercise of public duties and responsibilities, in relation to the fulfilment of legal and political aims and objectives, is effectuated by higher administrative authorities and government. To some extent, judicial review may have similar functions, at least in a system such as the Swedish environmental procedure, where the courts try challenges to administrative decisions on the merits and in relation to environmental aims and objectives.

But even if there are proper procedures for controlling the fulfilment of public responsibilities, we need to safeguard the relevant scope of such procedures. An administrative decision may intrude on the individual

---

[22] S. Westerlund, *Miljörättsliga grundfrågor 2.0* (Björklinge: Åmyra förlag, 2003), Chapter 4, esp. 65.
[23] Environmental Code (1998:808) Chapter 26 Section 1; Prop. 1997/98:45, Part I p. 494, and Part II p. 266.
[24] MÖD 2000:43 and 2000:44, drawn from RÅ 1995 ref. 55 and 1996 not. 190. Also MÖD 2003:19 on appeal of a decision not to act on a notification of a new installation. For statements by the Parliamentary Ombudsman see: JO 2002/2003 p. 357, and JO 2008/09 p. 384. See also: J. Darpö, 'Justitieombudsmannen, de närboende och miljön', in J. Ekroth and K. Swanström (eds.), *JO – Lagens väktare* (Stockholm: Riksdagens ombudsmän, riksdagstryckeriet, 2009), 71–100, at 72–5.

(environmental) interests of others, as well as public interests. Some of these interested parties do not have access to the procedure, for example future generations or nature itself. As discussed earlier, it is generally a public responsibility to advocate environmental interests, and to safeguard their appropriate protection. But public authorities have many interests to protect and promote, and environmental matters risk being overlooked when in competition with short-term economic interests, and so on. It is therefore necessary to safeguard a full and relevant procedural scope, for example through rules on decision-making procedures and materials to support those decisions. Swedish decision-making authorities have far-reaching duties under the '*ex officio* principle' to ensure there are sufficient materials to support their decisions.[25] They must gather information and consider any relevant materials made available to them. They will consult different authorities and other stakeholders, and consider their views and expertise on the matter. This should ensure that knowledge and information about interests not advocated by any directly concerned private party is brought into the regulatory procedure.

Another means of safeguarding sufficient procedural scope is giving other stakeholders procedural access. In contemporary environmental law the public concerned and NGOs will enjoy access to justice in environmental matters. Furthermore, a wider range of the public will have access to the decision-making procedure, and possibilities of speaking for environmental interests.[26] These rights are protected in the Aarhus Convention,[27] implemented by the EU and its Member States.

In summary, a more substantive perspective on the rule of law and legal certainty is reflected in public responsibilities in environmental matters and supported by different aspects of procedural law. First, competent

---

[25] Administrative Court Procedure Act (1971:29) Section 8, applied generally in the procedures of administrative courts and other authorities. See: SOU 2010:29 p. 79; RÅ 2006 ref. 15; JO 1997/78 p. 310 and JO 2006/08, 172; O. Lundin, 'Officialprincipen', in L. Marcusson (ed.), *Offentligrättsliga principer* (Uppsala: Iustus förlag, 2005), 169–94, at 172; A. K. Nilsson, *Enforcing Environmental Law. A Comparative Study of Environmental Administrative Law* (Uppsala University, 2011), 81–2, available at: http://uu.diva-portal.org/smash/record.jsf?pid=diva2:411546 (last accessed 27 June 2013); Sundberg, 'Förvaltningen och rättssäkerheten', 327–8.

[26] Concerned public and some NGOs enjoy access to the environmental court procedure: Environmental Code Chapter 16 Sections 12–14. In respect of the environmental impact assessment (EIA), Chapter 6, and in other consultation procedures, an even wider range of members of the public may participate in the environmental procedure.

[27] UNECE Convention on Access to Information, Public Participation in Decision-making and Access to Justice in Environmental Matters, UN Doc. ECE/CEP/43 (1998), 38 ILM 1999.

authorities have substantive and procedural duties and responsibilities to take action and to promote and protect environmental interests. There must, nevertheless, be proper procedures for substantive control of the exercise of wide administrative discretion in view of environmental aims and objectives, and procedural instruments to ensure the appropriate scope of such procedure. In the Swedish system, the courts can issue such control in the appeals procedure, where it is the duty of both the original decision-maker and of the court to ensure a full investigation is conducted. The court procedure is quite open, providing procedural access for many different kinds of parties. Thus environmental interests are brought into the procedure, and may trigger public responsibilities. Through these responsibilities, and the different means of controlling the exercise thereof, the legal order aims to ensure substantive legal certainty in environmental matters. This reflects an environmental perspective on the rule of law within administrative procedure in environmental matters.

However, even when public decision-makers are giving appropriate consideration and taking active efforts to fulfil environmental responsibilities, a main challenge of environmental regulation under the rule of law remains. The public authorities must be able effectively and appropriately to make individual actors change their behaviour to protect environmental interests and promote sustainability. Contemporary environmental law introduces new perspectives on public regulation and the rule of law. These will be discussed next.

4. The rule of law in a pluralistic reality of public power

4.1 The Rechtsstaat *under development*

The *Rechtsstaat* is today found in a new situation in which power of the state is diminishing, or being dispersed into a more pluralistic reality of public power. Different actors are involved in administration of public policy and exercise of power. Private actors are engaged to a greater extent, and public power is set in an internationalized context. This puts the rule of law in new a light.[28] Looking to parallel developments within environmental law regulation, we see that safeguards of the formal rule of law meet

---

[28] K. Tuori, 'Law Beyond the Nation State', in B. Diestelkamp, H. H. Vogel, N. Jörn, P. Nilsén and C. Häthén (eds.), *Liber amicorum Kjell Å Modeer* (Lund: Juristförlaget, 2007), 691–701; L. Vahlne Westerhäll, 'Rättsliga förändringar av social trygghet I Sverige under 1950–2000 i ett subsidiaritets- och solidaritetsperspektiv', 1–2 *Tidsskrift for Rettsvitenskap* (2005), 95–121.

state responsibilities of actively furthering environmental interests, but in a context of a decentralized method of public regulation. In this context, responsibilities for safeguarding environmental interests are common and shared, and the regulated actor is actively involved in the control of his or her own activities and in protection of the interests of others.

Public responsibilities for realizing environmental goals and protecting and promoting environmental interests have been discussed above as a substantial part of the rule of law. But the state does not carry environmental responsibilities alone. Each and every individual actor should be involved in management of natural resources. They have actor responsibilities. Even though public authorities take a leading role in ensuring necessary preconditions for such work, sustainable development and resource management should be decentralized and preventive in its approach. The aim is that individual actors should formulate their own environmental policy strategies, based on the framework and platform of environmental legislation.[29] Decision-making procedures are, moreover, opened up, inviting different stakeholders to participate.[30] These aspects of environmental responsibility entail further challenges to a traditional and formal concept of the rule of law.

4.2 Actor responsibilities and a new perspective on the rule of law

Swedish environmental law departs from general actor responsibility for each and every actor of significance for environmental regulation. Such responsibility applies to all actors causing harm, or the risk of such harm, to the interest protected and promoted in the Environmental Code. This may be a private person washing his car on the driveway, a small garage storing waste motor oil in barrels or a large industrial operation, for example a cement factory, or some other installation such as an airport or a motor cross arena, causing environmental nuisance and risks.

Rules reflecting actor responsibilities are duties of knowledge and evidence in Chapter 2 Sections 1–2 of the Code, and a duty of precaution (duty of care) in Section 3.[31] The duty of precaution is fundamental, requiring the taking of all reasonable and necessary precautionary measures to prevent, control and minimize environmental damage and nuisance.

---

[29] Prop. 1997/98:45 Part I pp. 159–161, 170 and 512–513. See also Decleris, *The Law on Sustainable Development*, 30–2, referring to Agenda 21.
[30] Prop. 1997/98:45 Part I p. 159.
[31] Prop. 2005/06:182 p. 36; SOU 2004:37 p. 121.

Duties of knowledge and evidence build on these precautionary duties, and require the actor to have sufficient knowledge and information about the activity and environmental risks involved, and how to control them. Moreover, a 'shifted burden of proof' requires a responsible actor to show to permitting or administrative supervision and enforcement procedures that they are in compliance with environmental law.

This basis of actor responsibility has been developed into a procedural order of self-supervision and control, and of reporting to the environmental authorities. The scope and content of self-supervision are regulated in more detail for operations with permit obligations, but apply generally for all environmental activities. The competent environmental authority can and will demand further investigations and reporting of information to the authorities, according to Chapter 26 Sections 19–22 of the Code. It is thus a general requirement that all actors control their own activities and provide the competent authority with the information needed for supervision and control under environmental law. The duties of self-supervision and control are seen as instruments for proving compliance with the general rules of consideration. This means that the addressee of administrative regulation measures will have to be an active party in the administrative procedure under environmental law, providing information and making investigations, and ensuring they have sufficient expertise in the environmental risks and how to control them. They will also carry the main burden of proof regarding compliance with environmental law. This should work so that uncertainty is detrimental to the person causing environmental risk or harm.

Actor responsibility connects to the polluter pays principle (PPP), the function of which is to impose costs of environmental harm on the party responsible for the pollution.[32] Analogy can also be made with strict civil liability for hazardous activities, which ensures the taking of appropriate safety precautions to avoid damage, and the internalization of costs. The actor should not benefit from putting others at risk.[33] Environmental actor responsibility also echoes principles underlying sustainable development, an essential feature of which is the idea of a decentralized world,

---

[32] The polluter pays principle is regulated in Art. 191.2 TFEU (Treaty on the Functioning of the European Union), and in the Swedish Environmental Code, see: Prop. 1997/98:45 Part I pp. 208–210. It is also formulated in the Rio Declaration Art. 16. See also A. Kiss and D. Shelton, *International Environmental Law*, 3rd edition (Ardsley: Transnational Publishers, 2004), 212–13.

[33] J. Hellner and M. Radetzki, *Skadeståndsrätt*, 8th edition (Stockholm: Norstedts juridik, 2010), 171–4. See also: SOU 1966:65, 72–5 and 278.

where sustainable development cannot be achieved without responsibilities and the participation of each and every actor, individually and collectively.[34] Environmental work is to be driven at grass-roots level, not just as top-down regulation.[35]

Actor responsibilities are, however, also rooted in legal history.[36] For polluting activities entailing more substantial risks to the health, property or welfare of others, a preventive and precautionary perspective has long since entailed extensive actor responsibilities for necessary preventive and reparative measures.[37] Scientific uncertainties and complexities have been recognized in this regulatory discourse since its inception. It was argued early on that actor responsibilities included precautionary duties of care, securing expertise and information, and planning and improving precautionary work. Active control measures were demanded in spite of damage having occurred, or even the certainty that damage would occur. In principle, hazardous activities were not permissible if sufficient precaution and control was not ensured. This entailed risk management, long before the precautionary principle was developed.[38]

In summary, actor responsibility is well established and boils down to the person causing or risking causing damage to legitimate environmental interests bearing responsibilities for control, prevention and precaution with regard to their own activities. The procedure for administrative regulation of these activities is based on environmental actors being the responsible and active parties, with the regulatory authorities taking a more supervisory, supporting and guiding role, and taking measures when necessary to control and enforce these duties on individual actors.

This order of things challenges general administrative procedure, where control functions lie with the decision-making authority, especially in onerous cases involving enforcement. The environmental authority

---

[34] Agenda 21, A/CONF.151/26/rev.1, Annex II, esp. Section 3, and Section 4, Subs. 40. See also: Decleris, *The Law on Sustainable Development*, 30–2, referring to Agenda 21.

[35] Prop. 1997/98:45 Part I pp. 160–161; SOU 1996:103 Part I p. 22, and Part II pp. 10–11.

[36] Use of water resources has a long regulatory history: 1880 Water Ordinance Section 12, stating a general responsibility to ensure that regulated materials did not get into the water; Section 2:58 of the 1918 Water Act (as amended in 1937), stating duty to take reasonable precautionary measures to protect ground water; 1942 Water Act regulation 8:23 on household sewage water, stating a duty to take necessary precautions to prevent pollution, if reasonable, and 8:32 on industrial sewage water, stating a principal prohibition that could be lifted if necessary precautionary measures were regulated.

[37] See NJA II 1942 pp. 79–80.

[38] Environmental Protection Act Section 5, SOU 1966:65 p. 211, note p. 221 on duties already at the risk of harm.

will instead rely on the duties of the actor to provide decision-making materials, to know the problems and the appropriate measures to take to abate these problems, and to prove compliance with law. The focus of the formal rule of law on protection of the addressee of public regulation is thus shifted. Administrative procedure relying on actor responsibility will not, to the same extent, favour the interests of the individual environmental actor.

Swedish regulation of actor responsibility thus reveals a new perspective on the rule of law in the administrative enforcement procedure. Environmental responsibilities and control functions are shared between the regulator and the regulated actor, and the actor carries primary responsibility for control of their activities. That includes procedural responsibilities, including showing the regulator that their activities are carried out in compliance with environmental law. The risk of uncertainties and situations of poor expertise or investigation will, in principle, be carried by the regulated actor. The described rules are perhaps unique to Sweden, but underlying general principles and doctrine of environmental law – PPP, precaution, sustainable development, and so on – provide a basis for actor responsibilities as fundamental to environmental law in other legal orders. However, arguing limits to individual freedom against state regulation is challenging, certainly where such freedom is connected to individual rights, and this will be explored next.

5. Rights, freedom and common interests

It could be argued that the described actor responsibilities and shifted burden of proof will infringe on the freedom and rights of the individual actor. Under the rule of law the individual is autonomous and protected against state involvement, sometimes with the support of fundamental human rights. Such rights may generally be delimited through regulation, but no further than what can be considered legitimate and proportionate. Administrative enforcement of environmental law will thus be formed by the idea of protection of fundamental rights and freedoms – typically property rights – but also by regulations delimiting such rights and freedoms. Environmental interests are considered to legitimate such delimitation, both in the case law of the European Court and in Swedish constitutional regulation.[39] Environmental standards are also applied to

---

[39] European Convention on Human Rights (ECHR), Protocol 1, Art. 1; *Fredin* v. *Sweden*, Judgment of 18 February 1991; Swedish Instrument of Government Chapter 2 Section 15.

determine the meaning of other established human rights. Certainly the right to home and private life comprises to some extent a right to live in a healthy environment.[40] Protection of the human environment is thus influential within the dynamic human rights discourse.[41] There is strong support and much regulation to provide grounds for administrative enforcement delimiting the rights and freedoms of the polluter.

To advance the discussion a little further into fundamental environmental law and sustainable development, it may be argued that natural resources such as air, water, fish or iron ore are fundamentally not free to be exploited or damaged. This argument is based in the doctrine of sustainable development, demanding inter- and intragenerational equity.[42] With the role of man as both creature and moulder of his environment follows both an equitable right to natural resources and a consequential responsibility to manage, protect and improve the environment for present and future generations.[43] The rights and duties are reciprocal, and the environmental actor must therefore respect the rights of other stakeholders. This idea of limited rights to natural resources could be argued as a wider principle of good neighbourliness.

The principle of sustainable development is established in international law, and implemented in Swedish law.[44] It must therefore reflect in the notion of a fundamental individual autonomy and property rights. This influences the interpretation of the fundamental idea of freedom, and thus brings something further to the conceptual discussion of the rule

---

See also: B. Bengtsson, 'En problematisk grundlagsändring', *Svensk Juristtidning* (1994), 920–33; G. Michanek, 'Markägare – med rätt att döda?, 2 *Miljörättslig tidskrift* (1995), 155–84; K. Åhman, 'Äganderätten i konflikt med andra skyddsvärda rättigheter eller intressen', in K. Åhman (ed.), *Äganderätten – dess omfattning och begränsningar* (Uppsala: Iustus förlag, 2009), 131–42, on conflicts between property rights and other rights and interests.

[40] *López Ostra v. Spain*, Judgment of 9 December 1994; *Hatton and Others v. the United Kingdom*, Judgment of 8 July 2003; *Taşkin and Others v. Turkey*, Judgment of 10 November 2004; and *Fadeyeva v. Russia*, Judgment of 9 June 2005. See also: P. Birnie, A. Boyle and P. Redgewell, *International Law and the Environment*, 3rd edition (Oxford University Press, 2009), 284; and Kiss and Shelton, *International Environmental Law*, 692.

[41] Birnie *et al.*, *International Law and the Environment*, 300–2; and Kiss and Shelton, *International Environmental Law*, 725–30.

[42] Report of the World Commission for Environment and Development, *Our Common Future*, 4, 8, 11, 29 and 46–9; Stockholm Declaration esp. preamble and Principles 1, 2, 9; Rio Declaration 1992 Principles 3, 5, 7 and 9. See also: Birnie *et al.*, *International Law and the Environment*, 119–23.

[43] Stockholm Declaration Principle 1; Kiss and Shelton, *International Environmental Law*, 665.

[44] Environmental Code Chapter 1 Section 1; Prop 1997/98:45 Part I pp. 1–2.

of law. This suggests that the individual is not autonomous with regard to management of common and shared resources, and that environmental sustainability is such a fundamental value that it constitutes a necessary precondition in the *Rechtsstaat* and part of legal certainty.[45] This perspective extends to procedural safeguards of legal certainty. The legal position of an actor denied the ability to cause risk or harm, or required to abate an environmental problem, does not seem that seriously infringed if he or she is fundamentally not free to cause harm. Environmental regulation and the procedural role of the individual must be viewed in that context. The administrative authority's procedural responsibilities will in the environmental case encounter actor responsibilities for knowledge, investigation and proof. The actor must participate in the control of his or her own activities. If taking action that could damage common resources, he or she must acquire sufficient information to facilitate a responsible and appropriate management decision.

With this contemporary perspective on the concepts of individual rights and freedoms in a context of environmental regulation and sustainable development, we find the basis for arguing a rule of law for nature, and the need to develop a legal discourse that expresses such arguments.

6. Concluding remarks

In conclusion, the rule of law is not to be understood as an absolute or eternal concept, but as a dynamic and practical conception of justice and protection against abuse of power. Is has developed from a demand for a formal concept of legality, to a wider and more substantive idea of justice and legal certainty – including environmental protection. In administrative enforcement this means that the authority must consider environmental protection as a legitimate counterweight to the protection of individual rights and freedoms. Today, the *Rechtsstaat* reflects plurality of interests and powers. Similarly, the idea of legal rights and responsibilities has developed into a more nuanced and interlinked conceptual understanding. Regulation is carried out in cooperation between public authorities, private individuals and organizations. The state can no longer be seen as the monopoly power regulating the defenceless individual citizen.

---

[45] Compare: A. Nilsson, *Rättssäkerhet och miljöhänsyn. En diskurs belyst av JO:s praxis I miljöärenden* (Stockholm : Santérus förlag, 2002), 97.

In this chapter the call for an environmental rule of law has been investigated in the context of a development of the rule of law that provides more room for the perspective of nature. The investigation has focused on procedural rules to support the rule of law, and noted developments of such procedural law in the context of Swedish administrative enforcement of environmental law. These involve public duties to protect environmental interests and realize environmental goals, and control of compliance with these responsibilities. Moreover, a wider range of participants have procedural rights and possibilities for advocating environmental interests. Last, but in no way least, there are well-developed actor responsibilities to actively carry out, and develop, preventive and precautionary measures to protect the environment and manage natural resources, and so on. The dynamics of fundamental rights and freedoms that support these instruments of a rule of law for nature have also been discussed. I conclude that an established and developing environmental counterweight to the formal rule of law protection of the polluter can be observed, and that a contemporary expression of the rule of law and legal certainty leaves room for arguments of appropriate environmental concern – and a responsibility for environmental lawyers to argue the case of nature.

16

Mechanisms for reviewing compliance with international environmental law open to private parties

CRISTINA VERONES

1. Introduction

The importance of environmental protection is recognized as a fundamental concern today. This is reflected by the large body of norms of International Environmental Law (IEL) that has developed over the past forty years, amounting to a true 'legal order for nature'. Yet, as several authors and reports point out, there exists a considerable amount of non-compliance with IEL, as well as a lack of enforcement, especially under traditional means of enforcing international law, that is inter-state mechanisms.[1]

Implementation, compliance and enforcement are all highly relevant for an effective rule of law for nature. Albeit denoting different aspects in a law-abiding process, the three notions are closely intertwined. Compliance denotes the fulfilment of (international) obligations incumbent on the state.[2] In order to fulfil these requirements, implementation is

---

This chapter is part of the author's research for her Ph.D. thesis. The model presented here is work in progress and may be subject to change. The author thanks Professor Jorge Viñuales for his helpful comments.

[1] E. Brown Weiss and H. Jacobson (eds.), *Engaging Countries – Strengthening Compliance with International Environmental Accords* (Cambridge, MA: MIT Press, 1998); United States General Accounting Office, *International Environment – International Agreements Are Not Well Monitored*, January 1992, GAO/RCED-92-43; B. Thompson, 'The Continuing Innovation of Citizen Enforcement', 1 *University of Illinois Law Review* (2000), 185–236, 189ff.

[2] UNEP, *Manual on Compliance with and Enforcement of Multilateral Environmental Agreements*, 2006, 59; A. Chayes, A. Handler Chayes and R. Mitchell, 'Managing Compliance: A Comparative Perspective', in E. Brown Weiss and H. Jacobson (eds.), *Engaging Countries – Strengthening Compliance with International Environmental Accords* (Cambridge, MA: MIT Press, 1998), 39–62, 39.

necessary, referring to all means adopted (by a state) to ensure an effective application of the rules in question.[3] Enforcement means 'compelling an actor to comply with a legal rule or agreement'.[4] Thus, if compliance is not voluntary, enforcement is necessary to ensure that the rule in question is respected. Enforcement does not necessarily refer only to legally binding judgments, but to any measure by any mechanism that will put enough pressure on the state to change its behaviour and comply with IEL.

Research has pointed to a number of reasons why states often do not comply with IEL, such as the lack of (human, financial or administrative) resources or the lack of will.[5] Furthermore, enforcement actions under traditional means of enforcing international law are often limited. In addition to the lack of institutions such as an international environmental court, this can be attributed to the lack of will of states. Moreover, in respect of global environmental resources such as the climate, it might be problematic to find a clear causal link between a polluter's conduct and actual damage,[6] making attribution under the International Law Commission's State Responsibility Articles challenging. For example, it cannot be conclusively held that, by operating one particular CO_2 emitting facility, a state directly contributes to damage occurring from climate change, such as rising sea-level. Consequently, there are also problems relating to standing,[7] since in order to bring a claim, a state needs to be 'injured', that is, the obligation in question needs to be individually owed to that state[8] or, when the obligation was owed to a group of states, that

---

[3] L. Boisson de Chazournes, 'La mise en œuvre du droit international dans le domaine de la protection de l'environnement: enjeux et défis', 99 *Revue Générale de Droit International Public* (1995), 37–76, 38; J. Ausubel and D. Victor. 'Verification of International Environmental Agreements', 17 *Annual Review of Energy and Environment* (1992), 1–43, 4.

[4] *Black's Law Dictionary*, 9th edn (St Paul: West, 2009); F. Yamin, 'NGOs and International Environmental Law: A Critical Evaluation of their Roles and Responsibilities', 10 *Review of European Community and International Environmental Law* (2001), 149–62, 153.

[5] A. Chayes and A. Handler Chayes, *The New Sovereignty* (Cambridge, MA: Harvard University Press, 1995), 13–14; M. Bothe, 'The Evaluation of Enforcement Mechanisms in International Environmental Law', in R. Wolfrum (ed.), *Enforcing Environmental Standards: Economic Mechanisms as Viable Means?*, Beiträge zum ausländischen öffentlichen Recht und Völkerrecht (Berlin: Springer, 1996), vol. 125, 13–38.

[6] J. Brunnée, 'Of Sense and Sensibility: Reflections on International Liability Regimes as Tools for Environmental Protection', 53:2 *International and Comparative Law Quarterly* (2004), 351–68.

[7] A. Thompson, 'The Rational Enforcement of International Law: Solving the Sanctioner's Dilemma', 1:2 *International Theory* (2009), 307–21, 309ff; B. Simma, *From Bilateralism to Community Interests in International Law* (Recueil des Cours, 1994), vol. 250.

[8] Article 42(a), International Law Commission, *Articles on Responsibility of States for Internationally Wrongful Acts*, 2001 (hereinafter ILC State Responsibility Articles).

state is specially affected by the breach,[9] which might either not be the case or be hard to prove. All these reasons contribute to a general lack of enforcement of IEL. In order to have a meaningful international legal system, it is, however, important that established rules are respected and non-compliers treated accordingly.[10] Otherwise, the legal system loses credibility.

To combat the weak action of states in ensuring an effective rule of law for nature, alternative approaches to state action have to be explored to strengthen enforcement and ultimately compliance with environmental rules. One solution that has been investigated in the literature is the use of a variety of international mechanisms open to private parties, such as individuals and NGOs, but also the private sector.[11] These mechanisms allow private parties to bring claims or information about a state's alleged non-compliance with IEL. Private parties are often interested in environmental protection since they are directly affected by environmental degradation. They could effectively use their access to these various mechanisms in order to bring claims related to IEL and environmental protection. Ultimately, if more pressure is put on states to respect IEL, environmental law is strengthened and a higher level of environmental protection can be reached.

The wide diversity of the possible mechanisms (see section 2 and Figure 16.5) makes the assessment of their contribution to the effectiveness of IEL particularly challenging. Different studies exist on specific mechanisms,[12] but an overall – comparative – assessment of the palette of mechanisms has yet to be provided. The purpose of this chapter is to provide a conceptual framework to allow for a comparative study. The framework is based on the criteria of access, applicable law and outcome

---

[9] Article 42(b), ILC State Responsibility Articles.
[10] H. Jacobson and E. Brown Weiss, 'A Framework for Analysis', in E. Brown Weiss and H. Jacobson (eds.), *Engaging Countries – Strengthening Compliance with International Environmental Accords* (Cambridge, MA: MIT Press, 1998), 1–18, 1.
[11] Many mechanisms also exist at the domestic level. See G. Pring and C. Pring, *Greening Justice – Creating and Improving Environmental Courts and Tribunals* (The Access Initiative, 2009).
[12] See T. Treves *et al.* (eds.), *Non-Compliance Procedures and Mechanisms and the Effectiveness of International Environmental Agreements* (The Hague: T.M.C Asser Press, 2009); D. Clark, J. Fox and K. Trakle (eds.), *Demanding Accountability – Civil-Society Claims and the World Bank Inspection Panel* (Lanham, MD: Rowman & Littlefiled Publishers Inc., 2003); L. Malone and S. Pasternack, *Defending the Environment – Civil Society Strategies to Enforce International Environmental Law* (Washington, DC: Island Press, 2006); K. Raustiala, 'Police Patrols & Fire Alarms in the NAAEC', 26 *Loyola Los Angeles International and Comparative Law Review* (2004), 389–413.

of the mechanisms. Putting these mechanisms in relation to each other according to these criteria results in an interesting picture of the 'state' of mechanisms open to private parties for the purpose of enforcement of IEL in a wide sense. It enables an overall comparison as well as comparison at the level of individual mechanisms.[13] Knowing which mechanisms are particularly useful for enforcing IEL contributes to strengthening IEL in at least two ways. It highlights the mechanisms that are most promising for private parties to use, and it will allow us to identify 'best' practices and features of mechanisms should we decide that an international mechanism generally related to IEL is necessary for strengthening environmental law.

In the next section, the chapter briefly introduces the mechanisms analysed. Then the comparative framework is explained, and some of the results of the theoretical framework outlined.

2. The mechanisms under consideration

As pointed out above, a wide variety of mechanisms exist that can be used by private parties to bring environmental claims. Only considering mechanisms directly related to multilateral environmental agreements would be too limiting, since there are other mechanisms that can directly apply IEL or work towards respect for the environment and environmental rules indirectly, for example by applying human rights.[14] This capacity to work for the benefit of nature and its rule of law directly or indirectly is one of the features describing the mechanisms included in this study. Another important characteristic of these mechanisms is that they are all open to private parties.

Mechanisms include non-compliance procedures under environmental treaties open to private parties, such as the Aarhus Convention non-compliance procedures (NCP), the accountability mechanisms of multilateral development banks, as well as investment mechanisms such as the International Centre for Settlement of Investment Disputes (ICSID). In addition, human rights mechanisms, for example the European Court of Human Rights, offer interesting possibilities for private parties wanting to act for the protection of the environment. Other mechanisms

---

[13] The author is currently working on her Ph.D. thesis, where she is comparing mechanisms based on the framework developed here as well as analysing the influence and importance of these mechanisms for the effective implementation of IEL.

[14] For an overview of all the mechanisms included here, see Figure 16.5 and footnote 36.

exist under soft law instruments, such as the Organisation for Economic Co-operation and Development (OECD) Guidelines on Multinational Enterprises.

Due to the large variety of mechanisms included here, the outcome varies according to the type of mechanism used (e.g. recommendations, legally binding judgments). Yet these outcomes have at least one element in common, namely the capacity to exert pressure on states. Most states are averse to such 'negative publicity'.[15] In addition to reputational pressure, pressure can be economic[16] or political. The presumption is that pressure will at the end of, or sometimes even during, the process in front of a mechanism[17] lead the state to change its behaviour and come (back) into compliance.[18] Achieving compliance is highly relevant for ensuring environmental protection and proper respect for the rule of law for nature.

3. Systematization of mechanisms

In order to classify all these international mechanisms and provide a more objective picture than by analysing each one in isolation, an analytical

---

[15] A. Thompson, 'The Rational Enforcement of International Law: Solving the Sanctioner's Dilemma', 1 *International Theory* (2009), 307–21; B. Richardson, 'Financing Sustainability: The New Transnational Governance of Socially Responsible Investment', 17 *Yearbook of International Environmental Law* (2006), 73–110, 77; E. Goodwin, 'The World Heritage Convention, the Environment, and Compliance', 20 *Colorado Journal of International Environmental Law and Policy* (2009), 157–98, 172.

[16] Consider, for example, the recommendation to suspend trade benefits of the non-complying party under the Convention on International Trade in Endangered Species of Wild Fauna and Flora (CITES) by the CITES secretariat, which can effectively amount to a trade ban with serious economic consequences for the state concerned. See P. Sand, 'Sanctions in Case of Non-Compliance and State Responsibility: *Pacta Sunt Servanda* – or Else?', in U. Beyerlin *et al.* (eds.), *Ensuring Compliance with Multilateral Environmental Agreements – A Dialogue between Practitioners and Academia* (Leiden: Martinus Nijhoff Publishers, 2006), 259–72.

[17] For example, concerning the deterioration of the Chichoj Lagoon in Guatemala, the association bringing the claim and the local government agreed during the public hearing in front of the Latin American Water Tribunal (LAWT) to an action plan to protect the lagoon, something that had not been possible before, presumably for lack of publicity and public pressure on the government. LAWT, *Afectación de la Laguna Chichoj, San Cristóbal Verapaz, Departamento de Alta Verapaz. República de Guatemala*, public hearing in September 2008, available at: http://tragua.com/wp-content/uploads/2012/04/veredicto_laguna_chichoj_guatemala_2008.pdf (last consulted 11 January 2013).

[18] M. Stephan, 'Environmental Information Disclosure Programs: They Work, but Why?', 83 *Social Science Quarterly* (2002), 190–205.

framework is proposed, based on three criteria: access, applicable law and available outcomes.

3.1 Access

The criterion of access refers to the question of 'how easy is it to gain the right to use a particular mechanism?' Here the issues of admissibility and standing play a crucial role.

Standing in international law can be defined as the capacity or right of an entity or person to present a legal claim to a particular body.[19] Thereby, we have to see how such a claim can be brought. We have to determine, for example, whether active steps have to be taken before access is granted, and if so, what kind of steps. These steps can be varied, for instance contacting another entity before bringing the claim[20] or exhausting local remedies.[21] Another aspect is whether the claimant has to pass via another entity, which will refer the case further. It is assumed that passing via another body makes access less direct, since the petitioner is dependent on other intermediary entities.

A last point to be considered is whether the claimant has to show that s/he is 'specifically affected' in order to bring a case. It is assumed that mechanisms requiring such a proof are less accessible, since without this condition it is possible for a greater number of interested private parties to take action.

The mechanisms are classified in five categories:

- **Immediately open:** Access is very easy. Mechanisms do not require particular steps to be taken nor to show specific affectedness before a case can be brought. There might be some preconditions to be fulfilled, such as being in a specific geographical area to use a particular body. However, these are general preconditions that need to be accepted as given, but not active steps that parties have to take when bringing a case. They are thus not taken into account here.
- **Direct:** Direct access refers to generally easy access, but with two possible limitations making these mechanisms slightly less accessible than

---

[19] H. Briggs, 'Barcelona Traction: the *jus standi* of Belgium', 65:2 *The American Journal of International Law* (1971), 327–45, 330; B. Garner (ed.), *Black's Law Dictionary*, 8th edn (St Paul: Thomson West, 2004), 1442.

[20] E.g. *Operating Procedure of the World Bank Inspection Panel*, Subject Matter of Request, §1.

[21] E.g. Article 35 of the European Convention on Human Rights.

those in the first category. The first limitation relates to the fact that some previous action in the sense of actively taking steps is imperatively needed before access can be granted. An example is the requirement to have prior contact with the World Bank Management before the complaint can be brought to the World Bank Inspection Panel. Although not a difficult condition, it is nevertheless a necessary procedural step. The second possible limitation – limiting the parties who are able to bring claims – is the obligation to show that the claimants are specifically affected by the alleged breach of the international norm. It is not necessary that both limitations are present at the same time.
- **Direct with legal condition:** Here the steps to be taken previously are legal steps, mainly referring to the exhaustion of local remedies. This does arguably require more time and resources to fulfil compared to writing a letter to the World Bank Management, for example. Therefore, it is considered that these mechanisms are slightly less accessible than the ones in the previous category.
- **Indirect:** These mechanisms are characterized by the fact that they cannot be reached directly, but petitioners have to pass via another entity, which will pass on the case. Petitioners clearly are dependent on the intermediary entity for whether or not the case will be forwarded. It is consequently considered that passing via another entity makes access less direct.
- **Restricted:** Mechanisms in this category, such as the European Court of Justice in relation to individual cases, have so many – personal but also procedural – conditions to be fulfilled by the petitioners that it is very difficult and sometimes even impossible for them to gain access.

Applying the above criteria to a set of thirty-four mechanisms, the picture set out in Figure 16.1 emerges.

Access does not seem to pose high hurdles. As is clearly visible from Figure 16.1, the majority of mechanisms can be found in the second category, that is in 'direct access'. Access in this category is not completely free, but not extremely difficult either, since only some prior non-legal steps have to be taken and/or it has to be shown that the plaintiffs are specifically affected. The second largest group of mechanisms can be found in the first category, where according to our definition access is very easy. Thus, the majority of mechanisms are characterized by relatively easy access conditions.

As far as the 'types' of mechanisms are concerned, there seems to be no uniformity. For example, both courts and NCPs can be found in different categories and are not concentrated in only one of them.

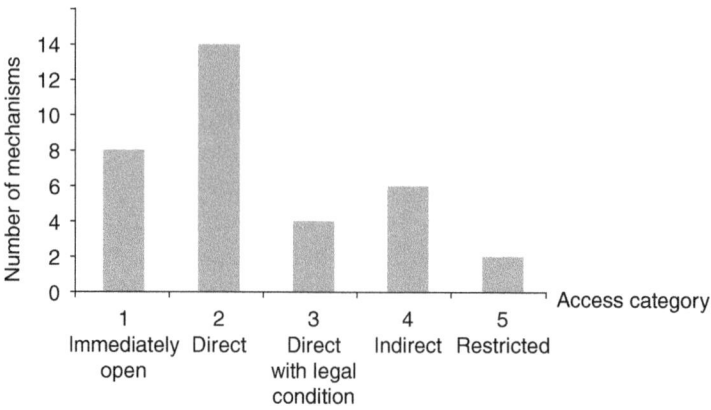

Figure 16.1 Number of mechanisms per access category

Interestingly, human rights mechanisms (including courts as well as committees) appear to be generally less easily accessible, since they are all to be found in categories three and four. A possible explanation could be that states are more sensitive when their human rights situation is assessed by a third mechanism than, for example, when their respect for IEL is dealt with by NCPs. Consequently, states put the access bar higher when creating human rights mechanisms by imposing requirements such as the exhaustion of local remedies.

3.2   Applicable law

Applicable law is the law applicable to solve the dispute on the merits, and thus not the law that is used to determine a mechanism's jurisdiction to hear a particular dispute.[22]

While some mechanisms specify which law they can apply,[23] others are silent on this point.[24] In the case of silence the applicable law has to be seen in relation to the jurisdiction of the mechanism. This restriction does not preclude the use of other branches of law for the purpose of interpreting the applicable law. However, the legal dispute is solved on the basis of the

---

[22] J. Collier and V. Lowe, *The Settlement of Disputes in International Law – Institutions and Procedures* (Oxford University Press, 1999), 239.
[23] E.g. arbitral tribunals under the ICSID Convention (Article 42 §1 ICSID Convention).
[24] E.g. the First Optional Protocol to the International Covenant on Civil and Political Rights (ICCPR) establishing the system of individual petitions to the Human Rights Committee.

applicable law, while the law used for interpretative purposes only helps in reaching the conclusion, but is not the legal basis of the verdict.[25]

A first distinction has to be made between mechanisms directly applying IEL and mechanisms that do not. This classification should be understood in a neutral sense. It is not claimed that mechanisms applying IEL are more (or less) effective than those that cannot. Environmental concerns can still be addressed even when applying human rights or investment law rather than IEL. Thus, environmental protection can be reached by applying laws other than IEL. Yet it has to be acknowledged that by using other branches of the law, environmental protection is usually more indirect and often limited.[26] For example, by using the right to property[27] it is first and foremost this right that is enforced and only indirectly and in a second step may the environment gain protection as well. Also for example, under human rights law only environmental concerns falling within an anthropocentric approach to the environment can be protected,[28] that is there needs to be imminent and direct harm to a human right. Thus, only environmental issues with a clear human focus can be dealt with, while other concerns such as biodiversity conservation are difficult or impossible to protect under human rights law. Arguably also, IEL treaties are limited to a particular subject, such as biodiversity conservation, but they have the potential to protect the environment where no protection through other rights would be possible. The difference in the applicable law matters not only from a legal but also from a practical perspective. Consequently, a distinction should be made between those mechanisms applying international environmental law and those not doing so, while at the same addressing environmental concerns.

It is not always clear which rules belong to IEL, since there is no universally accepted definition of IEL.[29] Trying to provide a definition of IEL

---

[25] J. Pauwelyn, 'Bridging Fragmentation and Unity: International Law as a Universe of Inter-connected Islands', 25 *Michigan Journal of International Law* (2004), 903–16.

[26] D. Shelton. 'Human Rights and the Environment: What Specific Environmental Rights Have Been Recognized?', 35 *Denver Journal of International Law and Policy* (2006), 129–71.

[27] E.g. *Peter A Allard* v. *Government of Barbados* in front of a UNCITRAL Tribunal, notice of dispute available at http://graemehall.com/legal/papers/BIT-Complaint.pdf (last consulted 20 December 2012). But see also *Case of Pialopoulos and Others* v. *Greece* in front of the ECtHR (*Case of Pialopoulos and Others* v. *Greece*, application no. 37095/97, ECtHR, Judgment, 15 February 2001).

[28] N. Gibson, 'The Right to a Clean Environment', 54 *Saskatchewan Law Review* (1990), 5–17; Shelton, 'Human Rights and the Environment'.

[29] For a discussion of different definitions of IEL see M. Fitzmaurice, *International Protection of the Environment* (The Hague: Receuil des Cours, 2001), vol. 293, 22–7;

goes far beyond this contribution. For our purpose a rather narrow conception of IEL is adopted, namely as those rules that purport to regulate or protect the natural environment or influences thereon. Thus, although human health and the environment are closely linked, for example, the human right to health is not considered an international environmental rule. It is true that the environment – and its pollution – has an impact on human health. Yet in order to have this impact, there first needs to be a pollution of an environmental resource. Only then will human health be affected and thus – as the other side of the coin – attempts at environmental protection through the human right to health will only benefit the environment indirectly, since it has to pass via another right (i.e. the human right to health) before reaching the environment as such.

A second distinction takes into account IEL 'hard' and 'soft' law or policy requirements, since from a legal point of view these are quite different sources.

A distinction in three categories is proposed:

- **IEL directly applicable:** Mechanisms are able to apply IEL directly, with or without the possibility of applying other branches of international law such as human rights as well. For the purposes of the *application* of IEL they are the 'best' mechanisms.
- **Overlapping rules:** Mechanisms cannot apply IEL. However, they can use IEL for interpretative purposes. Hence, it is possible to 'smuggle' IEL into their applicable law, which makes most of the mechanisms so called 'borrowed fora'.[30]
- **Soft IEL:** Mechanisms are concerned with soft law and policy requirements in environmental matters. Soft law can have important consequences and thus mechanisms in this category should not simply be ignored.

Figure 16.2 sets out the picture that results from the application of the criteria explained above.

It is promising to note that there are a large number of mechanisms able to apply IEL directly. This category includes mostly the NCPs of environmental treaties such as the Aarhus Convention, the Kyoto Protocol and the Alpine Convention. In addition, there are mechanisms

P. Birnie, A. Boyle and C. Redgwell, *International Law and the Environment*, 3rd edn (Oxford University Press, 2009), 2–6.

[30] J. Viñuales, 'Managing Abidance by Standards for the Protection of the Environment', in A. Cassese (ed.). *Realizing Utopia: The Future of International Law* (Oxford University Press, 2012), 326–39, 331–2.

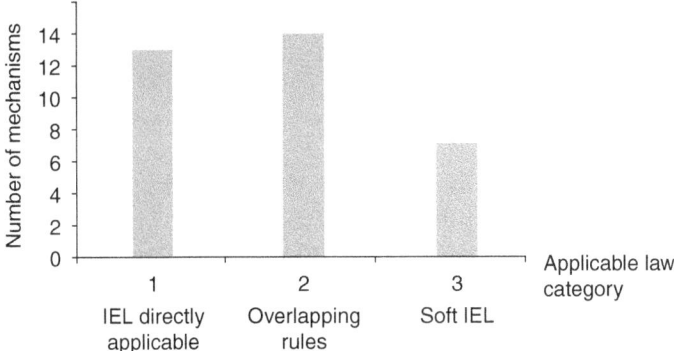

Figure 16.2 Number of mechanisms per applicable law category

such as the Complaints Mechanism of the European Investment Bank (EIB), the Latin American Water Tribunal (LAWT) and the International Court for Environmental Arbitration and Conciliation (ICEAC).[31] It has to be pointed out that with the exception of the European Court of Justice – applying European Environmental Law as well as IEL due to the fact that the EU is a member of several MEAs[32] – all courts and tribunals are to be found in category two, the one applying 'overlapping rules'. Thus, the rather disadvantaged position of IEL from the point of view of implementing mechanisms at the international level seems to be confirmed since, unlike other branches of international law, IEL does not have its own international court system. Most mechanisms in category one are NCPs of the corresponding environmental treaties. At the same time, Figure 16.2 confirms that other branches of law – such as human rights – can be used to address environmental issues. In this respect, it should be pointed out that human rights, compared to other branches of international law, such as investment law, is indeed the most reliable 'smuggling partner', an approach that has been recognized by the Human

---

[31] The mechanisms falling under this category are according to the current classification the following: the European Court of Justice (individual complaints and preliminary rulings), the NCPs of the Aarhus Convention, the 2003 Protocol on Pollutant Release and Transfer Registers, the 1999 Protocol on Water and Health to the 1992 Convention on the Protection and Use of Transboundary Water Courses and International Lakes, the Kyoto Protocol, the Alpine Convention, the secretariat-related mechanism under CITES, the Complaints Mechanism of the EIB, the European Ombudsman, the procedure under the North American Agreement on Environmental Cooperation, the LAWT and the ICEAC.

[32] The EU is a party to such treaties as the Aarhus Convention, the Convention on Biological Diversity and the Montreal Protocol on Substances that Deplete the Ozone Layer.

Rights Council in its study on the relationship between human rights and the environment.[33]

3.3 Outcome

The third criterion refers to the final outcome of a proceeding.

It might be appropriate to speak of 'remedies' here. However, when dealing with remedies references is often made to the whole 'process', ranging from access to justice to final reparation mechanisms.[34] Yet for the purpose of this third criterion, only the final decision is referred to, rather than the whole process. To avoid misunderstanding, the less legal term of 'outcome' rather than 'remedy' has been chosen.

A first distinction is made between legally binding and non-binding outcomes.

It is true that public pressure and 'bad publicity' can be effective tools for forcing an actor to change its behaviour, regardless of how legally binding an outcome may be.[35] Nevertheless, when deciding where to bring a case, the degree to which the final outcome binds an actor might be an important element for private parties. The importance of this distinction for the parties for choosing a mechanism should not be underestimated.

It has to be recalled that the idea behind the assumption that private parties want to take action for the environment before international mechanisms is that they are interested in environmental protection. An important element for establishing the outcome scale is based on the nature of IEL, that is its preventive rather than reactive character. It is consequently assumed that decisions that require the respondent to change its behaviour or system in the future, are more important for environmental protection than decisions that simply recognize that a violation has taken place in the past. This is not to claim that verdicts addressing the past are useless for the protection of the environment. However, in order to transform such findings for the purpose of environmental protection, some action is required. Thus, decisions themselves addressing this future element directly are more interesting for environmental protection as such.

---

[33] Human Rights Council, 19th session, *Analytical Study on the Relationship between Human Rights and the Environment*, A/HRC/19/34, 16 December 2011.

[34] GA Resolution 60/147, 16 December 2005 on *Basic Principles and Guidelines on the Right to a Remedy and Reparation for Victims of Gross Violations of International Human Rights Law and Serious Violations of International Humanitarian Law*.

[35] Chayes *et al.*, 'Managing Compliance', 55.

Consequently, two categories of outcomes are proposed: specific and general relief. Specific relief encompasses verdicts that address the violation of a norm owed to the claimant, that is they are focused on the specific case. Some of these mechanisms have the possibility of granting financial compensation, which might be an additional motivation to bring a case.

General relief is more focused on the future. These decisions require (and sometimes help) the respondent to change its system or behaviour and address the general policy rather than an individual violation, which makes clear that under this type of relief there is usually no possibility of financial compensation to the plaintiff.

The outcome scale is organized into five categories.

- **Specific, general and binding relief:** Mechanisms grant specific or general relief or any combination of the two. The mechanism can recognize the violation of a right owed to an individual or a group and potentially even award financial compensation, but at the same time it can also make recommendations on how the respondent should behave in the future. The decisions taken are legally binding, giving them more legal authority.
- **Specific, general and non-binding relief:** These mechanisms are very similar to those in category one in terms of type of relief, but the outcomes are not legally binding.
- **General and non-binding relief:** The claimant needs to have a high interest in environmental protection as such and an altruistic motivation, since the pronouncement addresses future general policy issues and not a specific past violation. The outcome is not legally binding.
- **Specific and binding relief:** The outcome only addresses the potential violation of a right owed to the claimant. These decisions are not directly very beneficial for the environment, since they address past violations rather than future respect of the norms. Yet these decisions are legally binding, giving them considerable legal authority.
- **Specific and non-binding relief:** The weakest outcome for the environmental protection is where the issue addressed is only the specific violation of the right of the claimant and where, in addition, the outcome is not legally binding.

Based on these categories, the result for 'outcome' presents itself as set out in Figure 16.3.

Given that the main logic of IEL is mostly preventive rather than reactive, general relief seems to be more interesting for environmental purposes, since it is directed towards the future and is potentially broader. At the same

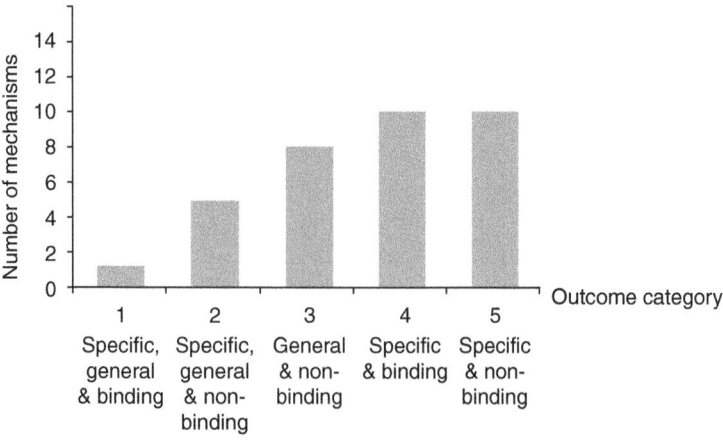

Figure 16.3 Number of mechanisms per outcome category

time, in order to motivate private parties to bring cases, it is understandable that most of them would like to 'get something' out of the proceedings. Thus, the 'best' mechanisms are those with the ability to grant a combination of specific and general relief, which is moreover binding. On the other hand, the 'worst' mechanisms for environmental protection under the aspect of outcome are those that grant only specific relief that is in addition not legally binding and thus often seen as 'toothless'. It is, therefore, rather disappointing to look at the data in Figure 16.3. Most mechanisms have rather unsatisfactory outcomes (namely only specific relief) from the environmental point of view. Only one mechanism – the Inter-American Court of Human Rights (IACtHR) – is to be found in category one, the 'best' category.

Unlike the other two criteria, the distribution of the different types of mechanisms is quite clear-cut. For example, all NCPs can be found in category three, while most courts are – not surprisingly – found in category four.

Based on the model presented in Figure 16.3, a few issues arise that should be analysed further in order to better understand the potential of the various mechanisms to contribute to a better implementation of IEL. One of these issues is the dilemma between access and outcome.

Figure 16.4 combines the data in Figures 16.1 and 16.3. It seems that while there are quite a number of mechanisms that are easily accessible, there are also quite a number of mechanisms whose outcome is not ideal form the environmental point of view, that is they grant mostly specific relief. If the criteria of access and outcome are further combined in

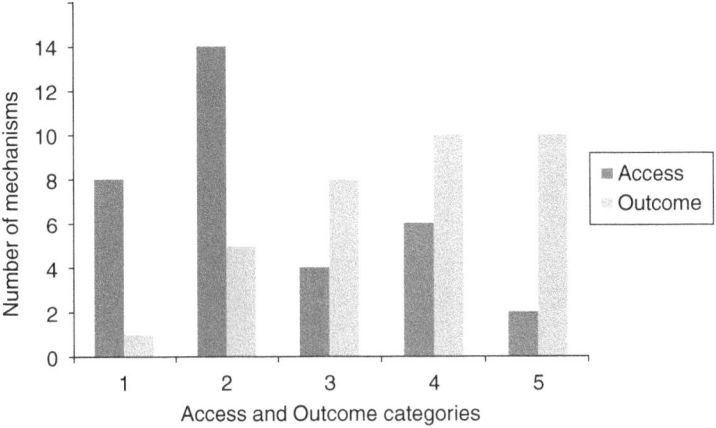

Figure 16.4 The access–outcome dilemma

a different representation (Figure 16.5), this dilemma of easy access but unsatisfactory results is confirmed not only in general terms but at the level of individual mechanisms as well.

In Figure 16.5[36] all the mechanisms are placed according to their position in the outcome and access categories. The 'best' mechanism would be located in cube 1-1 in the bottom left corner. There is at present no such ideal mechanism. Yet it is clearly visible that the biggest concentration of mechanisms can be found in the upper left corner, meaning that although they are easily accessible, they do not have a satisfactory outcome from the environmental point of view. At the same time, the 'best' mechanism in terms of outcome (the IACtHR) is accessible only indirectly, being thus located in cube 1/4.

It is well known that states are reluctant to have an independent third party decide on issues concerning their internal matters. Since almost all mechanisms, especially courts but also NCPs, have been created by states, it can be assumed that the creators were hesitant to give these mechanisms powers going beyond the consideration of a concrete case, for example in order to assess and make (binding) recommendations on the structural problems of a state. The weak point of other mechanisms, such as the

---

[36] Not commonly used abbreviations (alphabetical order): ADB = Asian Development Bank; EIB = European Investment Bank; EBRD = European Bank of Reconstruction and Development; IADB = Inter-American Development Bank; ICEAC = International Court for Environmental Arbitration and Conciliation; NAAEC = North American Agreement on Environmental Cooperation; WB = World Bank.

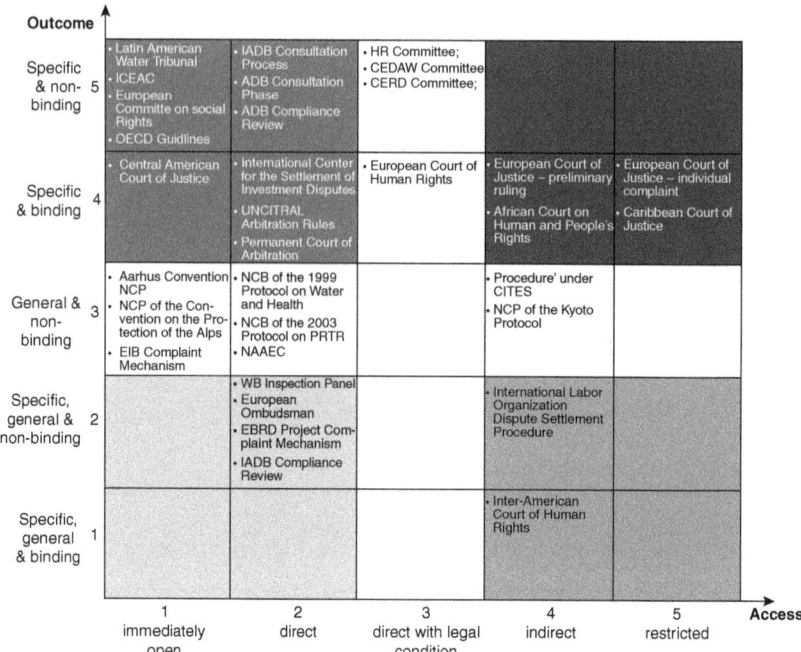

Figure 16.5 The access–outcome dilemma on the level of individual mechanisms

ICEAC,[37] is that they were not created by states and are thus often (politically and legally) less well accepted and cannot necessarily always make legally binding judgments.

4. Conclusion

In order to strengthen environmental protection and the rule of law for nature, compliance with existing IEL has to be ensured. While IEL is not the only solution to a cleaner environment, it is certainly an important part of that solution. If, however, these rules are repeatedly violated and under-enforced, this instrument of environmental protection is increasingly lost, and a veritable rule of law for nature cannot be established. As seen above, traditional state enforcement action is not sufficient. Therefore, granting access to private parties is an interesting alternative. By bringing cases, communications or requests to mechanisms, private

---

[37] The ICEAC was founded in 1994 by twenty-eight lawyers from twenty-two countries and is registered under Mexican law.

parties have the possibility of putting pressure on states finally to respect IEL and protect the environment. There are a considerable number of mechanisms that can be used in different contexts and for different violations, differing as to their outcome, access and applicable law. In order to determine which mechanisms are most promising to be used in this regard, it is thus necessary to have a viable comparison. In addition to a valuable 'inventory' of the current possibilities of using mechanisms to enforce IEL, this can provide the basis for further development or adjustment of (new) mechanisms. The model presented enables us to compare mechanisms that are open to private parties to bring claims relating to the environment. The conclusions that can be drawn promise to be more objective and 'overarching' (not limited to one set of mechanisms only), giving us a better appreciation of the situation and possibilities of private parties' IEL enforcement actions through international mechanisms, but also generating more insight into the characteristics of these mechanisms. Overall, the model has been able to show that the difficulty with these mechanisms does not seem to lie with their accessibility, but rather with their outcomes. Yet it should be stressed that the model as presented above is a theoretical model. Therefore, in the future the model has to be confronted with practice. Only this will give us a better understanding of the exact performance of various mechanisms. Some mechanisms are expected to underperform, that is they appear in a better position in the model than in practice, while others will overperform, meaning that they work better in practice than their position in the model would suggest. Based on this, it should be possible to draw lessons, identify 'best practice', determine what characteristics a 'good' mechanism has or whether we do indeed need a new international mechanism for the purpose of ensuring that the rule of law for nature is finally fully respected and ultimately a strong environmental protection reached.

Abbreviations

ADB	Asian Development Bank;
CEDAW	Committee on the Elimination of Discrimination against Women;
CERD	Committee on the Elimination of Ratial Discrimination;
CITES	Convention on International Trade in Endangered Species of Wild Fauna and Flora;
EIB	European Investment Bank;
EBRD	European Bank of Reconstruction and Development;

HR Committee	Human Rights Committee;
IADB	Inter-American Development Bank;
ICEAC	International Court for Environmental Arbitration and Conciliation;
NAAEC	North American Agreement on Environmental Cooperation;
OECD	Organisation for Economic Co-operation and Development;
PRTR	Pollutant Release and Transfer Registers;
UNCITRAL	United Nations Commission on International Trade Law;
WB	World Bank

PART VI

Rule of law for nature and the role of companies and markets

17

The green economy will not build the rule of law for nature

REBECCA M. BRATSPIES

"we're losing the fight, badly and quickly"
Bill McKibbon, "Global Warming's Terrifying Math,"
Rolling Stone (July 19, 2012)

1. Introduction

In June 2012 the world returned to Rio for the 2012 Conference on Sustainable Development (the Rio+20 Conference).[1] Marking the twentieth anniversary of the groundbreaking 1992 Rio Conference on Environment and Development,[2] Rio+20 aspired to build a more sustainable global society. This could have marked the rise of a different conception of sustainability; one recognizing nature as the irreplaceable foundation upon which the human economy is built. But, with no political will to fulfill the Brundtland Commission's demand that "human laws ... be reformulated to keep human activities in harmony with the unchanging and universal laws of nature,"[3] Rio+20 defaulted to embracing the "green economy"[4] rather than seizing the opportunity to formulate a new rule of law for nature.

This chapter benefitted from discussions at the 2011 meeting of the American Society for International Law, as well as the University of Oslo's Rule of Law for Nature Conference, and a CUNY Law faculty workshop. Special thanks to Dean Michelle Anderson, Don Anton, Anastasia Telesetsky, and Andrea McArdle for valuable feedback.

[1] United Nations Conference on Sustainable Development, June 20–22, 2012, available at: www.uncsd2012.org/rio20/index.html (last accessed June 11, 2013).
[2] United Nations Conference on Environment and Development, June 3–14, 1992, available at: www.un.org/geninfo/bp/enviro.html (last accessed June 11, 2013).
[3] UN Environment Program Governing Council, Report of the World Commission on Environment and Development, *Our Common Future*, UN Doc. UNEP/GC.14/13, ES-7 (March 20, 1987).
[4] Earthsummit 2012, Green Economy in the Context of Poverty Eradication and Sustainable Development, available at: www.earthsummit2012.org/conference/themes/green-economy-poverty-eradication (last accessed June 11, 2013).

The Rio+20 Conference took place against a backdrop of looming disaster.[5] Scientists around the world documented thousands of new high temperature records;[6] Greenland experienced unprecedented ice melts;[7] drought withered corn on the stalk across the United States;[8] and floods ravaged Australia,[9] China,[10] the Philippines,[11] and Korea.[12] While climate change is the most visible face of these emerging challenges,[13] it is not the only sustainability crisis. Indeed, global civil society is buffeted at all sides by a developing food crisis;[14] devastated ecosystems;[15] an ongoing economic and financial crisis;[16] and a burgeoning human population soon expected to top 10 billion,[17] bringing with it rapid urbanization[18] and

---

[5] Remarks by Achim Steiner at the opening of the World Congress on Justice, Governance and Law for Environmental Sustainability, June 18, 2012, available at: www.unep.org/newscentre/Default.aspx?DocumentID=2690&ArticleID=9176&l=en (last accessed June 11, 2013).

[6] NOAA, *State of the Climate Global Analysis* (June 2012), available at: www.ncdc.noaa.gov/sotc/global/2012/6 (last accessed June 11, 2013) (reporting, inter alia, 328 consecutive months with temperatures above the twentieth-century average).

[7] Alexandra Witze, "Greenland Enters Melt Mode," *Sciencenews* (August 3, 2012).

[8] Rob Preece, "Food Prices Set to Soar," *Daily Mail Online* (August 11, 2012), available at: www.dailymail.co.uk/news/article-2186936/U-S--drought-Food-prices-set-soar-corn-farmers-abandon-fields-size-Belgium-Luxembourg.html (last accessed June 27, 2013).

[9] Jim Andrews, "Major Flooding in Australia Continues," *Accuweather.com* (March 7, 2012).

[10] "Beijing Chaos After Record Floods," *BBC* (July 23, 2012).

[11] Floyd Whaley, "Rains Flood Manila Area, Sending Thousands Fleeing," *New York Times* (August 7, 2012).

[12] BBC, "North Korean Floods: Death Toll Raised, WFP Sends Food" (August 4, 2012), available at: www.bbc.co.uk/news/world-asia-19124495 (last accessed June 11, 2013).

[13] James E. Hansen, "Climate Change is Here and Worse than We Thought," *Washington Post* (August 3, 2012).

[14] Food and Agriculture Organization, *The State of Food Insecurity in the World 2011: How Does International Price Volatility Affect Domestic Economies and Food Security?* (Rome, 2011).

[15] Millennium Ecosystem Assessment, *Ecosystems and Human Well-being: Synthesis* 1–3 (2005), available at: www.maweb.org/documents/document.356.aspx.pdf (last accessed June 11, 2013).

[16] United Nations, *The Global Economic and Financial Crisis: Regional Impacts, Responses and Solutions* (2009), available at: www.un.org/regionalcommissions/crisispublication.pdf (last accessed June 11, 2013).

[17] United Nations, Department of Economic and Social Affairs, Population Division, *World Population Prospects: The 2012 Revision, Highlights and Advance Tables*, Fig. 1, Working Paper No. ESA/P/WP.227. (2013), available at: http://esa.un.org/wpp/documentation/pdf/WPP2012_%20KEY%20FINDINGS.pdf (last accessed June 27, 2013).

[18] UNFPA, *State of World Population 2007: Unleashing the Potential for Urban Growth*, available at: www.unfpa.org/swp/2007/presskit/pdf/sowp2007_eng.pdf (last accessed June 11, 2013).

relentlessly increasing consumption.[19] Each challenge, standing alone, poses a profound threat to human well-being. Yet we do not have the luxury of considering these interrelated crises individually; they demand an integrated response. As Professor Hans Christian Bugge pointed out, these challenges are cumulative, cross-sectoral, transboundary, and long-tail.[20] They are also what Ben Cashore calls "super wicked,"[21] meaning that those seeking to solve these problems are also helping to create them.[22]

These challenges stretch the capacity of law to manage human society, perhaps past its breaking point. Environmental scarcities and stresses are increasingly likely to trigger violent conflicts,[23] potentially jeopardizing the international law edifice that rose from the ashes of two world wars. Yet the answer proposed in Rio – embracing "the green economy" – did little to reshape human laws and markets to fit the logic of nature. Instead, at Rio+20 the "green economy" would allow the logic of markets to determine the future of nature.[24] For this reason, the Rio+20 Conference ended in disappointment[25] – leaving the world "continu[ing] to speed down an unsustainable path."[26] The Conference was doomed, at least in part, by

[19] Preparatory Committee for the United Nations Conference on Sustainable Development, 2nd Sess., Synthesis report on best practices and lessons learned on the objective and themes of the United Nations Conference on Sustainable Development 48, A.Conf.216/PC/8 (January 21, 2011) (hereafter PrepCom)
[20] Hans Christian Bugge, opening remarks, Rule of Law for Nature Conference, Oslo, May 9, 2012 (on file with the author). See also Chapter 1 by Hans Christian Bugge in this book.
[21] Steven Bernstein *et al.*, "Playing it Forward: Path Dependency, Progressive Incrementalism, and the 'Super Wicked' Problem of Global Climate Change" (February 28, 2007), 8, available at: http://environment.research.yale.edu/documents/downloads/0-9/2010_super_wicked_levin_cashore_bernstein_auld.pdf (last accessed June 27, 2013).
[22] During the 2009 Copenhagen Summit, the press emphasized the participants' carbon footprint. Sunanda Creagh, "Copenhagen Summit Carbon Footprint Biggest Ever," Reuters (December 14, 2009). The 2007 Bali Conference of the Parties drew similar allegations. Robin McDowell, "Climate Change Meeting Adds to Emissions," *Washington Post* (December 4, 2007).
[23] Thomas F. Homer-Dixon, *Environment, Scarcity and Violence* (Princeton University, 1999); Clionadh Raleigh and Henrik Urdal, "Climate Change, Environmental Degradation and Armed Conflict," 26 *Political Geography* (2007), 674–94.
[24] I adapted this phrase from Subhabrata Bobby Banerjee, "Corporate Social Responsibility: The Good, the Bad and the Ugly," 34 *Critical Sociology* (2008), 51–79, 65.
[25] For a survey of reactions to the conference, see Martin Leggett, "Rio+20 Outcome and Summary," *EarthTimes* (June 23, 2012), available at: www.earthtimes.org/politics/rioplus20-outcome-summary/2053 (last accessed June 11, 2013); see also Liz Ford, "Rio+20 Politicians Deliver 'New Definition of Hypocrisy' Claim NGOs," *Guardian* (June 21, 2012).
[26] Press Release: "Despite Agreed Environmental Goals World Still on Unsustainable Path" (quoting UNEP Director Achim Steiner).

its embrace of "the green economy" rather than the rule of law for nature as its primary sustainability goal. Only by grounding itself in ecological realities will international law develop a genuine roadmap for "more intelligent management of the natural and human capital of this planet."[27]

2. The roots of Rio+20

The 1992 Rio Conference, "the Earth Summit," was a transformative moment. The agreements that emerged from Rio, for all their flaws, reshaped international law. Not only did Principle 10[28] emphasize participation, but also the meeting itself modeled that participation. In addition to 108 heads of state, representatives from 178 countries, and 15,000+ citizens representing more than 9,000 NGOs came to Rio.[29] The 1992 Global Forum made wider participation irretrievably part of global environmental governance. This legacy was obvious at Rio+20. The Rio+20 Zero Draft drew on submissions from nations, political groups, constituency groups, and non-governmental organizations around the world – an inclusiveness that traces its lineage directly to 1992.

Key substantive ideas from Rio found their way into international law, including sovereign control over natural resources (Principle 2); the right to development (Principle 3); the precautionary principle (Principle 15); and the polluter pays principle (Principle 16).[30] These ideas were not new. Indeed, portions of the Rio Declaration were virtually identical to the 1972 Stockholm Declaration,[31] and many of the ideas had been discussed in detail in the 1987 Brundtland Report. But it was the Rio Declaration that brought them from the periphery of international legal discourse to its center. Even though the Rio Declaration was soft law, containing no legally binding commitments, it nevertheless represented a major step

---

[27] UNEP, *Towards a Green Economy: Pathways to Sustainable Development and Poverty Eradication*, Foreward (2011).

[28] Rio Declaration on Environment and Development, United Nations Conference on Environment and Development, Principle 10, at Annex 1, UN Doc. A/CONF.151/5/Rev.1 (1992).

[29] United Nations Dept. of Information, UNCED (May 23, 1997), available at: www.un.org/geninfo/bp/enviro.html (last accessed June 11, 2013).

[30] Rio Declaration on Environment and Development. The polluter pays principle dates back to the *Trail Smelter* Arbitration. See generally Rebecca M. Bratspies and Russel A. Miller (eds.), *Transboundary Harm in International Law: Lessons from the Trail Smelter Arbitration* (Cambridge University Press, 2006).

[31] Stockholm Declaration of the United Nations Conference on the Human Environment, GA Res. 2997, UN GAOR, 27th Sess., UN Doc. A/Conf.48/14/Rev.1.

toward embracing sustainable development – the promise of ensuring healthy and fulfilling lives for the current generation while entrusting to future generations the means to do the same[32] – as a core principle of international law.[33]

Yet, as the Rio+20 Zero Draft bluntly acknowledged, "sustainable development remains a distant goal."[34] It was this legacy of inaction that the world needed to confront at Rio+20. Legal documents and declarations had failed to produce real change.[35] At the dawn of the Anthropocene,[36] the world needed to do more than agree that there are three pillars to sustainable development.[37] Rio+20's urgent task was to make progress on integrating those pillars into a genuine rule of law for nature. That would have meant trading the old vision of development built on exploiting natural resources for a new vision, one premised on respecting the Earth as the source of all life.[38]

Yet Rio+20 failed to come to grips with this fundamental problem. Instead, the General Assembly doubled down on existing ideas about sustainable development by embracing "the green economy"[39] as the conference theme. The "green economy" was touted as "an instrument for mobilizing countries toward sustainable development."[40] Yet "the green economy" left the predominant economic model unquestioned, and continued to treat

---

[32] PrepCom, 3.
[33] Sustainable development is a central commitment of the UN Millennium Development Goals, available at: www.un.org/millenniumgoals (last accessed June 11, 2013). See United Nations Commission on Sustainable Development, http://sustainabledevelopment.un.org (last accessed June 11, 2013). The General Assembly declared 2005–2014 a decade of education for sustainable development. See GA Res. 57/254, 1, UN Doc. A/RES/S7/254 (December 20, 2002).
[34] United Nations Conference on Sustainable Development, June 20–22, 2012. "The Future We Want – Zero Draft of the Outcome Document," 13 (January 10, 2012) (hereafter Zero Draft), available at: www.uncsd2012.org/index.php?menu=140 (last accessed June 11, 2013).
[35] General Assembly 1/21/11 PrepCom Synthesis Report 13.
[36] A growing number of scientists believe that we have entered the Anthropocene – a new geological epoch in which the intensity and effects of human activities dwarf the geological or physical forces that dominated earlier millennia. See e.g., Jan Zalasiewicz, Mark Williams, Will Steffen, and Paul Crutzen, "The New World of the Anthropocene," 44 Environmental Science & Technology (2010), 2228–31; Paul J. Crutzen, "Geology of Mankind," 415 Nature (2002), 23. See also Chapter 3 by Nicholas Robinson in this book.
[37] The Brazil Country Submission echoed this point, cautioning that "Rio+20 should look to the future not to the past." Submission by Brazil to the Preparatory Process Rio+20 Conference (November 1, 2011), 5 (hereafter Brazil Submission), available at: www.uncsd2012.org/comp_memberstates.html (last accessed June 11, 2013).
[38] PrepCom, 6.   [39] Zero Draft.
[40] Brazil Submission, 23.

the environment as a supply of goods and services for meeting human wants rather than as the foundation for life itself. Like sustainable development, it papered over vast ideological, political, and economic disagreements.[41] Had Rio+20 negotiators instead tried to articulate a rule of law for nature, they would have been forced to confront this built-in tendency to focus on economic growth to the exclusion of other issues.[42]

3. The failure of sustainable development

Global economic integration has accelerated rapidly since 1992. One result of this integration has been the rise of new transnational actors with a heightened ability for economic activities across vast territorial and temporal scales. The environmental and social implications of their activities, however, remain subject to fragmented and partial state-based oversight. Relevant regulatory authority is often divided between multiple states. Many of these transnational actors rival states in wealth, power, and influence.[43] Their concentrated economic power gives them the ability to elude (and often control) the regulatory apparatus of individual states.[44] This power imbalance creates serious problems within states, and has produced a global trading system that prioritizes private economic objectives at the expense of social and environmental needs.

The economic benefits generated by this arrangement are distributed unevenly across and between societies.[45] The aggregate growth statistics touted by global trade's most vocal supporters often mask increasing inequality and further environmental degradation.[46] Too often,

---

[41] For a discussion of this point, see Rebecca Bratspies, "Rethinking Decisionmaking in International Environmental Law: A Process-Oriented Inquiry into Sustainable Development," 32 *Yale Journal of International Law* (2007), 363–91.

[42] PrepCom, 44.

[43] For the numbers behind this claim, see Rebecca M. Bratspies, "The Intersection of International Human Rights and Domestic Environmental Regulation," 38 *Georgia Journal of International and Comparative Law* (2010) 649–71, 652–3, and "Organs of Society: A Plea for Human Rights Accountability for Transnational Enterprises and Other Business Entities," 13 *Michigan State Journal of International Law* (2005) 9–38, 15.

[44] Edwin Mujih, "The Regulation of Multinational Companies Operating in Developing Countries: A Case Study of the Chad–Cameroon Pipeline Project," 16 *African Journal of International and Comparative Law* (March 2008), 83–99.

[45] Hannah Stoddart, Sue Riddlestone and Mirian Vilela, "Earthsummit 2012: Principles for the Green Economy" (2012) (identifying equitable distribution of wealth, economic equity, and intergenerational equity as essential to the green economy).

[46] This is true across many sectors of the economy. See, e.g., Dolagobinda Pradhan and Mark Flaherty, "National Initiatives, Local Effects: Trade Liberalization, Shrimp Aquaculture

development's benefits accrue to wealthier states, and to the wealthier segments within those states, while the costs are concentrated on poorer states, and on the poorest communities within those states.[47] Increased GDP, the statistic so heavily touted as economic globalization's main achievement, does not reliably translate into increased sustainability, decreased poverty, or a new focus on environmental protection.[48] Indeed, some suggest that the export-driven activities at the heart of economic globalization reinforce rather than undermine inequality.[49]

Sustainable development was supposed to ensure that did not happen. By setting economic growth on an equal footing with social and environmental protections, sustainable development was supposed to promote social and environmental health along with economic prosperity. Unfortunately, theory and practice did not converge. Given the multitude of actors cloaking their diverse and conflicting impulses under the guise of sustainable development, it is no wonder that there has been no grand compromise integrating environmental, economic, and human

    and Coastal Communities in Orissa, India," 21 *Society and Natural Resources* (2008), 63–76, 63–5; Calogero Carletto, Angeli Kirk, Paul Winters and Benjamin Davis, "Nontraditional Crops, Traditional Constraints: The Adoption and Diffusion of Export Crops Among Guatemalan Smallholders," *World Bank Policy Research Working Paper* 2–4 (2007), 4347; Center for Science in the Public Interest, "Cruel Oil: How Palm Oil Harms Heath, Rainforest and Wildlife" (2005), available at: www.cspinet.org/palm/PalmOilReport.pdf (last accessed June 11, 2013); Fantu Cheru, "Transforming Our Common Future: The Local Dimensions of Global Reform," 7 *Review of International Political Economy* (2000), 353–68.

[47] Millennium Declaration, para. 5 (noting that globalization's "benefits are very unevenly shared, while its costs are unevenly distributed").

[48] As part of a structural adjustment, the Peruvian government privatized a smelter in La Oroya, Peru, selling it to American-owned Doe Run. The agreement of sale committed Doe Run to install a host of environmental improvements. This was supposed to demonstrate that globalization can raise environmental standards and improve the health and welfare of local communities even as it generates economic gains. Yet, even though most of the children in La Oroya have unsafe blood lead concentrations, Doe Run failed to deliver on its environmental promises, citing competitive pressures from Chinese smelters. Anna K. Cederstav and G. Alberto Barandiaran, *La Oroya Cannot Wait* (Oakland, CA: Inter-American Association for Environmental Defense, 2002). In 2009 the Inter-American Commission on Human Rights accepted a case brought on behalf of the city's residents alleging that the failure to control pollution at the smelter amounted to a deprivation of the right to life and the right to bodily integrity. Inter-American Commission on Human Rights, "Admisibilidad Comunidad de la Oroya Peru," (2009), available at: www.cidh.oas.org/annualrep/2009sp/Peru1473-06.sp.htm (last accessed June 27, 2013).

[49] Center for Science in the Public Interest, "Cruel Oil"; Nyguyen L. Lebel *et al.*, "Industrial Transformation and Shrimp Aquaculture in Thailand and Vietnam: Pathways to Ecological, Social and Economic Sustainability?" 31 *Ambio: A Journal of the Human Environment* (2002), 311–23.

development objectives. Without that integration, twenty years of sustainable development failed to produce a globalization that promoted sustainability of the economic system, the environment, or of civil society. Part of the problem is that sustainable development is such a malleable concept.[50] Given its capacious and ambiguous boundaries, it should not be a surprise that it papered over rather than confronted its inherent contradictions.

Sustainable development did a far better job of incorporating "environmental assets" into economic systems than of giving priority to environmental or social concerns within economic decision-making. Theories about the fungibility of natural and economic capital[51] blunted the Rio Declaration's bold call for "intra- and intergenerational equity."[52] With environmental attributes primarily viewed as a set of resources for the economic system, sustainable development dwindled into demands for ever-more economic growth, regardless of the environmental or social cost.

The results have been deadly – more people suffer food insecurity than at any other time in human history,[53] even as we transgress planetary boundaries.[54] Indeed, the relatively low targets for poverty elimination[55] in the Millennium Development Goals (MDGs) underscore this failure to create a global community capable of "uphold[ing] the principles of human dignity, equality and equity at the global level."[56] What we need is

---

[50] National Research Council, *Our Common Journey: A Transition toward Sustainability* (1999) 22.

[51] Robert M. Solow, *An Almost Practical Step Toward Sustainability* (Washington, DC: Resources for the Future, 1992).

[52] *Our Common Future*, ES-7.

[53] Millennium Declaration, para. 4.

[54] Johan Rockström *et al.*, "Planetary Boundaries: Exploring the Safe Operating Space for Humanity,' 14:2 *Ecology and Society* (2009), 32 (proposing that human society has already transgressed the planetary boundaries for biodiversity loss, changes in the global nitrogen cycle, and climate change).

[55] International poverty elimination goals have become progressively less ambitious. The 1974 World Food Conference set a goal of eradicating hunger, malnutrition, and food insecurity by 1984. World Food Conference, Universal Declaration on the Eradication of Hunger and Malnutrition (1974), available at: www2.ohchr.org/english/law/malnutrition.htm (last accessed June 27, 2013). By 1996 the goal was to halve the number of people suffering food insecurity by 2015. Rome Declaration on World Food Security and Plan of Action (1996), available at: www.fao.org/docrep/003/w3613e/w3613e00.HTM (last accessed June 27, 2013). The Millennium Development Goals scaled down even further – aiming only to halve the percentage of people suffering food insecurity by 2015. We are unlikely to meet even that watered-down goal. Rebecca M. Bratspies, "Food Technology and Hunger," 8 *Law Culture and Humanities* (2012) 1–13, 6–8.

[56] United Nations Millennium Declaration, para. 2.

a new starting point for law and policy – one that treats the Earth as the source of all life rather than as a set of resources. In short, we need a rule of law for nature that recognizes humans as participants in the Earth's biogeophysical processes, rather than pretending that humans stand outside those processes and merely consume resources that exist a priori.

4. The contentless green economy

The world returned to Rio with the global economy in shambles,[57] a skyrocketing social inequality index,[58] and an environment in even worse shape.[59] The green economy was clearly a new attempt to integrate this broad suite of concerns.[60] The Zero Draft,[61] however, offered little in the way of transformative possibility, and failed to "redefine[e] the role and purpose of the economic system."[62] Despite calls to focus on integration,[63] the Final Document instead recycled the tired emphasis on balancing – reinforcing the notion that sustainable development embodies three separate sets of concerns. As a result, the green economy wound up being a global reaffirmation of unsustainable principles and practices. Worse, the particular iteration of the green economy embraced in Rio actually hinders the international community's ability to articulate and address sustainability challenges going forward.

If the international community was really committed to having the green economy serve as a means for integrating the pillars of sustainable development, it would need to begin by developing conceptual clarity

---

[57] IMF, World Economic Outlook: *Growth Resuming, Danger Remains* (April 2012), available at: www.imf.org/external/pubs/ft/weo/2012/01/pdf/text.pdf (last accessed June 11, 2013).
[58] Isabel Ortiz and Matthew Cummins, *Global Inequality: Beyond the Bottom Billion – A Rapid Review of Income Distribution in 141 Countries*, United Nations Children's Fund (UNICEF) Working Paper (April 2011).
[59] World Resources Institute, *Reefs At Risk Revisited* 3 (2011), available at: www.wri.org/publication/reefs-at-risk-revisited (last accessed June 27, 2013) (reporting that 75 percent of coral reefs are currently threatened); Millennium Ecosystem Assessment, *Synthesis* 2–16 (2005).
[60] PrepCom, 3–5 and 64.   [61] Zero Draft, 35.
[62] The Green Economy Coalition, *Introducing the Big Picture*, available at: www.greeneconomycoalition.org/big-picture/big-picture-%E2%80%93-overview (last accessed June 27, 2013).
[63] UN General Assembly President Nassir Abdulaziz al-Nasser cautioned that "we need to ensure that the words on the pages of the Rio+20 Outcome document have meaning." Remarks at the United Nations General Assembly's Informal Thematic Debate on "The Road to Rio+20 and Beyond" (May 22, 2012) (hereafter Remarks by al-Nasser).

about what constitutes a green economy. Unfortunately, policymakers were unable to agree upon even a loose definition.[64] The United Kingdom country submission helpfully explained that the green economy "is not a subset of the economy at large" but that instead "our whole economy needs to be green."[65] Yet many countries (including the UK) also qualified support for making energy-intensive industries "more energy and carbon efficient" to those situations *where it would be cost-effective* for them to do so."[66] These submissions conveyed the message that "we acknowledge biophysical planetary boundaries but would not want to constrain economic growth."[67] States expressed more concern that environmental standards might create new barriers to international trade than that unsustainable practices might jeopardize the very survival of human civilization.[68]

The world went to Rio without any agreement about what balance between economic, social, and environmental considerations the green economy should promote. There was no target for the green economy, and no way of marking its outer boundaries. The Outcome Document did not even offer a rough dividing line between what was clearly acceptable and what would be deemed clearly unacceptable in the green economy. Without some kind of core meaning,[69] the green economy cannot provide "principles, norms, rules and decision-making procedures around which actor expectations converge."[70] Worse, to the extent that embracing the

---

[64] PrepCom, 60; Preparatory Committee for the United Nations Conference on Sustainable Development, Progress to date and remaining gaps in the implementation of the outcomes of the major summits in the area of sustainable development, as well as an analysis of the themes of the Conference, Para. 57a, A/CONF.216/PC/2 (April 1, 2010).

[65] United Kingdom, *Submission to the United Nations Department of Economic and Social Affairs: UK Action on the Green Environment* 5 (2 November 2011) (hereafter UK Submission), available at: www.uncsd2012.org/content/documents/442UK%20 Contribution%20to%20Rio20.pdf (last accessed June 12, 2013).

[66] UK Submission, 31, 19) (emphasis added); Submission by the Government of the Republic of Indonesia to the Zero Draft of UNCSD2012, Outcome Document, 7–9 (hereafter Indonesia Submission), available at: www.uncsd2012.org/comp_memberstates.html (last accessed June 12, 2013).

[67] Kanchan Shrestra, "Next Up Rio+20 – Will It Be Inclusive This Time Round?" *Yale F&ES Blog* (December 23, 2011), available at: environment.yale.edu/blog/2011/12/23/next-up-rio20-will-it-be-inclusive-this-time-around (last accessed June 12, 2013).

[68] PrepCom, 69; Brazil Submission, 22; Republic of Ecuador Inputs for the Compilation Document for the United Nations Conference on Sustainable Development Rio+20, 1, available at: www.uncsd2012.org/comp_memberstates.html (last accessed June 12, 2013); Indonesia Submission; Inputs of the Russian Federation to the Outcome Document of the UN Conference on Sustainable Development 'Rio+20', 11 (October 28, 2011).

[69] Remarks by al-Nasser.

[70] Stephen Krasner, *International Regimes* (Ithaca: Cornell University Press, 1982), 2.

green economy obscures the value judgments embedded in existing economic structures and priorities, it actually thwarts our ability to make changes.

One major response have been calls to "green the supply chain." Indeed, the phrase has become a new shorthand for how to make economic globalization sustainable.[71] Unfortunately, tendencies toward sloganeering have outpaced genuine efforts at hybrid governance.[72] One of the most notorious examples is BP's *Beyond Petroleum* campaign. Prior to BP's disastrous Gulf of Mexico oil spill, BP had successfully constructed a veneer of environmental responsibility around itself, despite repeatedly violating environmental laws around the world.[73]

Any genuine attempt to "green the supply chain" must confront the profoundly unsustainable nature of our production system. Transnational corporations extract raw materials in response to demand signals generated by global markets, based on the consumption preferences of consumers dissociated from the externalized costs of that extraction. As articulated at Rio+20, the green economy did nothing to disturb, or even acknowledge, the power relationships behind this status quo. Existing production, distribution, and consumption relationships were the assumed starting point for discussions about the green economy. By normalizing this status quo, Rio+20 missed an opportunity to highlight the fundamental imbalances that drive environmental degradation. Instead, the green economy recommitted decisions about sustainability to the hands of those who historically have ignored social and environmental considerations in favor of short-term economic gains. It thus became a mechanism for perpetuating the very problems it was intended to address.

Before international law can guide a transition toward sustainability, it must first reconsider the defaults, the background givens against which the world takes up the question of sustainability. Unfortunately, the green economy obscures that prior inquiry. By focusing global attention on the next step from here – on improving what we have – Rio+20 had the

[71] UNEP and UNGC, *Unchaining Value: Innovative Approaches to Sustainable Supply* (2008) 2, available at: www.unep.org/resourceefficiency/Portals/24147/scp/unchaining/publications/Unchaining-Value-Final-Report.pdf (last accessed June 27, 2013).
[72] Maria C. Lemos and Arun Agrawal, "Environmental Governance," 31 *Annual Review of Environment and Resources* (2006), 297–325.
[73] Rebecca M. Bratspies, "A Regulatory Wakeup Call: Lessons from BP's Deepwater Horizon Disaster," *Golden Gate University Environmental Law Journal* (2011), 1–44, 5; Alyson Flournoy et al., *Regulatory Blowout: How Regulatory Failures Made the BP Disaster Possible* (October 2010), available at: www.progressivereform.org/articles/BP_Reg_Blowout_1007.pdf (last accessed June 12, 2013).

perverse effect of blunting investigation into an appropriate starting point for sustainability. Thus, in the Rio+20 preparatory documents the distributional aspects of proposed changes to the global economy associated with the green economy were front and center, while the distributional aspects of business as usual required no justification at all. The discourse proceeded as though the green economy alone meant picking winners and losers, or distributing benefits and costs. Such an approach naturalized the current situation. Change must be justified, but the ill effects of the status quo need not be. For example, the UK Submission emphasized "designing policy to work as efficiently as possible and highlighting where benefits justify costs,"[74] and "choosing the most efficient mix of interventions."[75] But without priorities and boundaries there is no way to identify what ends the green economy should strive towards, or the values it should seek to maximize.

To the extent that it prompted development of "a new model of consumption which did not compromise the needs of others or of future generations, nor damage the environment,"[76] the green economy might indeed promote a rule of law for nature. But there was little appetite for tackling this thorny question. The Outcome Document emphasized that commitments made under the Johannesburg Plan were voluntary,[77] and made no attempt to harden those commitments. Nor did the brief three paragraphs of the Outcome Document allotted to consumption and production contain any new proposals.[78] The message was clear – explicit discussions of the boundaries of the green economy were off the table, as was any acknowledgement that wealthy countries have currently (and historically) appropriated far more than their sustainable and fair shares of global resources.

Without this prior discussion of distributive justice, the green economy dwindles into mere verbiage. It is simply not possible to make fundamental changes while avoiding consideration of the power inequalities

---

[74] UK Submission, 20.   [75] Ibid., 19.
[76] *Unsustainable Consumption – the Mother of All Environmental Issues* (March 15, 2012), available at: www.eea.europa.eu/highlights/unsustainable-consumption-2013-the-mother (last accessed June 12, 2013) (quoting European Environmental Agency Executive Director Jacqueline McGlade).
[77] Draft Resolution Submitted by the President of the General Assembly, *The Future We Want*, UNGA Doc. A/66/L.56, 66th Sess. (June 24, 2012), 226 (hereafter *The Future We Want*).
[78] Brazil's proposed Global Pact for Sustainable Production and Consumption gained little traction and did not make it into the Outcome Document. Brazil Submission, 27–30.

that produced those unsustainable practices in the first place. Instead, it is a slippery slope from arguing to transnational business entities that there is a business case for sustainability, to allowing the business case to define when sustainability is appropriate. Arguments rooted in the proposition that managing supply chains for sustainability "makes good business sense"[79] risk reducing "the green economy" to a mere restatement of economic rationality. Rather than reshaping markets to fit the logic of nature, the green economy uses the logic of markets to determine the future of nature.

What happens, under this framing, when the sustainable choice does not "make good business sense?" The Roundtable on Sustainable Palm Oil (RSPO) offers a telling example of how the focus on greening an existing industry ignores an industry's overall unsustainable nature. It is a classic example of private governance that relies on voluntary participation rather than on public authority.[80] As such, it operates beside or around, rather than through the states in which it has activities.

The RSPO Principles and Criteria for Sustainable Palm Oil Production are typical of the kinds of soft law agreements that emerge from this kind of private governance.[81] Under the Principles, members ought not: to steal land;[82] to use forced labor;[83] or to expose workers to hazardous substances without providing training or protective gear.[84] RSPO members are not asked to avoid new negative impacts, or to remediate past negative impacts, let alone replace negative impacts with positive ones. All the RSPO asks of its members is "continual improvement" toward mitigating

---

[79] 2011 UNEP–Business and Industry Global Dialogue, Discussion Note: Strengthening the Role of the Private Sector in the transition to a Resource Efficient and Green Economy: On the Road to Rio+20 (April 1, 2011), 3, available at: www.accsr.com.au/pdf/20110412_unep_hohnen_background_paper.pdf (last accessed June 27, 2013).

[80] Benjamin Cashore, Greame Auld and Deanna Newsom, *Governing Through Markets: Forest Certification and the Emergence of Non-State Authority* (New Haven: Yale University Press, 2004).

[81] Roundtable on Sustainable Palm Oil, Principles and Criteria for Sustainable Palm Oil Production. Principle 2 (March 2006), available at: www.rspo.org/file/RSPO%20Criteria%20Final%20Guidance%20with%20NI%20Document.pdf (last accessed June 12, 2013).

[82] Ibid., Criteria 2.2, 2.3, interpreting Principle 2: Compliance with Applicable Laws and Regulations, and Criteria 6.4, interpreting Principle 6: Responsible consideration of employees and of individuals and communities affected by growers and mills; Criteria 7.6, interpreting Principle 7: Responsible development of new plantings.

[83] Ibid., Criteria 6.1, 6.5, interpreting Principle 6.

[84] Ibid., Criteria 4.6, 4.7, and 4.8, interpreting Principle 4: Use of appropriate best practices by growers and mills.

negative impacts.[85] If adhered to by its members, the RSPO Principles will undoubtedly improve current practices, which are notoriously rife with human rights and environmental abuses.[86] But improving existing practices, however worthy, is not the same thing as actually challenging inherently unsustainable markets and business models.[87] After all, even fully compliant members of the RSPO Principles are still engaged in large-scale monoculture of an alien species that depends on tremendous inputs of fertilizers and pesticides.[88] Worse, most palm oil plantations were planted by clear-cutting tropical primary forests, on lands that were expropriated from indigenous communities.[89] Even where not directly responsible for clear-cutting, the industry takes already cleared lands out of local food production – putting serious indirect pressure on remaining intact forests and jeopardizing local food security[90] – all to produce a product with an immense carbon footprint when used as a fuel,[91] and associated with serious ill-health consequences for those who consume it.[92]

The green economy, which starts with the existing industry and grafts on sustainability considerations, precludes assessment of the acceptability of the underlying activity. A rule of law for nature framing, by contrast, puts that question front and center. This is not to suggest that transnational enterprises should not work to green their supply chains, or that international law initiatives should not encourage or even require them to do

---

[85] Ibid., Principles 5, 6, and 8.
[86] Erik Wakker, *Greasy Palms: The Social and Ecological Impacts of Large-Scale Oil Palm Development in Southeast Asia* (London: Friends of the Earth UK, 2004), 15–18, available at: www.foe.co.uk/resource/reports/greasy_palms_impacts.pdf (last accessed June 12, 2013).
[87] UNEP and UNGC, *Unchaining Value*.
[88] E. Wakker and I. de Bruin, *Human–Wildlife Conflicts in and around Oil Palm Plantations* (Washington, DC: Center for Science in the Public Interest, 2004); I. E. Henson, *Environmental Impacts of Oil Palm Plantations in Malaysia*, Occasional Paper No. 33. Kuala Lumpur: Palm Oil Research Institute of Malaysia (1994).
[89] Center for Science in the Public Interest, "Cruel Oil."
[90] Ibid. See also World Rainforest Movement, *The Greening of the Dark Palm Oil Business* (March 2010), available at: www.wrm.org.uy/publications/briefings/RSPO.pdf (last accessed June 12, 2013).
[91] Greenpeace, *How the Palm Oil Industry is Cooking the Climate* (2007), available at: www.greenpeace.org.uk/files/pdfs/forests/cooking-the-climate-1.pdf (last accessed June 12, 2013).
[92] Center for Science in the Public Interest, "Cruel Oil"; National Institute of Diabetes and Digestive and Kidney Diseases, National Institutes of Health, *Prevent Diabetes Problems: Keep Your Heart and Blood Vessels Healthy*, NIH Publication No. 03–4283 (2003), available at: diabetes.niddk.nih.gov/dm/pubs/complications_heart/heart.pdf (last accessed June 12, 2013).

so. But ambitions for "a way forward, a new economic paradigm – one in which material wealth is not delivered perforce at the expense of growing environmental risks, ecological scarcities and social disparities,"[93] cannot be satisfied by taking fundamental issues off the table. To the extent that the green economy deflects attention away from core questions about social and environmental justice in a global economy, it makes meaningful progress toward sustainability more difficult.

5. Conclusion

States are the primary form of political organization – and will remain so for the foreseeable future. The key challenge is, therefore, how to reconcile an international legal system premised on sovereignty with a global market that allows transnational economic actors to elude state governance. This phenomenon gives rise to calls for governance in the absence of government.[94] The green economy is both recognition of that reality and also an attempt to assert state control over the space by "embed[ding] systems of governance in broader global frameworks of social capacity and agency that did not previously exist."[95] Yet at Rio+20 that attempt was half-hearted at best. The key subtext of many of the country submissions was that states dare not challenge the primacy of the market – they dare not prioritize other values, not even to the extent of recognizing them as genuinely co-equal pillars of sustainable development.

At Rio+20 the real and perceived trade-offs between economic and environmental outcomes should have been front and center. Much attention was devoted to the concern that sustainability meant environmental subsidies and environmental trade barriers. Yet the reality of existing *explicit* state subsidies that drive unsustainable practices[96] (let alone the

---

[93] UNEP, *Towards a Green Economy*, 14.
[94] James N. Rosenau, *Governance Without Government: Order and Change in World Politics* (Cambridge University Press, 1992).
[95] J. G. Ruggie, "Reconstituting the Global Public Domain – Issues, Actors and Practices," 19:4 *European Journal of International Relations* (2004), 499–531, 519.
[96] Global fossil fuel consumption subsidies were US$557 billion in 2008, and are projected to reach $660 billion in 2020. IEA, World Energy Outlook 2011: Analysis of Fossil Fuel Subsidies (October 4, 2011), available at: www.worldenergyoutlook.org/media/weowebsite/energysubsidies/ff_subsidies_slides.pdf (last accessed June 12, 2013). This staggering figure is actually an understatement. Doug Koplow, *Measuring Energy Subsidies Using the Price-Gap Approach: What Does It Leave Out?* (Winnipeg: International Institute for Sustainable Development, August 2009), available at: www.iisd.org/pdf/2009/bali_2_copenhagen_ff_subsidies_pricegap.pdf (last accessed June 12, 2013). For perspective, the

implicit subsidies in the form of degraded environments, pollution loads, and unsafe working conditions foisted on local populations)[97] prompted little scrutiny.[98] A side-event organized by the International Institute for Sustainable Development directly targeted fossil fuel subsidies.[99] The session emphasized that the subsidies are economically inefficient and lead to unsustainable, wasteful behaviors. Eliminating these subsidies would free up valuable fiscal resources that could be used to fund sustainable development priorities, while also reducing greenhouse gas emissions and promoting investment in renewable energy. Unfortunately, rather than embracing the bold call to eliminate fossil fuel subsidies, the Final Draft merely invited states to "consider rationalizing inefficient fossil fuel subsidies."[100]

Had the negotiations instead started from the recognition that current patterns of production and consumption were jeopardizing the survival of human civilization, the possibilities for success at Rio might have been very different. A rule of law for nature framing would have forced negotiators to confront the major transfer of resources from poorer, lower-consuming countries to richer, higher-consuming countries embedded in existing practices.[101]

By using the green economy to elide that point, the international community signaled its reluctance to confront the choices we are already making, and the balance we are already striking. Until we do, we will

estimated cost of reaching all the MDGs is $40–60 billion per year. World Bank, *Goals for Development: History, Prospects and Costs*, World Bank Policy Paper (April 2002), available at: www-wds.worldbank.org/external/default/WDSContentServer/IW3P/IB/2002/04/26/000094946_02041804272578/Rendered/PDF/multi0page.pdf (last accessed June 27, 2013).

[97] See Global Alliance for Workers and Communities, *Worker's Voices: an Interim Report on Worker's Needs and Aspirations in Indonesia* (2001), available at: http://web1.calbaptist.edu/dskubik/nike_rpt.pdf (last accessed June 27, 2013); Michael Rauscher, "On Ecological Dumping," 46 *Oxford Economic Papers* (1994), 822–40; Tito Cordella and Isabel Grilo, "Social Dumping and Relocations: Is There a Case for Imposing a Social Clause?" 31 *Regional Science and Urban Economics* (2001), 643–68, 645.

[98] PrepCom, 82.

[99] Rio+20 Side Event: Breaking Down Political Barriers to Fossil Fuel Subsidy Reform (June 21, 2012), available at: www.uncsd2012.org/index.php?page=view&type=1000&nr=234&menu=126 (last accessed June 12, 2013).

[100] *The Future We Want*, 225.

[101] United Nations Department of Economic and Social Affairs, *World Economic Situation and Prospects 2008*, available at: www.un.org/en/development/desa/policy/wesp/wesp_archive/2008wesp.pdf (last accessed June 27, 2013); Isabel Ortiz and Oscar Ugarteche, *Bank of the South: Progress and Challenges* (October 2008), available at: http://papers.ssrn.com/sol3/papers.cfm?abstract_id=1353450 (last accessed June 12, 2013).

continue to look past rather than at our core problems. We risk allowing the short-term costs to overshadow long-term intergenerational consequences. Such an approach belies the purported recognition at the heart of Rio+20 – "that the greatest risk is the risk of inaction that arises from resisting the scale of the change that is required."[102]

[102] PrepCom, 83.

18

Taking nature seriously

Can the UN Guiding Principles tame corporate profiteering?

SURYA DEVA

1. Introduction

Although companies have the potential to affect nature in both positive and negative ways, more often than not we see them profiteering at the cost of nature. Why is this so? This chapter examines whether the notion of sustainable development – one of the most common paradigms employed to preserve nature – is part of the problem. It is argued that sustainable development has proved to be a weak tool in taming corporate profiteering and in turn protecting the environment. We should then look for alternatives. I suggest that if we really take nature seriously, then a non-anthropocentric approach should be embraced and nature should be bestowed with autonomous rights. Doing so should allow a more equitable balancing between the needs of nature and the developmental needs of humans. Some developments already point to movement in this direction.

Taking nature seriously will also require that companies have direct environmental responsibilities under international law. While a patchwork of hard and soft law envisages certain direct corporate environmental responsibilities, there has been slow progress in concretizing legally binding environmental standards for companies at the international level. To illustrate this, this chapter reviews the 2011 United Nations Guiding Principles on Business and Human Rights (GPs).[1] Although the GPs unfortunately fail to articulate direct environmental responsibilities of companies, this omission should not be taken to mean that no such

---

The author would like to thank Mr Calvin Chun-ngai Ho for providing excellent research assistance.

[1] Human Rights Council, 'Guiding Principles on Business and Human Rights: Implementing the United Nations "Protect, Respect and Remedy" Framework', A/HRC/17/31 (21 March 2011) (hereafter HRC, 'Guiding Principles').

responsibilities exist or could be developed in future. In fact, a legally binding regulatory framework (including at the international level) might be critical for effectively preventing companies from profiteering in utter disregard of nature.

2. Nature, (sustainable) development and companies

What is the relationship between nature, (sustainable) development and companies? Nature is integral to the existence as well as survival of civilization and life in all forms. The same can be said about development – whether economic or political, cultural, linguistic and scientific – and the ideas of evolution and adjustment that underpin it. However, human behaviour and norms governing it can, at times, put nature and development on a collision course.

Sustainable development has been the main mantra employed to avoid or soften the impact of such collision. But has this strategy worked? Taking companies as an example, I show that the notion of sustainable development is not a potent device to tame corporate profiteering and in turn preserve nature. We might, therefore, need an alternative normative framework to strike a harmony between the needs of nature and development.

It should be stated at the outset that companies provide a useful reference point to this inquiry for at least two reasons. First of all, companies are not merely indispensable to the process of economic development; they are also key players having an impact – both positive and negative – on nature.[2] Second, since companies are generally driven by a desire to maximize profits,[3] their operations provide a good hard 'test case' to judge the robustness of any balancing framework.

2.1 Sustainable development and corporate profiteering

The 1987 report of the Brundtland Commission provides a seminal definition of 'sustainable development': 'meeting the needs of the present without compromising the ability of future generations to meet their own

---

[2] See S. Deva, 'Sustainable Good Governance and Corporations: An Analysis of Asymmetries', 18 *Georgetown International Environmental Law Review* (2006), 707–50, 712–14.
[3] Even the 'business case' for sustainable development underscores the importance of the 'bottom line'.

needs'.[4] Two key concepts that underpin sustainable development are 'needs' and the idea of 'limitations' imposed on the satisfaction of those needs so that the ability of future generations to satisfy their needs is not compromised.[5] Sustainable development in many instances concerns the 'attempts to reconcile the environmental protection and human development agendas'.[6] Sands argues that sustainable development embodies four separate but interrelated objectives: a commitment to preserve natural resources for the benefit of present and future generations; a prudent or appropriate use of natural resources; an equitable use of natural resources; and an integration of environmental considerations into economic and developmental plans, programmes and projects.[7]

Leaving aside the criticism that sustainable development is a contradiction in terms,[8] difficulties often arise in the application of ideas that underpin sustainable development. The problem begins with the conceptualization of 'needs' itself. Human needs, if not confined to bare minimum basic needs, are relative and contextual. Under the current model of development, the parameters of needs are often set by developed countries. Affluent people living in developing countries borrow these parameters and then the rest of the populace ends up conceiving their needs in terms of this infinitely upward cycle of consumerism: the need for a bicycle is replaced with the need for a scooter, then a car, and so on. Although some people in developed countries may in the meantime return to bicycles, it is too late for the trapped followers in developing countries. The context to this 'needs typology' is provided by the focus on creating choices for consumers in a free market economy and the consumption-based model of development. Just to illustrate, unhealthy (and also unsustainable) soft drinks have assumed the status of 'needs' for a large section of society,

---

[4] United Nations General Assembly, *Report of the World Commission on Environment and Development* (A/RES/42/187), available at: www.un-documents.net/a42r187.htm (last accessed 27 June 2013).

[5] D. Hunter, J. Salzman and D. Zaelke, *International Environmental Law and Policy*, 4th edn (New York: Foundation Press/Thomson Reuters, 2011), 123.

[6] A. P. Ross, *Sustainable Development Law in the UK: From Rhetoric to Reality* (Abingdon: Earthscan, 2012), 3.

[7] P. Sands, 'Environmental Protection in the Twenty-first Century: Sustainable Development and International Law', in R. L. Revesz, P. Sands and R. B. Stewart (eds.), *Environmental Law, the Economy, and Sustainable Development: The United States, the European Union and the International Community* (Cambridge University Press, 2000), 369, 374–5.

[8] S. Dresner, *The Principles of Sustainability* (London: Earthscan, 2002), 2; B. Bischoff, 'Sustainability as a Legal Principle', in K. Bosselmann and J. R. Engel (eds.), *The Earth Charter: A Framework for Global Governance* (Amsterdam: KIT Publishers, 2010), 167, 176.

thereby displacing the healthier and more sustainable option of drinking plain water.

Another problem in implementing sustainable development relates to the absence of independent representatives who can articulate the interests of future generations. If people representing the present generation have to deal with situations where there is a conflict between the needs of the present generation and the ability of future generations to meet their needs, there would be legitimate apprehension of a conflict of interest favouring the 'present' over the 'future'. While certain non-governmental organizations champion the cause of nature or future generations, their advocacy also operates within the normative boundaries set by the current majority.

The exercise of reconciling, balancing or integrating the environment and economic development also seems to be problematic, because in the absence of any prescribed normative hierarchy, development needs invariably supersede sustainability. Environmental impact assessments are conducted, in essence, to lend support to development projects rather than to assess their feasibility and potential withdrawal in appropriate cases. Since every developmental activity is likely to affect the environment adversely, sustainable development ends up becoming a gimmick to opt for 'lesser harm' instead of asking fundamental questions about the desirability of a particular developmental project and thus resulting in 'no harm'. Even if 'sustainable' precedes 'development' in sustainable development, if the focus remains on the development part, then it will result in 'business as usual' with some concessions to environmental concerns.[9]

These problems are multiplied when it comes to the application of sustainable development to and by companies, because companies are designed to maximize profits even at the cost of other competing common goods. Even when companies consider sustainability to be relevant, it is often for bottom-line reasons: sustainable business is good for business.[10] So 'going green' is driven more by a desire to gain competitive advantage over competitors and/or as part of risk management rather than by commitment to sustainable development. One can, for example, easily juxtapose BP and its green 'beyond petroleum' slogan with its role

---

[9] Bischoff, 'Sustainability as a Legal Principle', 177.
[10] See P. Malik, 'Environment as Profit Centre' (4 April 2011), available at: http://switchboard.nrdc.org/blogs/pmalik/environment_as_profit_center.html (last accessed 12 September 2012).

in contributing to the massive oil spill in the Gulf of Mexico by taking various time- and cost-saving decisions.[11]

If we apply the definition of sustainability advanced by Geoffrey Heal – 'doing things that we can safely continue indefinitely'[12] – it might be quite difficult to justify many of the existing corporate practices. Although excessive consumption is at the core of unsustainable development,[13] companies do everything possible to promote consumerism as a strategy to create new markets for their products.[14] Aggressive advertising,[15] offering broad arrays of product choices,[16] 'encouraging people to constantly change their belongings, often before the end of their productive life',[17] taking advantage of the 'human psychology'[18] and 'mega sales' are some of the tools used to promote consumerism. In some cases, consumers are encouraged to buy even potentially harmful products.[19]

When promotion of consumerism started raising eyebrows, companies turned to green consumerism. Although green consumerism may have triggered the development of environment-friendly products, this might not have reduced overall consumption levels[20] and has its limitations.[21] As Leonard highlights in 'The Story of Change', all sorts of 'green campaigns' start with the idea of 'buying better stuff' or 'recycling all that

---

[11] National Commission on the BP Deepwater Horizon Oil Spill and Offshore Drilling (US), *Deep Water: The Gulf Oil Disaster and the Future of Offshore Drilling* (2011), 125–6, available at: www.oilspillcommission.gov/final-report (last accessed 20 September 2012).

[12] G. Heal, 'Markets and Sustainability', in Revesz, Sands and Stewart (eds.), *Environmental Law, the Economy, and Sustainable Development* (Cambridge University Press, 2000), 410.

[13] 'Consumption is at the root of many of the world's greatest environmental challenges, including climate change, toxic waste, pollution, deforestation, and loss of biodiversity.' A. C. Lin, 'Virtual Consumption: A Second Life for Earth?', 47 *Brigham Young University Law Review* (2008), 47–114, 49 and generally 51–61.

[14] Deva, 'Sustainable Good Governance and Corporations', 719–20.

[15] Davidson contends that 'advertising is both a window on, and a product of' the current culture of consumerism. M. P. Davidson, *The Consumerist Manifesto: Advertising in Postmodern Times* (London: Routledge, 1992), 120.

[16] D. Dale, 'Spoilt for Choice', *Sydney Morning Herald* (9 June 2005), Spectrum 8–9.

[17] L. Crosbie and K. Knight, *Strategy for Sustainable Business: Environmental Opportunity and Strategic Choice* (New York: McGraw-Hill, 1995), 27.

[18] A. May, 'Consumption Therapy', *Sydney Morning Herald* (22 December 2004), 19.

[19] Deva, 'Sustainable Good Governance and Corporations', 721–3.

[20] Lin, 'Virtual Consumption', 79–80.

[21] See J. Hardner and R. Rice, 'Rethinking Green Consumerism', *Scientific American* (May 2002), 89.

stuff"[22] – thus promoting alternative consumption rather than reducing it. In other words, it appears that companies have been successful in improving their bottom-line by cultivating an image of being environmentally friendly but without necessarily making any positive contribution to reducing consumption and in turn conserving nature. In fact, it is arguable that green or ethical consumerism could be as detrimental to the environment as normal consumerism. The following criticism of Body Shop has some merit:

> The Body Shop have [sic] successfully manufactured an image of being a caring company that is helping to protect the environment and indigenous peoples, and preventing the suffering of animals – whilst selling 'natural' products. But behind the green and cuddly image lies the reality – the Body Shop's operations, like those of all multinationals, have a detrimental effect on the environment and the world's poor ... Companies like the Body Shop continually hype their products through advertising and marketing, *often creating a demand for something where a real need for it does not exist.*[23]

To some extent, the same could be said about companies promoting ecotourism or airlines offering 'carbon offset' for flights[24] – thus creating the impression such tourism or flights will not result in any detrimental impact on the environment. The push for biofuel raises similar concerns in that whatever benefits such fuel brings may be lost by the unsustainable growing of crops for making biofuel.[25]

Another variation of corporate 'greenwashing' is provided by first creating and promoting unsustainable products and then sprinkling them with a sustainability icing. Sale of drinkable water in disposable plastic bottles is a case in point. While the availability of safe drinking water is a basis necessity, the same cannot be said about the 'sale' of a natural resource in disposable plastic bottles,[26] which hardly existed two decades

---

[22] A. Leonard, 'The Story of Change: Annotated and Referenced Script', available at: www.storyofstuff.com/wp-content/uploads/manual/SoChange%20Annotated%20Script.pdf (last accessed 12 September 2012).

[23] Beyond McDonald's, 'What's Wrong with the Body Shop? – A Criticism of "Green" Consumerism', available at: www.mcspotlight.org/beyond/companies/bodyshop.html (last accessed 12 September 2012) (emphasis added).

[24] See Z. Kenny, 'Combating Global Warming Requires a Social Revolution' (15 August 2007), available at: www.greenleft.org.au/node/38122 (last accessed 12 September 2012).

[25] See United Nations Environment Programme, *Towards Sustainable Production and Use of Resources: Assessing Biofuels* (2009), available at: www.unep.org/pdf/biofuels/Assessing_Biofuels_Full_Report.pdf (last accessed 12 September 2012).

[26] Lin, 'Virtual Consumption', 57.

ago. Corporate campaigns for 'recycling' these plastic bottles to save the planet offer a symbolic and superficial treatment to unsustainable lifestyle choices created by companies. In fact, it is arguable that such business practices mask the environmental hazards inherent in the use of innocuous products.

One can thus conclude that sustainable development has not proved to be a potent tool for taming corporate profiteering. This scenario is unlikely to change in future. We should then look for alternatives. Some components of one such alternative are considered below.

2.2 Taking nature seriously

Taking nature seriously should entail that the autonomy and rights of nature are recognized and respected in their own right, rather than for the benefit of human beings (whether belonging to the present generation or future generations). But more importantly, such rights should carry enough weight so as not to become the subject matter of easy trade-offs. In other words, nature's rights should prevail, as a trump card, over economic development considerations unless the proposed economic development relates to the satisfaction of *basic* needs of the community or does not curtail nature's rights to the extent of becoming illusory. It will also be critical to have a robust legal framework – both at national and international levels – to enforce nature's rights against states as well as non-state actors such as companies.

The plea for recognizing nature's rights is not new.[27] As early as October 1982, the UN General Assembly had adopted the World Charter for Nature reflecting this sentiment.[28] The Charter declared, as one of the fundamental principles, that nature 'shall be respected and its essential processes shall not be impaired'.[29] It further stipulated that in 'the planning and implementation of social and economic development activities, due account shall be taken of the fact that the conservation of nature is an integral part of those activities'.[30] It was remarkable that the Charter did not limit the responsibility of preserving nature only to states; rather it expected non-state actors, including companies,

---

[27] See, for example, C. D. Stone's seminal piece 'Should Trees Have Standing?: Toward Legal Rights for Natural Objects', 45 *Southern California Law Review* (1972), 450–87.
[28] United Nations General Assembly, 'World Charter for Nature', A/RES/37/7 (28 October 1982), available at: www.un.org/documents/ga/res/37/a37r007.htm (last accessed 28 September 2012).
[29] Ibid., para. 1.   [30] Ibid., para. 7.

to conserve nature.³¹ The Charter also provided that all persons, 'in accordance with their national legislation … have access to means of redress when their environment has suffered damage or degradation'.³²

Although the Charter had arguably adopted a non-anthropocentric approach,³³ it still linked the preservation of nature to the survival of humanity.³⁴ In other words, nature has to be respected not for the sake of it, but because doing so is necessary for the well-being of humans. A clearer embracement of a non-anthropocentric approach is seen in more recent instruments. For example, the 2008 Constitution of the Republic of Ecuador includes the 'rights of nature' along with rights of people and communities.³⁵ Article 71 provides: 'Nature … where life is reproduced and occurs, has the right to integral respect for its existence and for the maintenance and regeneration of its life cycles, structure, functions and evolutionary processes. All persons, communities, peoples and nations can call upon public authorities to enforce the rights of nature.'

While the Indian Constitution of 1950 does not confer rights on nature, it imposes a *fundamental duty* on every citizen 'to protect and improve the natural environment including forests, lakes, rivers and wild life, and to have compassion for living creatures'.³⁶ More recently, in December 2010 Bolivia enacted the Law of the Rights of Mother Earth to recognize

---

[31] Paragraph 21 of the World Chapter for Nature provides:

> States and, to the extent they are able, other public authorities, international organizations, individuals, groups and corporations shall:
>
> (a) Co-operate in the task of conserving nature through common activities and other relevant actions, including information exchange and consultations;
> (b) Establish standards for products and manufacturing processes that may have adverse effects on nature, as well as agreed methodologies for assessing these effects.

[32] Ibid., para. 23.

[33] S. Emmenegger and A. Tschentscher, 'Taking Nature's Rights Seriously: The Long Way to Biocentrism in Environmental Law', 6:3 *Georgetown International Environmental Law Review* (1994), 545–92, 568–71.

[34] 'Mankind is a part of nature and life depends on the uninterrupted functioning of natural systems which ensure the supply of energy and nutrients … and living in harmony with nature gives man the best opportunities for the development of his creativity, and for rest and recreation.' UNGA, 'World Charter for Nature', Annex, Preamble.

[35] Constitution of the Republic of Ecuador 2008, Arts. 71–74, available at: http://pdba.georgetown.edu/Constitutions/Ecuador/english08.html (last accessed 28 September 2012). Article 67 of the Constitution of the Republic of Peru 1993 also requires the state to promote 'sustainable use of its natural resources'.

[36] Constitution of India 1950, Art. 51(g). Article 48A of the Constitution further provides that: 'The State shall endeavour to protect and improve the environment and to safeguard the forests and wild life of the country.'

the rights of Mother Earth, and the obligations of the state and society to ensure respect for these rights.[37] One can also refer here to the development in New Zealand of granting the Whanganui River a separate legal identity,[38] which should lead to the recognition of certain interests of the river. These rights of nature in due course may also include, what Laitos terms the right of 'nonuse',[39] thus imposing a duty on humans to leave nature alone.

One might ask what would be gained by bestowing nature with autonomous rights and how could these rights be enforced? One obvious advantage of conferring such rights on nature will be in terms of according them higher weight vis-à-vis other competing rights or social goals. This should, for instance, prevent states and individuals from claiming that while the environment is important, we need to develop.[40] The recognition of nature's rights will still require resort to a balancing exercise. Nevertheless, this should not result in skewed outcomes disadvantaging nature, because balancing will be between rights of equal importance (as it happens when two human rights come in conflict).

As far as the enforcement of nature's rights is concerned, there are well-developed legal mechanisms that can be relied upon. Corporate law, for example, specifies officers of the company that are empowered to enforce its rights and obligations. The notion of trustees under trust law provides another precedent that can be invoked. In either case, officers or trustees of nature – representing diverse community groups – can be appointed for a fixed duration to represent nature and protect its interests before various forums.

---

[37] Law of the Rights of Mother Earth, Art. 1, available at: http://f.cl.ly/items/212y0r1R0W2k2F1M021G/Mother_Earth_Law.pdf (last accessed 28 September 2012). See also J. Vidal, 'Bolivia Enshrines Natural World's Rights with Equal Status for Mother Earth', *Guardian* (10 April 2011) available at: www.guardian.co.uk/environment/2011/apr/10/bolivia-enshrines-natural-worlds-rights (last accessed 28 September 2012).

[38] K. Shuttleworth, 'Agreement Entitles Whanganui River to Legal Identity', *The New Zealand Herald* (30 August 2012), available at: www.nzherald.co.nz/nz/news/article.cfm?c_id=1&objectid=10830586 (last accessed 28 September 2012).

[39] J. G. Laitos, *The Right of Nonuse* (New York: Oxford University Press, 2012). See also Chapter 12 by Jan Laitos in this book.

[40] See, for example, the opposition to the recommendations made by the Gadgil Committee to preserve the Western Ghats, a UNESCO world heritage site in India. 'Western Ghats will Stifle Development', *The Indian Express* (21 November 2012), available at: www.indianexpress.com/news/-western-ghats-report-will-stifle-development-/1034104 (last accessed 30 December 2012).

3. Guiding principles and corporate responsibility towards nature

In June 2011 the United Nations Human Rights Council endorsed the GPs.[41] Since the GPs have been praised for breaking 'new ground'[42] and labelled as the 'game changer'[43] as well as a Universal Declaration of Human Rights-equivalent for business,[44] it will be useful to examine the extent to which they articulate responsibilities of companies to preserve nature. The analysis in this section should demonstrate that the GPs completely bypass the realm of nature or the environment, another clear instance of humankind not taking nature seriously.

3.1 Care for the environment: GPs' fatal omission?

The fact that companies can cause irreparable harm to the environment is well documented[45] – from the Bhopal gas disaster to the BP oil spill in the Gulf of Mexico.[46] Even the Special Representative of the Secretary General on the Issue of Human Rights and Transnational Corporations and Other Business Enterprises (SRSG) in his reports had expressly acknowledged that companies can adversely affect the environment, that states face challenges in regulating companies and that certain environmental initiatives/standards envisage responsibilities for business.[47]

---

[41] Human Rights Council, 'New Guiding Principles on Business and Human Rights Endorsed by the UN Human Rights Council' (16 June 2011), available at: www.ohchr.org/en/NewsEvents/Pages/DisplayNews.aspx?NewsID=11164&LangID=E (last accessed 17 June 2011).

[42] M. Otero, 'Keynote Address: UN Guiding Principles on Business and Human Rights' (8 December 2011), available at: www.state.gov/g/178545.htm (last accessed 20 September 2012).

[43] S. Jerbi, 'UN Adopts Guiding Principles on Business and Human Rights – What Comes Next?' (17 June 2011), available at: www.ihrb.org/commentary/staff/un_adopts_guiding_principles_on_business_and_human_rights.html (last accessed 20 September 2012).

[44] J. Kallman and M. Mohan, 'Reality Check: Just Tell It Like It Is', *Forbes Indonesia* (August 2011), 37.

[45] J. Jowit, 'World's Top Firms Cause $2.2tn of Environmental Damage, Report Estimates', *Guardian* (18 February 2010), available at: www.guardian.co.uk/environment/2010/feb/18/worlds-top-firms-environmental-damage (last accessed 31 December 2012).

[46] See Amnesty International, *Clouds of Injustice: Bhopal Disaster 20 Years On* (London: Amnesty International, 2004); National Commission on the BP Deepwater Horizon Oil Spill, *Deep Water*, n. 11.

[47] Commission on Human Rights, 'Interim Report of the Special Representative of the Secretary General on the Issue of Human Rights and Transnational Corporations and

Nevertheless, the GPs do not prescribe any *direct* environmental responsibilities of companies.[48]

The GPs are grounded on the 'Protect, Respect and Remedy' framework comprising three pillars: the state duty to protect human rights, corporate responsibility to respect human rights, and the access to remedy.[49] Under the first pillar (the state duty to protect human rights), there is no explicit mention of the duty to protect the environment. However, one can argue that states have such duty under both international law and national laws – irrespective of whether we treat the 'environment' as part of 'human rights' or not. At least in one respect the GPs do acknowledge that states should enforce laws – including environmental laws – where they directly or indirectly regulate business respect for human rights.[50]

The second pillar conceives that companies have a responsibility to respect human rights, which is independent of the duty of states. As I have argued elsewhere, this formulation suffers from several serious limitations.[51] For the current purpose, the key drawback lies in construing the term 'human rights' in such a narrow way that it is difficult, if not impossible, to include environmental responsibilities within its fold. Principle 12 reads as follows: 'The responsibility of business enterprises to respect human rights refers to *internationally recognized human rights – understood, at a minimum, as those expressed in the International Bill of Human Rights* and *the principles concerning fundamental rights set out*

Other Business Enterprises', E/CN.4/2006/97 (22 February 2006), paras. 15 and 29; Human Rights Council, 'Report of the SRSG: Business and Human Rights – Mapping International Standards of Responsibility and Accountability for Corporate Acts', A/HRC/4/35 (19 February 2007), paras. 20 and 51; Human Rights Council, 'Protect, Respect and Remedy: A Framework for Business and Human Rights', Report of the Special Representative of the Secretary General on the Issue of Human Rights and Transnational Corporations and Other Business Enterprises, A/HRC/8/5 (7 April 2008), paras. 12, 30, 34–35 and 61; Human Rights Council, 'Business and Human Rights: Towards Operationalizing the "Protect, Respect and Remedy" Framework', A/HRC/11/13 (22 April 2009), paras. 25 and 31; Human Rights Council, 'Business and Human Rights: Further Steps toward the Operationalization of the "Protect, Respect and Remedy" Framework', A/HRC/14/27 (9 April 2010), paras. 24, 29, 35, 40, 46, 69 and 91.

[48] See K. D. Jesse, 'The Responsibility of Transnational Corporations to Respect the Environment: A Plea to Supplement the Ruggie Framework', 10 *International and Comparative Corporate Law Journal* (2013) (forthcoming; on file with the author).

[49] For an analysis, see S. Deva, 'Guiding Principles on Business and Human Rights: Implications for Companies', 9:2 *European Company Law* (2012), 101–9.

[50] HRC, 'Guiding Principles', Commentary on Principle 3.

[51] S. Deva, *Regulating Corporate Human Rights Violations: Humanizing Business* (London and New York: Routledge, 2012), 110–13.

in the International Labour Organization's Declaration on Fundamental Principles and Rights at Work.'[52]

Not only is the environment missing from this 'minimal' list of human rights defined in Principle 12, there is also no mention of it in the illustrative list of 'additional standards' that companies may need to consider.[53] The closest reference that the GPs make to environmental responsibilities is in the following context: 'While processes for assessing human rights impacts can be incorporated within other processes such as risk assessments or *environmental and social impact assessments*, they should include all internationally recognized human rights as a reference point, since enterprises may potentially impact virtually any of these rights.'[54]

In short, one can conclude that unless one relies on the linkage between human rights and the environment,[55] the GPs do not articulate environmental responsibilities of companies as part of the minimum framework. Having said this, the GPs can still be used in a number of ways to press for the responsibilities of companies to preserve the environment. Let me highlight a few such possibilities here. The GPs use 'social expectations' as the normative basis to locate the corporate responsibility to respect human rights.[56] While the reliance on 'social expectations' is problematic for several reasons,[57] one can argue that such expectations cannot be static or confined to a limited set of human rights. In fact, as illustrated by regulatory initiatives mentioned in the section below, society already expects companies not to pollute the environment by their activities.

---

[52] HRC, 'Guiding Principles' (emphasis added).
[53] Ibid., Commentary on Principle 12.
[54] Ibid., Commentary on Principle 18 (emphasis added). Commentary on Principle 21 also refers to 'sustainability reports' as one of the formal reporting mechanisms.
[55] See A. Boyle, 'Human Rights and the Environment: Where Next?', 23 *The European Journal of International Law* (2012), 613–42; C. Gearty, 'Do Human Rights Help or Hinder Environmental Protection?', 1 *Journal of Human Rights and the Environment* (2010), 7–22; D. Shelton, 'Human Rights and Environment: Past, Present and Future Linkages and the Value of a Declaration' (2009), available at: www.unep.org/environmentalgovernance/Portals/8/documents/draftpaper%20Humanrightsnenvironment%20pastpresentandfuturelinkages.pdf (last accessed 31 December 2012).
[56] HRC, 'Protect, Respect and Remedy' (2008), para. 54. See also HRC, 'Guiding Principles', n. 1, para. 6 (Introduction to the Guiding Principles).
[57] See C. Lopez, 'The "Ruggie Process": From Legal Obligations to Corporate Social Responsibility?' in S. Deva and D. Bilchitz (eds.), *Human Rights Obligations of Business: Beyond the Corporate Responsibility to Respect?* (Cambridge University Press, 2013).

In the area of environmental protection, two interrelated challenges are often critical: first, the dilemma of 'how to behave in Rome' in view of divergent standards prevailing in different jurisdictions, and second, the need for extraterritorial regulation to deal with transboundary environmental issues/pollution. The GPs formulate the responsibility to respect human rights as 'a *global standard* of conduct expected for all business enterprises *wherever they operate*.'[58] This global approach can be employed to overcome the first challenge and, consequently, corporate compliance with only national environmental laws – which might be non-existent, low or lack enforcement – might not suffice if higher international standards are in place.[59] In relation to the second challenge, one can refer to the *permissive acknowledgment* of the GPs of the power of states to regulate the extraterritorial activities of companies domiciled in their territory and/or jurisdiction.[60]

The corporate responsibility to respect human rights under the GPs is not limited to own activities: companies are expected 'to prevent or mitigate adverse human rights impacts that are directly linked to their operations, products or services by their business relationships, even if they have not contributed to those impacts'.[61] If we apply this approach to environmental pollution, then a company should be responsible for pollution caused by its supply chain business partners. It is, however, unclear whether the GPs aim to make a parent company liable for human rights abuses committed by its subsidiary.[62] Logically speaking, a parent company should be held responsible for actions and omissions of its subsidiaries, especially if the responsibility might arise for the behaviour of independent contractors of the supply chain over which the parent company has lesser legal control.

'Due diligence' is the key process proposed by the GPs to enable companies to discharge their responsibility to respect human rights. The recommended process includes 'assessing actual and potential human rights impacts, integrating and acting upon the findings, tracking responses, and communicating how impacts are addressed.'[63] Due diligence is conceived

---

[58] HRC, 'Guiding Principles', Commentary on Principle 11 (emphasis added). See also ibid., Principle 23.
[59] For example, the Bhopal gas disaster might have been avoided had Union Carbide applied the safety standards practised in their US plant. See Deva, *Regulating Corporate Human Rights Violations*, 152–75.
[60] HRC, 'Guiding Principles', Principle 2 and Commentary.
[61] Ibid., Principle 13(b).
[62] Deva, 'Guiding Principles on Business and Human Rights', n. 49, 105.
[63] HRC, 'Guiding Principles', Principle 17.

as an 'ongoing' (rather than a one-time) exercise that will vary from company to company, depending on the size, nature and context of operations, and the severity of human rights risk.[64] On conducting an impact assessment, if it is found the adverse impact is caused or contributed to by a company, the company should take the necessary steps to cease or prevent the impact.[65] I have argued elsewhere that the application of due diligence to discharge the corporate responsibility to respect human rights is fraught with hidden dangers.[66]

Nevertheless, the utility of due diligence lies in estimating in advance the negative consequences of corporate projects and taking remedial steps to avoid harm – whether to human rights or the environment. In fact, considering that environmental impact assessment processes are already quite advanced, due diligence can prove equally, if not more, useful in guiding companies not to pollute the environment.

3.2 Do companies then have environmental responsibilities?

While the GPs fail to acknowledge that companies have any direct responsibilities to preserve nature, it would be inaccurate to say that no such responsibilities do exist. In fact, one can find several instances of corporate environmental responsibilities rooted in both hard and soft international law. Just to illustrate, the Convention on Civil Liability for Oil Pollution Damage stipulates that the owner of a ship – which could even be a company – 'shall be liable for any pollution damage caused by oil which has escaped or been discharged from the ship as a result of the incident'.[67] Similarly, the Convention on Civil Liability for Damage Resulting from Activities Dangerous to the Environment provides that the operator of a dangerous activity – which could again be a company – 'shall be liable for the damage caused by the activity as a result of incidents at the time or during the period when he was exercising the control of that activity'.[68]

---

[64] Ibid.   [65] Ibid., Commentary on Principle 19.
[66] S. Deva, 'Treating Human Rights Lightly: A Critique of the Consensus Rhetoric and the Language Employed by the Guiding Principles', in Deva and Bilchitz (eds.), *Human Rights Obligations of Business*, 78
[67] International Convention on Civil Liability for Oil Pollution Damage, UN Doc. 973 UNTS 4 (adopted 29 November 1969, entered into force 19 June 1975), Art. III(1) read with Art. I(2)/(3).
[68] Convention on Civil Liability for Damage Resulting from Activities Dangerous to the Environment, CSTS No. 150 (adopted 21 June 1993), Art. 6(1) read with Art. 2(5)/(6).

If we move from hard to soft law, several regulatory initiatives are worth noting. Although the 1992 Rio Declaration on Environment and Development did not explicitly refer to *direct* corporate responsibilities,[69] Chapter 30 of Agenda 21 focuses exclusively on the role of business and industry in the sustainable development project.[70] One may also refer to the UN Global Compact,[71] which recommends its participants to 'support a precautionary approach to environmental challenges', 'undertake initiatives to promote greater environmental responsibility' and 'encourage the development and diffusion of environmentally friendly technologies'.[72] The 2003 UN Norm[73] tried to frame environmental responsibilities of companies in a non-voluntary way. While this attempt did not materialize, paragraph 14 rightly reminded companies to 'carry out their activities in accordance with national laws, regulations, administrative practices, and policies relating to the preservation of the environment of the countries in which they operate as well as in accordance with relevant international agreements, principles, objectives, responsibilities, and standards with regard to the environment'.

Part VI of the Organisation for Economic Co-operation and Development (OECD) Guidelines for Multinational Enterprises – which came into effect on 21 June 1976[74] and were revised in June 2000[75] and updated in May 2011[76] – is another example of the environmental responsibilities of (multinational) companies. It provides that companies should, for instance, 'take due account of the need to protect the environment, public health and safety' and generally 'conduct their activities

---

See also the liability provisions of the Vienna Convention on Civil Liability for Nuclear Damage (adopted 21 May 1963; entered into force 12 November 1977).

[69] A/CONF.151/26 (Vol. I) (12 August 1992).
[70] 'Strengthening the Role of Business and Industry', available at: www.un-documents.net/a21-30.htm (last accessed 2 May 2012).
[71] It is worth mentioning that Professor John Ruggie was a key architect of the Global Compact. Ironically, however, when he drafted the GPs, the environmental responsibilities were not mentioned in them.
[72] UN Global Compact, 'The Ten Principles', Principles 7–9, available at: www.unglobalcompact.org/aboutthegc/thetenprinciples/index.html (last accessed 31 December 2012).
[73] Norms on the Responsibilities of Transnational Corporations and Other Business Enterprises with Regard to Human Rights, E/CN.4/Sub.2/2003/12 (2003).
[74] OECD Declaration on International Investment and Multinational Enterprises 1976, reprinted in 15 *International Legal Materials* (1976) 967–77.
[75] OECD Declaration on International Investment and Multinational Enterprises 2000, reprinted in 40 *International Legal Materials* (2001), 236–46.
[76] OECD Guidelines for Multinational Enterprises: Recommendations for Responsible Business Conduct in a Global Context (25 May 2011), available at: http://www.oecd.org/daf/inv/mne/48004323.pdf (last accessed 27 June 2011).

in a manner contributing to the wider goal of sustainable development'.[77] While the Guidelines are of course not legally binding and their efficacy in regulating corporate behaviour is limited,[78] they definitely indicate that companies are not outside the loop of environmental responsibilities.

On the basis of the above analysis, we can draw two general conclusions. First, the *failure* of the GPs to articulate direct environmental responsibilities of companies does not reflect accurately either the 'is' or 'ought' state of direct corporate responsibilities under international law. It is regrettable that rather than strengthening the existing framework incrementally, the GPs try to rewind the clock to send a message that the environment is not as important as human rights and that companies can pollute the environment at will without any consequences. Second, while soft voluntary measures are useful and regulation itself cannot bring about all the desired changes in corporate behaviour,[79] one should not underestimate the need for a legally binding international regulatory framework directed at companies. Soft regulatory instruments often rely on market forces, which are rarely effective in applying adequate and continuous pressure on all companies to meet their environmental responsibilities.

4. Conclusion

In 2001 Eden wrote that '[g]eography finally seems to be taking the environment, and particularly nature, seriously in conceptual terms'.[80] While we may have taken seriously the term 'nature' or 'environment' in a conceptual sense, our practice of regulating companies – which are

---

[77] Ibid., 40.
[78] See OECD Watch, *10 Years On: Assessing the Contribution of the OECD Guidelines for Multinational Enterprises to Responsible Business Conduct* (June 2010).
[79] Strasser observes: 'Living sustainably on the planet and passing a livable ecosystem on to our children will require business, and everyone else, to do things that must be motivated, indeed inspired, by other social controls and influences, things that regulation usually cannot command. Regulation is a useful policy tool to control particular conduct that causes specific, identifiable harms, but its commands are not very effective to reduce resource use, or to pursue ongoing adaptive management of environmental impacts through continuous improvement and technological innovation. In pursuing environmental protection, regulation is workably effective at policing the floor, but it is a poor tool to inspire or require a reach for the ceiling. Yet, sustainability requires that we do more than police the floor.' K. Strasser, 'Business Environmentalism: Good Works and Greenwash', 42 *Environmental Law Reporter News and Analysis* (2012), 10216–27, 10217.
[80] S. Eden, 'Environmental Issues: Nature versus the Environment?', 25:1 *Progress in Human Geography* (2001), 79–85.

indispensable actors having a bearing on the success of the project to preserve nature – indicates otherwise. This chapter provided two indicators of this state of affairs: the failure of sustainable development as a balancing tool in taming corporate profiteering, and the omission of the GPs to articulate direct environmental responsibilities of companies.

I suggested that if we really take nature seriously, then nature should be bestowed with autonomous rights that operate as trumps over other social goals. Both law and lawyers know well how this can be done and how balancing is done in such a way that the needs of nature are not scarified at the altar of economic development.

PART VII

A rule of law for the oceans

19

Conservation of marine biodiversity and the International Maritime Organization

TORE HENRIKSEN

1. Introduction

The UN Law of the Sea Convention (LOS Convention), which aims at establishing 'a legal order for the seas and oceans', celebrated its thirtieth anniversary on 10 December 2012.[1] The International Maritime Organization (IMO) is tasked under the LOS Convention with establishing common international ground rules for maritime safety and protection of the marine environment.[2] The assignment of such responsibility to the IMO can be viewed as a means of specifying and operationalizing the general obligations of flag states under the LOS Convention to protect and preserve the marine environment.[3] It also facilitates a dynamic development of the law by leaving states, through the IMO, to address topical issues through the adoption and amendments of treaties and other instruments. Under the LOS Convention states are required to take action to protect fragile or rare ecosystems and habitats of endangered species.[4] These obligations are supplemented and extended through the Convention on Biological Diversity (CBD).[5] The CBD is applicable to areas under national jurisdiction and to shipping irrespective of where it is taking place as an activity affecting biodiversity.[6] In addition to operational and accidental pollution, shipping affects marine biodiversity through the introduction of new species through fouling and ballast

---

[1] United Nations Convention on the Law of the Sea, 1833 United Nations Treaty Series, 3.
[2] James Harrison, *Making of the Law of the Sea. A Study in the Development of International Law* (Cambridge University Press, 2011), 154–5; LOS Convention Article 211(1).
[3] LOS Convention, Articles 192, 194(3)(b) and 94.
[4] Ibid., Article 194(5).
[5] Convention on Biological Diversity, 1760 United Nations Treaty Series, 79.
[6] Ibid., Article 4.

water exchange, debris such as plastic, noise, collision with marine mammals and physical impacts.[7] States parties to the CBD are required to assess and consider effects of shipping and other human activities on ecosystems and habitats and to take action to address adverse effects of shipping.[8] The obligation to protect habitats and ecosystems may require area-based regulation of shipping activities.

The IMO is important for the development and maintenance of the rule of law for the marine environment. The first question to be discussed is whether these developments in international environmental law have been introduced into IMO legislation: is conservation of marine biodiversity a relevant consideration, particularly in the adoption of area-based regulations? This would mean recognition of ecological and other qualities of marine biodiversity as legal constraints on shipping. The Particularly Sensitive Sea Area (PSSA) has been referred to as the IMO instrument for implementing the CBD. Therefore its impact on the adoption of area-based measures will be assessed.

The LOS Convention, which provides the legal framework for the implementation of these instruments, has a static character. It sets spatial and substantive limitations within which states may exercise jurisdiction.[9] The coastal state may be required under the CBD to regulate international shipping within its maritime zones to comply with its obligations. However, it is not competent to take unilateral measures in respect of foreign-flagged vessels navigating through its Exclusive Economic Zone (EEZ) in particular.[10] It is required to work through the IMO for the adoption of measures under its instruments to protect components of marine biodiversity under its jurisdiction. Part XII of the LOS Convention on the protection and preservation of the marine environment reflects the focus on prevention of pollution of the marine environment in the 1970s. The second question to be discussed is whether the LOS Convention setting out the rule of law for the seas and oceans is adequately addressing the threats to marine biodiversity by shipping.

---

[7] Assessment of the impacts of shipping on the marine Environment, Monitoring and Assessment Series, OSPAR 2009, available at: http://qsr2010.ospar.org/media/assessments/p00440_Shipping_Assessment.pdf (last accessed February 2013).
[8] CBD, Articles 7 and 8(l).
[9] Yoshifumi Tanaka, 'Zonal and Integrated Management Approaches to Ocean Governance: Reflections on a Dual Approach in International Law of the Sea', 19:4 *International Journal of Marine and Coastal Law* (2004), 483–514, 484–6.
[10] LOS Convention, Articles 21(2) and 211(5).

2. IMO and conservation of marine biodiversity

The objectives of the IMO are 'to encourage and facilitate the general adoption of the highest possible standards in matters concerning maritime safety, efficiency of navigation and prevention and control of marine pollution from ships'.[11] The objective of environmental protection was added following the Torrey Canyon incident.[12] In this chapter the focus will be on International Convention for the Prevention of Pollution From Ships (MARPOL 73/78) and the International Convention for the Safety of Life at Sea (SOLAS 74). MARPOL 73/78 was adopted in recognition of the need to 'preserve the human environment in general and the marine environment in particular'.[13] Its objective is to prevent pollution of the marine environment from discharges of harmful substances.[14] The Convention includes six annexes addressing different sources of pollution, including oil, garbage, sewage and air pollution. The Convention has gradually been expanded from dealing with oil pollution to addressing threats to the global environment. Preservation of the environment may include marine biodiversity and prevention of pollution contributes to the conservation of marine biodiversity. But neither the convention nor its annexes include any explicit reference to marine biodiversity. The objective of SOLAS 74 is to promote maritime safety.[15] Its Chapter V on navigation now includes environmental protection as a separate objective in the adoption of ship reporting and routeing systems.[16] The amendments came in recognition of the fact that vessels through their navigation may threaten the marine environment by pollution or by other impact such as physical damage. Neither the SOLAS nor its amendments include reference to marine biodiversity.

The two conventions include few if any provisions setting out general obligations or principles as a guide to their implementation. They mainly include decision-making procedures. Two of the IMO committees are

---

[11] Convention on the International Maritime Organization, Article 1(a), 289 UN Treaty Series.
[12] Alan Khee-Jin Tan, *Vessel-Source Marine Pollution. The Law and Politics of International Regulation* (Cambridge University Press, 2006), 76.
[13] International Convention for the Prevention of Pollution from Ships, as modified by the Protocol of 1978 relating thereto (MARPOL 73/78), 1340 UN Treaty Series, 62.
[14] MARPOL 73/78, Article 1.
[15] International Convention for the Safety of Life at Sea (SOLAS 74), 1184 UN Treaty Series, 278.
[16] Adoptions for amendments to the International Convention for the Safety of Lives at Sea, 1974, Resolution MSC.31 (63) Annex 1 and Resolution MSC.46 (65).

competent to amend them, by adopting technical regulations, rules and standards.[17] The Maritime Safety Committee (MSC)[18] may adopt amendments to SOLAS 74.[19] The Marine Environmental Protection Committee (MEPC)[20] has the same function under MARPOL 73/78.[21] The question is whether the conservation of biodiversity has been incorporated through the practice of these committees.

3. Regulating shipping by area-based measures

3.1 General measures

Area-based approaches are used in regulating shipping activities. They include special areas and emissions control areas, routeing measures for ships and PSSAs These area-based measures may be established in the territorial sea as well as in the EEZ of a coastal state and in adjacent areas of the high seas. The coastal state is competent to adopt some of the measures in respect of its territorial sea.[22] A special area and emission control area may be established under MARPOL 73/78 Annexes I, II, IV, V and VI (emission control area).[23] A special area is 'a sea area where for recognized technical reasons in relation to its oceanographical and ecological condition and to the particular character of its traffic the adoption of special mandatory methods for the prevention of sea pollution by oil is required'.[24] The mandatory methods may include stricter regulation of operational discharges for vessels than are applicable elsewhere. Ships' Routeing Systems (SRS) may be established under SOLAS 74 and the Convention on the International Regulations for Preventing Collisions at Sea (COLREGs)[25] 'for ensuring safety of life at sea, safety and efficiency of navigation and/or protection of the marine environment'.[26] The SRSs are geographically defined and can

---

[17] IMO Convention, Article 11.
[18] Ibid., Articles 27–31.
[19] SOLAS 74, Article VIII(a).
[20] IMO Convention, Article 38.
[21] MARPOL 73/78, Article 16(2).
[22] LOS Convention, Article 21.
[23] MARPOL 73/78 Annex I, Regulations 1.11, 15.2–3 and 34.3–5, Annex II Regulation 8, Annex IV Regulations 5bis and 11.3, Annex V Regulations 1.14 and 6 and Annex VI Regulation 2.8.
[24] Ibid. Annex I, Regulation 1.11.
[25] Convention on the International Regulations for Preventing Collisions at Sea, Rule 10, 1050 UN Treaty Series, 18. Rule 10 of COLREGs provides for traffic separation schemes.
[26] SOLAS 74, Regulation V/10.1.

include mandatory or recommended measures. A Particularly Sensitive Sea Area (PSSA) is an area in need of special protection because of its ecological, socio-economic or scientific attributes.[27] In contrast to the two above-mentioned area-based approaches, the PSSA does not have a treaty basis but is established through a non-legally binding instrument. The 'associate protective measures' adopted to protect the attributes of the PSSA must have legal basis in IMO conventions or in the LOS Convention Article 211(6).[28] The designation as a PSSA provides for addressing different threats from international shipping to an area. The PSSA has been described as the IMO implementation of CBD, both due to the values it seeks to protect and the comprehensiveness of its measures.[29] Since the measures adopted to protect the attributes of the PSSA are based in MARPOL 73/78, SOLAS 74 and other IMO treaties, the question is whether approval by the MEPC of a PSSA affects the decision-making under the relevant convention. Environmental protection is a relatively new consideration particularly under SOLAS 74. The first-mentioned area-based measures will now be investigated in order to assess whether they provide for marine biodiversity conservation.

3.2 Special areas and ships' routeing measures

3.2.1 Criteria

Guidelines have been adopted to supplement the procedural and substantial requirements under MARPOL 73/78 and SOLAS 74.[30] Although not legally binding, they include instructions to contracting parties and the MEPC and MSC on the interpretation and application of the provisions of

---

[27] Revised Guidelines for the Identification and Designation of Particularly Sensitive Sea Areas (hereafter PSSA Guidelines), Resolution A.982(24), paragraph 8.3.7.
[28] Ibid., paragraph 7.5.2.3.
[29] J. Roberts, *Marine Environment Protection and Biodiversity Conservation: The Application and Future Development of the IMO's Particularly Sensitive Sea Area Concept* (Berlin: Springer, 2007), 83 with further references in footnote 2 and 107–8; J. Roberts et al., 'Area-based Management on the High Seas: Possible Application of the IMO's Particularly Sensitive Sea Area Concept', 25 *The International Journal of Marine and Coastal Law* (2010), 483–522, 498.
[30] Guidelines for the Designation of Special Areas under MARPOL 73/78 and Guidelines for the Identification and Designation of Particularly Sensitive Sea Areas, Annex 1, IMO Assembly Resolution A.927(22) (hereinafter Special Area Guidelines); General Provisions on Ships' Routeing, as amended, IMO Assembly Resolution A.574 (14) (hereinafter General Provisions).

these two conventions.³¹ Therefore, they may provide information on the legal relevance of marine biodiversity under these instruments. The criteria for establishing special areas include ecological conditions, oceanographic conditions and vessel traffic characteristics. The relevant area is identified through ecological conditions, while the other two determine its vulnerability. The area may be defined by being the habitat of depleted or threatened species, containing a rare or fragile ecosystem or being of importance for larger marine ecosystems.³² These are descriptions of an ecologically sensitive area. The reference to ecosystems, breeding area and habitat is recognition that ecological boundaries must be considered and taken into account in regulating operational discharges. The CBD includes recognition of a broader set of biodiversity values. In addition to ecological values, its preamble lists scientific, socio-economic and cultural values. Not all of these ecological values and none of the socio-economic and cultural values are relevant in identifying a special area. When submitting a proposal for a special area, states may include information on these other values.³³ They may be relevant but not decisive in designating special areas.³⁴ Consequently, in addition to protecting a rare or vulnerable ecosystem, a special area may also be established to protect its scientific value.

Routeing measures have traditionally been established to improve safety within a particular area.³⁵ These measures may protect the marine environment as maritime casualties often inflict pollution damages. Protection of the environment is now a separate objective: routeing measures may be adopted to prevent pollution or other damage to the marine environment caused by groundings or collisions in or near 'environmentally sensitive areas'.³⁶ Other damage refers to physical impacts on seabed habitats and collisions with marine mammals. There is no definition of 'environmentally sensitive area'. This objective was included to ensure coordination with the PSSA concept, which includes ships' routeing as associated protective measures.³⁷ It is not known why 'particularly sensitive area' was not used and whether the intention was to give the concept

---

[31] Vienna Convention on the Law of Treaties, Article 31(3)(a) or (b) referring to subsequent agreement and practice of state parties.
[32] Special Area Guidelines, paragraph 2.5.
[33] Ibid., paragraph 3.3.
[34] Ibid., paragraph 2.3.
[35] General Provisions, paragraph 1.1.   [36] Ibid.
[37] See Amendment to General Provisions on Ships' Routeing, SN/Circ.155, June 1992; Roberts, *Marine Environmental Protection*, 121.

a different legal meaning.[38] Still, it is natural to read 'environmentally sensitive area' as at least including the ecological criteria for PSSA designation.[39] The ecological boundaries are recognized as relevant in regulating the navigation of vessels.

The vulnerability of an area is a function of its ecological values, and oceanographic and traffic characteristics. The states applying for these measures are required to undertake a risk assessment where these factors are included. One decisive factor in designating a special area is that it is used to a significant extent by vessels from which legal discharges under MARPOL 73/78 'would be unacceptable' in the light of the existing oceanographic and ecological conditions of the area.[40] It is the traffic pattern together with natural factors such as weather, ice conditions and tidal streams of the area that cause the risk of pollution to the environment and ecological values. Threats from other sources of pollution are included in this assessment.[41] Even a modest volume of traffic may cause unacceptable operational discharges if these affect an area with a fragile or vulnerable ecosystem.

Similarly, routeing measures aimed at protecting the marine environment must 'reasonably be expected to significantly prevent or reduce the risk of pollution or other damage to the marine environment of the area concerned'.[42] Other requirements indicate a high threshold for giving the ecological values decisive weight. In addition to the threshold in the risk assessment, the measures shall not have the 'effect of unreasonably limiting the sea area available for navigation'.[43] There are limits as to the size of the area to be covered by a routeing measure.[44] Irrespective of their purpose, the measures shall not impose 'unnecessary constraints on shipping' and shall be consistent with navigational rights of states under the law of the sea.[45] There is a preference for non-binding routeing measures as the threshold for making them mandatory is higher.[46] In comparison, when establishing special areas the navigational interests are safeguarded

---

[38] G. Peet, 'Particularly Sensitive Sea Areas – A Documentary History', 9 *International Journal of Marine and Coastal Law* (1994), 469–506, 486 and 494.
[39] PSSA Guidelines, paragraphs 4.4.1–4.4.11.
[40] Special Area Guidelines, paragraph 2.6.
[41] Ibid., paragraphs 2.8 and 2.9.
[42] General Provisions, paragraph 3.6.1.
[43] Ibid., paragraph 3.6.2.
[44] Ibid., paragraphs 2.1.13 and paragraph 5.5 setting out more specific requirements.
[45] Ibid., paragraph 3.7 with reference to SOLAS regulation V/10, paragraph 9.
[46] Ibid., paragraphs 3.5 and 6.17.

through an obligation for states with bordering coastlines to provide for adequate reception and treatment facilities.[47]

3.2.2 Area-based measures in practice

Conservation of marine biodiversity is a relevant consideration, but has it been applied in the adoption of area-based measures? The question will be addressed in the following by some case studies. The presentation is not meant to give an exhaustive assessment.

In its proposal for designating its southern continental shelf water a special area under MARPOL 73/78 Annex I, South Africa highlighted the need to protect threatened seabird populations and livelihood from operational discharges.[48] Further, this would help it meet its international obligations to conserve biological diversity. The area was defined by information on its ecological characteristics, its socio-economic value and scientific and cultural significance, concurrent with the criteria for designating a PSSA.[49] The application included information on measures taken to protect the environment,[50] including mandatory traffic separation schemes adopted under COLREGs. When discussed at the MEPC, the uniqueness of the oceanographic characteristics of the area and the fact that it hosted a large number of endemic species red-listed by the International Union for the Conservation of Nature (IUCN) was highlighted.[51]

On the initiative of Baltic Sea coastal states, Annex IV on sewage was amended to include special areas and the Baltic Sea was designated a special area.[52] In the application the Baltic Sea was described as a 'unique ecosystem with indispensable values ... particularly sensitive to changes in the

---

[47] MARPOL 73/78 Annex I, Regulation 38.4, Annex II Regulation 18.3, Annex IV Regulation 13 and Annex V Regulation 8. Special regulations applies to Antarctica as there are no reception facilities available: Annex I, Regulation 38.7.
[48] Identification and Protection of Special Areas and Particularly Sensitive Sea Areas Proposal for the designation of South Africa's southern continental shelf waters as a Special Area under MARPOL Annex I. Submitted by the Republic of South Africa, MEPC 54/8 (hereinafter South African Proposal).
[49] Ibid., Annex, item 3; PSSA Guidelines, paragraph 4.
[50] South African Proposal, Annex, paragraph 5.
[51] Report of the Marine Environment Protection Committee on Its Fifty-Fourth Session, paragraphs 8.7–8.16, MEPC 54/21.
[52] Amendments to the Annex of the Protocol of 1978 Relating to the International Convention for the Prevention of Pollution from Ships, 1973, Resolution MEPC.200(62), Report of the Marine Environment Protection Committee on its 62nd Session of MEPC, MEPC 62/24 Annex 12.

environment'.⁵³ Sewage from passenger vessels in particular contributed to the eutrophication of the sea, thus threatening the ecosystem.

Several of the ships' routeing measures are adopted to protect the marine environment.⁵⁴ They include a precautionary area, an area to be avoided and a no anchoring area.⁵⁵ A no anchoring area may be adopted to prevent physical damage to coral reefs.⁵⁶ The objective of areas to be avoided, the measure most frequently used, is normally to prevent pollution and damage to the environment. Some include both environmental protection and maritime safety objectives, while others are specifically established to protect sensitive sea areas. Some of these last-mentioned measures are included as associated protective measures under a PPSA while others are stand-alone measures.⁵⁷ An area to be avoided measure is also used to protect the habitats of whales in order to prevent ship strikes.⁵⁸

The format of proposals for routeing measures has developed in recent years. Many include descriptions of the ecological, social and cultural significance of the area as part of the reasons for establishing the measures.⁵⁹ The measures taken by states to protect the area are listed, including marine-protected areas. The proposals are modelled on the guidelines for PSSA designation. Other applications are less detailed but include descriptions of the environment, species or ecosystem to be protected.⁶⁰ The decisions on routeing measures seldom include any reasoning, but the information provided in the proposals suggests that the ecological significance and other values of the area are taken into account when establishing the measures. Proposals for mandatory routeing measures are more controversial.⁶¹ This was the case when Norway applied for a continuous

---

⁵³ Interpretations of, and amendments to, MARPOL and Related Instruments. Proposal to amend MARPOL Annex IV to include the possibility to establish Special Areas for the prevention of pollution by sewage and to designate the Baltic Sea as a special area under MARPOL Annex IV, MEPC.60/6/2.
⁵⁴ Ships' Routeing 2010 Edition, IMO.
⁵⁵ General Provisions, paragraph 2.12–2.14.
⁵⁶ Routeing of Ships, Ship Reporting and Related Matters, Mandatory No Anchoring Areas on Sharks Bank and Long Shoal, Barbados, NAV 53/12.
⁵⁷ Routeing Measures Other than Traffic Separation Schemes, Annex, SN/Circ.234.
⁵⁸ Routeing of Ships, Ship Reporting and Related Matters. Areas to be avoided 'In Roseway Basin, South of Nova Scotia', Canada, NAV 53/3/13.
⁵⁹ Routeing of Ships, Ship Reporting and Related Matters, Proposed area to be avoided, submitted by New Zealand, NAV/49/3.
⁶⁰ Routeing of Ships, Ship Reporting and Related Matters, Mandatory No Anchoring Areas on Sharks Bank and Long Shoal, Barbados, NAV 53/12.
⁶¹ Report to the Maritime Safety Committee, paragraph 3.10, NAV 49/19.

and mandatory traffic separation scheme in its EEZ from East Finnmark to the Lofoten Islands.[62] The proposal was supported by the risks posed by the increasing number of oil tankers to the environment. It included information on oceanography of and the ecological, social and economic and scientific importance of the area. The application met opposition in the relevant sub-committee on Safety of Navigation (NAV), as it meant a mandatory traffic separation scheme of 560 nautical miles.[63] The revised proposal of Norway consisting mostly of recommended sea routes was 'not likely to cause a disproportionate burden to the shipping industry'.[64]

These examples suggest that ecological values and other biodiversity characteristics are relevant in establishing area-based measures. But regard for navigation and maritime safety are still outweighing conservation of biodiversity in establishing routeing measures.

3.3 Particularly sensitive sea area designation

A PSSA has been described as 'nothing more (and nothing less) than a qualification and a basis on which protective measures may be taken through IMO-measures'.[65] This assertion calls for an investigation of the effects of a designation as a PSSA on the adoption of measures: does identifying the vulnerability of an area affect the decision?

To be designated as a PSSA, an area must satisfy three conditions: first, it must meet any of the ecological, social, cultural and economic or scientific and educational criteria. Second, it must be vulnerable to damage from international shipping activities, and third, there must be measures available under IMO instruments or the LOS Convention to protect the area from the identified threats.[66]

The MEPC undertakes an initial assessment of a proposal whether all these conditions are met and may designate the area a PSSA 'in principle'.[67] This may be regarded as recognition that ecological and other biodiversity values warrant restrictions on shipping activities. It is the relevant

---

[62] Routeing of Ships, Ship Reporting and Related Matters. New mandatory traffic separation scheme off the coast of Norway from Vardø to Røst Submitted by Norway, NAV 52/3/6.
[63] Report to the Maritime Safety Committee, Paragraph 3.36, NAV 52/18.
[64] Ibid., paragraph 3.37.
[65] Peet, 'Particularly Sensitive Sea Areas', 469–70.
[66] Revised Guidelines for the Identification and Designation of Particularly Sensitive Sea Areas, paragraphs 4, 5 and 6 respectively; IMO Assembly Resolution 982 (24).
[67] PSSA Guidelines, paragraphs 8.1–8.2 (assessment of substantive criteria), 8.3.1–8.3.2 (procedure).

IMO Committee or sub-committee (NAV) that may adopt the proposed associated protective measures consistent with the criteria of the relevant instrument.[68] The final designation as a PSSA is made when the measures have been approved.[69]

Whether the preliminary designation has any effect on the adoption of associated measures was tested with the Galapagos Archipelago PSSA. In its proposal to designate the archipelago a PSSA, Ecuador included a request for a mandatory area to be avoided.[70] The extensive size of the area raised questions on the role of the NAV in the designation of PSSAs. The Dutch delegation stated: 'it was clearly the authority of MEPC to decide whether an area can be designated as a PSSA and to determine which Associated Protective Measures would best protect the environment in the area concerned.' But it was the NAV that was most competent to determine which measure would best protect the safety of navigation.[71] The area to be avoided was adjusted and made recommendatory.[72] In the revised 2006 PSSA guidelines it was confirmed that the MSC and its sub-committees have separate responsibility to determine whether the criteria under the relevant instrument are fulfilled.[73] The proposal to designate the Baltic Sea a PSSA included several mandatory areas to be avoided.[74] The NAV noted that the proposal did not justify the establishment of mandatory areas and established them as two non-mandatory areas to be avoided.[75]

These examples illustrate that PSSA designation does not necessarily have a greater effect on the design of routeing measures compared with

---

[68] PSSA Guidelines, paragraph 8.3.3 and paragraph 7.10 (the proposal for associated protective measure shall also be sent directly to the relevant IMO Committee/sub-committee.
[69] Ibid., paragraph 8.3.4.
[70] Identification and Protection of Special Areas and Particularly Sensitive Sea Areas Designation of the Galapagos Archipelago as a Particularly Sensitive Sea Area Submitted by Ecuador, MEPC 51/8/2; Designation of the Galapagos Archipelago as a Particularly Sensitive Sea Area; MEPC 53/24/Add.1.
[71] Report to the Maritime Safety Committee; paragraph 2.20–3.23, NAV 51/19.
[72] Ibid., Annex 5.   [73] PSSA Guidelines, paragraph 8.3.3.
[74] Routeing of Ships, Ship Reporting and Related Matters. New traffic separation schemes in Bornholmsgat and North of Rügen, recommended deep-water route in the eastern Baltic Sea, amendments to the traffic separation schemes Off Gotland Island and South of Gedser and new areas to be avoided at Hoburgs Bank and Norra Midsjöbanken. Submitted by Denmark, Estonia, Finland, Germany, Latvia, Lithuania, Poland and Sweden, NAV 51/3/6; Designation of the Baltic Sea Area as a Particularly Sensitive Sea Area, Resolution Mepc.136(53), Report of the Marine Environment Protection Committee on Its Fifty-Third Session, MEPC 53/24.Add.2.
[75] Report to the Maritime Safety Committee, paragraph 3.50–3.51, NAV 51/19.

those adopted directly under SOLAS 74. Areas to be avoided and other routeing measures to protect the environment are usually made recommendatory, irrespective of being associated protective measures or adopted directly under SOLAS 74 or COLREGs. The balancing between the consideration of conservation of biodiversity and the interests of navigation does not seem to be different.

Another effect of a PSSA designation may be the expansion of measures. First, the objectives of existing measures may be broadened to include a wider set of biodiversity values. Second, new measures may be developed to address threats to marine biodiversity. An area must be characterized by ecological values, socio-economic values or scientific and educational values to be designated a PSSA.[76] There is an overlap between these three sets of values and the values to be promoted through the CBD. None of the IMO instruments have been designed to protect scientific, educational and cultural values. They have gradually been amended to protect different types of ecological values. The non-ecological values of biodiversity do not enjoy separate protection but remain considerations subordinate to ecological values. There are few examples that PSSA designation leads to the adoption of new measures. Proposals to ban single hull tankers carrying heavy oil from sailing through the Western European PSSA[77] or a mandatory pilotage scheme through the Torres Strait PSSA[78] met resistance within both the MEPC and MSC as they arguably lacked adequate legal basis and conflicted with freedom of navigation under the law of the sea. They did not result in amendments of the instruments. Instead the single hull ban was made generally applicable through amendment to MARPOL 73/78 Annex I and the pilotage scheme for Torres Strait was made recommendatory.[79] When MARPOL 73/78 Annex IV was amended primarily to designate the Baltic Sea special area, this measure was not argued on the status of the Baltic Sea as a PSSA.[80]

This suggests that PSSA designation does not necessarily mean more weight is given to ecological and other biodiversity values when regulating shipping. There are few if any examples that designation directly prompts

---

[76] PSSA Guidelines, paragraph 4.4.
[77] Report of the Marine Environment Protection Committee on its Forty-Ninth Session, Paragraph 8.12–8.14 and 8.20–8.24, MEPC 49/22.
[78] Report to the Maritime Safety Committee, NAV 50/19 paragraphs 3.14–3.29 and Report of the Legal Committee on the Work of its Eighty-Ninth Session, paragraphs 222–241, LEG 89/16.
[79] Report of the Maritime Safety Committee on its Seventy-Ninth Session, paragraph 10.11–10.16, MSC.79/23.
[80] See footnotes 61 and 62.

new measures or expands their objective. However, the indirect effects of the PSSA concept should not be disregarded.[81] The objective of routeing and ship reporting measures under SOLAS 74 was amended explicitly to include environmental protection. The arguments in applications both for routeing measures and special areas have increasingly been designed according to the PSSA format and criteria. It has obviously led to the increased use of such measures, introduction of new (no anchoring area) measures and more weight being given to environmental protection.[82]

4. Area-based measures and the law of the sea

The special areas and routeing measures are adopted through IMO instruments but are to be implemented through the law of the sea.[83] But does the law of the sea provide an adequate legal framework for the implementation of these measures?

It is the flag states that are the subjects of obligations under the IMO instruments, which require them to implement these obligations through legislation and enforcement.[84] These obligations are also part of the LOS Convention through the use of rules of reference in Article 94(5) and Article 211(2): the flag states parties to the LOS Convention are required to exercise jurisdiction over their vessels to ensure conformity with generally accepted international regulations, standards, procedures and practices. The area-based regulations adopted through SOLAS 74 and MARPOL 73/78 are consequently applicable to the flag state irrespective of whether or not it is a party to the relevant IMO instrument. Flag states are further required to enforce these regulations and standards irrespective of where they are violated (LOS Convention Article 217(1)).

The area-based measures adopted through IMO instruments are based on initiatives of the coastal states concerned, often as part of their work to implement their obligations to conserve ecological and other biodiversity values.[85] The right of coastal states to legislate and enforce area-based regulations in respect of foreign-flagged vessels within their maritime zones

---

[81] Markus J. Kachel, *Particularly Sensitive Sea Areas. The IMO's Role in Protecting Vulnerable Marine Areas* (Berlin: Springer, 2008), 286–7.
[82] Amendments to the General Provisions on Ships' Routeing, SN/Circ.215, proposed by the USA, NAV 46/3/2.
[83] J. Roberts, 'Protecting Sensitive Marine Environments: The Role and Application of Ships' Routeing Measures', 20:1 *International Journal of Marine and Coastal Law* (2005), 135–59, 141.
[84] SOLAS 74, Article I and MARPOL 73/78, Article 1.
[85] CBD, Article 8.

depends on international law as reflected in the LOS Convention. Within its 12 nautical miles territorial sea the coastal state enjoys sovereignty over foreign-flagged vessels.[86] It is competent to restrict operational discharges and to adopt routeing measures to prevent accidental pollution and other damage to the marine environment, such as those referred to above, and to enforce violations of these measures.[87] Although it would ensure their legitimacy, the coastal state is not required to have such area-based measures adopted or approved through IMO conventions.[88] The sovereignty of the coastal state is restricted by the obligation to respect the right of innocent passage and not to hamper this right.[89] Establishing an area to be avoided, practically banning navigation through a large part of its territorial sea, may conflict with navigational rights.

In the adjacent EEZ the coastal state enjoys more limited environmental jurisdiction over foreign-flagged vessels.[90] It may adopt legislation consistent with generally accepted international norms to prevent pollution of the marine environment.[91] In order to regulate operational discharges and navigation within an ecologically sensitive sea, the coastal state needs the measures to be adopted through MARPOL 73/78 and SOLAS 74. Most routeing measures such as areas to be avoided are recommendatory and non-binding. The coastal state is not competent to prohibit shipping that violates these measures. The jurisdiction of the coastal state under LOS Convention Part XII is further limited to the prevention of pollution.[92] It does not provide a right to prevent other damage to the marine environment: even if approved by the NAV, it may not establish 'no anchoring areas' or 'areas to be avoided' if their purpose is to prevent physical damage to seabed habitats or to prevent collisions between vessels and marine mammals. The enforcement jurisdiction of the coastal state in respect of area-based measures in the EEZ is more limited.[93] Violation of recommendatory measures may not be enforced. When a violation of mandatory measures does not result in discharges causing or threatening pollution, the coastal state may only ask for the identity of the vessel and its next port of call. It may take enforcement measures if the vessel calls

---

[86] LOS Convention, Article 2(3).
[87] Ibid., Article 21(1).
[88] Roberts, 'Protecting Sensitive Marine Environments', 151.
[89] LOS Convention, Article 24(1).
[90] Ibid., Article 56(1)(b).
[91] Ibid., Article 211(5).
[92] Ibid.
[93] Ibid., Article 220(3)–(6).

voluntary at one of its ports or it may request the flag state to enforce the violation.[94] If a vessel violates a ban on operational discharges in a special area, the coastal state has extensive jurisdiction in the EEZ. The coastal state may not enforce violations of mandatory routeing measures in the EEZ unless they led to collisions or groundings causing discharges.

The general obligation under LOS Convention Article 192 to protect and preserve the marine environment as supplemented by the CBD suggests that shipping is to be undertaken within ecological boundaries. However, the provisions regulating the implementation of the obligation in the EEZ do not provide a clear allocation of responsibility between the flag state and the coastal state. The IMO has a very limited role in ensuring compliance with the area-based measures. When these measures are recommendatory, it is more or less left to the flag state to implement them. They will probably be respected where they do not restrict navigation. The coastal state comes closest to having the power to regulate shipping but still has limited jurisdiction. This is particularly evident where the threat to biodiversity comes from damage other than pollution. It has been argued that the sovereign rights over natural resources under LOS Convention Article 56 provide an adequate basis for coastal states to regulate shipping in these situations.[95] But then the aim of regulating shipping must be to prevent activities that directly threaten living marine resources. Arguably, shipping activities such as anchoring and whale strikes that inflict damage on habitats and species are included in the sovereign rights. Such development may be viewed as infringements of the freedom of navigation and qualify for what is described as creeping jurisdiction. The involvement of IMO instruments in establishing routeing measures to prevent such physical damage may prevent disputes.[96]

5. Conclusions

At the age of thirty the LOS Convention provides for flexibility, leaving the IMO as the competent international organization to develop international standards and rules for the preservation and protection of the marine environment from shipping activity. With the exception of the

---

[94] Ibid., Articles 220(1) and 217(4)–(8).
[95] Lindy Johnson, *Coastal State Regulation of International Shipping* (Dobbs Ferry: Oceana Publications, 2004), 116–17 and 127–33; Erik Molenaar, 'Arctic Marine Shipping: Overview of the International Legal Framework, Gaps, and Options', 18 *Journal of Transnational Law & Policy* (2009), 289–325, 305–6.
[96] Roberts, 'Protecting Sensitive Marine Environments', 139–41.

2004 Ballast Water Convention (BWC),[97] the IMO conventions have not explicitly addressed the threats to marine biodiversity from shipping. The assessment of the practice under SOLAS 74 and MARPOL 73/78 and the PSSA Guidelines is evidence that that conservation of marine biodiversity is relevant in regulating international shipping. Area-based measures are established in respect the boundaries of nature as defined by ecosystems, habitats and threatened species. The IMO has contributed to the necessary development of the rule of law for nature. This assessment suggests that the main influence of the PSSA concept is its indirect effects. Irrespective of whether the area status is designated as a PSSA or not, the MSC and NAV are reluctant to let ecological and other biodiversity values dictate mandatory routeing measures. Therefore, its potential has not been exploited. A more explicit and comprehensive and legal approach to conservation of marine biodiversity by the IMO is needed.

The main challenge to the implementation of the area-based measures is lack of adequate means. The rule of law for the sea and oceans do not allow for all threats to marine biodiversity. Things have not been made easier by using non-binding measures, which may be seen as a compromise between the interests of the coastal states and the interests of navigation. There are two dangers with this. First, in proposing routeing measures the coastal state will be more concerned with its legitimacy among the flag states than addressing the ecological values threatened. Alternatively, the coastal state will base its regulations on its sovereign rights over living marine resources. This may lead to state practice challenging the freedom of navigation and create conflicts. The question is whether the coastal states and flag states can find acceptable solutions through the IMO developing the rule of law for nature.

---

[97] International Convention for the Control and Management of Ships' Ballast Water and Sediments (not in force), IMO Doc. BWM/CONF/36, of 16 February 2004.

20

Implementing the rule of law for nature in the global marine commons

Developing environmental assessment frameworks

ROBIN WARNER

1. Introduction

The Anthropocene era[1] has brought with it increased threats to the biodiversity of the world. Nowhere are these threats more apparent than in the world's oceans where the marine environment and its biodiversity is at risk from a wide array of human impacts including pollution, overfishing, destructive fisheries practices and climate change.[2] The obligation to identify the environmental impacts of human activities and to mitigate their adverse effects is a critical element of the rule of law for nature.[3] While legal and governance frameworks to implement this obligation are well established for terrestrial and marine areas under national jurisdiction, legal and governance structures to protect the marine environment from adverse human impacts beyond national jurisdiction are still fragmentary and underdeveloped. Until the latter half of the twentieth century, human use of the oceans beyond a narrow coastal belt was largely confined to navigation, fishing and whaling,[4] and from the mid nineteenth century the laying of submarine cables and pipelines.[5] With the development of the continental shelf and the exclusive economic zone, coastal states have

---

[1] See Chapter 3 by Nicholas Robinson in this book.
[2] Robin Warner and Clive Schofield, 'Climate Change and the Oceans: Legal and Policy Portents for the Asia Pacific Region and Beyond', in Robin Warner and Clive Schofield (eds.), *Climate Change and the Oceans. Gauging the Legal and Policy Currents in the Asia Pacific and Beyond* (Cheltenham: Edward Elgar Publishing, 2012), 1.
[3] See Chapter 14 by Massimiliano Montini in this book.
[4] Sylvia Earle, *Sea Change: A Message of the Oceans* (New York: G. P. Putnam's Sons, 1995), 21.
[5] Alastair Couper (ed.), *The Times Atlas and Encyclopaedia of the Sea* (London: Times Books Ltd, 1990), 200 notes that the first successful submarine cable was laid between England and France in 1851.

extended their jurisdictional reach to a wider offshore domain for purposes such as resource exploitation, marine scientific research and the generation of energy from wind and waves.[6] Other developments such as the depletion of inshore fish stocks, an increase in global maritime trade and transport and the search for new resources have led to greater human activity in marine areas beyond national jurisdiction (ABNJ) – the global marine commons.[7] These activities have expanded to include more frequent and invasive marine scientific research expeditions, associated bioprospecting for marine genetic resources, exploration for deep seabed minerals and geo-engineering experiments utilizing the capacity of the ocean to absorb excess carbon dioxide from the Earth's atmosphere.[8]

The extended spectrum of human activities now taking place in ABNJ has the potential to harm the highly interconnected and sensitive ecosystems of these areas if not carefully managed now and into the future. International law can play a vital role in preventing and mitigating the adverse impacts of human activities on the rich repository of marine biodiversity in ABNJ through the further development of environmental impact assessment and related processes such as strategic environmental assessment for these areas. The term 'environmental assessment' is used in this chapter to refer to all the different elements of the environmental assessment process including prior environmental impact assessment, strategic environmental assessment and ongoing and post-activity monitoring of environmental impacts.[9] Environmental impact assessment is acknowledged as a key element in the suite of tools for biodiversity conservation, and its application to activities affecting the marine environment has been endorsed in many international law instruments and policy statements. The 1982 United Nations Convention on the Law of the Sea (LOSC) imposes a general obligation on States Parties to assess the potential effects of activities under their jurisdiction or control that may cause substantial pollution of, or significant and harmful changes to

---

[6] 1982 United Nations Convention on the Law of the Sea, 1833 UNTS 3 (LOSC), Arts. 56 and 77.
[7] Kristina Gjerde and Charlotte Breide (eds.), *Towards a Strategy for High Seas Marine Protected Areas: Proceedings of the IUCN, WCPA and WWF Experts Workshop on High Seas Marine Protected Areas*, 15–17 January, Malaga, Spain (Gland: IUCN, 2003), 6–7.
[8] Ibid., 7.
[9] Strategic environmental assessment refers to the formal, systematic and comprehensive process of identifying and evaluating the significant environmental implications of proposed plans, programmes and policies to ensure that they are fully considered and addressed at the earliest stages of decision-making. See Chapter 14 by Massimiliano Montini in this book.

the marine environment. This obligation has been elaborated and implemented through regional and sectoral instruments that contain more specific provisions on environmental impact assessment in different contexts.[10] The application of strategic environmental assessment to marine areas is less common. Currently there is limited legal and institutional provision for the implementation of environmental assessment processes generally in ABNJ.

This chapter examines international law obligations for environmental assessment in the world's oceans and the complex challenges involved in implementing these in ABNJ. The fragmentary nature of the legal and institutional framework for environmental governance in ABNJ is discussed, as well as some initiatives being taken at the global level to develop a more comprehensive framework for environmental assessment in these extensive areas of the ocean. Finally, the need to strengthen environmental assessment in ABNJ as an important component of the rule of law for nature and ways in which this might be achieved are assessed.

2. The international law basis for environmental assessment in marine areas

Environmental assessment involves a complex mix of obligations derived from multiple sources of international law. These sources include conventional international law instruments, customary international law principles and the decisions of international tribunals.[11] These obligations have grown in specificity and now encompass not only prior environmental impact assessment (EIA), but also ongoing monitoring of impacts on the marine environment, strategic environmental assessment (SEA) and transboundary environmental impact assessment. Both the International Court of Justice (ICJ) and the International Tribunal for the Law of the Sea (ITLOS) have addressed the obligation to conduct EIA of activities with the potential to significantly affect the global environment.[12]

---

[10] These instruments include the regional seas conventions, the 1991 Protocol on Environmental Protection to the Antarctic Treaty (Madrid Protocol), the UN Fish Stocks Agreement and the International Seabed Authority's Regulations for exploration contractors. Some of these instruments are discussed further below.

[11] Neil Craik, *The International Law of Environmental Impact Assessment* (Cambridge University Press, 2008), 88–9.

[12] See section 2.2 on 'The customary international law status of the obligation to conduct EIA'.

2.1 Conventional international law sources and policy documents for environmental assessment

2.1.1 United Nations Convention on the Law of the Sea (LOSC)

The LOSC contains general obligations to conduct assessment and monitoring of activities with the potential for significant effects on the marine environment but no further detail on how these obligations should be implemented in different offshore zones. Article 206 specifies that 'where States have reasonable grounds for believing that planned activities under their jurisdiction or control may cause substantial pollution of, or significant and harmful changes to, the marine environment, they shall ... assess the potential effects of such activities on the marine environment'. These obligations are not limited to areas within national jurisdiction. States must also keep under surveillance the effects of any activities they engage in or permit, to determine whether these activities are likely to pollute the marine environment (Article 204(2)). These general obligations are supplemented by the more specific EIA principles and procedural provisions that have been developed in international environmental law instruments and associated guidelines.

2.1.2 United Nations Environment Programme (UNEP) Goals and Principles of EIA

One of the earliest global elaborations of the fundamental components of an EIA process is found in the 1987 UNEP Goals and Principles of EIA.[13] Principle 1 specifies that an EIA should include, at a minimum:

- A description of the proposed activity;
- A description of the potentially affected environment;
- A description of the practical alternatives;
- An assessment of the likely or potential environmental impacts of the proposed activity and alternatives;
- An identification and description of measures available to mitigate adverse environmental impacts of the proposed activity and alternatives, and an assessment of those measures;

---

[13] UNEP, *United Nations Environment Programme Goals and Principles of EIA* (UNEP Principles), available at: www.unep.org/Documents.Multilingual/Default.asp?DocumentsID=1008ArticleID=1658 (last accessed 13 June 2013).

- An indication of gaps in knowledge and uncertainties that may be encountered in compiling the required information; and
- An indication whether the environment of any other state or of areas beyond national jurisdiction are likely to be affected by the proposed activity or alternatives.

This statement of minimum requirements is significant for ABNJ as it highlights the need to include in EIAs an indication of whether proposed activities will affect these areas. ABNJ is also mentioned in Principle 11, which specifies that states should endeavour to conclude bilateral, regional or multilateral arrangements to provide reciprocal notification, exchange of information and agreed-upon consultation on the potential environmental effects of activities under their control or jurisdiction likely to significantly affect other states or ABNJ.

The general obligation to consult with interested stakeholders on an EIA before a decision is made to proceed with an activity is recognized in Principle 7, which provides that:

> government agencies, members of the public, experts in relevant disciplines and interested groups should be allowed appropriate opportunity to comment on the EIA.

For activities affecting ABNJ, this immediately raises the question of who qualifies as an interested stakeholder and which organization is responsible for administering and responding to such consultation. In the case of ABNJ, stakeholders could include intergovernmental and non-governmental organizations as well as multinational corporations and concerned individuals. Currently there is no one intergovernmental organization responsible for protection of the marine environment beyond national jurisdiction with a process in place to administer such consultation and respond to questions.

2.1.3 Convention on Biological Diversity (CBD)

The 1992 Convention on Biological Diversity (CBD) links Contracting Parties' obligations to conduct environmental assessment more directly to the conservation of biodiversity in both marine and terrestrial environments.[14] Under its provisions, Contracting Parties must introduce appropriate procedures requiring EIA of proposed projects that

---

[14] Convention on Biological Diversity, opened for signature 22 May 1992 (entered into force 29 December 1993), 31 ILM 822.

are likely to have significant adverse effects on biodiversity with a view to avoiding or minimizing such effects (Article 14(1)(a)). This obligation applies to processes and activities, regardless of where their effects occur, carried out under the jurisdiction or control of Contracting Parties in areas under their national jurisdiction or in ABNJ (Article 4(b)). The critical importance of collaboration between states in minimizing adverse impacts to biodiversity in ABNJ is emphasized in Article 14(1)(c). This requires Contracting Parties to promote reciprocal notification, exchange of information and consultation on activities under their jurisdiction or control that are likely to have a significant adverse effect on the biodiversity of other states or on ABNJ. In the case of imminent or grave danger or damage, originating under their jurisdiction or control, to biodiversity under the jurisdiction of other states or in ABNJ, Contracting Parties must immediately notify the potentially affected states as well as initiate action to prevent or minimize such danger or damage. Contracting Parties also have obligations to identify processes and categories of activities that have or are likely to have significant adverse impacts on the conservation and sustainable use of biological diversity, and monitor their effects through sampling and other techniques (Article 7(c)).

The obligations in the CBD have been augmented by Voluntary Guidelines on Biodiversity-Inclusive Impact Assessment (CBD Guidelines) that emphasize the importance of including biodiversity-related criteria in the screening process.[15] The Guidelines reflect a best practice standard for EIAs of activities with the potential to significantly affect all aspects of biodiversity, including those components situated in ABNJ. They depend on a detailed level of knowledge of species, habitats and ecosystems and their interconnections in a particular marine area. A later section of this chapter on global initiatives will refer to the process currently being undertaken in the CBD to define the special considerations to be taken into account in EIAs of activities with the potential to significantly affect biodiversity in marine and coastal areas, including ABNJ.

---

[15] *Biodiversity in Impact Assessment.* Background Document to Decision VIII/28 of the Convention on Biological Diversity. Voluntary Guidelines on Biodiversity-Inclusive Impact Assessment, available at: www.cbd.int/doc/publications/imp-bio-eia-and-sea.pdf (last accessed 27 June 2013).

2.2 The customary international law status of the obligation to conduct EIA

The customary international law status of EIA including its marine components has been commented on, but not without ambiguity in the recent jurisprudence of the ICJ and ITLOS. The general tenor of comments is that the obligation to conduct prior EIA is an emerging principle of customary international law but is not yet fully crystallized. In the *Gabcikcovo-Nagymaros* case the ICJ considered assessment, notification and consultation, effectively the elements of an EIA process, to be a necessary step in a state's implementation of the duty to prevent transboundary harm and the concept of sustainable development.[16] In this case, Judge Weeramantry, in a separate opinion recalling his earlier dissenting opinion in the *Nuclear Tests* case, which linked EIA to the duty to prevent harm, also notes that EIA should not be limited to prior EIA but should also extend to ongoing monitoring of impacts.[17] In the *Pulp Mills* case, the ICJ found that:

> it may now be considered a requirement under general international law to undertake an environmental impact assessment where there is a risk that the proposed industrial activity may have a significant adverse impact in a transboundary context, in particular, on a shared resource.[18]

In the *Mox Plant* Case, ITLOS concluded that the United Kingdom had breached its obligations under Article 206 of the LOSC by failing to carry out an adequate assessment of the potential impacts of a nuclear fuel reprocessing plant in Cumbria on the marine environment of the Irish Sea.[19] The 2011 advisory opinion of ITLOS on the Responsibilities and Obligations of States Sponsoring Persons and Entities with Respect to

---

[16] *Gabcikovo-Nagymaros Project (Hungary/Slovakia)* (1997) ICJ Rep. 7, para. 141; Alan Boyle, 'The Gabcikovo-Nagymaros Case: New Law in Old Bottles', 8 *Yearbook of International Environmental Law* (1997), 18; Craik, *The International Law of Environmental Impact Assessment*, 114.

[17] *Gabcikovo-Nagymaros Project (Hungary/Slovakia)* (1997) ICJ Rep 7, paras. 111–113; Craik, *The International Law of Environmental Impact Assessment*, 114–15.

[18] *Pulp Mills on the River Uruguay Case (Argentina/Uruguay) (Provisional Measures)* (2006) ICJ Rep., para. 204.

[19] *Mox Plant Case (Provisional Measures)* ITLOS No. 10 (2001), para. 82; Alan Boyle, 'Environmental Jurisprudence of the International Tribunal for the Law of the Sea', 22(3) *International Journal for Marine and Coastal Law* (2007), 377; Marie Cordonnier Segger, Marcus Gehring and Andrew Paul Newcombe, *Sustainable Development in World Investment Law* (Alphen aan den Rijn: Kluwer Law International, 2011), 152.

Activities in the Area, also acknowledged the customary international law status of the obligation to conduct EIAs for activities with the potential for significant impacts on the marine environment, including for ABNJ, specifically the Area.[20]

3. Regional implementation of environmental assessment in ABNJ

3.1 Regional seas conventions

There are broad obligations on environmental assessment in most of the UNEP and non-UNEP regional seas agreements. Parties to these conventions are typically responsible for developing EIA guidelines, legislation and processes that prevent or minimize harmful effects on the Convention Area with the assistance of competent global, regional and sub-regional organizations. In most cases the Convention Area is limited to marine areas within the national jurisdiction of the parties, although there are some regional seas conventions that include ABNJ in their scope of application.[21] The conventions do not incorporate screening, scoping and content prescriptions for EIA, leaving this responsibility to the more detailed legislative enactments of their member states. Different versions of the duty to notify and consult on EIAs with other parties and the relevant regional seas organization appear in many of the conventions, but most are relatively loose prescriptions urging rather than obligating states to disseminate results of EIAs and consult with affected parties.[22]

The 1995 Convention for the Protection of the Marine Environment and Coastal Region of the Mediterranean (Barcelona Convention) makes specific mention of notification and consultation among Contracting Parties where activities are likely to have a significant adverse effect on ABNJ. Article 4(3)(c) provides that:

---

[20] International Tribunal of the Law of the Sea, *Advisory Opinion on Responsibilities and Obligations of States Sponsoring Persons and Entities with Respect to Activities in the Area*, 1 February 2011, p. 44, para. 145, available at: www.itlos.org/fileadmin/itlos/documents/cases/case_no_17/adv_op_010211.pdf (last accessed 13 June 2013) (herafter ITLOS Advisory Opinion).

[21] The scope of application of the 1986 Convention for the Protection of the Natural Resources and Environment of the South Pacific Region (Noumea Convention), the 1992 Convention for the Protection of the Marine Environment of the North-east Atlantic (OSPAR Convention) and the 1995 Convention for the Protection of the Marine Environment and the Coastal Region of the Mediterranean (Barcelona Convention) extend to ABNJ.

[22] Craik, *The International Law of Environmental Impact Assessment*, 145.

the Contracting Parties shall promote cooperation between and among States in environmental impact assessment procedures related to activities under their jurisdiction or control which are likely to have a significant adverse effect on the marine environment of other States or *areas beyond the limits of national jurisdiction* on the basis of notification, exchange of information and consultation.

This provision recognizes the mandatory responsibility of Contracting States to protect and preserve the marine environment beyond national jurisdiction in their region.

The OSPAR Commission established to implement the 1992 Convention for the Protection of the Marine Environment of the Northeast Atlantic (OSPAR Convention) is moving towards more collaborative arrangements between competent regional and global authorities for EIA and SEA of activities, plans, programmes and policies affecting ABNJ marine protected areas (MPAs) within the Convention's area of responsibility. The OSPAR Ministerial Meeting in 2010 established six MPAs in ABNJ encompassing four seamounts, an area of the deep seabed beyond national jurisdiction in the southern area of the Charlie Gibbs Fracture Zone and an area to the north of the Azores Islands in the Atlantic.[23] A collective arrangement between OSPAR and global and regional organizations with responsibilities for managing activities such as fisheries, deep seabed mining and ships routeing in these MPAs, including the North East Atlantic Fisheries Commission, the International Seabed Authority and the International Maritime Organization, is in the course of negotiation. Under this arrangement, joint management plans will be prepared for each of the six MPAs including provisions for cooperation on EIAs and SEAs.[24]

3.2 Protocol on Environmental Protection to the Antarctic Treaty (Madrid Protocol)

The test applied for screening activities for EIA under the Madrid Protocol to the Antarctic Treaty is more complex and multilayered than many other international instruments and clearly applies to ABNJ, although there are

---

[23] OSPAR Commission, *OSPAR Network of Marine Protected Areas*.
[24] 'Designation and Management of OSPAR MPAs Beyond National Jurisdiction in the North-East Atlantic', Presentation by Dr Henning von Nordheim and Tim Packeiser, IUCN/German Federal Agency for Nature Conservation Seminar on the Conservation and Sustainable Use of Marine Biodiversity beyond National Jurisdiction, 3–6 December 2011, Bonn, Germany.

significant exceptions to its application to certain activities.[25] The screening process has three levels – the preliminary assessment, initial environmental evaluation and comprehensive environmental evaluation.[26] A preliminary assessment is carried out at the national level for all activities subject to the Protocol with less than a minor or transitory impact. If an activity has no more than a minor or transitory impact, an initial environmental evaluation must be carried out, and if it has more than a minor or transitory impact, a comprehensive environmental evaluation must be carried out. All activities, both governmental and non-governmental, in the Antarctic treaty area (south of 60° S latitude) are subject to these provisions, except for fishing, sealing, whaling and emergency operations, as these are covered by other international instruments.[27]

4. Sectoral implementation of environmental assessment in ABNJ

Some sectors of activity in ABNJ have implemented unilateral environmental assessment measures tailored to particular types of activities.

4.1 Fisheries sector

Parties to the UN Fish Stocks Agreement[28] must assess the impacts of fishing, other human activities and environmental factors on target stocks and species belonging to the same ecosystem or associated or dependent ecosystems, and develop data collection and research programmes to assess the impact of fishing on non-target and associated or dependent species and their environment.[29] This obligation has been further elaborated in the 2009 Food and Agriculture Organization (FAO)

---

[25] Protocol on Environmental Protection to the Antarctic Treaty, opened for signature 4 October 1991 (entered into force 14 January 1998) 30 ILM 1455 (hereafter Madrid Protocol).
[26] Madrid Protocol, Article 8(1); K. Bastmeijer and R. Roura, 'Environmental Impact Assessment in Antarctica', in K. Bastmeijer and T. Koivurova, *Theory and Practice of Transboundary Environmental Impact Assessment* (Leiden: Martinus Nijhoff Publishers, 2008), 182.
[27] Madrid Protocol, Article 8(2).
[28] Agreement for the Implementation of the Provisions of the United Nations Convention on the Law of the Sea of 10 December 1982 relating to the Conservation and Management of Straddling Fish Stocks and Highly Migratory Fish Stocks, opened for signature 4 August 1995 (entered into force 11 December 2001) 267 UNTS 3 (hereafter UN Fish Stocks Agreement).
[29] UN Fish Stocks Agreement, Articles 5(d) and 6(3)(d).

International Guidelines for the Management of Deep Sea Fisheries in the High Seas (Deep Sea Fishing Guidelines), which were developed to help states and regional fisheries management organizations (RFMOs) implement a call from the United Nations General Assembly (UNGA) to prevent significant adverse impacts on vulnerable marine ecosystems or not to authorize the bottom fishing activity (UNGA Resolution 61/105 paragraphs 80–91).[30] Significant adverse impacts are defined as those that compromise ecosystem integrity (i.e. ecosystem structure or function) in a manner that:

(i) impairs the ability of affected populations to repair themselves;
(ii) degrades the long-term natural productivity of habitats; and
(iii) causes, on more than a temporary basis, significant loss of species richness, habitat or community types.[31]

The Guidelines also specify that impacts should be evaluated individually, in combination and cumulatively.[32] They call for states to conduct assessments of individual bottom fishing activities and to adopt measures to prevent significant adverse impacts on vulnerable marine ecosystems (VMEs). These procedures include identifying areas or features where VMEs are known or likely to occur, identifying the location of fisheries in relation to these areas and features, and then developing data collection and research programmes to assess the impact of fishing on target and non-target species and their environment.[33] The Guidelines list the characteristics of VMEs that should be subject to assessments and give examples of potentially vulnerable species groups, communities and habitats, as well as features that potentially support them.[34]

4.2 Deep seabed mining sector

Deep seabed mining activities in ABNJ are subject to a well-developed framework of environmental assessment obligations. An exploration contractor must submit to the International Seabed Authority (ISA) an assessment of the potential environmental impacts of proposed activities with an application for approval of a plan of work together with a description of proposed measures for the prevention, reduction and control of

---

[30] FAO, *International Guidelines for the Management of Deep Sea Fisheries in the High Seas* (2009), available at: www.fao.org/docrep/011/i0816t/i0816t00.htm (last accessed 27 June 2013).
[31] Ibid., 4, para. 17.   [32] Ibid.   [33] Ibid., 9–11.   [34] Ibid., 4, paras. 14–16.

possible impacts on the marine environment.[35] The Recommendations for the Guidance of Contractors for the Assessment of the Possible Environmental Impacts Arising from Exploration for Polymetallic Nodules in the Area, issued by the Authority's Legal and Technical Commission in revised form in 2010, specify the particular activities of exploration contractors that are subject to EIA.[36] The sponsoring state of an exploration contractor is under a due diligence obligation to ensure that an exploration contractor fulfils all these obligations.[37]

5. Legal and institutional challenges in implementing environmental assessment obligations in ABNJ

Although the obligation to conduct environmental assessment of activities with the potential for significant impacts on the marine environment is well established in both customary and conventional international law, implementation of this obligation for ABNJ is still at a nascent stage. There is no overarching international agreement that develops in more specific terms the obligation contained in Article 206 of the LOSC to assess the potential effects for ABNJ sites of planned activities under the jurisdiction or control of a state. Similarly, institutional coverage for ABNJ is far from comprehensive, with no global body having overarching responsibility for protection and preservation of the marine environment or conservation of marine biodiversity beyond national jurisdiction, and only a few regional seas programmes having specific environmental protection responsibilities for these areas. The ISA has comprehensive environmental protection powers for seabed mining activities affecting the Area, but this advanced environmental governance situation for the deep seabed beyond national jurisdiction is not matched by a global institution with

---

[35] Agreement Relating to the Implementation of Part XI of the United Nations Convention on the Law of the Sea of 10 December 1982, opened for signature 28 July 1994 (entered into force 28 July 1996) 33 ILM 1309 (Part XI Implementation Agreement), Annex, para. 7; Regulations for Prospecting and Exploration of Polymetallic Nodules (hereafter Polymetallic Nodule Regulations), Regulation 18(c) and (d), available at: www.isa.org.jm/files/documents/EN/Regs/PN-en.pdf (last accessed 13 June 2013).

[36] Recommendations for the Guidance of Contractors for the Assessment of the Possible Environmental Impacts Arising from Exploration for Polymetallic Nodules in the Area, para. 10, available at: www.isa.org.jm/files/documents/EN/7Sess/LTC/isba_7ltc_1Rev1.pdf (last accessed 13 June 2013).

[37] ITLOS Advisory Opinion, 43–4, paras. 141–3; Polymetallic Nodules Regulation 31(6) and Regulations for Prospecting and Exploration of Polymetallic Sulphides (Polymetallic Sulphides Regulations), Regulation 33(6), available at: www.isa.org.jm/files/documents/EN/Regs/PolymetallicSulphides.pdf (last accessed 27 June 2013).

comparable environmental protection powers for the high seas water column. For activities such as bioprospecting and marine geo-engineering taking place in high seas areas there are no mandatory environmental protection laws and regulations at the global or regional level.

Lack of an integrated system of environmental governance for ABNJ presents considerable problems for implementing comprehensive environmental assessment processes in these vast areas of the ocean and is a key deficiency in the rule of law for nature. The predominant form of jurisdiction in ABNJ is flag state jurisdiction for shipping navigating these areas of the oceans. It therefore falls to individual flag states rather than any regional or global body to regulate and enforce the activities of their flag vessels in ABNJ including their impacts on the marine environment. This results in variable levels of compliance with environmental standards, no auditing of individual flag state performance or sanctioning of substandard performance. Many stages in an environmental assessment process require a coordinating authority, a body that is lacking in the disjunctive system of flag state governance applicable to most ABNJ activities. These include the initial screening process to select which activities are subject to environmental assessment, the scoping process to decide the terms of reference for an environmental assessment, the public notification and consultation process to engage relevant stakeholders, the post EIA decision-making phase and the ongoing monitoring of environmental impacts. A global environmental governance body for ABNJ, together with a coordinated system of regional environmental governance bodies, could perform these tasks and monitor emerging activities with the potential for adverse impacts on the marine biodiversity of these areas.[38]

With the intensification of activities in ABNJ, the establishment of a global environmental governance instrument and institutional infrastructure to conserve the marine biodiversity of these areas is becoming increasingly urgent. Environmental assessment obligations for deep seabed mining exploration in the Area apply to all exploration contractors under the ISA's regulations described above, but in the fisheries sector the FAO's Deep Sea Fishing Guidelines apply only to bottom fishing activities

---

[38] For further reading on this issue see Rosemary Rayfuse and Robin Warner, 'Securing a Sustainable Future for the Oceans Beyond National Jurisdiction: The Legal Basis for an Integrated, Cross Sectoral Regime for High Seas Governance in the 21st Century', 23(3) *International Journal of Marine and Coastal Law* (2008), 399–421; Robin Warner, *Protecting the Oceans beyond National Jurisdiction: Strengthening the International Law Framework* (Leiden: Martinus Nijhoff Publishers, 2009), 207–34.

rather than all high seas fishing and aquaculture activities and rely predominantly on the variable standards inherent in flag state implementation by individual flag states, or on limited reciprocal inspection and enforcement arrangements through RFMOs. A wide range of current and emerging activities involving ships in ABNJ such as oil and gas exploration on the extended continental shelf in relation to the impacts on the high seas water column above the shelf, bioprospecting, marine scientific research, survey activities, marine geo-engineering, deep-sea tourism and military activities are not subject to any EIA process. In most cases the EIA obligations in regional seas conventions do not require member states to assess the impact of their activities on the marine environment beyond national jurisdiction because the geographic scope of the conventions does not extend to these areas.

Environmental governance in ABNJ is further complicated by the array of international instruments applicable in these areas, many with overlapping mandates. Antarctica is a case in point with the Antarctic Treaty system conventions, the LOSC, the CBD, the Convention on Migratory Species[39] and the International Convention on the Regulation of Whaling[40] all applying to ABNJ below 60° S latitude. A more comprehensive and integrated environmental governance framework for ABNJ could develop environmental assessment processes for new and emerging activities in ABNJ and coordinate existing sectoral and regional processes. It could also perform the role of prescribing and monitoring best practice standards for environmental assessment in ABNJ. The rule of law for nature could also be strengthened by introducing a more objective and independent system of environmental assessment in ABNJ, where international panels drawn from interested stakeholders such as the regional seas organizations and intergovernmental and non-governmental environmental organizations conducted environmental assessments, rather than these processes being undertaken by proponents of particular industrial activities. Mandatory implementation of the mitigation measures and recommendations not to proceed with activities having unacceptable levels of adverse impact on the ABNJ environment would be a further strengthening factor.

---

[39] Convention on Migratory Species, opened for signature 23 June 1979 (entered into force 1 November 1983) 19 ILM 15 (CMS).
[40] International Convention for the Regulation of Whaling opened for signature 2 December 1946 (entered into force 10 November 1948) 161 UNTS 72 (ICRW).

6. Global initiatives to strengthen the international law framework for environmental assessment in ABNJ

6.1 United Nations General Assembly (UNGA) initiatives

In the five meetings since its inception in 2004, the United Nations General Assembly (UNGA) Ad Hoc Open-ended Informal Working Group, created to study issues related to the conservation and sustainable use of marine biological diversity beyond areas of national jurisdiction (BBNJ Working Group), has consistently identified EIA for activities affecting marine areas beyond national jurisdiction as an important component of its work. In 2011 the Co-Chairpersons recommended to the UNGA that a process be initiated by the General Assembly, to ensure that the legal framework for the conservation and sustainable use of marine biodiversity in ABNJ effectively addresses relevant issues including EIA by identifying gaps and ways forward. These issues would be dealt with through the implementation of existing instruments and the possible development of a multilateral agreement under the LOSC. In particular, it was recommended that the process address measures such as EIA.[41] The UNGA in its annual Oceans and Law of the Sea Resolution on 24 December 2011 endorsed the BBNJ Working Group recommendations.[42] A recommendation to support the initiation of a process to develop an implementation agreement under the LOSC that would address the conservation and sustainable use of marine biodiversity in ABNJ including EIA was also endorsed by the UN Conference on Sustainable Development (Rio+20) in June 2012.

6.2 CBD initiatives

The Conference of the Parties of the CBD has also been proactive in investigating the scientific and technical aspects of EIA for activities in ABNJ.

---

[41] Letter from the Co-Chairs of the Ad Hoc Open-ended Informal Working Group to the President of the General Assembly, 30 June 2011, Annex, Section I, paras. (a) and (b).

[42] Oceans and the Law of the Sea; Resolution adopted by the UNGA on 24 December 2011 (A/RES/66/231 of 28 November 2011), para. 167; UN Conference on Sustainable Development – Rio+20, *The Future We Want*, UN Doc A/66/L.56, 24 July 2012, para. 162.

It convened an Expert Workshop on Scientific and Technical Elements of the CBD EIA Guidelines that focused on ABNJ in November 2009.[43] This highlighted some of the governance and practical challenges related to the implementation of EIA for activities in ABNJ.

It emphasized the practical difficulties associated with conducting EIAs including:

- The industry proposing the activity and the national flag state jurisdiction are often far from the marine area affected;
- The conduct of EIA and management, control, monitoring, surveillance and follow-up activity were likely to be more costly and may be less effective for a given budget; and
- Capacity-building needs for EIA in ABNJ would be greater as customs of practice are less established, methodologies less mature, and multiple assessment cultures may converge in the same area.[44]

The complex and fragmentary nature of the law and institutions governing ABNJ were accentuated, including:

- The split legal framework for ABNJ – high seas (LOSC Part VII) and deep seabed beyond national jurisdiction; the Area (LOSC Part XI and Part XI Implementation Agreement);
- The diverse institutional framework for ABNJ including States, non-State actors and global and regional organizations and the need for cooperation between all these actors to conserve biodiversity;
- The fact that stakeholders are harder to define for ABNJ because communities do not have immediate proximity to these areas; and
- The variable standards of compliance among states with environmental assessment obligations in international conventions.[45]

The Workshop's Report was considered by the tenth Conference of Parties of the CBD in 2010, which endorsed the development of voluntary guidelines for the consideration of biodiversity in EIAs for marine and coastal areas drawing on the guidance from the Workshop.[46] The Guidelines

---

[43] Report of the Expert Workshop on Scientific and Technical Aspects relevant to Environmental Impact Assessment in Marine Areas beyond National Jurisdiction, UNEP/CBD/EW-EIAMA/2, 20 November 2009, available at: www.cbd.int/doc/?metting=EWEIAMA-01 (last accessed 13 June 2013).
[44] Ibid., Annex II, paras. 10–14.
[45] Ibid., Annex II, paras. 7–9.
[46] Report of the Tenth Meeting of the Conference of the Parties to the Convention on Biological Diversity, UNEP/CBD/COP/10/27, 20 January 2011, Annex, Decision X/29, para. 50, available at: www.cbd.int/cop10/doc (last accessed 13 June 2013).

have been developed for all marine and coastal areas rather than simply for ABNJ, emphasizing the interconnections between ocean ecosystems across jurisdictional boundaries. This initiative represents an important step in articulating the peculiar characteristics of EIA for activities in ABNJ and should provide a repository of information on EIA for all sectors operating in ABNJ.

7. Conclusion

There is an established obligation to conduct prior EIAs of activities with the potential for significant impacts on the marine environment, including ABNJ, in both customary international law and conventional international law, but its implementation in ABNJ is still at an early stage. There is as yet no such established obligation to undertake the other elements of environmental assessment referred to in this chapter, including SEA and ongoing and post-activity monitoring of environmental impacts on ABNJ. This chapter has examined some limited examples of EIA for ABNJ activities in regional and sectoral contexts. The establishment of a more comprehensive and integrated system of environmental assessment in ABNJ faces considerable hurdles, including the lack of global and regional institutions with the responsibility to monitor new activities in ABNJ and administer environmental assessment processes. Increasing human impacts on the oceans provide a strong impetus for strengthening the legal and institutional infrastructure for environmental assessment of all human activities affecting ABNJ. A number of options are available to the international community for a legally binding instrument on environmental assessment in ABNJ, including a stand-alone instrument or relevant provisions in a potential implementation agreement under the LOSC for the conservation of marine biodiversity in ABNJ. Developing comprehensive obligations and global standards for prior environmental impact assessment and ongoing monitoring of the impacts of activities in ABNJ is an essential step forward in strengthening the rule of law for nature and its role in conserving this pristine element of the Earth's environment. The sensitivity and unique nature of the marine environments in ABNJ underscores the importance of establishing and implementing best environmental assessment practices in ABNJ. The potential negotiation of an international instrument to conserve biodiversity in ABNJ, through the BBNJ Working Group, could provide a catalyst for more international cohesion in implementing environmental assessment for

ABNJ. Implementation of such an agreement will require cooperation between relevant global and regional organizations, as well as states with jurisdiction or control over activities with the potential for significant effects on ABNJ. Its advent would open up the possibility for increased global scrutiny of and intervention in environmental assessment processes for ABNJ.

21

Using the public trust doctrine to achieve ocean stewardship

MARY TURNIPSEED, MICHAEL C. BLUMM, DUNCAN E. J. CURRIE, KRISTINA M. GJERDE, PETER H. SAND, MARY C. WOOD, JULIE A. HAMBROOK BERKMAN, RYKE LONGEST, GAIL OSHERENKO, STEPHEN E. ROADY, RAPHAEL D. SAGARIN AND LARRY B. CROWDER

1. Introduction

Although we depend on the ocean for food, livelihoods, energy, and transportation (not to mention global climate regulation and nutrient cycling), to date society has been largely unable to strike a balance between human use of ocean ecosystems and their long-term conservation. One reason is that the opacity and sheer enormity of ocean space challenge the development of effective governance regimes. For instance, censusing a population of fish is not as easy as counting trees; and the oceans, covering over 70 percent of the Earth's surface and providing 99 percent of the world's available living space, often conceal considerable illegal and overfishing and habitat destruction.[1] In addition, an array of ecosystems, human enterprises, and complex jurisdictions inhabit the vast oceans, rendering

---

This chapter is contributed in recognition of the life and work of Jon M. Van Dyke. The authors would like to thank University of Oregon law students Erin B. Toft-Dupuy and Seth Bichler for their indispensable assistance in preparing this contribution. Mary Turnipseed gratefully acknowledges support from a Packard Foundation grant to the National Center for Ecological Analysis and Synthesis. Mary Turnipseed also thanks Darragh Hare for his helpful feedback on an earlier version of this chapter and the Mesa Refuge in Point Reyes Station, California, for providing the space, in all senses of the word, for drafting this chapter.

[1] *Ocean Facts: The Ocean is Home to the Greatest Diversity of Major Plant, Animal, and Microbial Groups on Earth,* National Oceanic and Atmospheric Administration, United States Department of Commerce, available at: oceanservice.noaa.gov/facts/ocean_life.html (last visited January 11, 2013).

comprehensive ocean governance at the national and international levels an often distant prospect.

This contribution focuses on the rule of law for oceans and, in particular, on the 61 percent of the world's oceans (and 43 percent of the world's surface) falling outside national jurisdiction.[2] This area, often called the "high seas," raises particularly challenging problems, as laws and regulations there are generally fragmented, weak and difficult to enforce. At last estimate, high seas fisheries comprised approximately 12–15 percent of the total global marine fish catch by volume and 25 percent by value,[3] and accounted for 13–50 percent of the value of global illegal, unreported and unreported (IUU) fishing.[4]

At the Earth Summit in June 2012, government leaders took a step towards improving ocean governance for marine areas beyond national jurisdiction. In the outcome document, *The Future We Want*, they recognized their responsibility as ocean stewards by agreeing as follows:

> We therefore commit to protect, and restore, the health, productivity and resilience of oceans and marine ecosystems, and to maintain their biodiversity, *enabling their conservation and sustainable use for present and future generations*, and to effectively apply an ecosystem approach and the precautionary approach in the management, in accordance with international law, of activities having an impact on the marine environment, to deliver on all three dimensions of sustainable development.[5]

Additionally, in paragraphs 158–177 of *The Future We Want*, the leaders committed (or recommitted) to addressing persistent threats to the world's oceans, such as marine pollution, overfishing, illegal fishing, and habitat destruction, as well as emerging issues related to climate change, ocean acidification, and sea-level rise.[6]

This language did not appear out of the blue. For nearly a decade, governmental officials meeting at the United Nations have stressed

---

[2] Boris Worm and David Vanderzwaag, "High Seas Fisheries: Troubled Waters, Tangled Governance, and Recovery Prospects," 64:5 *Behind the Headlines* (2007), Canadian Inst. of Int'l Affairs & Ctr. for Int'l Governance Innovation, 4, available at: http://papers.ssrn.com/sol3/papers.cfm?abstract_id=2101249 (last visited June 27, 2013).

[3] Ibid., 5.

[4] Marine Resources Assessment Group, *IUU Fishing on the High Seas: Impacts on Ecosystems and Future Science Needs* (2005), 7, available at: www.illegal-fishing.info/uploads/illegal-fishing-mrag-impacts_ecosystem.pdf (last visited June 13, 2013).

[5] *The Future We Want*, GA Res. 66/288, para. 158, UN Doc. A/RES/66/288 (September 11, 2012) (emphasis added), available at: www.un.org/ga/search/view_doc.asp?symbol=A/RES/66/288&Lang=E (last visited June 13, 2013).

[6] Ibid., paras. 158–77.

the importance of addressing these issues.[7] As a result, many governments (and stakeholders) had hoped to achieve a commitment at the 2012 Earth Summit to launch negotiations for a new international agreement to implement the far-reaching environmental provisions of the UN Convention on the Law of the Sea (UNCLOS) in the high seas.[8] However, due to the inability to gain consensus on more action-oriented language, government leaders committed to make a decision on a new international instrument by the end of 2014.[9] While this approach delays progress on establishing a more comprehensive legal framework for the high seas, it provides an opportunity to further consider how states may better steward the global oceans, including areas beyond national jurisdiction.

We propose mobilizing an often overlooked legal concept, the public trust doctrine (PTD), to help governments and international bodies to achieve protection of high seas resources. The PTD embodies the ancient and widespread principle that certain common natural resources must be managed by governments on behalf of their citizens.[10] Traditionally trust resources comprised riverbeds and tidelands, but in some jurisdictions the scope has been widened to include fish and other wildlife, forests, ocean ecosystems, and even groundwater and the atmosphere.[11] The beneficiaries of the trust include both current and future citizens, which means that governmental trustees must protect the ability of current beneficiaries to access and use trust resources while simultaneously

---

[7] Since 2006 these efforts have included an ad hoc informal working group of the United Nations General Assembly. See Kristina M. Gjerde *et al.*, "Ocean in Peril," *Marine Pollution Bull* (forthcoming). See also Liane Veitch *et al.*, "Avoiding Empty Ocean Commitments at Rio+20," 336 *Science* (2012), 1383.

[8] Veitch *et al.*, "Avoiding Empty Ocean Commitments," 1385.

[9] *The Future We Want*, para. 174.

[10] Joseph L. Sax, "The Public Trust Doctrine in Natural Resource Law: Effective Judicial Intervention," 68 *Michigan Law Review* (1970), 471, 484 (arguing that "certain interests are so particularly the gifts of nature's bounty that they ought to be reserved for the whole of the populace").

[11] Mary Turnipseed, Stephen E. Roady, Raphael Sagarin and Larry B. Crowder, "The Silver Anniversary of the United States' Exclusive Economic Zone: Twenty-Five Years of Ocean Use and Abuse, and the Possibility of a Blue Water Public Trust Doctrine," 36:1 *Ecology Law Quarterly* (2009), 1, 10–25; Mary C. Wood, "Advancing the Sovereign Trust of Government to Safeguard the Environment for Present and Future Generations (Part I): Ecological Realism and the Need for a Paradigm Shift", 39:43 *Environmental Law* (2009), 80 (discussing expansion of public trust); *Bonser-Lain v. Texas Commission on Environmental Quality*, No. D-1-GN-11-002194, 2012 WL 3164561 (Dist. Ct. Tex. 201st August 2, 2012) ("The public trust doctrine includes all natural resources of the State, including the air and atmosphere").

ensuring that the body of the trust remains intact for future generations.[12] If the trustees abandon this fiduciary duty, the PTD empowers the citizen beneficiaries (or representatives thereof) to seek judicial relief.[13]

Although the phrase "public trust doctrine" arose in US courts, the notion that governments must make decisions about common natural resources in the interests of the people who elect them has arisen many times throughout history.[14] US courts have traced the origin of the American PTD back through English common law to Roman and natural law.[15] Today the PTD also appears as a central principle in legal systems of many other states; and, according to Michael Blumm and Rachel Guthrie, the doctrine is "leading a vibrant and significant life abroad."[16] Additionally, core elements of the PTD (e.g., the notion of stewardship or trusteeship on behalf of current and future citizens) appear in many international legal instruments, including UNCLOS, the preeminent treaty regarding states' jurisdiction over their adjoining seas, the deep seabed, and the high seas.[17]

Courts worldwide have made clear that the beneficiaries of public trusts include both present and future generations of citizens.[18] As a tangible right protecting future generations, the PTD provides legal force to the notion of "intergenerational equity," the principle that meeting the needs of the current generation cannot sacrifice the ability of future generations to meet their needs.[19] Intergenerational equity forms a clear prerequisite for the ubiquitous goal of achieving sustainable development, defined as "development that meets the needs of the present with-

---

[12] Turnipseed et al., "The Silver Anniversary," 17–18.
[13] Wood, "Advancing the Sovereign Trust of Government," 75–6.
[14] See Charles F. Wilkinson, "The Headwaters of the Public Trust: Some Thoughts on the Source and Scope of the Traditional Doctrine," 19 *Environmental Law* (1989), 425.
[15] Ibid., 429.
[16] Michael C. Blumm and Rachel D. Guthrie, "Internationalizing the Public Trust Doctrine: Natural Law and Constitutional and Statutory Approaches to Fulfilling the Saxion Vision," 45 *University of California Davis Law Review* (2012), 741, 746. See also Mary Turnipseed et al., "Reinvigorating the Public Trust Doctrine: Expert Opinion on the Potential of a Public Trust Mandate in US and International Environmental Law," 52:6 *Environment* (2010), 13 (discussing functional equivalents).
[17] See text accompanying footnotes 51–60.
[18] See, e.g., *Oposa v. Factoran*, G.R. No. 101083, 224 S.C.R.A. 792 (July 30, 1993) (Phil.).
[19] Edith B. Weiss, *In Fairness to Future Generations: International Law, Common Patrimony, and Intergenerational Equity* (Tokyo: United Nations University Press, 1989); Catherine Redgwell, *Intergenerational Trusts and Environmental Protection* (Yonkers: Juris, 1999).

out compromising the ability of future generations to meet their own needs."[20]

The need for new institutions to address "the legitimate interests of future generations" was one of the key themes in planning the 2012 Earth Summit.[21] This chapter presents the public trust as a foundation for such a new institution for the high seas. Although not a "new" legal concept, the PTD has been largely overlooked in past decades when environmentalists were largely focused on developing, strengthening, or defending environmental statutes. Many of the authors of this chapter have argued that the PTD stands uniquely poised to contribute a foundational basis to achieving effective natural resources governance regimes at national and international scales. In this chapter we first discuss the broad parameters of the PTD in national and international contexts and then describe how a more fully realized PTD mandate could contribute a strong stewardship mandate to a high seas ocean governance regime.

2. The public trust doctrine – substance and context

2.1 The substance of the public trust doctrine

The PTD springs from an early understanding that some natural resources are "so vital to public welfare and human survival that they cannot be exclusively exploited through private property ownership and control."[22] Fundamentally a concept of property law applied to both land and water (especially tidelands), the PTD affirms a common property right to assets held in trust for the benefit of this and future generations.[23] The PTD enables governmental trustees to intervene when uses significantly affect trust resources. Additionally, the PTD enables citizens to take action against governmental trustees to protect trust assets for future generations. As

---

[20] UN Secretary-General, *Report of the World Commission on Environment and Development: Our Common Future*, Chapter 2, 1, and Annex 1, 2, UN Doc. A/42/427 (August 4, 1987).

[21] Third Nobel Laureate Symposium on Global Sustainability, The Stockholm Memorandum: Tipping the Scales towards Sustainability 5 (May 18, 2011), available at: http://globalsymposium2011.org/wp-content/uploads/2011/05/The-Stockholm-Memorandum.pdf (last visited June 13, 2013).

[22] Mary C. Wood, "You Can't Negotiate with a Beetle: Environmental Law for a New Ecological Age," 50 *Natural Resources Journal* (2010), 167, 200.

[23] Wood, "Advancing the Sovereign Trust of Government," 45. Though there is no legally recognized category of "common property" in the United States, application of the PTD leads to the conclusion that US law does contain an element of common property. Ibid., 82–3.

an assertion of *jus publicum* (the public's ownership interest), the PTD underlies private title[24] and provides an established defense to the government against takings claims.[25]

As a doctrine of property law, the PTD represents a formidable legal tool available to citizens to enforce sustainable resource management.[26] However, the PTD is not without controversy, since it rankles certain private property advocates who see it as condoning government "takings" of private assets.[27] Others have argued that environmental protection should be left to a more precise realm of statutory law than common law (i.e., judge-made law).[28] Nevertheless, there is surging interest in the PTD and other common laws, which many think may be more adaptable to the changing needs of society than statutory and regulatory law.[29]

A trust presents a basic type of ownership in which one manages property for the benefit of another.[30] Governmental trustees have fiduciary obligations, one of the most important of which is to protect the assets of the trust for future generations.[31] As formulated by the US Supreme Court in one of the early landmark cases, the trust includes resources of "special character" and "public concern" in which the citizens have a crucial

---

[24] See Michael C. Blumm, "The Public Trust Doctrine and Private Property: The Accommodation Principle," 27 *Pace Environmental Law Review* (2010), 649.

[25] See *Esplanade Properties* v. *City of Seattle*, 307 F.3d 978, 987 (9th Cir. 2002).

[26] Harrison C. Dunning, "The Public Trust: A Fundamental Doctrine of American Property Law," 19 *Environmental Law* (1989), 515, 516 ("The public trust is a fundamental doctrine in American property law"). See also Gail Osherenko, "New Discourses on Ocean Governance: Understanding Property Rights and the Public Trust," 21 *Journal of Environmental Law and Litigation* (2006), 317, 366 n. 258.

[27] See Randy T. Simmons, "Property and the Public Trust Doctrine," 39 *Property and Environment Research Center (Policy Series)* (2007), 1; James L. Huffman, "A Fish out of Water: The Public Trust Doctrine in a Constitutional Democracy," 19 *Environmental Law* (1989), 527.

[28] See Richard J. Lazarus, "Changing Conceptions of Property and Sovereignty in Natural Resources: Questioning the Public Trust Doctrine," 71 *Iowa Law Review* (1986), 631.

[29] See Clifford L. Rechtschaffen and Denise E. Antolini (eds.), *Creative Common Law Strategies for Protecting the Environment* (Washington, DC: Environmental Law Institute Press, 2007).

[30] Wood, "Advancing the Sovereign Trust of Government," 45.

[31] See *Geer* v. *Connecticut*, 161 U.S. 519, 534 (1896) ("[I]t is the duty of the legislature to enact such laws as will best preserve the subject of the trust, and secure its beneficial use in the future to the people of the state"), overruled by *Hughes* v. *Oklahoma*, 441 U.S. 322 (1979); George G. Bogert *et al.*, *Bogert's Trusts and Trustees* § 582 (St Paul: Thomson West, 2012) ("The trustee has a duty to protect the trust property against damage or destruction"); C. Lords, "Protection of Public Trust Assets: Trustees' Duty of Loyalty in the Context of Modern American Politics," 23 *Journal of Environmental Law and Litigation* (2008), 519–42.

interest.[32] The legislature is usually the primary trustee; and the executive branch, as agent of the trustee, is bound by the same public trust obligation.[33] Finally, the role of the judiciary is vital. As the Hawaiian Supreme Court clarified, "[t]he check and balance of judicial review provides a level of protection against improvident disposition of an irreplaceable res."[34]

The roots of the PTD trace to ancient Roman law, in the Institutes of Justinian, which famously declared: "By the law of nature these things are common to mankind – the air, running water, the sea, and consequently the shores of the sea."[35] England incorporated this doctrine into its laws,[36] and early US courts determined that upon independence from Britain, the thirteen original states inherited the doctrine as part of accepting British common law.[37] The modern-day PTD owes much of its development to US case law and legislation: over the past forty years courts and legislatures in many US states have expanded the scope of the public trust law to include – in various measures – fish and terrestrial wildlife, freshwater sources, beaches, and entire ecosystems. Today the PTD has a presence in all states, assuming varied roles in court decisions, natural resources statutes, and state constitutions.[38] Although the concept of a "federal" public trust has rarely been asserted, many legal scholars emphasize a federal trust duty and its applicability to resources such as the oceans and atmosphere.[39]

---

[32] *Illinois Central Railroad Co. v. Illinois*, 146 U.S. 387, 454–55 (1892).

[33] See *In re Iao Ground Water Management Area*, 287 P.3d 129 (Haw. 2012); *Center for Biological Diversity v. FPL Group*, 83 Cal. Rptr. 3d 588, 600–01 (Cal. Ct. App. 2008); *In re Water Use Permit Applications* (*Waiahole Ditch*), 9 P.3d 409 (Haw. 2000).

[34] *Waiahole Ditch*, 9 P.3d at 455. See also *In re Iao*, 287 P.3d at 182; *Arizona Center for Law in Public Interest v. Hassell*, 837 P.2d 158, 169 (Ariz. Ct. App. 1991) ("Just as private trustees are judicially accountable to their beneficiaries for dispositions of the res ... so the legislative and executive branches are judicially accountable for their dispositions of the public trust").

[35] *The Institutes of Justinian* 1.2.1, 2.1.1, Thomas C. Sandars trans. (Chicago: Callaghan & Co., 1876). However, throughout history, various societies have independently arrived at and protected the common right of their citizens to access seashores and ocean resources. See generally Wilkinson, "The Headwaters of the Public Trust."

[36] Lord Hale, "De Jure Maris," in: Stuart A. Moore (ed.), *History of the Foreshore and the Law Relating Thereto*, 3rd edn (London: Stevens, & Haynes, 1888), 384–406.

[37] See *Martin v. Lessee of Waddell*, 41 U.S. 367, 416 (1842).

[38] See Turnipseed *et al.*, "The Silver Anniversary," 10–11; Alexandra B. Klass, "Modern Public Trust Principles: Recognizing Rights and Integrating Standards," 82 *Notre Dame Law Review* (2006), 699, 714.

[39] See Osherenko, "New Discourses on Ocean Governance," 156–8. See also Brief for Law Professors as Amicus Curiae Supporting Plaintiff at 6, *Alec L. v. Jackson*, No. 3:11-cv-02203 (December 7, 2011), available at: http://ourchildrenstrust.org/sites/default/files/Sax%20Amicus_0.pdf (last visited June 13, 2013); Wood, "Advancing the Sovereign Trust of

The PTD also appears in numerous other countries' court cases, environmental statutes, and constitutional provisions.[40] In some states, generally common-law countries or those with mixed common and civil law heritage (e.g., India, the Philippines, and South Africa), courts and legislatures have applied the PTD by name to protect a wide variety of natural resources and citizens' rights to access them.[41] In other states (e.g., Ecuador, Switzerland, and Nigeria), the concept of governmental stewardship of natural resources on behalf of citizens has arisen independent of a common law heritage. In these states, "PTD-like" laws and jurisprudence protect public access to common natural resources or impose trusteeship-like governmental responsibilities over common-pool resources but do not necessarily use the term "public trust."[42]

The Supreme Court of India has issued some of the most articulate and far-reaching pronouncements of the trust principle. For example, in a landmark 1996 case, *M.C. Mehta* v. *Kamal Nath*, the Supreme Court of India declared the PTD to be "part of the law of the land":[43]

> The State is the trustee of all natural resources which are by nature meant for public use and enjoyment. [The] public at large is the beneficiary of the seashore, running waters, airs, forests and ecologically fragile lands. The State as a trustee is under a legal duty to protect the natural resources. These resources meant for public use cannot be converted into private ownership.[44]

In the Philippines, the PTD provided the fulcrum principle in an ambitious order issued by the Supreme Court forcing a dozen government

---

Government," 85 ("Where the federal government has a national interest in the resource, it is a co-trustee along with the states"); M. Casey Jarman, "The Public Trust Doctrine in the Exclusive Economic Zone," 65 *Oregon Law Review* (1986), 1 (arguing for application of the public trust doctrine to federal ocean waters); Turnipseed *et al.*, "The Silver Anniversary," 45 ("If state public trust duties accompany the sovereign authority of state governments to govern, then it follows that a federal public trust burden also conveys with the sovereign authority of the federal government to govern.").

[40] Blumm and Guthrie, "Internationalizing the Public Trust Doctrine," 748.

[41] Ibid. These global "legal transplants" are part of what historian Arnold Toynbee defined as mimesis; that is, "the reception and adoption of elements of culture that have been created elsewhere and have reached the recipients by a process of diffusion." Arnold J. Toynbee, *Study of History: Reconsiderations* (Oxford University Press, 1961), 343. See also Alan Watson, *Legal Transplants: An Approach to Comparative Law*, 2nd edn (Athens, GA: University of Georgia Press, 1993).

[42] Peter H. Sand, "Sovereignty Bounded: Trusteeship for Common Pool Resources?" 4 *Global Environmental Politics* (2004), 47, 50; Blumm and Guthrie, "Internationalizing the Public Trust Doctrine."

[43] *M.C. Mehta* v. *Kamal Nath* (1997) 1 S.C.C. 388 (India).   [44] Ibid.

agencies to clean up Manila Bay.[45] Fifteen years prior to this decision, the same court halted logging of the country's old-growth forests, declaring a sovereign obligation existing "from the inception of humankind" to protect natural resources for present and future generations.[46] Lastly, in South Africa the ecological scope of the PTD extends beyond tidal waters and seashores, and includes "sensitive ecosystems, wetlands, biological diversity and genetic resources, mineral and petroleum resources";[47] and the National Environmental Management Act (NEMA) and the Integrated Coastal Management Act both assert the PTD.[48] For example, NEMA declares, "The environment is held in public trust for the people, the beneficial use of environmental resources must serve the public interest and the environment must be protected as the people's common heritage."[49]

2.2   Manifestations of public trusteeship in international law

Although the concept of public trusteeship has primarily been advanced at the national level, elements of the PTD are discernible in a number of treaties and proceedings of international bodies,[50] starting with the preamble of the 1946 International Convention for the Regulation of Whaling, which formally recognizes "the interest of the nations of the world in safeguarding for future generations the great natural resources represented by the whale stocks."[51] The notion of trusteeship for current and future generations also appears in the 1972 World Heritage Convention, which establishes the primary duty for each state to ensure "the identification, protection, conservation, presentation and transmission to future generations of the cultural and natural heritage" situated on

---

[45] *Metropolitan Manila Development Authority v. Concerned Residents of Manila Bay*, G.R. Nos. 171947–48, 574 S.C.R.A. 661 (S.C. December 18, 2008) (Phil.).
[46] *Oposa v. Factoran*, G.R. No. 101083, 224 S.C.R.A. 792 (July 30, 1993) (Phil.).
[47] Blumm and Guthrie, "Internationalizing the Public Trust Doctrine," 792. See also Elmarie Van der Schyff, "South African Natural Resources, Property Rights, and Public Trusteeship: Transformation in Progress," in: David Grinlinton and Prue Taylor (eds.), *Property Rights and Sustainability: The Evolution of Property Rights to Meet Ecological Challenges* (Leiden: Martinus Nijhoff, 2011), 323–39.
[48] National Environmental Management Act: Integrated Coastal Management Act 24 of 2008 §§ 11(1), 12(a) (South Africa); National Environmental Management Act 107 of 1998 § 2(4)(o) (South Africa).
[49] National Environmental Management Act 107 of 1998 § 2(4)(o) (South Africa).
[50] Sand, "Sovereignty Bounded," 52.
[51] International Convention for the Regulation of Whaling, Preamble, December 2, 1946, 62 Stat. 1716, 161 UNTS 74.

its territory.⁵² Similarly, the 1992 UN Framework Convention on Climate Change declares a duty of nations to "protect the climate system for the benefit of present and future generations of humankind."⁵³

The principle of trusteeship for current and future generations is also contained in UNCLOS.⁵⁴ UNCLOS declares that the international seabed Area (i.e., the seabed, ocean floor, and subsoil beyond national jurisdiction) and its mineral resources are "the common heritage of mankind,"⁵⁵ vests all rights in these resources in "mankind as a whole"⁵⁶ and requires activities in the Area to "be carried out for the benefit of mankind."⁵⁷ The common heritage concept as expressed in UNCLOS has been described as "a form of international trusteeship,"⁵⁸ even as "one of the most developed applications of trusteeship or fiduciary relationship in an environmental context."⁵⁹ However, the extent of its application to activities other than the extraction of minerals from the seabed remains undefined.

3. A new treaty for the high seas based on an international ocean trust

A real challenge exists in enforcing both national laws and international treaties in the vast oceans, especially those waters and seabed Areas beyond national jurisdiction.⁶⁰ This difficulty has manifested in,

---

⁵² Convention Concerning the Protection of the World Cultural and Natural Heritage, Art. 4, November 16, 1972, 27 UST 37, 1037 UNTS 151.

⁵³ United Nations Framework Convention on Climate Change, Art. 3, May 9, 1992, 1771 UNTS 107.

⁵⁴ United Nations Convention on the Law of the Sea, December 10, 1982, S. Treaty Doc. No. 103–39 (1994), 1833 UNTS 397 (hereinafter UNCLOS).

⁵⁵ Ibid. Art. 136 (reaffirmed by GA Res. 48/263, UN Doc. A/Res/48/263 (July 28, 1994)) (Agreement Relating to the Implementation of Part XI of the United Nations Convention on the Law of the Sea, July 28, 1994, 1836 UNTS 41).

⁵⁶ Ibid. Art. 137(2).   ⁵⁷ Ibid. Art. 140(1).

⁵⁸ Alan E. Boyle, "Remedying Harm to International Common Spaces and Resources: Compensation and Other Approaches," in: Peter Wetterstein (ed.), *Harm to the Environment: The Right to Compensation and Assessment of Damages* (Oxford University Press, 1997), 83, 84.

⁵⁹ Catherine Redgwell, "Reforming the United Nations Trusteeship Council," in: W. Bradnee Chambers and Jessica F. Green (eds.), *Reforming International Governance: From Institutional Limits to Innovative Reforms* (Tokyo: United Nations University Press, 2005), 179; Patricia Birnie, Alan E. Boyle and Catherine Redgwell, *International Law and the Environment*, 3rd edn (Oxford University Press, 2009), 198.

⁶⁰ Worm and Vanderzwaag, "High Seas Fisheries." See also Sarika Cullis-Suzuki and Daniel Pauly, "Failing the High Seas: A Global Evaluation of Regional Fisheries Management Organizations," 34 *Marine Policy* (2010), 1036.

for example, unsustainably high rates of fishing in the high seas, despite strong language in international treaties to promote biodiversity conservation and sustainable fishing. For instance, the 1995 UN Fish Stocks Agreement requires states to, inter alia, ensure the sustainability of straddling (i.e., transboundary) and highly migratory fish stocks and minimize the risk of long-term or irreversible effects of fishing operations.[61] Yet, at last estimate, more than half of the highly migratory oceanic sharks and nearly two-thirds of straddling and high seas stocks were overexploited or depleted.[62] Thirty percent of highly migratory tuna and other tuna-like species were similarly overexploited or depleted.[63]

World leaders at the 2012 Earth Summit recognized the need to build capacity for "monitoring, control, surveillance, compliance and enforcement" systems throughout the global oceans.[64] We concur, but identify the need to develop a foundational governance framework for these enhanced capacities that guides all decision-making to better protect the interests of future generations. The PTD is well positioned to contribute to this new governance regime. In a high seas governance framework centered on the PTD, the living marine resources of the high seas and seabed Area would comprise the corpus of the "International Ocean Trust" (IOT) and global citizens, both current and future, would be the trust beneficiaries.[65] All states and designated international bodies would be endowed with fiduciary duties toward the trust. It would also be essential to specifically endow an existing international institution (e.g., the UN General Assembly) with the authority to oversee the execution of the IOT. Alternatively, the authority could be vested in far-reaching institutional innovations, such as an International High Seas Commission (e.g., modeled on the UN Human Rights Council) or a UN High Commissioner for Oceans or independent Ocean Guardian.[66]

---

[61] Agreement for the Implementation of the Provisions of the United Nations Convention on the Law of the Sea of 10 December 1982 Relating to the Conservation and Management of Straddling Fish Stocks and Highly Migratory Fish Stocks, Preamble, Art. 5–7, UN Doc. A/CONF.164/37 (September 8, 1995) (entered into force December 11, 2001).

[62] FAO Fisheries and Aquaculture Department, *The State of World Highly Migratory, Straddling, and Other High Seas Fishery Resources and Associated Species 2006* (2007), 68, available at: ftp.fao.org/docrep/fao/009/a0653e/A0653E00.pdf (last visited June 13, 2013).

[63] Ibid.   [64] *The Future We Want*, para. 170.

[65] Enclosing international ocean resources in a trust has been suggested before. See, e.g., Montserrat Gorina-Ysern et al., "Ocean Governance: A New Ethos Through a World Ocean Public Trust," in: Linda K. Glover and Sylvia A. Earle (eds.), *Defying Ocean's End: An Agenda for Action* (Washington, DC: Island Press, 2004), 197–212.

[66] See Independent World Commission on the Oceans, *The Ocean: Our Future* (Cambridge University Press, 1998), 136 ("[C]onsideration should be given to the appointment of an

Peter Sand concludes, "[A] transfer of the public trust concept from the national to the global level is conceivable, feasible, and tolerable,"[67] because, inter alia, the trust concept responds uniquely to vexing transboundary issues. While national statutes generally stop at political borders, "[a] notable strength of the [PTD's] property framework is that it creates logical rights to shared assets that are not confined within any one jurisdictional border."[68] What results from this "transnational environmental trusteeship," as Peter Sand explains, "is the democratic accountability of states for their management of trust resources in the interest of the beneficiaries – the world's 'peoples'."[69]

States sharing planetary common-pool resources (such as the atmosphere and oceans) are characterized as "co-tenant trustees" because they share reciprocal, corollary duties towards the shared resources.[70] This concept draws from a US federal district court case that described governments with shared property interests in a public trust asset as "co-trustees," each encumbered with fiduciary obligations to protect the trust asset.[71] With regard to ocean ecosystems that transcend state and international boundaries, defining co-tenant trusteeship in this way could support the establishment of bilateral, regional, and multilateral efforts, as appropriate, to manage trust ecosystems.

Under classic trust law, several duties of trustees prove salient to this conceptualization of a new high seas governance regime. First, the powers of co-trustees are "held jointly by the trustees and all must unite in

---

independent Ocean Guardian, with a mandate to take up grievances concerning alleged non-compliance with international marine agreements, or misuse of the oceans and their resources").

[67] Sand, "Sovereignty Bounded," 57.
[68] Wood, "Advancing the Sovereign Trust of Government," 84.
[69] Sand, "Sovereignty Bounded," 57–8.
[70] See Mary C. Wood, *Nature's Trust: Environmental Law for an Ecological Age* (forthcoming, Cambridge University Press, 2013), Chapter 10. Mary C. Wood, "Atmospheric Trust Litigation Around the World," in: Ken Coghill, C. J. G. Sampford and Tim Smith (eds.), *Fiduciary Duty and the Atmospheric Trust* (Farnham: Ashgate, 2012), 126. Other international spaces include Antarctica, outer space, and the moon. See Paul A. Berkman, "'Common Interests' as an Evolving Body of International Law: Applications to Arctic Ocean Stewardship," in: Susanne Wasum-Rainer, Ingo Winkelmann and Katrin Tiroch (eds.), *Arctic Science, International Law and Climate Change: Legal Aspects of Marine Science in the Arctic Ocean* (Berlin: Springer, 2012), 155–74.
[71] *United States v. 1.58 Acres of Land*, 523 F.Supp.120, 122–23 (D. Mass. 1981). See also *Puget Sound Gillnetters Association v. U.S. District Court (Boldt)*, 573 F.2d 1123, 1126 (9th Cir. 1978) (describing state and tribal sovereign interests in shared fishery as analogous to a co-tenancy that precludes waste of the common property). For discussion, see Wood, "Advancing the Sovereign Trust of Government," 84–7.

their exercise," and co-trustees have duties to take action against other co-trustees when necessary to protect the estate for the beneficiaries.[72] Translated to the execution of the IOT, a state or intergovernmental trustee would be accountable for its management of trust resources to both international beneficiaries[73] and its co-tenant trustees and could arguably seek judicial remedy if another state trustee shirked its responsibility.

The trusteeship duty to preserve the resources of the trust is also relevant. In general, courts protect trust resources against "substantial impairment," which places a heavy prejudice against the authorization of activities that could cause significant or lasting harm, individually or in combination with other activities.[74] Trustees of the IOT could be held responsible for ensuring that part of the revenues generated from the economic development of trust resources (e.g., high seas fisheries) are reinvested in the trust for the purposes of managing trust resources and remediating damage to them.[75]

Additionally, the duties to administer the trust in the sole interest of its beneficiaries (both present and future) and to provide information to beneficiaries about the status of the trust could be vital to this new high seas framework.[76] To protect the interests of future citizens, trustees must manage public access to trust resources while resisting short-term interests seeking to capture the decision-making process in their favor. And, because "a [public trustee] must always be able to make a full accounting of his stewardship,"[77] a robust high seas treaty based on an IOT would require state and international trustees to keep the citizen beneficiaries informed about the status of ocean resources and the activities affecting those resources.

Both of these duties could strongly promote comprehensive ocean management. For instance, the duty to provide "full accounting" requires

---

[72] Bogert, *Bogert's Trusts*, § 91.
[73] Sand, "Sovereignty Bounded," 55.
[74] See, e.g. *McQueen v. S.C. Coastal Council*, 354 S.C. 142, 149 (2003) ("The State ... cannot permit activity that substantially impairs the public interest in marine life, water quality, or public access"); *Orion Corp. v. Washington*, 747 P.2d 1062, 1072–73 (holding that a landowner "could make no use of the tidelands which would substantially impair the trust").
[75] Christopher D. Stone, "Mending the Seas Through a Global Commons Trust Fund," in: Jon M. Van Dyke, Durwood Zaelke and Grant Hewison (eds.), *Freedom for the Seas in the Twenty-First Century: Ocean Governance and Environmental Harmony* (Washington, DC: Island Press, 1993), 171–86.
[76] See Restatement (Third) of Trusts § 2 (2003).
[77] Antony Scott, "Trust Law, Sustainability, and Responsible Action," 31 *Ecological Economics* (1999) 139, 144.

the trustees to first ascertain what resources the trust encompasses. In typical private trusts involving money or property, this analysis is straightforward. But where marine ecosystems form the corpus of the trust, the trustee must conduct sufficient studies to establish key baseline information about the composition and functioning of the ecosystems. Recognizing that complete information is never possible, the precautionary principle would obligate state trustees to take all reasonable steps to secure baseline data before making decisions on how to manage the trust resources.[78] Environmental impact assessments, strategic environmental assessments, and other mechanisms to assess potential impacts of high seas activities would be essential to ascertaining how to prevent significant adverse impacts. These trusteeship duties could also support efforts to map the spatial distribution of ocean resources and ocean-borne activities and evaluate trade-offs among the activities.[79]

Ultimately, as the basic procedural dimension of an international public trusteeship is "legal accountability for the exercise of social power,"[80] the accountability of governments to "peoples,"[81] including future generations, is what endows the concept of a high seas treaty based in principles of trusteeship with particular heft. As governments and international bodies around the world increasingly look for ways to achieve sustainable development of the world's high seas resources, greater application of the PTD via the creation of an IOT can assist these efforts by (1) ensuring they are bounded by the overarching duty to make prudent decisions for current and future citizens; (2) providing to policymakers and resource managers both the authority and duty to act in the interest of long-term sustainability; and (3) promoting the creation of mechanisms for international monitoring and dispute settlement through which citizen beneficiaries may ensure protection of their interests.

---

[78] See *In re Water Use Permit Applications* (*Waiahole Ditch*), 9 P.3d 409, 466 n.59 (Haw. 2000), 426 ("Where scientific evidence is preliminary and not yet conclusive regarding the management of fresh water resources which are part of the public trust, it is prudent to adopt 'precautionary principles' in protecting the resource"). For discussion of the precautionary principle as a fiduciary duty, see Wood, *Nature's Trust*, Chapter 9.

[79] Mary Turnipseed, Larry B. Crowder, Raphael D. Sagarin and Stephen E. Roady, "Legal Bedrock for Rebuilding America's Ocean Ecosystems," 324 *Science* (2009), 183.

[80] Phillip Allott, *Eunomia: New Order for a New World*, 2nd edn (Oxford University Press, 2001), 336. See also Peter H. Sand, "Global Environmental Change and the Nation State: Sovereignty Bounded?" in: G. Winter (ed.), *Multilevel Governance of Global Environmental Change: Perspectives from Science, Sociology and the Law* (Cambridge University Press, 2006), 519–38.

[81] John Rawls, *The Law of Peoples* (Cambridge, MA: Harvard University Press, 1999), 23.

4. Conclusion

> That generations of trustees have slept on public rights does not foreclose their successors from awakening.[82]

Setting natural resource use on a sustainable course will require striking a balance between the use of nature and its conservation. Establishing a vigorous "rule of law" will be integral to achieving this balance. In this chapter we have argued that a vital step towards securing the sustainable use and conservation of high seas ecosystems beyond national jurisdiction will be through widely mobilizing a well-established but often overlooked legal concept, the PTD. The PTD serves a useful dual function. As a shield, it can be applied proactively to anticipate and resolve contentious debates over how to manage natural resources for the long-term benefit of national and global citizenries. As a sword, it is enforceable both by governmental trustees and against governments (by citizen beneficiaries) to halt activities that compromise public trust resources.

The time has arrived for states to support the creation of a new high seas governance regime based on the concept embodied by the IOT, described herein. The "trust" aspect of the PTD is vital to its utility: in providing rights to global citizens and responsibilities to governmental and intergovernmental bodies, the PTD converts aspirational stewardship goals to substantive trusteeship duties. While the public trust is a common law concept, the fundamental precepts of the PTD are broad enough to accommodate the world's legal systems and support integrated and accountable decision-making with regard to the high seas.[83] Applied in tandem with comprehensive approaches to governance, such as ecosystem-based management[84] and marine spatial planning,[85] an expanded, fully invigorated PTD would help clarify the role of state governments and international bodies in developing and implementing laws to manage the oceans, as trustees for both current and future global citizens.

---

[82] *Arizona Center for Law in Public Interest v. Hassell*, 172 Ariz. 356, 369 (Ariz. Ct. App. 1991).
[83] Amicus Brief, 11 ("The public trust doctrine assumes Constitutional force as an inherent attribute of sovereignty").
[84] Heather M. Leslie and Karen L. McLeod, "Confronting the Challenges of Implementing Marine Ecosystem-Based Management," 5 *Frontiers in Ecology and Environment* (2007), 540.
[85] Oran R. Young *et al.*, "Solving the Crisis in Ocean Governance," 49 *Environment* (2007), 20.

INDEX

academic studies, 52
administrative enforcement
   actors, 267
   basis of actor responsibility, 269
   challenges, 270
   discretion, 266
   duties, 265
   formal legal certainty, 261
   grass-roots, 270
   judiciary, 267
   legal history of actor responsibility, 270
   nuisance, 262
   procedures, 265
   public authority, exercise of, 262
   public responsibilities, 268
   Rechtsstaat under development, 267
   shifted burden of proof, 269
   state responsibilities for protecting legitimate interests, 263
   substantive review, 265
   Sweden, 271
administrative justice, 135
animal welfare, 5
Anthropocene, *see* Epochs
anthropocentric values, 215

beliefs, 86
biological foundations for law, 49–56
bottom-up empowerment, 36–8

challenges to humanity, 50
civilization
   dependence on conditions, 97
climate change, 44
complexity theory, 68

compliance
   meaning, 275
constitutional order
   principles, 133
consumption, 5, 115, 125, 297
   current patterns, 310
   degradation, and, 222
   efficiency, 120
   environmental, 118
   green, 76
   limit, 5
   model of development, 314
   new model, 306
   norms and, 68
   over, 68
   preferences, 305
   reducing levels, 316
   sustainability, and, 146, 316
context of nature, 82–7
   cultural, 83
   culture of self-constraint, 86
   environmental grundnorm, 83–4
   environmental reductionism, 83
   human and natural sphere, 85–6
   lack of recognition, 82
   natural law, 84
   socio-economic, 83
contrat naturel, the, 129
corporate responsibility
   absence of environment, 323
   care for the environment, 321–5
   conclusion, 327
   due diligence, 324
   environmental protection, 324
   environmental responsibilities, do companies have, 325–7
   failures, 325

GPs' fatal omission, 322
guiding principles, and, 321–7
hard and soft law, 326
human rights, 322, 324
OECD Guidelines for Multinational Enterprises, 326
social expectations, 323
cost–benefit analysis, 14, 129, 168
creationism, 53

Darwinism, 50, 53, 57
Social, 53
deep ecology, 216, 217
doctrinal construction, 156
domination or participation, 100–2
human needs and, 102
natural resources, 101
obvious problems, 101
other, the, 101
private rights, 101
property, 101
public interest, 101

Earth jurisprudence, 103, 106
Earth laws, 104
economic development, 5, 22, 29, 31, 32, 135, 160, 186, 318, 328
agenda, 147
balancing, 315
companies, 313
planning, 318
sustainability, and, 244
economic growth, 5, 61, 63, 83, 89, 232, 243, 300, 302, 304
implications, 300
limit, 5
sustainability, and, 301
ecosystems
decision-making, 169
degradation and approach, 158–9
destroy or conserve, 171
governance, 168
importance, 151
integration, *see* integration
moving forward, 172–4
rational choices, 169
tipping points, 96·

understanding of function, 170
value judgements, 168
worth, 170
enforcement
actions, 276
causal links, 276
failure to comply, 276
lack of, 277
legal system of credibility, 277
meaning, 276
mechanisms, *see* mechanisms
environment as property, 226
environmental assessment, 349
CBD initiatives, 361
conclusion, 363–4
Convention on Biological Diversity (CBD), 351–2
conventional basis, 350–2
Customary International Law Status of the Obligation to Conduct EIA, 353
deep seabed mining sector, 357
establishing governance, 359
extent of instruments, 360
fisheries sector, 356
global initiatives to strengthen the international law framework for environmental assessment in ABNJ, 361–3
lack of integrated governance, 359
legal and institutional challenges in implementing environmental assessment obligations in ABNJ, 358–60
obligation to conduct, 358
protocol on environmental protection to the Antarctic Treaty, 356
regional implementation of environmental assessment in ABNJ, 354–6
regional seas conventions, 354–5
sectoral implementation of environmental assessment in ABNJ, 356–8
United Nations Convention on the Law of the Sea (LOSC)/(UNCLOS), 350

environmental assessment (*cont.*)
  United Nations Environment Programme (UNEP) Goals and Principles of EIA, 350–1
  United Nations General Assembly (UNGA) initiatives, 361
environmental impact assessment (EIA)
  application, 247
  critical approach, 246–50
  differences in approach, 248
  first time, 246
  information, 248
  mandatory projects, 247
  national approaches, 248
  procedures, 247
  public participation, 250
  reason for, 315
  scope, 250
  shortcomings, 247
  standards, 249
environmental law
  acceleration, 106
  actors, 31
  agreements, 38
  commitments, 40
  discretion of regulatory authorities, 259
  discretionary rules, 164–6
  emergence, 28
  enforcement, 95
  focus of research, 259
  formal legal certainty in enforcement of, 261–3
  fragmentation, 163–4, 349
  growth, 32
  improving, 96
  international, 28, 29
  international developments, 106–8
  local communities, 206
  love of nature, and, 59
  main concern, 101
  national, 28, 30
  other law, and, 31
  principles, 25
  role, 348
  soft law, 29, 39
  strophe, as, 49
  use of principles, 166–7

environmental legal research
  implications, 91–3
  new era, 91–3
environmental problems, 9–24
  administrative borders, crossing, 18–19
  cause, 4
  complexity in decision-making, 21–4
  corruption, 20–1
  dilemma of attacking at source, 24–6
  economic and social borders, crossing, 17–18
  invisible issues, 10
  laws of nature, cannot influence, 9–10
  long-term effects, 19
  nature has no voice, 11–12
  plurality of values, 21–4
  pricing values and harms, difficulty with, 14–15
  public goods, as economic, 12–14
  small decisions paradox, 15–17
  uncertainties, marked by, 10–11
environmental rights, 51
  constitutions, and, 69
Epochs
  Anthropocene, 27, 32, 33, 34, 37, 44, 45, 46, 47, 49–54, 56, 59, 60, 64, 65, 66, 68, 71, 175, 179, 299
  geological, 27
  Holocene, 27, 32, 33, 49, 70
  Pleistocene, 33
evolution, 65
evolutionary biology, 47, 49, 54
  environmental law, and, 59
  legal scholarship, and, 56
evolved norms, 47–9
  biophilia, 51, 55, 59, 62–5
  caring, 67
  constructs, and, 58
  cooperation, 51, 55, 60–2
  foresight, 51, 67
  importance, 60
  instincts, and, 58
  justice for humans and nature, 68–71
  law, and, 70

INDEX 383

nature, 55
religion, and, 64
resilience, 51, 55, 65–8
sharing, 51, 67

food insecurity, 302
fundamental legal rights
  conflicts, 104
  right to exist, 104
  right to play ecological role, 104

goals, 97
going green, 315
governance
  failure of, 95–8
Great Jurisprudence, 103
green economy, the, 297, 298, 300, 303
  activities, 309
  alone, 306
  balancing, 304
  boundaries, 306
  commitment, 303
  conclusion, 309
  contentless, 303–9
  definition, 304
  distributive justice, and, 306
  green the supply chain, 305
  no target, 304
  obscuring, 305
  Rio+20 conference, and, 303
  risk, 307
  rule of law of nature, 306
  sustainability, 305
  theme, 299
  value judgments, 305
greenhouse gas emissions, reducing, 47, 120
greenwashing, 317
guidelines
  legal status, 120

hegemony, 49
holistic impact assessment
  common framework, 254, 256
  conclusion, 257–8
  evaluating activities, 255
  need for merging SEA and EIA, 253–5
  new single instrument to promote a holistic sustainability approach, 255–7
  procedural integration, 255
  public participation, 256
  reasons, 255
  spatial planning, 255
  sustainability, 256
  value of procedures, 256
  way forward, 253–7
human exceptionalism
  illusion of, 104

implementation
  meaning, 275
information technology, 34, 35
instincts
  ecological, 46, 49, 55
  economic, 46, 49, 50, 55
  human, 46, 48, 50, 54, 59, 62, 66, 68
  hunter-gatherer, 46
integration, 147
  balancing, 149
  conservation vs. utilization, 159
  delimiting balancing process, 150
  ecosystem approach, 159–62
  environmental integrity, 151
  example, 149
  functions, 152
  governance interests, 159
  governance sectors, 160
  implications, 149
  interests, 150
  limits, 152–4
  measures, 149
  multitude of elements, 149
  protection, and, 151
  purpose, 151–2
  regulatory frameworks, 161
  regulatory subject-matters, 161
  resource management, 150
  and sustainable development, 138, 142, 147–55, 172, 302, 314
  what does it mean, 148–50
International Maritime Organization (IMO), 331
  conservation of marine biodiversity, 333
  importance, 332

International Maritime Organization
    (IMO) (cont.)
  objectives, 333
intrinsic values, 215
irreversible impacts, 175, 195

justice, 32

kaleidoscopic world, the, 34–8
  challenges, 44
  concluding reflections, 43–5
  legal instruments for the
      future, 38–43

language, 58
laws of nature, 54, 103
  principles of legality, and, 103
leadership
  lack of, 77
legal certainty
  protection of environmental
      interests, 264–7
legal coherence
  importance, 172
  minor legislative changes, 173
  obstacles to, 162–7
legal innovations, 50
  environmental law, and, 70
legal profession
  responsibility, 156
  sustainability, on, 157

marine biodiversity
  area-based measures and law of the
      sea, 343–5
  area-based measures in practice,
      338–40
  areas to be avoided, 339
  assessment for PSSA, 341
  balancing, 365
  conclusions, 345–6
  conditions for PSSA, 340
  conservation of, 333
  criteria, 335–8
  effect of PSSA designation, 341
  Exclusive Economic Zone, 344
  flagstate power, 345
  format of proposals, 339
  general regulation, 334–5
  global concerns, 348
  international law basis for assess-
      ment, 349–54
  language, 366
  legal frameworks, 347
  no anchoring areas, 339
  obligations, 343
  particularly sensitive sea area
      designation, 340–3
  pollution, and, 336
  precautionary areas, 339
  protection, 337
  regulating shipping by area-based
      measures, 334–43
  risks to, 347
  routeing measures, 336
  special areas and ships' routeing
      measures, 335–40
  threats to, 366
  values, 340
  vulnerability of an area, 337
mechanisms
  access, 280–2
  applicable law, 282–6
  binding and non-binding
      outcomes, 286
  categories, 289
  classification, 283
  consideration, under, 278–9
  direct, 280
  direct with legal condition, 281
  distinctions, 282
  distribution, 288
  diversity of possible, 277
  hard and soft law, 284
  IEL directly applicable, 284
  IEL, soft, 284
  immediately open, 280
  indirect, 281
  outcome, 286–91
  outcome scale, 287
  overlapping rules, 284
  private parties, 286
  restricted, 281
  rules, 283
  systematization, 279–90
Millennium Ecosystem Assessment
    report, 95
myths, 85

natural law, 57, 84
natural resources
　first-generation resource use
　　laws, 209
　fourth-generation publicly held
　　resource nonuse laws, 213–14
　freedom, and, 272
　goals of law, 212
　legal perspective, 213
　management, 221
　non-anthropocentric protection of
　　nonuse values, 215–18
　scarcity of, 114
　second-generation conservation
　　laws, 210
　third-generation resource nonuse
　　laws, 211–13
　types, 209
nature
　applying rule of law, 232–4
　benefits in bestowing rights, 320
　challenges in protecting, 3
　concept of, 6–9
　constructs of, 111
　development and companies,
　　313–20
　ethical questions, 5
　human species and, 102
　implementing rights, 229–30
　inherent rights of, 227–9
　legal status, 3
　legal subjects, as, 105
　moral status of, 5
　obligations to, 5
　profiteering at cost, 312
　recognizing rights, 226–30
　right of standing in court
　　proceedings, 111
　role of protection, 111
　taking seriously, 312, 318–20
　universe is the primary law-giver, 232
neoclassical economic model, 244
neo-liberal anthropocentrism, 131
new cultural Renaissance, 97

OECD Guidelines on
　Multinationals, 119

policy integration, 25

politics
　rhetoric, 5
power imbalance, 300
principled priority guide, 154
problem, as, 25
promotion of consumerism, 316
proportionality
　analogy, suggesting an, 114
　breadth, 114
　demands, 115
　eco-, 128
　ecological, 115–18
　economics, 119
　French legal systems, 113
　German Federal Nature Protection
　　Law, 121
　German legal systems, 113
　international agreements, 123
　international law, 127
　legal norm, 121–4
　legal status, 118–26
　limitation of power, 114
　minimizing encroachments, 127
　Natura 2000, 121
　origins, 112
　overlapping, 126–9
　preconditions, 112
　public interest, 121
　reasonable objective, 116
　references by formal law, 125
　social and legal norms
　　combined, 124–6
　social norm, 118–20
　society, 114
　socio-, 128
　sociological to ecological, from, 112–18
　summarized examples, 122
　terminology, 114
　test for eco-, 115
　test of alternatives, 116, 117
　tests, 112
　tradition of, 112–14
　undercutting thresholds, 125
　unregulated areas, 124
public trust doctrine (PTD), 367, 368
　application, 372
　classic trust law, 376
　conclusion, 379
　effects, 370

public trust doctrine (PTD) (*cont.*)
  importance, 370
  manifestations in international law, 373
  new institutions, 369
  new treaty for the high seas based on an international ocean trust, 374–8
  ocean management, and, 377
  procedural, 378
  roots, 371
  substance, 369–73
  substance and context, 369–74
  trusteeship duty, 377
purpose of law, 99–100
  good system, 99
  interdependent conditions, 100
  introducing new legislation, 99
  meta, 99

regulatory model
  need for new, 243–5
restoration
  concluding thoughts, 189–90
  duty, 177
  duty for transboundary cooperation, 184
  duty to rehabilitate and restore degraded ecosystems, 183–4
  ecoscape and state practice, 181–3
  ecoscapes, 179–89
  emerging legal principle of ecoscape, 183–9
  harm, 178
  principle of ecological integrity of territory as an extension of human environmental security, 186–9
  principle of non-regression, 185–6
  remedial mitigation, as, 177–9
  science and ecoscapes, 180–1
rights of waterways, 222
  conclusions, 238
  defining 'healthy' waterways, 236
  enforcing, 237
  flawed results, 223
  future on this path, our, 225
  good intentions, 222

good intentions fail us, how did, 224
  implementing in California, 234–8
  modernizing the law to protect the rights of waterways and aquatic species, 235–6
rights of waterways, 226–30
Rio+20 conference, 3, 31, 40, 41, 42, 76, 97, 230, 297, 306
  backdrop, 295
  declaration, 107
  disappointment, 297
  failures, 299, 309
  Green Economy, 108
  intentions, 146
  key ideas, 298
  normliazing status quo, 305
  recognition, 148
  roots of, 298–300
  rule of law, and, 300
  task, 299
  The Future We Want, 76
  trade-offs, 309
RSPO Principles and Criteria for Sustainable Palm Oil Production, 307
rule of law, 11, 132–4
  about, 78–82
  actor responsibilities, 268–71
  administrative regulation, 260
  ancient Greek philosophers, 78
  ancient Roman philosophers, 78
  approaches, 98
  attitude, 78
  benefit humans, not nature, 209–14
  challenges, 27, 77
  components of nature should have rights, which, 216, 217
  concept of, 6–9
  concluding remarks, 273
  constitutional law, 133
  constitutional value, 133
  countries that provide for ecocentric resource nonuse protections, 218
  democracy, and, 75
  Dicey, 79

differences, 98
duty towards nature or a nature-held right of nonuse, 216
ecological approach, 90
emerging, 49
environment, and the, 155–7
environmental constitutionalism, 136
European conceptions, 80–2
extending to nature, 134–6
Finnis, 77
formal at the core of *Rechtsstaat*, 260–3
Fuller, 98
goodness of laws, 135
grounding during crisis, 6–9
Hayek, 79
hierarchy, and, 77
Hobbes, 79
ignorance, and, 76
importance, 132
king is law, 98
law is king, 98
legal certainty, 261
legal certainty in a substantive perspective, 263–7
litigation strategy, 135
meaning, 75, 78
moral ideals, 80
natural resources, *See* natural resources
nature legitimating non-anthropocentric nonuse values, 215–21
necessary to protect fundamental rights, 230–2
new-order, 133
oceans, for, 366
orthodox manifestation, 135
path to the future, 32–46
path to today, 28–32
pluralistic reality of public power, 267–71
principles of legality, 98
procedural, 132
proportionality, *See* proportionality
protecting over socio-economic interests, 144
purpose and contet of the right, what should be, 217
raise for nature, who may, 219–21
Rawls, 79
Raz, 79
reconceptualization, 98
reimagining, 102–5
rights, freedom and common interests, 271–3
shifting focus, 176
South Africa, 133, 136–9
standard of constitutionality, 134
substance, 132
sustainability, 147
sustainable development, and, 136–9
traditional formulations, 102
rule of law for nature, 11–12, 14–15, 17–21, 23, 26, 27, 32, 43, 46, 49, 56, 71, 91, 100, 131–2, 134–6, 138, 153, 176, 190, 215, 220, 273, 275–9, 290, 295, 299–303, 306, 308, 310, 346, 347–9, 359–63

scientific effects, 33–4
sector responsibility, 25
sociobiology, 47, 48, 52, 53, 54
evidence, 71
juridical studies, 70
rule of law for nature, and, 56–60
socio-economic development, 142
ecological considerations, and, 142
justifiable, 143
need for, 141
regulation, 143
strategic environmental assessment (SEA)
application, 251
critical appraisal, 250–3
effectiveness, 252
EIA, and, 251
first time, 250
scope, 251
screening procedure, 252
shortcomings, 253
sub-Saharan African region
checks and balances, 197
climate change, 204
conclusions, 205–6

sub-Saharan African region (*cont.*)
  conservation, 203
  forest degradation, 203
  forest governance and climate change, 202–5
  forests and culture, 199–200
  global objectives in environmental governance, meeting, 195
  indigenous peoples' rights, 205
  local governance, 197, 205
  modern governance, 196
  nature to livelihoods and poverty eradication, contribution, 199–202
  peoples, forests, values, 191–5
  population, 196
  resource extraction, 198
  traditional knowledge and norms in forest governance, application of, 200–2
  traditional norms, 196–9
  value of nature, 191
successes, 94
sustainability, 6, 60, 87, 88, 146, 184, 251, 378
  abstract political value, as, 130
  achievements, and, 86
  achieving, 91
  boundaries, 302
  business case, 307
  case for, 87, 90
  commitments to, 41
  common rationale, 255
  company relevance, 315
  compromises, 153
  considerations, 136
  constitutional objective, 143
  continuity, 144
  contradiction, 314
  corporate practices, 316
  corporate profiteering, and, 313–18
  courts, 131
  crises, 296
  crisis, 75
  cultures, 87
  defaults, 305
  defining, 78
  development, 130–2, 143–5
  development, as a general principle, 154–5
  different conception, 295
  Earth's capacity to, 95
  ecological core, 89–90
  economics, and, 301
  failure of development, 300–3
  first modern statute, 88
  foundational principle, as a, 87–90
  fundamental value, 273
  globalization, and, 302
  green economy, and, 298
  hierarchy, 315
  history, 87, 88
  holistic, 255
  imperative, 93
  implementing development, problems, 315
  importance, 146
  inherent problems, 147
  integration, 147
  judicial appraisal, 139–42
  judicial role, 144
  maintaining, 91
  measures, 25
  no absolutes, 143
  normative content, 154
  obligation to ensure, 144
  perspective, 92
  policy, 25
  principle of, 244
  promoting protection, 131
  promotion, 245
  proportionality, and, 129
  reasons for failure, 147
  reconceptualizing, 132
  rule of law, and, 86, 259
  shortcomings of the SEA and EIA, 246–53
  South Africa, 131, 136–9
  strong, 77, 245
  sub-Saharan African region, 198
  water resources, 4
  weak approach, 244
sustainable development, 3, 6, 19, 24, 29, 32, 39–42, 49–50, 76–7, 89–91, 94–5, 111, 130–57, 166, 171, 175, 195, 230, 244, 246, 254, 259, 264, 268–73, 299, 300–3, 309–15, 318, 326–8, 353, 368, 378

trade-offs, 150
traditional humanistic dualism, 54
transformation of law, 105–8
 justice, 108
 unlawfulness, 108

UN General Assembly had adopted the World Charter for Nature, 318
UN Law of the Sea Convention (LOS Convention), 331
 legal framework, 332
UNEP Global Environmental Outlook, 4
United Nations Conference on the Human Environment, 3
United Nations Environment Programme (UNEP), 28, 30, 95
United Nations Framework Convention on Climate Change, 40, 101
 conference, 203

United Nations Guiding Principles on Business and Human Rights (GPs), 312

value judgements, exercise of, 173
voluntary actions, 38

Western political-economic worldview, 86
wide margin of appreciation, 150
 challenges of, 167–72
 importance of life-supporting systems, 171–2
 incommensurable and incomparable values, 168–70
 uncertainty about the functioning of the ecological system, 170–1
wild laws, 103, 106
World Commission on Environment and Development (WCED)
 strategic imperatives, 24